The history of the
OLYMPICS

The history of the
OLYMPICS

Edited by Martin Tyler

Marshall Cavendish
London and New York

Published by Marshall Cavendish Publications Limited,
58 Old Compton Street, London W1V 5PA
© Marshall Cavendish Limited, 1969, 1970, 1971, 1975
Some of this material has previously appeared in the partwork *The Game*
First printing 1975
ISBN 0 85685 126 4
Printed in Great Britain by Severn Valley Press Limited

Introduction

There is no sporting occasion quite like the Olympic Games. No other event can capture its international appeal, its intensity of competition in a whole range of sports, the excellence of its athletic performance, and its basic ideology.

The History of the Olympics traces the history of this unique institution from its rebirth in Athens in 1896—when a mere 285, all-male entrants comprised the first modern Olympic Games—through the beginning of the Winter Olympics in 1924 to the lavish 26–sport spectacle of Sapporo and Munich in 1972. No other book has ever provided such a thorough documentation of this great festival, bringing it to life in words, in a lavish gallery of photographs (many of them rare), and in comprehensive statistics.

The History of the Olympics enables you to experience the monumental moments of Olympic performance from arenas as far apart in time as in distance; from St Louis to Stockholm, from London to Los Angeles, from Melbourne to Munich, from St Moritz to Squaw Valley. The feats of competitors like Jesse Owens, Emile Zatopek, Jean-Claude Killy and Mark Spitz are vividly recalled—as are those of countless other men and women who became folk heroes to the world simply because they were great winners in this most prestigious of tournaments.

The History of the Olympics also looks to Montreal, a vital moment in the story of this great event. The sheer size and near impossibility of organizing all the necessary events for the summer games, and a reputation tarnished by arguments over professionalism and by the events of 1972 mean that the Canadian celebration must inevitably point the way of the future. But some parts of that future are assured; its history, its pageantry, its competitiveness and, in general, its friendliness, cannot be ignored and the Olympic Games, even if in a reduced form, will most certainly and rightly survive as the world's most important sporting event.

Endpapers: *Baton-changing in the 4 by 400 metres relay at Munich.*
Previous page overleaf: *The opening of the 1964 Tokyo Games.*
Opposite: *French slalom champion Augert on the slopes.*

Contents

Left: Double gold medallist Pierre d'Oriola clears a fence on Nagir at Mexico City, where he won a silver in the show jumping team event. D'Oriola's gold medals were won in 1952 and 1964 in the individual event.

Foundation and Growth

No sporting event grips the world's imagination like the Olympic Games. The World Cup can fascinate the television viewers of Europe and South America—the baseball World Series transfixes the population of the United States—and the Melbourne Cup brings the state of Victoria to a dead stop. But the Olympics belong to the whole world. Participation in the Games is looked on not only as an achievement, but as an honour. Little-known Africans become household names all over the world . . . American sprinters are offered huge fees to play professional football . . . and Russian soldiers gain promotion . . . simply because they win a small medal in the Olympic Games.

Various legends purport to account for the inception of the Olympic Games in ancient Greece. Pindar tells of how Hercules initiated the Games after cleansing the Augean stables. Augeas, ruler of Elis, made Hercules clean out his enormous stables in a single day. Hercules extracted a promise from the king that if he did so he would be given a tenth of the king's herds. Unwisely, the king did not keep to his side of the bargain, and Hercules promptly killed Augeas and his family, made himself a present of the entire stock of cattle, and instituted the Olympic Games to mark the occasion. This is only a legend, but the Greeks did hold religious Games as a part of everyday life. Homer, in the *Iliad*, describes the ritual Games at the funeral of Patroclus, in about 1100 BC.

The Olympic Games were only one of a number of similar celebrations in Greece, but they became the most important, and a list of champions from the year 776 BC exists. At first the Games occupied only one day, and consisted of a single event—a running race for one length of the stadium (about 210 yards). In time they were extended, lasting five days (with two more days devoted to religious observances). The programme eventually included four running events—the one-stadium-length dash, a race over two lengths of the stadium, a long-distance race (the *dolichos*) of about 2¾ miles, and a race in armour. Combat sports included boxing and the *pankration*—a no-holds-barred event in which only gouging and biting were forbidden. Further elaborations of the programme included a chariot race for *quadrigas*—chariots drawn by four horses—and a pentathlon. As its name implies, the pentathlon consisted of five events, but it was, by some accounts, an elimination contest. The order of the first four events,

Central Press

Radio Times Hulton Picture Library

the long jump, javelin, discus, and a sprint, is uncertain, but it is generally accepted that wrestling was the fifth event, and was resorted to only if the competition was not already decided.

But the Olympics were essentially religious affairs, and the Greeks always proclaimed a sacred truce—the *hieromenia*—for the duration of the Games, and for the people travelling to and from Olympia. The competitors and spectators had to be male free-born Greeks, though the circumscription on women spectators was later lifted. To the Greeks it was important to win well, and any competitor found guilty of an unfair practice had to pay a fine which was used to build a statue of Zeus at the entrance to the stadium. In all the history of the ancient Games, only 13 of these were erected.

Gradually, the Games lost their reputation, especially after the Roman Emperor, Nero, entered and was allowed to win the chariot race in AD 66. Finally, in AD 393, the Olympic Games were abolished by a decree from the emperor Theodosius, and in the 5th century the once sacred buildings were demolished. In time, earthquakes and floods buried the site beneath about 20 feet of soil.

The modern Olympics

Happily, the memory and ideals of the Greeks' Olympic organization did not crumble with the ruins of Olympia. In the 19th century, archaeologists began excavating the site of the temple of Zeus, and between 1875 and 1881 most of the Olympia complex was uncovered. With the growing interest in sports of all kinds in the 19th century, it was, perhaps, inevitable that the ideals of the Greek Olympic Games should be revived. The credit for this belongs to the Frenchman Baron Pierre de Coubertin (1863-1937). He thought that at least one reason for the flowering of Greece during the 'Golden Age' was sport and the ideals of the Olympic Games. He also saw a parallel in the stature of 19th-century Britain in the games played at the famous public schools. Furthermore, nothing could be lost—and a great deal gained—by bringing together the youth of the world in friendly competition. The new Olympic Games would be a period of concord in which all differences of status, religion, politics, and race would be forgotten. It was with these thoughts in mind that he summoned an international meeting at the Sorbonne in Paris in 1894, and two years later his

ideas took a concrete form at the first celebration of the modern Olympic Games, in Athens.

In 1894, de Coubertin also founded the International Olympic Committee, which consisted of members chosen by him for their devotion to the Olympic movement. This body has seen the Olympics grow from a small gathering of enthusiasts (285 strong in 1896) to vast gatherings: 5,215 men and 844 women competed at Mexico City in 1968. The IOC awards the Games to a city, rather than a country, some six years before they are due to be held. And because of the commercial gains to be made from hosting the Games, city councils will go to great lengths to impress the IOC. At a special IOC meeting all the cities applying for the Games state their cases with the help of films, models, and press hand-outs. The stadiums are normally built especially for the Olympics, and they remain as amenities for the population afterwards.

The Olympics are held in the first year of an Olympiad, which is a period of four years beginning in a year divisible by four (ie 1896 or 1968). It is a rule of the IOC that the Games must be celebrated in the first year of an Olympiad, and they cannot be postponed. The first modern Olympics were, therefore, held in the first year of the first modern Olympiad—1896—and so on The Games were to be universal, and so they are held all over the world. Thus, as early as 1904, the Games went to America—St Louis. The Greeks wanted to keep the Olympics in Greece, and in 1906 an Interim Games was held in Athens. But this was the only such 'intercal-

3

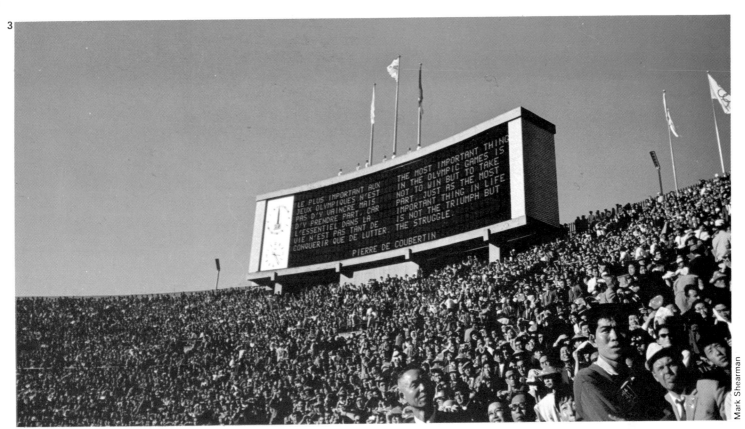

Mark Shearman

4

London Express News & Feature Service

1 The first Olympic torch relay, part of the 1936 celebrations, passed through eastern Europe on its way from Olympia to Berlin.
2 Baron Pierre de Coubertin, the founder of the modern Olympic Games, saw his brain-child grow from a small gathering at Athens in 1896 to world-wide meetings of the world's best sportsmen.
3 De Coubertin's words, the ideal underlying the Olympic movement, are displayed on the scoreboard at the opening ceremony of every Olympic Games. 4 The Olympic torch begins its journey from the host city of Olympia, and is carried in a relay until 5 it burns throughout the Games in the stadium.

5

Mark Shearman

ated' celebration.

The Games of 1900 and 1904 were subordinate to concurrently held trade fairs, and this detracted from their importance. Such unfortunate treatment was amended at the 1908 Games in London, which can justifiably by regarded as the prototype for all subsequent Games.

The first women to compete in the Olympic Games were entrants to the tennis and golf events in 1900. But it was not until 1912 at Stockholm that women's swimming events were included in the Games; and athletics events for women formed part of the programme for the first time at Amsterdam in 1928. Meanwhile, in 1924, a separate Winter Olympic Games had been established, the first of them being held at Chamonix. Before 1932, the Games had been outside Europe only once, but that year both Games were held in the United States—the Winter Games at Lake Placid in New York State and the full Games in Los Angeles. An Olympic Village was established for the first time at the

Los Angeles Games.

As communications became easier more people were able to compete in and visit the Olympics wherever they were held. And as the Games became more important, the host cities endeavoured to outdo the previous hosts. The apotheosis of such one-upmanship came at the Berlin Games of 1936 which were used by the Nazis as a shop-window. Later, nobody wanted to be compared with Germany under the Nazis, and after 1936 the Olympics tried to remain as free from politics as possible. But as the Games have grown as the major international spectacle, receiving unprecedented exposure, they have become more vulnerable to political pressure groups seeking maximum exploitation to further their claims. The threatened boycott by the Africans, and the taking hostage of Israeli team members by Palestinian guerrillas, both at Munich, served as unwanted reminders that politics and sport were linked more than ever before.

World War II necessitated the cancellation of two Olympic Games—the 1940 Games first scheduled for Tokyo and in 1938 awarded to Helsinki, and the 1944 Games scheduled for London. But after 12 years the 1948 Games were held—at short notice—in London. No new sports arenas were built for these Games, but London already had a number of suitable venues.

In 1956 the Olympics were held in Melbourne, the first time they had not been celebrated in Europe or America. But because of the strict Australian quarantine laws the equestrian events had to be held separately, in Stockholm. This remains the only instance of one sport being held in a different country from the main Games.

Tokyo was the host city for the 1964 Games, the first to be held in Asia. The Japanese organized their Games with amazing efficiency and flair, while the hospitality of the people won them many friends. More than £200,000,000 was spent on providing suitable facilities for the Games, including a vast programme of new roads.

There was no more controversial choice of venue for the Olympics than Mexico in 1968. The main criticism was that the rarefied air of the city put 'sea-level' athletes at a grave disadvantage. Though this was a valid point, the Games proved a splendid success. What shocked many, however, was the enormous cost of staging the Games when, it was pointed out, the Mexicans might have put the money to far better use by building decent homes for the thousands of poorly paid and unemployed who are forced to live in a squalor which compares badly with Mexico City's superficial affluence.

The Olympic Games are confined to amateurs. Any amateur sport widely practised—in 40 countries in 3 continents in the case of men's sports and 20 countries in 2 continents in the case of women's (according to the 1970 regulations)—can be considered for inclusion in the Games. Entry standards have been laid down in athletics, although every country is entitled to enter one competitor in every event. In team events, only one team is allowed from any country, but reserves can be used.

The opening and closing ceremonies follow the same basic pattern from one Games to another, although minor changes are made. At the opening ceremony, the words of Baron Pierre de Coubertin are displayed on the scoreboard: 'The important thing in the Olympic Games is not winning, but taking part. The essential thing in life is not conquering but fighting well.' The head of state of the host country enters with the president of the IOC and the president of the organizing committee, and they take their places. The scoreboard then displays the words 'Citius, Altius, Fortius'—faster, higher, stronger. The teams enter, and in accordance with tradition the Greek team leads and the host country brings up the rear. The others march in alphabetical order.

This completed, the president of the organizing committee requests the president of the IOC to ask the head of state or his representative to open the Games. The Olympic flag is raised to the strains of the Olympic hymn, and the official flag of the Games (presented by the Belgian Olympic Committee at the Antwerp Games of 1920) is handed over to the mayor of the host city who keeps the flag until the next celebration. Thousands of pigeons are released, a salute of three guns is fired, and then the final runner in the torch relay from Olympia enters—a feature of the Games which was introduced in 1936. The flame is lit, and the Olympic oath is taken by a competitor of the host country. It reads: 'In the name of all competitors I promise that we will take part in these Olympic Games, respecting and abiding by the rules which govern them, in the true spirit of sportsmanship, for the glory of sport and the honour of our teams.' The Olympic Games have begun.

The closing ceremony is shorter. The central feature is a march of representatives of the competing nations in a single body regardless of their nationality. The name of the host country is displayed on the scoreboard, the Olympic flame is allowed to go out, and the Olympics are over for another four years.

The Olympic opening ceremony is one of the most colourful pageants to be seen anywhere. 1 The Olympic flag is borne into the stadium. 2 Some teams parade in their national dress—Mongolia's flag bearer at the 1968 Games.
3 The host country's team always brings up the rear of the procession—Mexico's team at Mexico City in 1968.

International Olympic Committee

The International Olympic Committee (IOC) is the body responsible for the most important amateur sporting festival in the world, the Olympic Games. It was established in 1894 by the founder of the modern Olympics, Baron Pierre de Coubertin, and the members were chosen personally by him for their devotion to the Olympic movement.

The IOC was, and is, a self-perpetuating body, and its members are considered not as delegates from their countries, but as ambassadors from the IOC. This system has engendered much censure, but the IOC's success is seen in each Olympic Games, and its independence from national influences has much to commend it.

Successive strong presidents have given the IOC its authority, none more so than Avery Brundage, who became president in 1952. His idealistic views have been the subject of much criticism and ridicule, but his uncompromising attitude may have saved the IOC from the worst aspects of commercialism.

Members must speak French or English, and are elected by the IOC themselves, and in general no country has more than one member on the 60-70-strong body. Members are elected for life, but as a rule must retire at 72 years of age. On election, the new member is welcomed by the president and then undertakes to safeguard the Olympic ideals. All members must be free from political, sectarian, and commercial influences.

Every detail of the Olympic Games is controlled by the IOC, and it is the IOC's responsibility to decide, some six years ahead, the venue of both summer and winter celebrations. Regular meetings, and conferences with the representatives of national Olympic committees and international sporting organizations, ensure that the views of every sport and national body are known at first hand to the men who are the most important members of the international amateur sporting fraternity.

Above: Avery Brundage, the president of the IOC from 1952 to 1972 and probably the staunchest defender of the amateur faith in sport.
Right: The skiers, with their brand-carrying equipment and star image, often bore the brunt of Brundage's anti-commercialism attitudes.
Below: The opening of the Mexico City Olympics—the culmination of many years of planning by the IOC.

PRESIDENTS OF THE INTERNATIONAL OLYMPIC COMMITTEE	
1894-1896	Dimitrios Vikelas (Greece)
1896-1925	Baron Pierre de Coubertin (France)
1925-1942	Count Henri de Baillet Latour (Belgium)
1946-1952	Sigfrid Edstrom (Sweden)
1952-1972	Avery Brundage (USA)
1972-	Lord Killanin (Ireland)

A myriad of sports, and disciplines within those sports, comprise the 'summer' Olympic Games. Athletics, or track and field, is the sport that holds the public more than most, thanks to extensive television coverage and the obvious drama and explosive talent it provides. Swimming, too, has the ability to throw up the instant super-star for the media to exploit. Yet the Olympic Games is much more: in 1972, for example, some 21 sports were contested.

Away from the glare of the main Olympic arena, boxers, weightlifters, gymnasts and others draw the spectators indoors; often well away from the Olympic village, rowers, canoeists, cyclists, yachtsmen, and horsemen (and women) draw their own adherents.

The horse is involved in another event apart from the three equestrian disciplines. This is the modern pentathlon, which requires the courage of the horseman, the steady hand of the marksman, the élan of the fencer, and the durability of the runner and swimmer.

The Summer Olympic Games

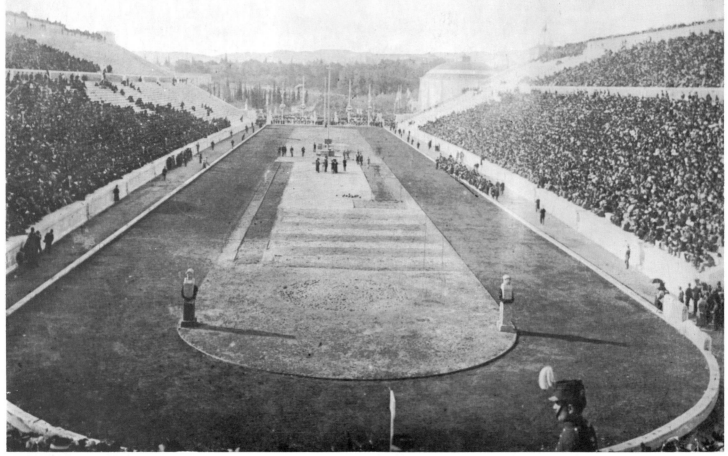

Athens Olympic Games (1896)

The first modern Olympic Games, revived about 1,500 years after the original Games died, produced moments of drama and periods of sheer farce—but, mostly the latter. The epic victory of Greek shepherd Spiridon Louis in the marathon, and the high jump won at a shade under 6 ft, cannot be denied as genuine athletic achievements. But then there was the dapper Frenchman who ran his 100-metre heat in white kid gloves . . . the American 100-metre swimmer who dived into the icy sea water, screamed 'I'm freezing!' and hastily climbed out . . . the English tourist who casually entered the tennis tournament—and won it.

It all started in the mind of a French nobleman, Baron Pierre de Coubertin. His great interest was public education, and he believed strongly (and heretically for those days) that you could not separate mental and physical development. He became increasingly despondent about commercialism in sport, and eventually dreamed up an antidote—a revival of the ancient Olympic Games. He envisaged amateur athletes from all parts of the world meeting every four years to compete in a selected number of sports.

In 1894 the baron presided over a congress of 13 nations at the Sorbonne, in Paris. Twenty-one other nations wrote in, also pledging their support. The assembled nations unanimously resolved that: 'in order to maintain and promote physical culture, and particularly to bring about a friendly intercourse between the nations, sports competitions should be held every fourth year on the lines of the Greek Olympic Games and every nation should be invited to participate.'

De Coubertin had planned to hold the first of these modern Games in Paris, in 1900, as part of the Paris International Exposition. But the Greek delegates put in an eloquent plea, based on tradition and history, for Athens as the inaugural seat of the Games. This was agreed, and the date fixed for 1896.

With a scant two years to prepare, the Greek authorities were suddenly faced with a fund-raising problem. They eventually prevailed upon George Averoff, a wealthy Greek philanthropist living in Alexandria, to foot the bill for a million drachmas (nearly £40,000 in those days). With this windfall, plus the money from commemorative stamps and public appeals, the Greeks proceeded to restore the Pan-Athenaic Stadium of Herodis. The 2,000-year-old ruins were rebuilt in marble, with a capacity of about 70,000 spectators. The stadium was about 200 yards long, and the 400-metre track had corners that were impossible to negotiate at speed.

Thirteen nations sent representatives (most of them unofficial) to compete in nine sports: cycling, fencing, gymnastics, lawn tennis, shooting, swimming, athletics, weight-lifting, and wrestling. Rowing had also been on the agenda, but was cancelled because of bad weather. Total entries for all sports were under 500.

The unofficial 13-man American team (five of whom came from the Boston Athletic Association) were unaware that Greece was still using the Julian calendar (which differed from the Gregorian by some 11 days). They did not arrive in Athens until the eve of the Games. To add to their troubles, they had barely recovered from a long and tedious journey by boat and train before they were paraded in front of a hospitable Greek crowd and persuaded to drink innumerable toasts late into the night.

The Panathenaic Stadium, splendidly restored in glistening white marble, formed an apt setting for the first modern Olympic Games.

The opening ceremony of the first modern Olympic Games took place on Easter Monday, April 6, 1896—the 75th anniversary of Greece's independence from Turkey—before 80,000 spectators. In the presence of Queen Olga, Crown Prince Constantine, Baron de Coubertin, and a throng of other VIPs, King George announced: 'I hereby proclaim the opening of the First International Olympic Games in Athens.' The opening ceremony closed with a cantata, and a bugle-call announced the first event.

There were 12 events in the athletics programme. Performances were disappointing, even for those days, even allowing for the horseshoe track and the horribly loose cinders. American athletes won nine of the events; two—the 800 and 1,500 metres—went to a former Australian mile champion then resident in England; and one —the marathon, the last and greatest event of the programme —was won by a Greek.

The first Olympic champion was James B. Connolly, from Boston.

who won the triple jump with a distance of 44 ft 11¾ in. A Greek came second, more than a yard behind. In those days the event was hardly known outside Greece, and competitors were allowed to take two hops and a jump—today's rules specify a hop, a step, and a jump. The world record of 48 ft 6 in had been set by an American three years before.

Throwing the discus followed. This was another event hardly known outside Greece but, in spite of this, three Greeks, three Danes, an Englishman, an American, a Frenchman, a Swede, and a German took part. Bob Garrett, the American, had never even seen a proper discus before reaching Athens, and was relieved to discover that the real thing was much easier to handle than the crude imitation he had been hurling across the Princeton campus. In the event, the Greeks took full marks for grace, but Garrett led the field by 8 inches. The American later added the shot to his discus triumph.

On the second day, the Americans continued to dominate the track and field events. Ellery Clark won both the long jump and the high jump, and sprinter Tom Burke easily took the 400-metre title in 54.2 sec. Burke had been American champion in 1895 and a few months after the Games clocked a time almost 6 seconds faster for the event—an indication of the atrocious running conditions in Athens. Burke also won the 100-metre final.

The fourth double victor was the Australian Edwin Flack, a member of the London Athletic Club. He beat Arthur Blake of Boston by a yard in the 1,500 metres, easily won the 800 metres on the third day, and soon afterwards departed for Marathon to try his luck in the long-distance race.

This final athletics event was the highlight of the Games. When the programme was being discussed, Michel Bréal, a French student of Greek mythology, suggested the idea of commemorating the feat of a legendary Greek hero with a long-distance race. In 490 B.C. on the plains of Marathon, nearly 25 miles from Athens, the heavily outnumbered Athenians repelled a Persian invasion. According to the legend, Pheidippides, a Greek soldier and champion Olympic runner, was entrusted to carry the good news to the capital. Exhausted after the battle, Pheidippides nevertheless loped off towards Athens and finally staggered into the market place there. He delivered his message, collapsed, and died.

The idea of commemorating the event caught on, and a race was arranged to start on the plains of Marathon over the route that Pheidippides had allegedly covered —a distance of about 40 kilometres (nearly 25 miles) to the stadium in Athens. The host nation had come

nowhere in the track and field events. If they were to salvage anything from the Games, it was now or never.

Among the 25 starters, all of whom had spent the previous night at Marathon, was a 25-year-old, handsome, moustachioed Greek shepherd called Spiridon Louis. During army service he had shown great stamina and all Greece pinned high hopes on him. The competitors started to the sound of a pistol shot from the bridge of Marathon at 2 p.m. precisely. They were accompanied

by a troop of soldiers, acting as marshals; a posse of doctors trundled behind in carts.

After 30 minutes the leader, Lermusiaux of France, reached the village of Pikarni. With rather an optimistic sense of pace he had already surged more than a mile ahead of Flack, in second place. Louis was nowhere, but still supremely confident. At the halfway stage the order was France, Australia, United States. Lermusiaux was so far ahead at Karvati that he was prematurely crowned by the villagers with a victor's gar-

land. But after 32 km he had had enough and dropped out of the race, exhausted. Louis, who had steadily been working his way through the field, came up to Flack's shoulder. At the 36th kilometre Flack suddenly collapsed.

As Louis jogged on, approaching the stadium, the murmur from the crowd swelled to a roar. Hundreds of doves were released. Prince George and Crown Prince Constantine rushed to the entrance, and when the shepherd hero trotted in, a full seven minutes ahead of his nearest rival, they ran round the track beside him on his final lap. Gifts of all kinds were pressed on the victor. As it happened, five of the first six men were Greeks, so honour was saved. Louis had been promised, if he won, a number of 'fringe benefits', such as free haircuts for life, free groceries, free transport, and similar attractions.

The scenes of jubilation had interrupted the pole vault, which was going on in the stadium. Americans took first and second places in the event, helped by poles of extraordinary length which enabled them to jump the (then) fabulous height of 3.30 metres (10 ft 9¾ in).

There were 10 weight-lifters

1 Today, the rebuilt Panathenaic Stadium is preserved as a perpetual monument to the Olympic Games. As a tribute to athletics in general, the closing ceremony of the 1969 European championships was held in the stadium. 2 The start of the 110 metres hurdles manifests a variety of styles, with US winner Tom Curtis getting down on four points. 3 Spiridon Louis, marathon champion, poses after the victory ceremony. In addition to the gold medal and olive branch, awarded to each winner, Louis was also presented with a silver cup and an ancient vase. 4 Baron Pierre de Coubertin, whose vision and untiring efforts led to the world-wide revival of the ancient Olympic Games.

13

tinidis, the eventual winner, not only had the handicap of a lengthy signature, but managed to break his bicycle shortly after the turn. He borrowed the starter's machine and soon regained his lead. But again he fell off, wrecked the second bicycle, and was overtaken once more. Bloody, but nothing daunted, he jumped onto a friend's bike and pedalled home to victory a good 20 minutes ahead of the second man.

The tennis tournament was a somewhat light-hearted affair held in a shed on the shores of the Illissos. It was won by an English tourist called Boland, who entered because he happened to be there at the time. Sir George Stuart Robertson, the Greek scholar and hammer-throwing Oxford Blue, also entered the tennis tournament —because it was the only way he could get the use of a court. He also took part in the shot-put and discus, and composed and recited the valedictory Greek ode.

Of the 160 entrants for the 200-metre shooting event, 150 were Greeks. The six gymnastics events included an item labelled 'arm exercises with smooth cord', more easily recognizable, perhaps, as rope-climbing. Fencing consisted of a foils contest (in which Frenchmen came first and second), sabres (won by a Greek), and a special foils contest for 'fencing masters'—that is, professionals!

For the record, although the figures are quite without significance, the United States won 11 firsts, Greece 8, Germany 6½, France 5, Britain 2½, Australia, Austria, and Hungary 2 each, and Denmark and Switzerland 1 apiece.

The presentation of prizes, on the tenth and final day, took place in pouring rain. King George of Greece presented each winner with a gold medal and an olive branch. Runners up received a bronze medal and a laurel branch. The specially composed Greek ode was recited, and the winners paraded slowly round the stadium. As the band played and the crowd cheered, a special ovation was reserved for Spiridon Louis, marching proudly and happily in the front row of the champions of the First Olympiad.

competing. Launceston Elliott, from England, won the single-handed lift, but he seems to have attracted more attention for the beauty of his person than for his prowess with the weights. After the contest, a servant who was ordered to remove the weights, found the task beyond him. Prince George came to his aid and, picking up the heaviest weight with ease, threw it a considerable distance.

Launceston Elliott's good looks were of no help to him in the wrestling, in which there were no weight limits. Herr Schumann of Germany, who won the event, seized him round the middle and 'threw him to the ground in the twinkling of an eye', according to a contemporary report.

The swimming events were somewhat parochial. Some were held in the ice-cold water of the Bay of Zea, to the consternation of swimmers who had trained in heated pools. Only 3 of the 29 entries for the 500-metre race took part, and three Greeks were the only swimmers to compete in the race 'for sailors of the Royal Navy'.

Cycling consisted of six events. Three of them, all won by Frenchman Paul Masson, were short— the longest being the 10,000 metres, which Masson narrowly won from his compatriot Léon Flamaud. The latter gained some consolation by winning the 100 km (one of the three long events), consisting of some 300 dizzying laps of the Velodrome. The cycling marathon started in Athens, wended its way to Marathon, where the six competitors had to sign their names on a parchment in the presence of a special commissioner, and returned to the Velodrome in Athens. A. Konstan-

1 Three marathon runners of the 1896 Games get down to a spot of road work with not a horseless carriage in sight.
2 A proud victor receives his olive branch from King George of Greece. **3** The Games are over, and the winners parade slowly round the stadium for the last time.

ATHENS OLYMPIC GAMES, 1896 (Gold Medallists)

Athletics

100 metres	Thomas Burke	USA	12.0 sec
400 metres	Thomas Burke	USA	54.2 sec
800 metres	Edwin Flack	Australia	2 min 11.0 sec
1,500 metres	Edwin Flack	Australia	4 min 33.2 sec
Marathon	Spiridion Louis	Greece	2 hr 58 min 50.0 sec
Hurdles	Thomas Curtis	USA	17.6 sec
High Jump	Ellery Clark	USA	5 ft 11¼ in
Pole Vault	William Hoyt	USA	10 ft 10 in
Long Jump	Ellery Clark	USA	20 ft 10 in
Triple Jump	James Connolly	USA	44 ft 11¾ in
Shot	Robert Garrett	USA	36 ft 9¾ in
Discus	Robert Garrett	USA	95 ft 7½ in

Cycling

Event	Winner	Country	Result
333⅓ metres	Paul Masson	France	24.0 sec
2,000 metres	Paul Masson	France	4 min 56.0 sec
10,000 metres	Paul Masson	France	17 min 54.2 sec
100 km	Leon Flamand	France	3 hr 08 min 19.2 sec
12 hours race	Felix Schmal	Austria	195¾ miles
Marathon (50 miles)	A. Konstantinidis	Greece	3 hr 22 min 31.0 sec

Fencing

Event	Winner	Country	Result
Foil	E. Gravelotte	France	
Foil (for fencing masters)	Leon Pyrgos	Greece	
Sabre	Jean Georgiadis	Greece	

Gymnastics

Event	Winner	Country	Result
Parallel Bars (individual)	Alfred Flatow	Germany	
Horizontal Bars	Hermann Weingartner	Germany	
Pommelled Horse	Louis Zutter	Switzerland	
Long Horse	Karl Schumann	Germany	
Rings	Jean Mitropoulos	Greece	
Rope Climbing	Nicolaos Andriakoupolos	Greece	23.4 sec
Team Events		Germany	

Lawn Tennis

Event	Winner	Country	Result
Men's Singles	P. Boland	GB	
Doubles	P. Boland (GB), Fritz Thraun (Germany)		

Shooting

Rifle Match 300 metres	Georges Orphanidhis	Greece	
Rifle Match 200 metres	Pantelis Karasseudas	Greece	
Revolver 25 metres	John Paine	USA	
Revolver 30 metres	Sommer Paine	USA	
Pistol 25 metres	Jean Phrangoudis	Greece	

Swimming

Event	Winner	Country	Result
100 metres	Alfred Guttmann	Hungary	1 min 22.2 sec
500 metres	Paul Neumann	Austria	8 min 12.6 sec
1,200 metres	Alfred Guttmann	Hungary	18 min 22.2 sec
100 metres (sailors' race)	Jean Malokinis	Greece	2 min 20.4 sec

Weight Lifting

Event	Winner	Country	Result
One Hand	Launceston Elliot	GB	156 lb (71.0 kg)
Two Hands	Viggo Jensen	Denmark	245 lb (111.5 kg)

Wrestling

	Karl Schumann	Germany	

Paris Olympic Games (1900)

In conjunction with the Paris International Exhibition of 1900, various sporting events were held in the French capital from May 14 to October 28. Exactly which of these sports, 15 altogether, can be termed 'Olympic' in the true sense of the word is debatable. A realistic view would seem to be that a number of sports were promoted, and it is a matter of choice which of them should be regarded as official. For instance, there were 23 shooting events with all kinds of weapons: the fencing embraced amateurs and professionals: the swimming competitions—listed in the FINA handbook—included an underwater swim for distance and an obstacle race. There was a tug-of-war in which a joint Danish and Swedish contingent beat the United States, and a tennis tournament in which the Doherty brothers were prominent.

The athletics events—at least some of them—may be regarded as Olympic, although the programme was headed 'Republique Francaise, Exposition Universelle de 1900, Championnats Internationaux'. Even so, the events were haphazardly arranged, and included some contentious handicaps. They were scheduled to take place over two days on a 500-metre grass track laid out in the Bois de Boulogne. The turf was very thick, and was heavily watered. The sprint course and the long jump run-up were said to be downhill, and as part of the course was among trees it was impossible for the timekeepers to see the starter from the winning post. The competitions, such as they were, were marred by the scratching of some Americans who refused to compete on a Sunday.

The star of the athletics was Alvin Kraenzlein of Pennsylvania, who won four events—the 60 metres dash, the 110 and 200 metres hurdles, and the long jump. Another American, Ray Ewry, won three titles—the standing high jump, long jump, and triple jump.

The double-champions in athletics included John Tewksbury, who took the 200 metres and the 400 metres hurdles, and was second in the 100 metres, third in the 200 metres hurdles, and fourth in the 60 metres. Irving Baxter won the high jump and the pole vault, rather luckily in each case because his more favoured rivals refused to compete in the Sunday's finals; Baxter was also second in the standing high and long jumps.

British entries had a field day in the middle-distance events. Alfred Tysoe took the 800 metres in 2 min 1.2 sec, Charles Bennett the 1,500 metres in 4 min 6.2 sec, and in a British clean-sweep of the

1 Irving Baxter—winner of high jump and pole vault at the 1900 Olympic Games.
2 The first great all-rounder in the modern Olympic Games was Alvin Kraenzlein who won the long jump, 60 metres, and both hurdles events.
3 Britain's Charles Bennett won the 1,500 metres and was a member of Britain's winning 5,000 metres team.
4 The great Irish-American hammer thrower John Flanagan won the first of three successive Olympic titles.

4,000 metres steeplechase J. T. Rimmer edged out Bennett for first place. Tysoe, Bennett, and Rimmer all ran for Britain in the 5,000 metres team race in which they defeated a French team. Some idea of the comic opera nature of these 'Games' can be gathered from the fact that another member of Britain's team, Stan Rowley, was an Australian who had previously come third in the 60, 100, and 200 metres sprints.

In the throwing events America won all three titles. Robert Garrett, defending his shot and discus titles, had an unhappy time. In the shot he improved on his Athens performance by nearly 4 ft. but was still beaten into third place by his team-mates Richard Sheldon and Josiah McCracken. In the discus throw, he had trouble throwing the implement straight down a lane of trees, and was unplaced. John Flanagan won the first Olympic hammer title with a respectable 163 ft. 2 in.

The arrangements for the marathon typified the whole proceedings. The race was run on July 19, and the course of 25 miles followed the old Parisian fortifications. As soon as the runners left the Bois and entered the city through the Passy Gate, they were mobbed by a crowd of cyclists and early cars. Only 7 men of the 19 starters finished, and the winner by over 5 minutes was Michel Theato, a Parisian baker's roundsman said to be fully familiar with the course—and the short cuts.

The swimming was held in the River Seine. Britain's John Jarvis

won the 1,000 and 4,000 metres events by considerable margins, and Australia's Freddy Lane the 200 metres freestyle and a 200 metres obstacle race. His prize for the 200 metres was a replica of the Louvre, weighing more than 50 pounds, and for the obstacle race a similar sized bronze of a peasant girl.

PARIS OLYMPIC GAMES, 1900 Champions

Athletics

Event	Champion	Country	Result
60 metres	Alvin Kraenzlein	USA	7.0 sec
100 metres	Frank Jarvis	USA	11.0 sec
200 metres	John Tewksbury	USA	22.2 sec
400 metres	Maxwell Long	USA	49.4 sec
800 metres	Alfred Tysoe	Great Britain	2 min 1.2 sec
1,500 metres	Charles Bennett	Great Britain	4 min 6.2 sec
Marathon	Michel Theato	France	2 hr 59 min 45.0 sec
5,000 metres team race		Great Britain	26 points
2,500 metres steeplechase	George Orton	USA	7 min 34.4 sec
4,000 metres steeplechase	John Rimmer	Great Britain	12 min 58.4 sec
110 metres hurdles	Alvin Kraenzlein	USA	15.4 sec
200 metres hurdles	Alvin Kraenzlein	USA	25.4 sec
400 metres hurdles	John Tewksbury	USA	57.6 sec
High jump	Irving Baxter	USA	6 ft 2¾ in
Pole vault	Irving Baxter	USA	10 ft 10 in
Long jump	Alvin Kraenzlein	USA	23 ft 6¾ in
Triple jump	Myer Prinstein	USA	47 ft 5¾ in
Standing high jump	Ray Ewry	USA	5 ft 5 in
Standing long jump	Ray Ewry	USA	10 ft 6½ in
Standing triple jump	Ray Ewry	USA	34 ft 8¼ in
Shot	Richard Sheldon	USA	46 ft 3 in
Discus	Rudolf Bauer	Hungary	118 ft 3 in
Hammer	John Flanagan	USA	163 ft 2 in
Tug-of-war		Denmark-Sweden	

Swimming

Event	Champion	Country	Result
200 metres freestyle	Freddie Lane	Australia	2 min 25.2 sec
1,000 metres freestyle	John Jarvis	Great Britain	13 min 40.0 sec
4,000 metres freestyle	John Jarvis	Great Britain	58 min 24.0 sec
5 x 40 metres relay		Germany	—
Underwater swim	M. de Vaudeville	France	60 metres
200 metres obstacle race	Freddie Lane	Australia	2 min 38.4 sec

St Louis Olympic Games (1904)

The International Olympic Committee's official figures for participation at the 1904 Olympics is a mere 496 men from 10 nations, and no women. Other sources claim as many as 9,000 competitors. All that is certain is that some sort of Olympic celebrations were held in St Louis between May and September 1904. The Games were first scheduled to take place in Chicago, but were later handed over to the Louisiana Purchase Exposition of St Louis, and as a result the Games were in reality of very little importance compared with the exhibition itself. 'All sports', the semi-official report runs, 'given under the auspices of the Exposition must bear the name "Olympic",' and under this banner were held all sorts of events: interscholastic events open only to schoolboys from the state of Missouri, open handicaps for residents of Missouri, YMCA championships, and so on. It is quite impossible to tell which events were truly Olympic and which were not.

The vast majority of gold medals went to the United States, and in track and field athletics there was only one non-US winner—Etienne Desmarteau of Canada, a policeman from Montreal, who won the 56-lb weight throw. Indeed, the only non-American medallists of any kind were John Daly of Ireland (second in the steeplechase), Paul Weinstein of Germany (third in the high jump), and Nicolaos Georgantas of Greece (third in the discus). The United States made a clean sweep of seven boxing events, with O. L. Kirk winning the bantamweight and featherweight titles, cycling (Marcus Hurley won four events), and rowing (11 events in all), and won all but one gymnastics event. Only in fencing, where Cuba won five out of six contests, and in swimming, where Hungarians and Germans took six events to the

1 Freddie Lane, who at Paris in 1900, won Australia's first swimming titles, beating Hungary's Zoltan Halmay by 5.8 seconds in the 200 metres freestyle and also winning the 200 metres 'obstacle' race. The obstacle race, sometimes called 'hurdle swimming', was an amusing affair, but it is not surprising that this was the only time it was in the Olympic programme. The competitors had to struggle through barrels every 50 metres in this 200 metres race. Lane, from Sydney, won by 1.6 seconds from Otto Wahle of Austria, and it was probably his size—he weighed only 9½ stone—that helped him to victory. Lane used a double overarm stroke, similar to the trudgen but with a narrow kick, which was considered too strenuous until this rugged little man won the New South Wales title in 1899.
2 Alvin Kraenzlein, the first man to win four gold medals in one Olympic Games: in the 60 metres, 110 metres hurdles, 200 metres hurdles, and long jump at Paris. In 1898 and 1899, he had set world best performances in three different events.

ST LOUIS OLYMPIC GAMES, 1904 Gold Medallists			
Athletics			
60 metres	Archie Hahn	USA	7.0 sec
100 metres	Archie Hahn	USA	11.0 sec
200 metres	Archie Hahn	USA	21.6 sec
400 metres	Harry Hillman	USA	49.2 sec
800 metres	James Lightbody	USA	1 min 56.0 sec
1,500 metres	James Lightbody	USA	4 min 5.4 sec
Marathon	Thomas Hicks	USA	3 hr 28 min 53 sec
2,500 metres steeplechase	James Lightbody	USA	7 min 39.6 sec
4 mile team race	New York AC	USA	
110 metres hurdles	Fred Schule	USA	16.0 sec
200 metres hurdles	Harry Hillman	USA	24.6 sec
400 metres hurdles	Harry Hillman	USA	53.0 sec
High jump	Samuel Jones	USA	5 ft 11 in
Pole vault	Charles Dvorak	USA	11 ft 6 in
Long jump	Myer Prinstein	USA	24 ft 1 in
Triple jump	Myer Prinstein	USA	47 ft 0 in
Standing high jump	Ray Ewry	USA	4 ft 11 in
Standing long jump	Ray Ewry	USA	11 ft 4¾ in
Standing triple jump	Ray Ewry	USA	34 ft 7¼ in
Shot	Ralph Rose	USA	48 ft 7 in
Discus	Martin Sheridan	USA	128 ft 10½ in
Hammer	John Flanagan	USA	168 ft 1 in
56 lb weight	Etienne Desmarteau	Canada	34 ft 4 in

United States' five, was there anything that could be described as serious foreign competiton.

In the track and field events, held over six days from August 29 to September 3, there were four triple winners—Archie Hahn in the 60, 100, and 200 metres, James Lightbody (800 metres, 1,500 metres, and steeplechase), Harry Hillman (400 metres flat and 200 and 400 metres hurdles), and Ray Ewry, who repeated his 1900 hat-trick of winning the three standing jumps—high, long, and triple. The best performances came from Hahn, who won the 200 metres over a straight course in 21.6 sec, and Hillman, who ran the 200 metres hurdles in 24.6 sec.

The marathon event, run over 40 kilometres, provided the Games with an element of drama. Run on a hot day on roads deep in dust, the race caused 17 of the 31 starters to retire, including one Fred Lorz. He gave up at 9 miles, but having had a lift in a car he ran the last 5 miles into the stadium, where he was hailed as the winner. His prank was soon discovered, and Lorz was suspended for life, although he did compete in, and win, the Boston Marathon the following year. The actual winner, Thomas Hicks, finished 6 minutes in front of the next man. His spirits were kept up in the closing stages by ministrations of strychnine, raw eggs, and brandy.

The swimming events were held in an ornamental lake with the swimmers starting from a raft. Hungary's Zoltan Halmay won the 50 and 100 yards, not without having to compete in a swim-off for the 50 yards title after the judges had failed to agree and passions had been inflamed to fighting pitch. New York AC won the 4 x 50 yards relay and the water polo in these Games, the only time that individual club sides have contested an Olympic swimming competition. But then this was no ordinary Olympics.

1 Harry Hillman soars over the final hurdle in the 200 metres event. Hillman, of New York AC, also won the 400 metres hurdles and the 400 metres dash on the track.
2 James D. Lightbody of the Chicago AA won the 800 and 1,500 metres, and the 2,500 metres steeplechase, and thus gained the award for amassing most individual points.
3 Etienne Desmarteau, a Montreal policeman, stopped the United States winning all the events by coming out on top in the 56-lb weight throw.
4 Standing jump expert Ray Ewry won the high, long, and triple jumps, retaining all the titles he had won four years previously at the Olympic meeting in the Bois de Boulogne.

Interim Olympic Games

(Athens, 1906)

The first modern Olympic Games, held in Athens in 1896, proved such a success that the Greek organizers asked to keep the Games permanently in their country. Baron de Coubertin, the acknowledged resuscitator of the Olympics, believed that they should be fully international in character, and not the preserve of one country. Had he not received the full support of the International Olympic Committee, it is doubtful that the Olympics would have secured the status they now possess. But the Greeks, though bitterly disap-

1 The start of the 1906 84 km cycle race, an event which ended in a tie between two French competitors. 2 Prince George applauds the winner of the marathon, William Sherring.

pointed at the IOC's decision, obtained permission to stage a Games in Athens on the tenth anniversary of their revival. They planned that there should be a Games in Athens every ten years, but the 1906 venture was in fact unique.

Known variously as the 'Intercalated' or 'Interim' Games, the 1906 Games were opened on April 22 by King George of Greece in the presence of other

A rather fancifully posed shot of Georgantas, winner of the stone putting event. He threw the 14 lb weight an impressive 65 ft. 4 in.

INTERIM OLYMPIC GAMES, 1906 Gold Medallists

Athletics

100 metres	Archie Hahn	USA	11.2 sec
400 metres	Paul Pilgrim	USA	53.2 sec
800 metres	Paul Pilgrim	USA	2 min 1.2 sec
1,500 metres	Jim Lightbody	USA	4 min 12.0 sec
5 miles	H. Hawtrey	Great Britain	26 min 26.2 sec
Marathon	William Sherring	Canada	2 hr 51 min 23.6 sec
1,500 metres walk	George Bonhag	USA	7 min 12.6 sec
110 metres hurdles	R. Leavitt	USA	16.2 sec
High jump	Con Leahy	Great Britain	5 ft 9¾ in
Pole vault	Fernand Gonder	France	11 ft 6 in
Long jump	Myer Prinstein	USA	23 ft 7½ in
Triple jump	Peter O'Connor	Great Britain	46 ft 2 in
Standing high jump	Ray Ewry	USA	5 ft 1½ in
Standing long jump	Ray Ewry	USA	10 ft 10 in
Shot	Martin Sheridan	USA	40 ft 5 in
Discus	Martin Sheridan	USA	136 ft 0 in
Discus (Greek style)	Werner Jarvinen	Finland	115 ft 5 in
Javelin	Erik Lemming	Sweden	175 ft 6 in
Pentathlon	H. Mellander	Sweden	
Tug-of-War		Germany	
Rope climb (10 metres)	D. Aliprantis	Greece	11.4 sec
Lifting the bar bell (both hands)			
	D. Tofalos	Greece	317.6 lb
Lifting the bar bell (each hand separately)			
	H. Steinbach	Austria	168 lb
Throwing the stone (14 lb)			
	G. Georgantas	Greece	65 ft 4 in

Cycling

333⅓ metres time trial	Francesco Verri	Italy	22.8 sec
1,000 metres scratch	Francesco Verri	Italy	1 min 42.2 sec
5,000 metres	Francesco Verri	Italy	8 min 35.0 sec
2,000 metres tandem	J. Matthews & A. Rushen	Great Britain	
20 km paced race	W. J. Pett	Great Britain	29 min 0 sec
Road race (84 km)	{ Vast	France	2 hr 41 min 28.0 sec
	Bardonneau	France	

Fencing

Foil—individual	M. Dillon-Cavanagh	France
Epee—individual	Comte de la Falaise	France
Epee—team		France
Sabre—individual	Jean Georgiadis	Greece
Sabre—team		Germany
Football		Denmark

Gymnastics

Team competition		Norway

Lawn Tennis

Men's singles	Max Decugis	France
Men's doubles	Max Decugis & M. Germot	France
Ladies' singles	Miss Semyriotou	Greece
Mixed doubles	Max & Mme Decugis	France

Rowing

Canoe race	Delaplane	France
Coxed pairs (1,000 m)	E. Brunna, E. Fontanella, G. Cerana (cox)	Italy
Coxed pairs (1,600 m)	E. Brunna, E. Fontanella, G. Cerana (cox)	Italy
Coxed fours (2,000 m)		Italy

Shooting

There were 15 shooting contests. Norway and Switzerland each won five, France three, Great Britain one, and Greece one.

Swimming

100 metres freestyle	Charles Daniels	USA	1 min 13.0 sec
400 metres freestyle	Otto Scheff	Austria	6 min 23.8 sec
1,600 metres freestyle	Henry Taylor	Great Britain	28 min 28.0 sec
1,000 metres team		Hungary	16 min 52.4 sec
High diving	Gottlob Walz	Germany	156.00 pts

assorted royal persons and a packed crowd of 60,000 in the Panathenaic stadium built for the 1896 celebrations. The track, the surface of which was soft and invited some criticisms, was quite unsuited to stern competitions: it had straights some 200 yards long, and the turns were sharp. In addition, the races were run in a clockwise direction.

Athletics contests were held in some 24 events, including rope-climbing, tug-of-war, and weightlifting. The United States, with a team selected for the first time as the result of special 'tryouts', was most formidable, winning 11 events. Archie Hahn, the 1904 victor over 60, 100, and 200 metres, was restricted to winning the 100 metres, the only sprint on the programme, and Jim Lightbody repeated his 1,500 metres victory. But Lightbody could not duplicate his 800 metres success of 1904, losing to Paul Pilgrim, a late addition to the United States team who was also successful in the 400 metres. Great Britain gained three wins: H. Hawtrey in the 5 miles, Con Leahy (an Irishman) in the high jump, and Peter O'Connor (another Irishman) in the triple jump. O'Connor, the world record holder, was runner-up in his speciality, the long jump, to the American Myer Prinstein, who had set his final world record of 24 ft. 7¼ in. in 1898. Olympic champion Ray Ewry won the standing high and long jumps, while Martin Sheridan, the 1904 discus champion, won the shot and the discus. The Greek-style discus throw, however, went to the first of the great Jarvinen family, Werner, who beat the Greek hero George Georgantos. Greece failed to win any of the regular track and field events, but excelled in the more esoteric competitions —the rope climb, 'lifting-the-barbell-with-both-hands', and throwing the 14-lb stone.

Paul Pilgrim just beats Jim Lightbody to the tape in the 800 metres. Pilgrim was also successful in the 400 metres.

Charles Daniels, the American who had won two swimming events at St Louis, won the 100 metres freestyle in a slow time of 1 min. 13.0 sec. This was understandable as the event was held in the sea at Phaleron. Otto Scheff won the 400 metres and Henry Taylor the mile—both in times well in excess of their best.

French players dominated the lawn tennis, with Max Decugis winning three events, the singles, doubles (with M. Germot), and the mixed doubles with his wife.

The Greeks, the ancient founders of the Olympics, succeeded in fulfilling a great need at the beginning of the 20th century. The disorganised competition at Paris in 1900 and the cumbersome arrangements for the 1904 Games in St Louis—both of which were run concurrently with and subordinate to a trade fair—had, despite their shortcomings, shown that international competitions were wanted by sportsmen and public alike. The 1906 Games saw the beginning of the Olympics in a form which has persisted, roughly, ever since.

London Olympic Games (1908)

Two of the strangest sights in all sporting history were seen in the the new Shepherd's Bush stadium built especially for the Olympic Games of 1908. The first was the British Lieutenant Wyndham Halswelle 'running over' to win the 400 metres, and the second was the Italian candy-maker Dorando Pietri collapsing in the stadium at the end of the marathon.

There were a number of Olympic celebrations in London that year. The summer sports were held in July, and so-called autumn sports —boxing, football, lacrosse, and skating—later in the year. The 1908 Games were the last at which the host country had full jurisdiction over the sports. There were so many protests from the visitors that international bodies were soon formed to iron out various problems of rule-interpretation and amateurism.

The athletics, swimming, wrestling, gymnastics, and cycling events were held in the stadium; the rowing over the 1½-mile course at Henley; shooting at Bisley and Uxendon; and other sports at local venues more suited to them. But motor-boat racing was held on the Solent, and the 12-metre yachting on the Clyde.

A strong American team dominated the athletics events on the newly laid ⅓-mile track. Their most successful competitor was Melvin Sheppard who won the 800 metres and 1,500 metres. His 800 metres time, 1 min 52.8 sec, was a world record, and in the 1,500 metres he beat the British world record

holder, Harold Wilson, by a couple of yards, with another Briton, Norman Hallowes, third. And in the 1,600 metres relay (200+200+400+800 metres), Sheppard anchored the United States team, to win his third gold medal of the Games.

Americans won most of the more 'technical' events. Forrest Smithson in the 110 metres hurdles and Charles Bacon in the 400

metres hurdles set world records in winning. Ray Ewry gained his customary double in the standing jumps; John Flanagan won his third hammer gold medal; and Martin Sheridan walked off with both discus titles. Only Sweden's Erik Lemming (in the two javelin events) and Ireland's Timothy Ahearne who was competing for Britain in the triple jump broke the American stranglehold in the

1 Harold Blackstaffe wins the 1908 Olympic single sculls.
2 The start of the 100-kilometre cycle race in the new stadium.
3 John Flanagan won his third consecutive hammer title with a throw of 170 ft. 4¼ in. Other Americans were second and third.

field events.

The British Empire supplied the winners of the shorter sprints, through South Africa's Reggie Walker in the 100 metres and Canada's Bobbie Kerr in the 200 metres. But the big talking point of the track races was the victory of Halswelle in the 400 metres. In the final he was opposed by three Americans. The race was not run in lanes, and one of the Americans, J. C. Carpenter, appears to have edged Halswelle wide as they entered the finishing straight. A shout of 'Foul' went up, and the British officials broke the tape before the finish. Carpenter was disqualified and a re-run was ordered, but when the time for the re-run arrived the other two Americans, W. C. Robbins and J. B. Taylor, refused to take part. So Halswelle ran over—the only instance of such an occurrence in the history of the Games.

Despite the controversy of the 400 metres, the most famous race was the marathon. Run from Windsor Great Park along the roads of West London to the stadium in hot, windless weather, the race was attempted by 56 men of whom only 27 finished. The little Italian, Dorando Pietri, did not follow the initial fast pace, and after 15 miles the South African Charles Hefferon was in the lead. He held this advantage until the 24th mile, when first Pietri and then the American John Hayes passed him. But the Italian's effort had so exhausted him that he was almost unconscious when he entered the stadium. He collapsed on the track, officials put him back on the right course (an act which immediately disqualified him), and the brave man struggled on and was helped to the tape. Hayes, who had run a sensible race in the heat, was just over half-a-minute behind Pietri at the finish, and he was awarded the gold medal. Pietri's heroic effort so affected the British queen that she presented him with a special gold cup.

British athletes, out of contention in the marathon, had a field day in the other distance events. Emil Voigt won the 5 miles, Arthur Russell the 3,200 metres steeplechase, and George Larner the 3,500 metres and 10 miles walks. And the British team in the 3-mile team race packed five men into the first seven places to win comfortably.

Second in importance to the athletics was the swimming, where Britain's Henry Taylor from Chadderton in Lancashire won three gold medals. In the 100-metre pool he won the 400 and 1,500 metres events in world record times, and anchored Britain to a fine 4 by 200 metres relay win. Fred Holman of Britain won the 200 metres breaststroke from his team-mate 38-year-old W. W. Robinson. But probably the best swimmer on display was the American sprinter Charles Daniels, who won the

100 metres in a world best time. Britain won the water polo, and in the team was Paul Radmilovic, who also won a gold in the relay—the only man ever to win golds in both swimming and water polo.

A collapsible tower had been built for the diving events, and European divers won six of the seven medals awarded, there being a tie for third place in the fancy diving. Swedes, headed by Hjalmar Johansson, made a clean sweep of the plain diving, and Albert Zurner led a German assault in the fancy diving—Kurt Behrens was second and Gottlob Walz third, tying with America's George Gaidzik.

A 660-yard cycle track, built round the running track, completed the new arena, but the events were marred by continual rain and a large number of punctures. British cyclists took every gold medal except the tandem—won by France—and the 1,000 metres sprint which was declared void after the riders had exceeded the time limit.

Outside the stadium, British sportsmen were no less successful, winning all the lawn tennis championships, rowing, and yachting, as well as the polo, racquets, six of the shooting events, and two of the three motor-boat titles. For the eights at Henley a veteran Leander crew had been in training to beat the Belgian European champions. With a magnificently histrionic gesture, the Belgians tossed their cigar butts into the Thames before embarking, but they went down narrowly to Leander in one of the greatest races seen at any regatta.

Of the 'autumn' sports, the boxing was a clean sweep for the home country. Future England cricket captain, Johnny Douglas, won the middleweight gold. Britain also won the soccer, hockey, and ladies figure skating. But in the rugby final a visiting Australian team beat the English county champions, Cornwall, 32-3, while Canada not surprisingly beat Britain 14-10 at lacrosse.

The summer sports ended with a ceremonial prizegiving by Queen Alexandra. Gold, silver, and bronze medals, and diplomas of merit were awarded. Lord Desborough, who had organized the Games with tremendous flair, called for three cheers for the Queen, and the Games of the Fourth Olympiad passed into history.

1 Reggie Walker (right) won the 100 metres in 10.8 sec.
2 John Hayes, the eventual winner of the marathon, passes through Willesden. He finished 32 sec behind the disqualified Pietri.
3 Ulrich Salchow won the first ever Olympic figure skating title, which was held as part of the London Games.
4 12-metre yachts contested their event on the river Clyde in Scotland.

Official Report of 1908 Olympics

5 J. C. Carpenter crosses the finishing line in the 400 metres final as British officials break the tape and signal a 'no race'.
6 Carpenter was disqualified as a result of an examination of the runners' footprints. The race was not run in lanes.

Mansell

LONDON OLYMPIC GAMES, 1908 Gold Medallists

Archery
York round (men)	W. Dod	Great Britain	
National round (women)	Q. Newall	Great Britain	
50 metres Continental	E. G. Grisot	France	

Athletics
100 metres	Reginald Walker	South Africa	10.8 sec
200 metres	Robert Kerr	Canada	22.6 sec
400 metres	Wyndham Halswelle	Great Britain	50.0 sec
800 metres	Melvin Sheppard	USA	1 min 52.8 sec
1,500 metres	Melvin Sheppard	USA	4 min 3.4 sec
5 miles	Emil Voigt	Great Britain	25 min 11.2 sec
Marathon	John Hayes	USA	2 hr 55 min 46.4 sec
Relay (2 x 200 + 1 x 400 + 1 x 800 metres)		USA	3 min 29.4 sec
110 metres hurdles	Forrest Smithson	USA	15.0 sec
400 metres hurdles	Charles Bacon	USA	55.0 sec.
3,200 metres steeplechase	Arthur Russell	Great Britain	10 min 47.8 sec
3 miles team race		Great Britain	
3,500 metres walk	George Larner	Great Britain	14 min 55 sec
10 miles walk	George Larner	Great Britain	1 hr 15 min 57.4 sec
Standing high jump	Ray Ewry	USA	5 ft 2 in
Standing long jump	Ray Ewry	USA	10 ft 11¼ in
High jump	Harry Porter	USA	6 ft 3 in
Pole vault	Edward Cooke	USA	} 12 ft 2 in
	Alfred Gilbert	USA	
Long jump	Frank Irons	USA	24 ft 6½ in
Triple jump	Timothy Ahearne	Great Britain	48 ft 11¼ in
Shot	Ralph Rose	USA	46 ft 7½ in
Discus (free style)	Martin Sheridan	USA	134 ft 2 in
Discus (Greek style)	Martin Sheridan	USA	124 ft 8 in
Hammer	John Flanagan	USA	170 ft 4¼ in
Javelin (free style)	Erik Lemming	Sweden	178 ft 7½ in
Javelin (conventional)	Erik Lemming	Sweden	179 ft 10½ in
Tug of War		Great Britain	

Boxing
Bantamweight	H. Thomas	Great Britain
Featherweight	R. K. Gunn	Great Britain
Lightweight	F. Grace	Great Britain
Middleweight	John Douglas	Great Britain
Heavyweight	A. L. Oldham	Great Britain

Cycling
One lap (660 yards)	Victor Johnson	Great Britain	
1,000 metres sprint	final declared void		
5,000 metres	Ben Jones	Great Britain	8 min 36.2 sec
20 kilometres	C. B. Kingsbury	Great Britain	34 min 13.6 sec
100 kilometres	C. H. Bartlett	Great Britain	2 hr 41 min 48.6 sec
Team pursuit (3 laps)		Great Britain	2 min 18.6 sec
2,000 metres tandem	Maurice Schilles	} France	
	Andre Auffray		

Fencing
Epee—individual	Gaston Alibert	France
Epee—team		France
Sabre—individual	Jeno Fuchs	Hungary
Sabre—team		Hungary
Football—Association		Great Britain
Football—Rugby		Australia

Gymnastics
Combined exercises	Alberto Braglia	Italy	317 pts
Team		Sweden	438 pts
Hockey	England team	Great Britain	
Lacrosse		Canada	

Lawn Tennis—Grass courts
Singles—men	M. J. G. Ritchie	Great Britain
Singles—women	Dorothea Lambert Chambers	Great Britain
Doubles—men	George Hillyard	} Great Britain
	Reginald Doherty	

Lawn Tennis—Covered courts
Singles—men	Arthur Gore	Great Britain
Singles—women	G. Eastlake Smith	Great Britain

Doubles—men	Arthur Gore, Herbert Roper-Barrett	} Great Britain

Motor Boats
Unrestricted	E. B. Thubron	France	(in Camille)
Under 60 ft long	Tom Thornycroft	Great Britain	(in Gyrinus)
6½-8 metre racing cruisers	Tom Thornycroft	Great Britain	(in Gyrinus)
Polo		Great Britain	

Racquets
Singles—men	E. B. Noel	Great Britain
Doubles—men	V. H. Pennell & J. J. Astor	} Great Britain

Rowing (course 1½ miles)
Single sculls	Harry Blackstaffe	Great Britain	9 min 26 sec
Coxless pairs	J. Fenning, Gordon Thomson	} Great Britain	9 min 41 sec
Coxless fours		Great Britain	8 min 34 sec
Eights		Great Britain	7 min 52 sec

Shooting
National rifle teams		USA
Individual rifle, 1,000 yards	J. K. Millner	Great Britain
Open rifle teams		Norway
Open rifle, 300 metres	A. Helgerud	Norway
Miniature rifle teams		Great Britain
Miniature rifle—individual	A. A. Carnell	Great Britain
Miniature rifle—disappearing target	W. K. Styles	Great Britain
Miniature rifle—moving target	A. F. Fleming	Great Britain
Revolver—team		USA
Revolver—individual	P. van Asbroek	Belgium
Running deer—team		Sweden
Running deer—individual	Oscar Swahn	Sweden
Running deer—double shot	W. Winans	USA
Clay pigeon—individual	W. H. Ewing	Canada
Clay pigeon—team		Great Britain

Skating
Figures—men	Ulrich Salchow	Sweden
Figures—women	Madge Syers	Great Britain
Pairs	Anna Hubler, Heinrich Burger	} Germany
Special figures	N. Panin	Russia

Swimming
100 metres freestyle	Charles Daniels	USA	1 min 5.6 sec
400 metres freestyle	Henry Taylor	Great Britain	5 min 36.8 sec
1,500 metres freestyle	Henry Taylor	Great Britain	22 min 48.4 sec
200 metres breaststroke	Frederick Holman	Great Britain	3 min 9.2 sec
100 metres backstroke	Arno Bieberstein	Germany	1 min 24.6 sec
4 x 200 metres relay		Great Britain	10 min 55.6 sec
Plain high diving	Hjalmar Johansson	Sweden	83.76 pts
Fancy diving	Albert Zurner	Germany	85.5 pts
Water Polo		Great Britain	

Tennis (Jeu de Paume)
	Jay Gould	United States

Wrestling—Catch as catch can
Bantamweight	George Mehnert	USA
Featherweight	George Dole	USA
Lightweight	G. de Relwyskow	Great Britain
Middleweight	Stanley Bacon	Great Britain
Heavyweight	G. C. O'Kelly	Great Britain

Wrestling—Greco-Roman
Lightweight	Enrico Porro	Italy
Middleweight	Fritjof Martensson	Sweden
Light-heavyweight	Werner Weckman	Finland
Heavyweight	Richard Weisz	Hungary

Yachting
6-metre class	G. U. Laws	Great Britain	(in Dormy)
7-metre class	C. J. Rivett-Carnac	Great Britain	(in Heroine)
8-metre class	Blair Cochrane	Great Britain	(in Cobweb)
12-metre class	T. C. Glen-Coats	Great Britain	(in Hera)

Stockholm Olympic Games (1912)

The 1912 Olympic Games surpassed the previous three promotions in organization, participation, and performance. Held with typical Scandinavian flair in the Swedish capital, the Games attracted 2,484 men and 57 women competitors who took part in a programme that included no fewer than 18 shooting events, 3 gymnastic team events, and indoor and outdoor tennis. Women's swimming events were included in the Olympics for the first time, and there was a new sport—the modern pentathlon—which was designed to find the best all-round athlete in the world.

This last event was the brain-child of Baron Pierre de Coubertin, the founder of the Games, and he was doubtless pleased at the way in which the new sport caught on. Swedes gained the first four places, with the gold medal going to Gustaf Lilliehook. The first foreign finisher was G. S. Patton, Jr, of the United States, later famous as General 'Blood and Guts' Patton of World War II. The inclusion of women's swimming events was a break-through for female emancipation in athletic sports, although women's events had previously been held in archery, tennis, and skating.

The outstanding features of the track and field athletics were the all-round excellence of the Ameri-

1 Already garlanded, Ken McArthur wins the Stockholm marathon for South Africa. **2** The modern pentathlon gold medallist, Gustaf Lilliehook of Sweden. **3** The great Jim Thorpe, who was stripped of his two titles. **4** Eventual gold medallist Ted Meredith wins his 800 metres semi-final from Hanns Braun of Germany. **5** The tall Englishman, Arnold Jackson, wins the 1,500 metres in a blanket finish. **6** Hannes Kolehmainen beats Jean Bouin for the 5,000 metres gold. **7** Double sprint champion Ralph Craig grits his teeth as he wins the 200 metres. **8** Hawaiian Duke Kahanamoku began his reign with a convincing 100 metres freestyle victory at Stockholm. **9** First and second for Australia in the women's 100 metres: Fanny Durack (right) set a world record in the heats; Wilhelmina Wylie got the silver.

can team and the emergence of Finland as a strong nation of runners. Americans won 16 of the athletics events, although later two were rescinded. Individually, the stars of the Games were Hannes Kolehmainen of Finland and Jim Thorpe of the United States. Kolehmainen, nicknamed 'Hannes the Mighty' for his feats at the Games, won individual gold medals in the 5,000 metres (in a world record 14 min 36.6 sec), the 10,000 metres, and the cross-country race. He set a second world record in the heats of the 3,000 metres team race (8 min 36.8 sec), but the Finnish team failed to make the final. Kolehmainen gained a silver medal as well, as the Finnish team were narrowly beaten into second place in the cross-country.

But few people dispute that the best athlete—perhaps the greatest of all time—was America's Jim Thorpe. Yet his name does not even appear in the official records. In Stockholm he competed in four events, and won the track and field pentathlon and decathlon events with some ease. The following year, however, it was revealed that he had taken part in some professional baseball matches, and on the orders of the International Olympic Committee, Thorpe's name was struck from the records. But Thorpe is remembered: he won the 10-event decathlon by almost 700 points according to the tables then in use; he was first in all of the five events in the pentathlon, and in individual events came seventh in the long jump and equal-fourth in the high jump. In 1913, Thorpe became a professional footballer and made his mark in

this sport as surely as he had done in track and field.

America's other outstanding performer was 19-year-old James 'Ted' Meredith, who set two world records in the 800 metres final. His winning 800 metres time was 1 min 51.9 sec, and he ran on the extra 4.67 metres to set a world 880 yards record of 1 min 52.5 sec. Defending champion Mel Sheppard was relegated to second place, 0.1 sec behind Meredith, and was even less successful in defending his 1,500 metres crown two days later, being unplaced. This race resulted in an unexpected victory for Britain's Arnold Jackson after a remarkably severe sprint down the home straight, with only 0.8 sec separating first from fifth.

In addition to Thorpe and Kolehmainen, two other men won two gold medals. Finland's Armas Taipale won the discus and the 'discus throw—two hands' which was the only time this event featured in the Games (as was the case with the shot and javelin two-handed aggregate events). The American Ralph Craig won the 100 and 200 metres sprints. In the 100 metres, five of the six finalists were Americans, and this race was notable for there being no fewer than eight false starts.

Elsewhere, honours were fairly evenly divided. South Africa's Ken McArthur won the marathon from his team-mate Chris Gitsham; Canada's George Goulding won the 10,000 metres walk; Gustaf Lindblom won the triple jump to give Sweden a gold medal; and Constantin Tsiclitiras won a rare gold medal for Greece, in the standing long jump.

Official Report of 1912 Olympics

The Leander eight retained their Olympic title in 1912.

Outside the newly constructed athletics stadium, the swimming was being held in a pool built in an inlet of Stockholm harbour. But the water was perfectly calm, and a number of world records were set. Duke Kahanamoku of Hawaii made his first Olympic appearance, winning the 100 metres freestyle. Canada's George Hodgson set a world 1,500 metres record and won that event and the 400 metres. Germany's Walter Bathe won both breaststroke events in most impressive style, and an Australasian team won the 4 by 200 metres relay. This team comprised three Australians and one New Zealander, Malcolm Champion—the first and for at least 60 years the only New Zealander to win an Olympic swimming gold medal. The new women's events were a great success. Australia's Fanny Durack won the 100 metres freestyle from her team-mate Wilhelmina Wylie, and Great Britain won the free-style relay. Domestic honour was satisfied when Greta Johansson

won the high diving for Sweden.

Britain had a successful time in the rowing. William Kinnear won the single sculls, and the Leander Club crew won the eights from a New College VIII. The second Olympic soccer tournament resulted in a second victory for the Great Britain team, who beat Denmark 4-2 in the final. This game was played in burning heat, and Britain were perhaps lucky to win as a number of the Danes had been injured in their semi-final match with the Netherlands.

It was fortunate for the Olympic movement in general that these Games had been so well organized. Apart from the Thorpe incident—which in any case did not arise until months after the Games were over—and the tragic death of a Portuguese marathon runner named Lazaro, the Games passed without any of the acrimony that had been so typical of the London Games four years previously. It was for this reason that they were so promptly revived after the 'war to end wars', which put paid to the 1916 Games scheduled to be held in Berlin.

STOCKHOLM OLYMPIC GAMES, 1912 Gold Medallists

Athletics			
100 metres	Ralph Craig	USA	10.8 sec
200 metres	Ralph Craig	USA	21.7 sec
400 metres	Charles Reidpath	USA	48.2 sec
800 metres	Ted Meredith	USA	1 min 51.9 sec
1,500 metres	Arnold Jackson	Great Britain	3 min 56.8 sec
5,000 metres	Hannes Kolehmainen	Finland	14 min 36.6 sec
10,000 metres	Hannes Kolehmainen	Finland	31 min 20.8 sec
Marathon	Kenneth McArthur	South Africa	2 hr 36 min 54.8 sec
110 metres hurdles	Frederick Kelly	USA	15.1 sec
4 x 100 metres relay		Great Britain	42.4 sec
4 x 400 metres relay		USA	3 min 16.6 sec
8,000 metres cross-country			
—individual	Hannes Kolehmainen	Finland	45 min 11.6 sec
—team		Sweden	
3,000 metres team race		USA	
10,000 metres walk	George Goulding	Canada	46 min 28,4 sec
Running high jump	Almer Richards	USA	6 ft 4 in
Running long jump	Albert Gutterson	USA	24 ft 11¼ in
Pole vault	Harry Babcock	USA	12 ft 11½ in
Triple jump	Gustaf Lindblom	Sweden	48 ft 5 in
Standing high jump	Platt Adams	USA	5 ft 4¼ in
Standing long jump	Constantin Tsiclitiras	Greece	11 ft 0¾ in
Shot—one hand	Pat McDonald	USA	50 ft 4 in
Shot—both hands	Ralph Rose	USA	90 ft 10½ in
Discus—one hand	Armas Taipale	Finland	148 ft 4 in
Discus—both hands	Armas Taipale	Finland	271 ft 10¼ in
Javelin—one hand	Eric Lemming	Sweden	198 ft 11½ in
Javelin—both hands	Julius Saaristo	Finland	358 ft 11¾ in
Hammer	Matt McGrath	USA	179 ft 7 in
Pentathlon	Ferdinand Bie	Norway	
Decathlon	Hugo Wieslander	Sweden	
Tug-of-War		Sweden	
Modern Pentathlon	Gustaf Lilliehook	Sweden	
Soccer		Great Britain	
Swimming—Men			
100 metres freestyle	Duke Kahanamoku	USA	1 min 3.4 sec
400 metres freestyle	George Hodgson	Canada	5 min 24.4 sec
1,500 metres freestyle	George Hodgson	Canada	22 min 0.0 sec
200 metres breaststroke	Walter Bathe	Germany	3 min 1.8 sec
400 metres breaststroke	Walter Bathe	Germany	6 min 29.6 sec
100 metres backstroke	Harry Hebner	USA	1 min 21.2 sec
4 x 200 metres relay		Australasia	10 min 11.2 sec
Springboard diving	Paul Gunther	Germany	
Plain high diving	Erik Adlerz	Sweden	
Fancy high diving	Erik Adlerz	Sweden	
Swimming—Women			
100 metres freestyle	Fanny Durack	Australasia	1 min 22.2 sec
4 x 100 metres relay		Great Britain	5 min 52.8 sec
High diving	Greta Johansson	Sweden	
Water Polo		Great Britain	

Swedish Olympic Committee

British Olympic Association

Above: **Ralph Rose, here winning the shot at London, retained his Olympic title in Stockholm.** *Left:* **'Mighty' Matt McGrath, Tipperary-born but a gold medallist for the United States.**

Antwerp Olympic Games (1920) [1]

'Firsts'—quite apart from those that won gold medals—were the order of the day at the VIIth Olympic Games held in the Belgian city of Antwerp in 1920. It was the first stumbling attempt at a global get-together in a world recently shattered. The Olympic flag was unfurled for the first time, and the Olympic oath was first introduced. Most exciting of all, perhaps, Paavo Nurmi, the 'Phantom Finn', made his Olympic debut.

The disappointingly sparse attendances betrayed the haste with which the Games had been organized. Belgium had had but one year's notice in which to prepare, and her war-weary people were in no mood for games of any kind. In spite of a new 30,000-seat stadium and a nominal admission fee, the crowds did not much exceed 20,000.

The Belgians did not invite any of the Central Powers (Austria, Bulgaria, Germany, Hungary, or Turkey), but the the new countries of Czechoslovakia and Estonia, and newly independent Finland took part. There were 29 countries represented in 22 sports, and the total number of contestants was something under 3,000.

The Games proper were opened on August 14 by King Albert of the Belgians, in the presence of Baron de Coubertin, founder of the modern Olympic Games. Fifteen nations shared the 150 gold medals, the United States claiming 41 of them, followed by Sweden with 19 and Finland with 15. Belgium, Britain, Italy, and Norway reached double figures. Tiny Finland, spearheaded by the redoubtable Nurmi, dug deep into her track and field talent to produce nine gold medals for those events. The Finns tied with the United States, the first and only time the Americans have been equalled in track and field.

In athletics Paavo Nurmi was incomparably the man of the Games. Although he stood only on the threshold of his glittering career, Nurmi won two individual gold medals and one silver—after inexperience had cost him his first race (the 5,000 metres) to Joseph Guillemot of France. During the next 10 years the Finn was to compete successfully in two more Olympic Games and set world records at every event from 1,500 metres to 1 hour.

Hannes Kolehmainen, the first

Press Association

ANTWERP OLYMPIC GAMES, 1920 Gold Medallists

Archery

Fixed Bird Target—Men

Individual	(Small Bird)	E. Van Meer	Belgium
	(Large Bird)	E. Clostens	Belgium
Team	(Small Bird)		Belgium
Team	(Large Bird)		Belgium

Moving Bird Target—Men

	(28 metres)	H. Van Innis	Belgium
	(33 metres)	H. Van Innis	Belgium
	(50 metres)	Louis Brule	France
Team	(28 metres)		Netherlands
	(33 metres)		Belgium
	(50 metres)		Belgium
60- and 50-yard Individual —Women		Miss Q. Newall	GB

Association Football

Belgium

Athletics

Track and Field events

100 metres	Charles W. Paddock	USA	10.8 sec
200 metres	Allan Woodring	USA	22.0 sec
400 metres	Bevil G. D. Rudd	S Africa	49.6 sec
800 metres	Albert G. Hill	GB	1 min 53.4 sec
1,500 metres	Albert G. Hill	GB	4 min 01.8 sec
3,000 metres team race		USA	
5,000 metres	Joseph Guillemot	France	14 min 55.6 sec
10,000 metres	Paavo Nurmi	Finland	31 min 45.8 sec
Marathon	Hannes Kolehmainen	Finland	2 hr 32 min 35.8 sec
110 metres Hurdles	Earl J. Thompson	Canada	14.8 sec
400 metres Hurdles	Frank F. Loomis	USA	54.0 sec
3,000 metres Steeplechase	Percy Hodge	GB	10 min 00.4 sec
Cross Country (10,000 metres)			
Individual	Paavo Nurmi	Finland	27 min 15 sec
Team		Finland	
3,000 metres Walk	Ugo Frigerio	Italy	14 min 55 sec
10,000 metres Walk	Ugo Frigerio	Italy	48 min 06.2 sec
4x100 metres Relay		USA	42.2 sec
4x400 metres Relay		GB	3 min 22.2 sec
High Jump	Richard W. Landon	USA	6 ft 4¼ in
Pole Vault	Frank K. Foss	USA	13 ft 5 in
Long Jump	William Pettersson	Sweden	23 ft 5½ in
Triple Jump	Vilho Tuulos	Finland	47 ft 7 in
Shot	Ville Porhola	Finland	48 ft 7 in
Discus	Elmer Niklander	Finland	146 ft 7¼ in
Hammer	Patrick Ryan	USA	173 ft 5¼ in
Javelin	Jonni Myyra	Finland	215 ft 9¾ in
Pentathlon	Eero Lehtonen	Finland	
Decathlon	Helge Lovland	Norway	
Tug of War		GB	

Boxing

Flyweight	Frank De Genaro	USA
Bantamweight	Clarence Walker	S Africa
Featherweight	Paul Fritsch	France
Lightweight	Samuel Mosberg	USA
Welterweight	T. Schneider	Canada
Middleweight	Harry Mallin	GB
Light-Heavyweight	Edward Eagan	USA
Heavyweight	R. Rawson	GB

Cycling

1,000 metres Sprint	Maurice Peeters	Netherlands	1 min 38.3 sec
2,000 metres Tandem	Harry Ryan, Thomas Lance	GB	2 min 49.4 sec
4,000 metres Team Pursuit		Italy	5 min 20 sec
Road Race—Individual	Harry Stenquist	Sweden	4 hr 40 min 01.8 sec
—Team		France	19 hr 16 min 43.2 sec

Equestrian Sports

Grand Prix (Jumping)

Individual	Tommaso Lequio	Italy
Team		Sweden
Grand Prix (Dressage)	Janne Lundblad	Sweden
Three Day Event—Individual	Helmer Morner	Sweden
—Team		Sweden

Fencing

Foil —Individual	Nedo Nadi	Italy
—Team		Italy
Epee —Individual	Armand Massard	France
—Team		Italy
Sabre—Individual	Nedo Nadi	Italy
—Team		Italy

Gymnastics

Combined Exercises —Individual	Giorgio Zampori	Italy

Hockey

GB

Ice Hockey

Canada

Lawn Tennis

Men's Singles	Louis Raymond	S Africa
Ladies' Singles	Mlle Suzanne Lenglen	France
Men's Doubles	O. G. Turnbull & Max Woosnam	GB
Ladies' Doubles	Mrs J. McNair & Miss Kitty McKane	GB
Mixed Doubles	Max Decugis & Mlle S. Lenglen	France

Modern Pentathlon

Gustaf Dyrssen — Sweden

Polo

GB

2

3

4

5

1 (overleaf) US high flyer Frank Ross soared to a world record of 13 ft 5$\frac{9}{16}$ in. in the pole vault, in spite of a waterlogged track. He left his nearest rival 13 inches below him.
2 Britain's Percy Hodge, with a wealth of cross-country experience behind him, won the steeplechase in a fraction over 10 min. It was at Antwerp that this event was finally standardized at its present length of 3,000 metres.
3 Pat Ryan, one of a succession of Irish-American 'whales', tossed the hammer a little over 173 ft for the gold medal and a new world record. He later established a mark of 189 ft 6½ in that stood unbeaten

for nearly a quarter of a century—a lengthy record period for any event.
4 Iron man Frank Loomis of America also broke a world record—he skimmed over the 400-metre hurdles in a time of 54 sec dead. He had previously won the American championship in the same event, and also held the 220-yard low hurdles title.
5 Earl 'Tommy' Thomson, the Canadian hurdler, brought a tinge of gold to the maple leaf when he captured the 110 metres high hurdles for his country in world record time. Thomson had more than a little American help in his great win— he had trained for many years in the US.

of the flying Finns, who had thrilled the fans at the 1912 Olympics with his three gold medals in the middle distance events, won a sensational marathon at Antwerp by 13.2 seconds—the closest Olympic marathon ever. In addition to Nurmi's and Kolehmainen's contributions, Finland won four field events and the track and field pentathlon.

The United States took the two sprints and the sprint relay. The spectacular Charley Paddock, the first of many to be dubbed 'the world's fastest human', collected a gold for the 100 metres, but in the 200 metres ran out of steam 20 metres before reaching the tape. Canada won the 110 metres hurdles through the efforts of Earl 'Tommy' Thomson who, in spite of

a leg injury, broke the Olympic record. English-born Bevil Rudd won the 400 metres for South Africa, and Britain won the 4x400 metres relay to add to her victories in the 800 and 1,500 metres, the steeplechase, and the tug-of-war.

In the swimming, the United States made almost a clean sweep, winning seven out of ten of the men's events and four out of five of the women's. Sweden collected the remaining three men's events and a Danish girl won the women's high diving. The Hawaiian, Duke Kahanamoku, swimming for the United States, won the 100 metres freestyle in a new world record time and picked up a second gold medal as a member of the record-breaking 4x200 metres relay team. Another mem-

ANTWERP OLYMPIC GAMES, 1920 Gold Medallists (continued)

Rowing				200 metres Breaststroke	Haken Malmroth	Sweden	3 min 04.4 sec
Single Sculls	John Kelly	USA	7 min 35.0 sec	400 metres Breaststroke	Haken Malmroth	Sweden	6 min 31.8 sec
Double Sculls	John Kelly,	USA	7 min 09.0 sec	4x200 metres Relay		USA	10 min 04.4 sec
	Paul Costello			Platform Diving	Clarence Pinkston	USA	
Coxless Pairs	E. Olgeni, G. Scatturin	Italy	7 min 56.0 sec	Plain High Diving	Arvid Wallman	Sweden	
Coxed Fours		Switzerland	6 min 54.0 sec	Springboard Diving	Louis Kuehn	USA	
Eights		USA	6 min 05.0 sec	**Swimming and Diving**—Women			
Rugby Football		USA		100 metres Freestyle	Ethelda Bleibtrey	USA	1 min 13.6 sec
				300 metres Freestyle	Ethelda Bleibtrey	USA	4 min 34.0 sec
Shooting				4x100 metres Relay		USA	5 min 11.6 sec
Pistol and revolver (50 metres)				Platform Diving	Stefani Fryland-Clausen	Denmark	
—Individual	Carl Frederick	USA		Springboard Diving	Aileen Riggin	USA	
—Team		USA		**Water-Polo**		GB	
Pistol and revolver (30 metres)				**Weight lifting**			
—Individual	Guilherme Paraense	Brazil		Featherweight	F. de Haes	Belgium	485 lb
—Team		USA		Lightweight	Alfred Neyland	Estonia	567 lb
Running Deer				Middleweight	B. Gance	France	540 lb
—Individual singles	Otto Olsen	Norway		Light-Heavyweight	E. Cadine	France	639 lb
—Individual doubles	Ole Lilloe-Olsen	Norway		Heavyweight	Filippo Bottini	Italy	595 lb
—Team doubles		Norway		**Wrestling**			
Small Bore (Miniature) Rifle				Freestyle			
—Individual	Lawrence Nuesslein	USA		Featherweight	Charles Ackerley	USA	
—Team		USA		Lightweight	Kalle Antilla	Finland	
Military Rifle (300 metres)				Middleweight	Eino Leino	Finland	
2 positions —Individual	Morris Fisher	USA		Light-Heavyweight	Anders Larsson	Sweden	
—Team		USA		Heavyweight	Robert Roth	Switzerland	
Standing —Individual	Carl Osburn	USA		**Graeco-Roman Style**			
—Team		Denmark		Featherweight	Oskari Friman	Finland	
Prone —Individual	Otto Olsen	Norway		Lightweight	Emil Ware	Finland	
—Team		USA		Middleweight	Carl Westergren	Sweden	
Military Rifle (300 and 600 metres)				Light-Heavyweight	Claes Johansson	Sweden	
Prone —Team		USA		Heavyweight	Adolf Lindfors	Finland	
Military Rifle (600 metres)				**Yachting**			
Prone —Individual	Hugo Johansson	Sweden		12-metre class (old type)		Norway	
—Team		USA		(new type)		Norway	
Clay Pigeon—Individual	Mark Arie	USA		10-metre class (old type)		Norway	
—Team		USA		(new type)		Norway	
Skating				8-metre class (old type)		Norway	
Figure—Men	Gillis Grafstrom	Sweden		(new type)		Norway	
—Women	Magda Julin-Mauroy	Sweden		7-metre class (old type)		GB	
Pairs	Ludovika Jakobsson &	Finland		6-metre class (old type)		Belgium	
	Walter Jakobsson			(new type)		Norway	
Swimming and Diving—Men				6·5-metre class		Netherlands	
100 metres Freestyle	Duke Kahanamoku	USA	1 min 00.4 sec	40-metre class		Sweden	
400 metres Freestyle	Norman Ross	USA	5 min 26.8 sec	30-metre class		Sweden	
1500 metres Freestyle	Norman Ross	USA	22 min 23.2 sec	12 ft centreboard boat		Netherlands	
100 metres Backstroke	Warren Kealoha	USA	1 min 15.2 sec	18 ft centreboard boat		Netherlands	

ber of that renowned team was
Norman Ross, who also won
the 400 and 1,500 metres freestyle races.

Among the women, three gold
medals went to the American girl
Ethelda Bleibtrey, all with new
Olympic records, in the 100 and
300 metres freestyle and the 4x100
metres freestyle relay. The American Aileen Riggin was just 13 years
old when she won the springboard
diving competition.

Largely through the prowess of
John Kelly, a young bricklayer
from Philadelphia, the United
States won three of the five rowing
events. Kelly, father of Princess
Grace of Monaco, was probably
the greatest individual oarsman in
history. In 1919 and 1920 he won
126 consecutive races. At Antwerp
he beat Britain's Jack Beresford in
the single sculls by 1 second and,
half an hour later, teamed with his
cousin Paul Costello to take the
double sculls. They repeated this
victory in 1924 at Paris. Beresford
eventually competed in five Olympics, winning three gold and two
silver medals.

The 14 yachting events were held
at Ostend in very rough seas.
Norway had by far the largest
entry of the six nations taking part
and won seven of the events. The
Netherlands took three, Sweden
two, and Belgium and Britain one
apiece. The solitary British victory
was in the 7-metre (old type) class,
with Dorothy Winifred acting as
helmswoman. After these Games
it was decided that conditions of
entry in the yachting events should
be standardized, and the whole
programme was put under the
control of the International
Yachting Federation.

Fifteen teams took part in the
football. Britain was hustled out
by Norway in the first round, and
the final was fought between
Belgium and Czechoslovakia. On
their way to the final, the Belgians
had beaten Spain (3–1) and the
Netherlands (3–0). The Czechs
had beaten Yugoslavia (9–0),
Norway (4–0), and France (4–1).

The final itself was a debacle.
The referee weakened before a
large Belgian crowd, and when he
sent a Czech player off in the
second half there was trouble. The
Czech's furious team-mates joined
him off the field, and the jury
awarded the match to Belgium.

The boxing titles were fairly
evenly distributed. The United
States won three, Britain two, and
France, Canada, and South
Africa one each. Edward Eagan,
who won the light-heavyweight
title, gained a bobsleigh gold
medal 12 years later at Lake
Placid, New York, the only competitor ever to win golds at both
summer and winter Games. He
later became chairman of the New
York State Boxing Commission.
The American Frank de Genaro,
who took the flyweight crown,
later became professional flyweight
champion of the world. Harry
Mallin, who won the middle-

weight title for Britain, repeated
his success four years later in Paris.

The Scandinavian countries
scooped all 15 places in the five
wrestling events. Finland was most
successful with five victories in the
two classes. Finnish grapplers won
two gold medals in the freestyle,
and three gold, four silver, and a
bronze in the graeco-roman.

Italians won five of the six
fencing events, but the individual
epée gold medal went to Armand
Massard of France, who in 1946
was to become a member of the
International Olympic Committee.
A Belgian fencer, Victor Boin, had
the honour of taking the Olympic
oath, for the first time, on behalf
of the assembled athletes.

The star of the tennis competitions was Suzanne Lenglen, pride
of France and, according to many

1 Jonni Myrrä, the Finnish
javelin champion, took the gold
medal for this event at
Antwerp with a throw of
215 ft 9¾ in. Scandinavian
athletes have had a long
tradition of success in the
javelin, and Myrrä enhanced
this reputation by repeating
his success four years later at
the Paris Olympics, but this
time with a throw that was
more than 9 ft shorter.
2 American ace sprinter
Charley Paddock, first of the
'world's fastest humans', was
renowned for his flying leap at
the tape. Here he hurls himself
through the air to win the
100 metre title in 10.8 sec. He
collected a second gold medal
for anchoring the victorious
US 4 x 100 metre relay team.

experts, the greatest-ever woman
tennis player. She swept up the
singles and, with her partner Max
Decugis, the mixed doubles titles,
and was a finalist in the women's
doubles. The veteran Decugis had
won the singles and, with his wife,
the mixed doubles, 14 years earlier
in the interim Games at Athens.

Belgium, France, and the
Netherlands were the only
countries to enter the archery
competitions. They had been held
once before, in 1908, but after
Antwerp they were dropped. In
the cycling events the 4,000 metres
team pursuit race was held for the
first time, and in the equestrian
competitions figure riding was
included for the first and last
time. The British polo team won
the gold medal, beating Spain
13—11 in the final. Polo had been
included in the 1908 Games and
was to make its final appearance
in the Berlin Olympics of 1936.

There were only four events in
the gymnastics, and only four
nations—Denmark, Italy, Norway, and Sweden—competed, with
Italy winning two gold medals.
But there were no less than 21
competitions in the shooting programme, including pistol and
revolver, military rifles, and mini-
ature rifles. The United States took
the lion's share of medals, with
Norway coming a poor second.
Ice hockey was first introduced at
the Antwerp Games, and the
Canadians started as they meant
to continue by winning the first
championship.

Finally, it should be added for
the record that the United States
walked off with the rugby championship, and to prove that it was
no fluke, repeated the victory four
years later in Paris—an oddity
equalled only by their humiliation
of the England soccer team in the
1950 World Cup.

Press Association
Harold Abrahams

Paris Olympic Games (1924)

The second Olympics to be held in Paris were a great contrast to the chaotic sports meeting of 1900. The Olympic celebrations began at Chamonix at the end of January 1924 with the first ever Winter Olympic Games, and in May and June continued with rugby and association football competitions. In the rugby, only three teams took part: France, the United States, and Romania. The games involving Romania were a formality, France winning 61-3 and the United States 37-0. But in the deciding match the United States beat France 17-3. Twenty-three teams competed in the soccer, and in the final Uruguay beat Switzerland 3-0. The South Americans—whose team included such future stars of the World Cup as Scarone, Cea, and Petrone—scored 17 goals and conceded only 2 throughout the five rounds.

Athletics

The Games proper began on July 5, and the athletics events saw one of the greatest exhibitions of middle-distance running ever. The man responsible was the Finn Paavo Nurmi, who won five gold medals. Over six consecutive days he took part in seven races, and won them all. First he won his heats of the 5,000 and 1,500 metres on two consecutive days, and then on the third day within the space of 1½ hours he won the 1,500 metres in an Olympic record time of 3 min 53.6 sec, and the 5,000 in 14 min 31.2 sec—another Olympic record. The day after this double triumph, Nurmi led his team home in the heat of the 3,000 metres team race, and without even a day's rest won the 10,000 metres cross-country event. The day was extremely hot, and of the 39 starters only 15 completed the course. The other 24 had collapsed, overcome by the heat and exhaustion, but Nurmi entered the stadium at the end hardly perspiring. On the next day he led the Finnish team to victory in the 3,000 metres team race, coming home first in 8 min 32.0 sec, less than 2 seconds outside his own world record.

The small Finnish contingent won a further five gold medals. Ville Ritola, runner-up to Nurmi in the 5,000 metres and the cross-country and second man home in the 3,000 metres team event, took the 10,000 metres and the 3,000 metres steeplechase. Albin Stenroos, who was 35 years old and had been third in the 10,000 metres at Stockholm in 1912, finished almost six minutes ahead of the field in the marathon. Jonni Myrra, the world record holder, retained his javelin title with a modest 206 ft. 7 in., and in the track and field pentathlon Eero

Lehtonen also won his second Olympic gold medal.

The most successful athletics nation, in terms of gold medals, was the United States with 12 titles. Jackson Scholz beat his team-mate Charley Paddock (the world record holder) in the 200 metres. In the 110 metre hurdles three Americans reached the final, where Dan Kinsey just edged out South Africa's Syd Atkinson for the gold medal. And in the 400 metres hurdles Morgan Taylor won by over a second from the Finn Erik Vilen. Taylor's time—52.6 sec—beat the existing world record by 1.4 seconds, but as he knocked a hurdle over it was not accepted under the existing rules. Taylor reached two more Olympic finals in this event, finishing third at Amsterdam in 1928 and Los Angeles in 1932.

In the high jump, Harold Osborn won with an Olympic record leap of 6 ft. 6 in., and later gained a unique double victory with a win in the decathlon.

1 The innocence of the early Olympics—the Austrian standard bearer gives the Olympic salute later adopted by the Nazis.
2 Paavo Nurmi breaks the tape to win the 1,500 metres title and
3 leads the field in the tough 10,000 metres cross-country race.
4 An American victory in the 200 metres: Jackson Scholz beats leaping Charley Paddock (left) to the line to win in 21.6 sec.
5 Harold Osborn clears 6 ft. 6 in. to win the high jump gold.
6 The great inter-war walker Ugo Frigerio added the 1924 10,000 metres title to his previous wins at 3,000 and 10,000 in 1920.
7 William DeHart Hubbard wins the long jump with 24 ft. 5 in.
8 Gold for Britain—Harold Abrahams wins the 100 metres dash.
9 Triple swimming champion Johnny Weissmuller won gold medals in the 100 and 400 metres freestyle, and the 4 by 200 metres team.
10 Australia's 'Boy' Charlton was a sensation in the 1,500 metres, breaking the world record by over a minute.

Americans continued their unbroken run of success in the pole vault, winning all three medals. Glenn Graham and Lee Barnes tied with 12 ft. 11½ in., but the 17-year-old Barnes won the jump-off and the gold medal. Another American 1-2 came in the long jump, with William DeHart Hubbard clearing 24 ft. 5 in. to beat Ed Gourdin, the world record holder, whose best was 23 ft. 10½ in. As it turned out, the world's best long jumper was not competing. This was Robert Le-Gendre, who had not qualified for the long jump in the American trials but excelled himself to clear 25 ft. 5¾ in.—a new world record—during the pentathlon the day before the long jump was held.

Clarence Houser led an American clean sweep of the shot-put medals, and then won the gold medal in the discus. Another American triumph came in the hammer. Fred Tootell (174 ft. 10 in.) beat 46-year-old Matt McGrath (166 ft. 9½ in.) by 8 feet. McGrath thus gained his second Olympic silver—his first came in 1908—to add to the gold he won in 1912. His Olympic record of 179 ft. 7 in., set in 1912, was not beaten until 1936.

The other field event, the triple jump (then known as the 'hop,

step, and jump'), was won by Australia's 30-year-old Anthony Winter with a world record effort of 50 ft. 11¼ in., 4 inches more than the runner-up Luis Brunetto of Argentina.

Great Britain gained three victories on the track, in the 100, 400, and 800 metres. In the 100 metres Harold Abrahams equalled the Olympic record of 10.6 sec on three occasions. In the second round he returned his first 10.6, which equalled Willie Applegarth's 10-year-old British best, and though he was left badly at the start of his semi-final he still finished ahead of two Americans, defending 100 metres champion Charley Paddock and Chester Bowman. But there was no doubt about the final, which came four hours later. Abrahams led from start to finish to win by a clear yard from America's Jackson Scholz with New Zealand's Arthur Porritt third.

Abrahams also reached the final of the 200 metres, but his running lacked all inspiration and he finished sixth and last. Third was Britain's Eric Liddell, the British 100 yards record holder whose religious beliefs prevented his competing in the 100 metres (the first round of which was held on a Sunday). He did, however, take part in the 400 metres, and though he was not one of the pre-Games favourites he made the most of his proven speed when it came to the final. He set off at a seemingly suicidal speed, and was timed at 22.2 sec for the first 200 metres, most of which (the track was 500 metres round) was down the straight. He held on to his lead to win by 0.8 sec in 47.6 sec, which was an Olympic record and was also accepted as a world record, though it was inferior to Ted Meredith's 440 yards time set in 1916, and is no longer included in the official list.

Britain's third gold medal came through Douglas Lowe in the 800 metres. On form, the most likely winner was Hyla Stallard, Lowe's team-mate who has won the AAA title in a fast 1 min 54.6 sec. But in the final Stallard was suffering from an injured foot and faltered down the home straight, as Lowe and Switzerland's Paul Martin swept past him. Lowe beat Martin for first place by a fifth of a second, and Stallard just lost third place to Schuyler Enck of the United States on the line. Stallard had some small consolation two days later when he won the bronze medal in the 1,500 metres, with Lowe fourth.

The United States teams won both relays, and set world records in each of them—41.0 sec for the 4 by 100 metres, in which Great Britain were second, and 3 min 16.0 sec for the 4 by 400 metres. None of the American 400 metres entries ran in their 4 by 400 metres team, and only one of the 100 metres men (Loren Murchison) in the 4 by 100.

Swimming

It was a vintage Olympic Games in the open-air swimming pool. Johnny Weissmuller won three gold medals, and Duke Kahanamoku appeared in his third Olympic Games—at the age of 33—and won the silver medal in the 100 metres. The men's 1,500 metres record was slashed by over a minute. The women's programme included backstroke and breaststroke events for the first time.

Weissmuller won the first three of his five Olympic golds—in the 100, 400, and 4 by 200 metres freestyle. He won the 100 metres by an enormous margin—2.4 sec —from Kahanamoku, the champion in 1912 and 1920. Weissmuller's second victory, in the 400 metres, was somewhat closer: he beat Sweden's Arne Borg by 1.4 sec. Third in the 400 metres was Andrew 'Boy' Charlton of Australia, at 16 the baby of the big boys in Paris, and his moment of glory was to come in the 1,500 metres. In the heats Arne Borg trimmed his own world record of 21 min 15.0 sec to 21 min 11.4 sec, but in the final two days later Charlton won by over half-a-minute from Borg in 20 min 6.6 sec. Third was Australia's Frank Beaurepaire—aged 33— who had also won the bronze in this event in 1908 and 1920. And fourth was Britain's Jack Hatfield, 31 years old, who 12 years earlier had been second in the 400 and 1,500 metres.

In the backstroke events, Warren Kealoha retained his men's title, and his American team-mate Sybil Bauer won the women's—4.2 seconds in front of the runner-up, Britain's Phyllis Harding. Aileen Riggin, who was third in this race, became the only competitor to win Olympic medals for swimming and diving when she came second in the springboard event.

After the United States, Britain were the next most successful team in the women's competitions. One Briton reached the first five of every event, the freestyle relay squad were runners-up to the United States, and Lucy Morton became Britain's first woman Olympic swimming champion by winning the 200 metres breaststroke, in which other British girls were third and fifth.

Other Sports

John B. Kelly, who had won the single sculls gold medal in Antwerp four years previously, did not defend his title, but he brought his tally of Olympic golds to three by partnering his cousin Paul Costello to their second victory in the double sculls. The single sculls title went to Britain's Jack Beresford, the Antwerp runner-up, who lost to America's William Garrett-Gilmore in his heat but won his way through the repechage to get his revenge in the final. A second gold came

29

Britain's way in the coxless fours: Trinity College, Cambridge, beat a Canadian crew by 1¼ lengths.

The Paris Games were the last at which lawn tennis featured as a championships event. The women's singles title went to the Californian Helen Wills, that year's Wimbledon runner-up. The Wimbledon champion, Britain's Kitty McKane, went out to France's Mlle Vlasto in the semi-finals. Miss Wills gained another gold medal by partnering Mrs Wightman—the instigator of the Britain v United States ladies match—in the doubles, in which they beat the British pair of Miss McKane and Mrs Covell. Frank Hunter and Vincent Richards, that year's Wimbledon doubles champions, beat the French idols Henri Cochet and Jacques Brugnon in the men's doubles.

The boxing events saw two countries winning two golds each in the eight events: the United States, with Fidel La Barba (flyweight) and John Fields (featherweight), and Great Britain, with Harry Mitchell (light-heavyweight) and Harry Mallin. Mallin became the first man to retain an Olympic boxing title, beating team-mate John Elliott in the middleweight final.

PARIS OLYMPIC GAMES, 1924 Gold Medallists

Athletics

Event	Name	Country	Time/Distance
100 metres	Harold Abrahams	Great Britain	10.6 sec
200 metres	Jackson Scholz	USA	21.6 sec
400 metres	Eric Liddell	Great Britain	47.6 sec
800 metres	Douglas Lowe	Great Britain	1 min 52.4 sec
1,500 metres	Paavo Nurmi	Finland	3 min 53.6 sec
5,000 metres	Paavo Nurmi	Finland	14 min 31.2 sec
10,000 metres	Ville Ritola	Finland	30 min 23.2 sec
Marathon	Albin Stenroos	Finland	2 hr 41 min 22.6 sec
3,000 metres team race		Finland	
110 metres hurdles	Dan Kinsey	USA	15.0 sec
400 metres hurdles	Morgan Taylor	USA	52.6 sec
3,000 metres steeplechase	Ville Ritola	Finland	9 min 33.6 sec
10,000 metres cross-country	Paavo Nurmi	Finland	32 min 54.8 sec
Cross-country team		Finland	
4 x 100 metres relay		USA	41.0 sec
4 x 400 metres relay		USA	3 min 16.0 sec
10 kilometres walk	Ugo Frigerio	Italy	47 min 49.0 sec
High jump	Harold Osborn	USA	6 ft 6 in
Pole vault	Lee Barnes	USA	12 ft 11½ in
Long jump	William DeHart Hubbard	USA	24 ft 5 in
Triple jump	Anthony Winter	Australia	50 ft 11¼ in
Shot	Clarence Houser	USA	49 ft 2¼ in
Discus	Clarence Houser	USA	151 ft 5 in
Hammer	Fred Tootell	USA	174 ft 10 in
Javelin	Jonni Myrra	Finland	206 ft 7 in
Pentathlon	Eero Lehtonen	Finland	14 points
Decathlon	Harold Osborn	USA	7,710.775 points

Boxing

Event	Name	Country
Flyweight	Fidel La Barba	USA
Bantamweight	William Smith	South Africa
Featherweight	John Fields	USA
Lightweight	Hans Nielsen	Denmark
Welterweight	Jean Delarge	Belgium
Middleweight	Harry Mallin	Great Britain
Light-heavyweight	Harry Mitchell	Great Britain
Heavyweight	Otto von Porat	Norway

Cycling

Event	Name	Country	Time
1,000 metres sprint	Lucien Michard	France	
2,000 metres tandem	Jean Cugnot, Lucien Choury	France	
50 kilometres track race	Jacobus Willems	Netherlands	1 hr 18 min 24 sec
4,000 metres team pursuit		Italy	5 min 12 sec
188-km Road Race			
—individual	Armand Blanchonnet	France	6 hr 20 min 48 sec
—team		France	

Equestrian

Event	Name	Country
Dressage	Ernst Linder	Sweden
Show jumping—individual	Alphons Gemuseus	Switzerland
—team		Sweden
Three day event—individual	Adolph van Zijp	Netherlands
—team		Netherlands

Fencing—Men

Foil —individual	Roger Ducret	France
—team		France
Epee —individual	Charles Delporte	Belgium
—team		France
Sabre—individual	Sandor Posta	Hungary
—team		Italy

Fencing—Women

Event	Name	Country
Foil—individual	Ellen Osiier	Denmark

Gymnastics

Event	Name	Country
Combined exercises		
—individual	Leon Stukelj	Yugoslavia
—team		Italy
Parallel bars	August Guttinger	Switzerland
Horizontal bar	Leon Stukelj	Yugoslavia
Pommel horse	Josef Wilhelm	Switzerland
Rings	Franco Martino	Italy
Vault—lengthwise	Frank Kriz	USA
—sideways	A. Seguin	France
Rope climbing	Bedrich Supcik	Czechoslovakia

Lawn Tennis

Event	Name	Country
Men's singles	Vincent Richards	USA
Ladies' singles	Helen Wills	USA
Men's doubles	Vincent Richards, Frank Hunter	USA
Ladies' doubles	Helen Wills, Hazel Wightman	USA

Event	Name	Country
Mixed doubles	Hazel Wightman, R. N. Williams	USA
Modern Pentathlon	Bo Lindman	Sweden
Polo		Argentina

Rowing

Event	Name	Country	Time
Single sculls	Jack Beresford	Great Britain	7 min 49.2 sec
Double sculls	Paul Costello, John B. Kelly	USA	6 min 34.0 sec
Coxless pairs	E. Rosingh, A. Beynan	Netherlands	8 min 19.4 sec
Coxed pairs	Edouard Candeveau, Alfred Felber, Emil Lachapelle (cox)	Switzerland	8 min 39.0 sec
Coxless fours		Great Britain	7 min 8.6 sec
Coxed fours		Switzerland	7 min 18.4 sec
Eights		USA	6 min 33.4 sec
Rugby Football		USA	

Shooting

Optional rifle—team		USA
—individual	Morris Fisher	USA
Miniature rifle—team		France
—individual	Charles Coquelin de Lisle	France
Automatic pistol		
—team		USA
—individual	H. N. Bailey	USA
Running deer:		
single shot—team		Norway
—individual	John Boles	USA
double shot—team		Great Britain
—individual	Ole Lilloe Olsen	Norway
Clay pigeon—team		USA
—individual	Gyula Halasy	Hungary
Soccer		Uruguay

Swimming—Men

Event	Name	Country	Time
100 metres freestyle	Johnny Weissmuller	USA	59.0 sec
400 metres freestyle	Johnny Weissmuller	USA	5 min 4.2 sec
1,500 metres freestyle	Andrew Charlton	Australia	20 min 6.6 sec
200 metres breaststroke	Robert Skelton	USA	2 min 56.6 sec
100 metres backstroke	Warren Kealoha	USA	1 min 13.2 sec
4 x 200 metres freestyle relay		USA	9 min 53.4 sec
Springboard diving	Albert White	USA	
Plain high diving	Richmond Eve	Australia	
Fancy high diving	Albert White	USA	

Swimming—Women

Event	Name	Country	Time
100 metres freestyle	Ethel Lackie	USA	1 min 12.4 sec
400 metres freestyle	Martha Norelius	USA	6 min 2.2 sec
200 metres breaststroke	Lucy Morton	Great Britain	3 min 33.2 sec
100 metres backstroke	Sybil Bauer	USA	1 min 23.2 sec
4 x 100 metres freestyle relay		USA	4 min 58.8 sec
Springboard diving	Elisabeth Becker	USA	
Plain high diving	Caroline Smith	USA	
Water Polo		France	

Weightlifting

Event	Name	Country	Weight
Featherweight	Paolo Gabetti	Italy	887¼ lb
Lightweight	Edmond Decottignies	France	970 lb
Middleweight	Carlo Galimberti	Italy	1,085¾ lb
Light-heavyweight	Charles Rigoulot	France	1,107¾ lb
Heavyweight	Giuseppe Tonani	Italy	

Wrestling

Freestyle

Bantamweight	Kustaa Pihlajamaki	Finland
Featherweight	Robin Reed	USA
Lightweight	Russel Vis	USA
Light-middleweight	Hermann Gehri	Switzerland
Middleweight	Fritz Haggmann	Switzerland
Light-heavyweight	John Spellman	USA
Heavyweight	Harry Steele	USA

Graeco-Roman

Event	Name	Country
Bantamweight	Eduard Putsep	Estonia
Featherweight	Kalle Anttila	Finland
Lightweight	Oscari Friman	Finland
Middleweight	Edvard Vesterlund	Finland
Light-heavyweight	Carl Westergren	Sweden
Heavyweight	Henry Deglane	France

Yachting

Event	Name	Country
12-ft centreboard	Leon Huybrechts	Belgium
8-metre class	'Bera'	Norway
6-metre class	'Elisabeth V'	Norway

Amsterdam Olympic Games (1928)

The Games of the IXth Olympiad, held in July and August of 1928, were chiefly remarkable for the rather grudging inclusion of women track and field competitors for the first time—and a somewhat less grudging welcome to a 300-strong team of German athletes, the first since World War I. A total of 700,000 spectators flocked to the capital of the Netherlands to watch more than 3,900 competitors from 46 different countries take part. There were 109 separate competitions in the 17 sports.

A new stadium was built on marshy ground, to accommodate 40,000 spectators. The splendid 400-metre running track was surrounded by a 500-metre cycle track, with a football pitch in the centre. There was also a marathon tower, 150 ft high, bearing a bowl at the top in which a flame burnt throughout the period of the Games.

Prince Hendrick, the Prince Consort, acting for Queen Wilhelmina, performed the opening ceremony on July 28, and 35,000 sports fans were there to cheer the march past of the nations. They were unable to cheer the French contingent, who pointedly absented themselves from the parade because of alleged insults by a pro-German Dutch gatekeeper. In contrast to the enormous squads from Germany and the United States, Haiti, Cuba, and Panama each sent a solitary athlete.

Twenty-eight nations gained at least one gold medal each. As usual, the United States were way out in front with an impressive 22 gold medals, followed by Germany with 10, Sweden 9, and Finland 8. Britain won 3—two in track and field events and one in rowing; Canada had 4, and Australia, India, New Zealand, and South Africa one apiece.

Japan secured her first-ever gold medal through Mikio Oda, who won the triple jump with a leap of 15.21 metres (49 ft 10¾ in). Some 36 years later, at the Tokyo Olympics, Oda was a member of the organizing committee. His historic Japanese medal was commemorated in 1964 by a flagpole, bearing the Olympic flag and exactly 15.21 metres high.

With no hint of what lay in store for his boys in the prestigious track events, Major General Douglas MacArthur, president of the U.S. Olympic Committee, encouraged the folks back home with the following words: 'The opening of the Games finds the American team at the peak of form. We have assembled the greatest team in our athletic history.' Unfortunately for the General and his audience, the United States obtained only one gold medal in the 10 individual track events—the 400 metres being won by a star football player from Syracuse named Ray Barbuti. But they redeemed themselves by winning both the relay races, the high jump, long jump, pole vault, shot, and discus.

The solitary Haitian, Silvio Cator, distinguished himself by coming second in the long jump. He gained further fame four years later by becoming the world's first 26-ft long jumper. To this day he remains the only Haitian ever to win an Olympic medal.

Percy Williams, a curly-headed ex-waiter from Canada, achieved the coveted 'double' by winning both the 100 and 200 metre sprints, and Britain's Douglas Lowe repeated his Paris success in the 800 metres, the first man to do so at this distance. The powerful Finns won four track events and the decathlon. Paavo Nurmi, having won two gold medals in Antwerp and four in Paris, added another gold and two silver to his burgeoning collection. For most of the marathon two Japanese, a Finn, and an American battled grimly for the lead. But a few

1 The Amsterdam Olympics saw a member of the British peerage win a gold medal for a track event: Lord Burghley (later the Marquess of Exeter) took the 400 metres hurdles in 53.4 sec.
2 The Canadian team smashed the world record for the women's 4 x 100 metres relay, laying claim to their gold medals with a time of 48.4 sec. It was the first time that women had been allowed to compete in track and field events in the Olympic Games.
3 South African sprinter Sydney Atkinson (497) clocks a time of 14.8 sec to gain the coveted gold medal in the 110 metres hurdles.

miles from the tape, El Abdel Ouafi, a 29-year-old Arab, strode through the pack to win the gold for France by 150 yards.

The Irish Free State gained her first win as an independent country through the mighty Patrick O'Callaghan, appropriately throwing the hammer, an event in which Irish-Americans had excelled for many years. Altogether, nine new Olympic records (four of them also world records) were set in the men's track and field events.

The women had to content themselves with three track and two field events: 100 metres, 800 metres, sprint relay, high jump, and discus. Canada won the high jump through Ethel Catherwood, and the Canadian team also gained golds in the sprint relay. In the 800 metres, won by Germany's Linda Radke, many of the competitors (some of whom had never run the distance before) showed signs of distress. The organizers were so disturbed that the event was subsequently dropped; the distance, they concluded, was too great for the weaker sex. Nearly a quarter of a century elapsed before it was reintroduced into the Games.

Thirty-three competitors from 11 countries were eager to display their talents in the modern pentathlon. The competition consists of five events—shooting, swimming, fencing, cross-country running, and cross-country riding. At these Olympics, the points awarded for each event corresponded to the position in which the competitor finished, and the competitor with the lowest total was the overall winner. Sweden gained her fourth successive victory in this event through Sven Thofelt.

There were eight swimming events for men and seven for women. The United States won 10 of these, the remaining five each going to a different country. The American Johnny Weismuller, who subsequently created the film role of Tarzan, gained gold medals

in the 100-metres freestyle and in the relay. These he added to the three golds already won in the Paris Olympics for the 100 metres and 400 metres freestyle, and the relay.

Arne Borg of Sweden maintained his swimming reputation in the 400 metres and 1,500 metres. In 1924 he had taken a silver medal in the 400 metres; this time, he had to be content with a bronze. But in the 1,500 metres, for which four years earlier he had won a silver medal, he came home with a gold. Similarly with Australian Andrew 'Boy' Charlton. In Paris he had swum his way to a bronze medal in the 400 metres; in Amsterdam he turned it into a silver. He won a second silver in the 1,500 metres— the event that he had won in 1924.

After·a tremendous struggle in the platform diving event, Pete Desjardins of the United States snatched victory from the American-trained Egyptian, Farid Simaika, by 0.16 of a point. Desjardins also took first place in the springboard diving. Altogether, nine world records were set up in the swimming and diving events.

Eighteen teams competed in the association football championships, but Britain was a notable absentee. It was alleged that many of the competing countries were paying their players for 'broken time' (time lost from their ordinary jobs) and Britain opted out in protest at this breach of amateurism. The holders, Uruguay, met near neighbours Argentina in the final. The pitch resembled a battlefield at times, and with the score at 1–1 after 15 minutes of extra time both teams were happy to lick their wounds in preparation for the replay. In the second final Argentina scored first with a disputed goal. Uruguay equalised, and eventually retained the championship 2–1.

The eight boxing divisions attracted nearly 150 fighters from 29 countries. Italy came off best with three gold medals, but it was

Sport in Beeld

1 Paavo Nurmi, perhaps the best known name in the history of athletics, won the 10,000 metres crown and came second in the 5,000 metres and 3,000 m steeplechase.
2 Master French swordsman Lucien Gaudin took the foils and epée title.
3 Germany's Linda Radke sets a world record of 2 min 16.8 sec for the 800 metres, leaving Miss Hitomi (265) trailing in second place.
4 French Arab El Abdel Ouefi jogs home an easy winner in the 1928 marathon.
5 Norway's entry *Norna* took the gold medal in the 6-metre class at Amsterdam.
6 American footballer Ray Barbuti powers his way to the tape in the 400 metres, in a shade over 47 sec.

the judging that won the headlines—some of it was so bad as to be unbelievable. It seems that mauling, butting, and boring were all one to the gentlemen who did the scoring.

German fencer Helen Mayer, who took the gold in the individual foil, the only women's event, won every match throughout the competition and received only nine hits in the process. German fencers also came third and fourth in this event. France, Italy, and Hungary each scored doubles in the six men's events.

Switzerland won three of the five gymnastic events. Women gymnasts had given exhibitions at previous Games, but at Amsterdam a women's team event was included for the first time. They had to wait another 24 years before more gymnastic events for women competitors were staged.

Among the oarsmen only the Americans gained more than a single victory. Paul Costello won his third gold medal in successive Olympics in the double sculls, this time with Charles McIlvaine as his partner. An American crew also won the eights, for the third time in succession, roared on mercilessly to victory by their vociferous cox, Don Blessing. Bobbie Pearce of Australia won the single sculls by a good four lengths.

Hockey, dropped from the 1924 Games, was reintroduced—much to India's satisfaction. They gained the first of six Olympic wins in succession, scoring 29 goals throughout the competition without conceding one. There were no shooting events, because of trouble over amateurism, and the tennis competitions were dropped (for ever) because of a similar controversy.

Perhaps the last word on the Amsterdam Olympic Games should rest with General MacArthur, who described them with somewhat exaggerated if not pardonable pride as 'a model for all future Olympics'.

AMSTERDAM OLYMPIC GAMES, 1928 Gold Medallists

Association Football		Uruguay	
Athletics—Men			
100 metres	Percy Williams	Canada	10.8 sec
200 metres	Percy Williams	Canada	21.8 sec
400 metres	Ray Barbuti	USA	47.8 sec
800 metres	Douglas G. A. Lowe	GB	1 min 51.8 sec
1500 metres	Harry E. Larva	Finland	3 min 53.2 sec
5000 metres	Ville Ritola	Finland	14 min 38 sec
10000 metres	Paavo Nurmi	Finland	30 min 18.8 sec
Marathon	A. El Ouafi	France	2 hr 32 min 57 sec
4x100 metres relay		USA	41.0 sec
4x400 metres relay		USA	3 min 14.2 sec
110 metres hurdles	Sydney Atkinson	S Africa	14.8 sec
400 metres hurdles	Lord David Burghley	GB	53.4 sec
3000 metres steeplechase	Toiva A. Loukala	Finland	9 min 21.8 sec
High Jump	Robert W. King	USA	6 ft 4⅜ in
Long Jump	Edward Hamm	USA	25 ft 4¾ in
Triple Jump	Mikio Oda	Japan	49 ft 10¾ in
Pole Vault	Sabin W. Carr	USA	13 ft 9¼ in
Shot	John Kuck	USA	52 ft 0¾ in
Discus	Clarence Houser	USA	155 ft 3 in
Hammer	Patrick O'Callaghan	Ireland	168 ft 7 in
Javelin	Erik Lundqvist	Sweden	218 ft 6 in
Decathlon	Paavo Yrjola	Finland	8053.29 pts
Athletics—Women			
100 metres	Elizabeth Robinson	USA	12.2 sec
800 metres	Linda Radhe	Germany	2 min 16.8 sec
4x100 metres relay		Canada	48.4 sec
High Jump	Ethel Catherwood	Canada	5 ft 2½ in
Discus	Helena Konopacka	Poland	129 ft 11¾ in
Boxing			
Flyweight	Anton Kocsis	Hungary	
Bantamweight	Vittorio Tamagnini	Italy	
Featherweight	L. van Klaveren	Netherlands	
Lightweight	Carlo Orlandez	Italy	
Welterweight	Edward Morgan	New Zealand	
Middleweight	Piero Toscani	Italy	
Light-Heavyweight	Victorio Avendano	Argentina	
Heavyweight	Rodriguez Juvado	Argentina	
Cycling			
1000 metres	R. Beaufrand	France	
1000 metres time trial	Willy Falk-Hansen	Denmark	1 min 14.4 sec
2000 metres tandem	B. Leene, D. van Dijk	Netherlands	
4000 metres team pursuit		Italy	5 min 01.8 sec
Road Race—Individual	Henry Hansen	Denmark	4 hr 47 min 18.0 sec
Team		Denmark	15 hr 9 min 14.0 sec
Equestrian Events			
Dressage—Individual	Carl von Langen	Germany	
Team		Germany	
Show Jumping—Individual	F. Ventura	Czechoslovakia	
Team		Spain	
Three Day Event—Individual	Lt. Ferdinand Pahud de Mortanges	Netherlands	
Team		Netherlands	
Fencing—Men			
Foil—Individual	Lucien Gandin	France	
Team		Italy	
Epee—Individual	Lucien Gandin	France	
Team		Italy	
Sabre—Individual	Odon Tersztyansky	Hungary	
Team		Hungary	
Fencing—Women			
Foil— Individual	Helene Mayer	Germany	
Gymnastics—Men			
Vaulting Horse	Eugen Mack	Switzerland	
Pommelled Horse	Hermann Hanggi	Switzerland	
Horizontal Bar	George Miex	Switzerland	
Parallel Bars	Ladislav Vacha	Czechoslovakia	
Rings	Leon Stukelji	Yugoslavia	
Combined Individual	George Miex	Switzerland	
Combined Team		Switzerland	
Women's Team		Netherlands	
Hockey		British India	
Lacrosse		USA	
Modern Pentathlon	Sven Thofelt	Sweden	
Rowing			
Single Sculls	Henry Pearce	Australia	7 min 11 sec
Double Sculls	Paul Costello, Charles McIlraine	USA	6 min 41.4 sec
Coxwainless Pairs	K. Moeschler, B. Muller	Germany	7 min 6.4 sec
Coxed Pairs	H. Schochlin, C. Schochlin, H. Bourquin (cox)	Switzerland	7 min 42.6 sec
Coxwainless Fours		GB	6 min 36.0 sec
Coxed Fours		Italy	6 min 47.8 sec
Eights		USA	6 min 3.2 sec
Swimming—Men			
100 metres freestyle	John Weismuller	USA	58.6 sec
400 metres freestyle	Albert Zorilla	Argentina	5 min 1.6 sec
1500 metres freestyle	Arne Borg	Sweden	19 min 51.8 sec
100 metres backstroke	George Kojac	USA	1 min 8.2 sec
200 metres breaststroke	Yoshiyuki Tsurata	Japan	2 min 48.8 sec
4x200 metres freestyle relay		USA	9 min 36.2 sec
Springboard Diving	Pete Desjardins	USA	
Highboard Diving	Pete Desjardins	USA	
Swimming—Women			
100 metres freestyle	Albina Osipovich	USA	1 min 11.0 sec
400 metres freestyle	Martha Norelius	USA	5 min 42.8 sec
100 metres backstroke	Marie Braun	Netherlands	1 min 22.0 sec
200 metres breaststroke	Hilde Schrader	Germany	3 min 12.6 sec
4x100 metres freestyle relay		USA	4 min 47.6 sec
Springboard Diving	Helen Meany	USA	
Highboard Diving	Elizabeth Pinkston	USA	
Water-Polo		Germany	
Weightlifting			
Featherweight	Franz Andrysek	Austria	634 lb
Lightweight	Kurt Helbig*	Germany	711 lb
	Hans Haas	Austria	
Middleweight	Francois Roger	France	738 lb
Light-Heavyweight	Said Nosseir	Egypt	782 lb
Heavyweight	Josef Strassberger	Germany	810 lb
Wrestling			
Freestyle			
Bantamweight	Kaarie Makinen	Finland	
Featherweight	Allie Morrison	USA	
Lightweight	Osvald Kapp	Estonia	
Welterweight	Arve Haavisto	Finland	
Middleweight	Ernst Kyburz	Switzerland	
Light-Heavyweight	Thure Sjostedt	Sweden	
Heavyweight	John C. Richtoff	Sweden	
Graeco-Roman style			
Bantamweight	Karl Leucht	Germany	
Featherweight	Voldemar Vali	Estonia	
Lightweight	Lajos Keresztes	Hungary	
Middleweight	Vaino A. Kokkinen	Finland	
Light-Heavyweight	Ibrahim Moustafa	Egypt	
Heavyweight	Rudolph Svensson	Sweden	
Yachting			
6-metre class	Prince Olav	Norway	
8-metre class	Mme V. Heriot	France	
12-foot dinghy	Sven Thorell	Sweden	

*Results and bodyweights being equal Helbig and Haas were declared joint champions.

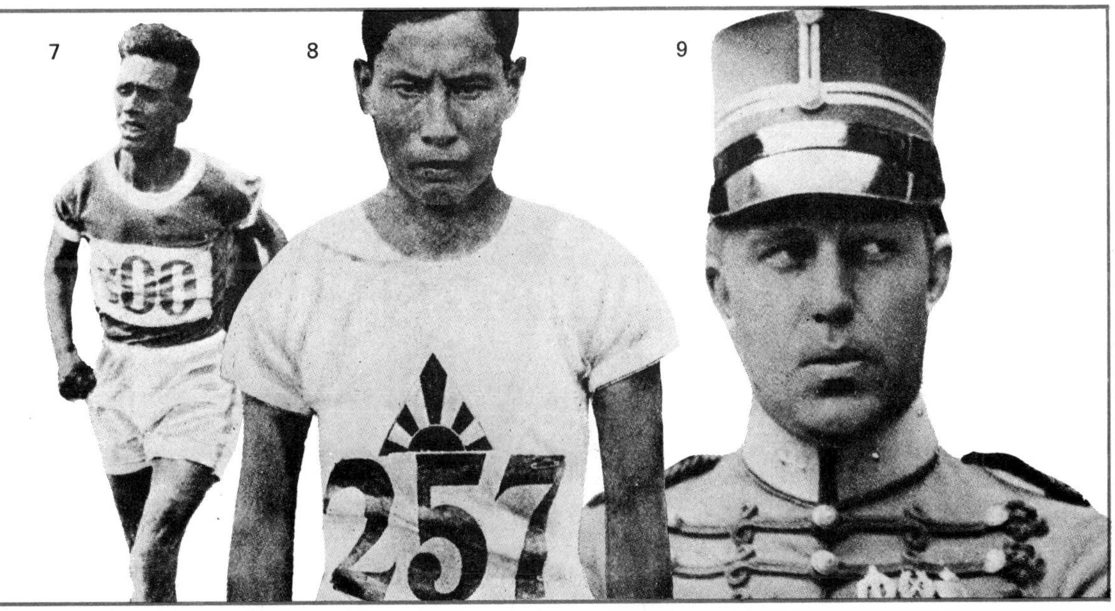

7 The dynamic Finn, Willie Ritola, relentlessly upheld his country's great tradition in the distance events, already established by Kolehmainen and Nurmi. At Amsterdam in the 10,000 metres he matched Nurmi stride for stride until the last lap, but was beaten at the tape by less than a second. A few days later he had his revenge by defeating his great rival in the 5,000 metres.
8 Grim-faced Mikio Ada produced a historic leap of nearly 50 ft in the triple jump to win Japan's first ever gold medal.
9 Sven Thofelt won the modern pentathlon for Sweden with a total of 47 points on the old reckoning.

Los Angeles Olympic Games (1932)

The ninth in the series of modern Olympic Games was held at Los Angeles in late July and early August 1932, the first Games to be held in the Americas since the St Louis celebrations of 1904. In many ways they were the first of the highly organized promotions that typified the Games afterwards. For the first time an 'Olympic village', housing the 1,300 male athletes, was especially constructed, while the 120 women competitors (in three sports—athletics, swimming, and fencing) were located in an hotel. Although 40 countries were represented in Los Angeles, the travelling distance and the time and expense involved resulted in very small entries from the European countries.

Athletics

Thirty-four nations sent some 400 men and women to Los Angeles to compete for 23 men's and 6 women's titles. The United States, of course, had a full team, but other countries could not afford to be so well represented. The women were competing in their second track and field Olympics, and their programme had been expanded by the inclusion of the 80 metres hurdles and javelin, but the 800 metres was dropped.

The United States won 11 men's titles, with Finland the next most successful team with 3. American women won five out of the six events, while their only failure was in the 100 metres, won by Stanislawa Walasiewicz—representing Poland, her native country, but a resident—known as Stella Walsh —in the United States since she was two years old. The track events were notable for the introduction of an experimental electric timing mechanism, while hand-operated stop watches and a movie camera were also used.

Eddie Tolan became the first coloured man to win a gold medal in the 100 or 200 metres. In fact he won both, beating his fellow-American Ralph Metcalfe by an inch in the 100 metres and equalling the world record of 10.3 sec. In the 200 metres he beat George Simpson (also of the United States) by two yards in 21.2 sec with Metcalfe third. The only European to reach either final was Arthur Jonath of Germany, who took the bronze in the 100 metres and was fourth in the 200. Tolan was not included in America's 4 by 100 metres relay team, and nor was Metcalfe. But the quartet showed the United States' remarkable depth of sprinting ability, winning by 10 yards in 40.0 sec, a world record.

The 400 metres final was also an all-American battle, between Bill

Official Report of the 1932 Olympics

1 The scene in the Los Angeles Coliseum as the Games of the Xth Olympiad were opened on July 30, 1932.
2 George Gulack won a gold medal for America on the rings. American gymnasts won 5 of the 11 gymnastic events contested in the Games. 3 Jean Shiley won the high jump after a jump-off with her American teammate Mildred Zaharias. Both girls were credited with a world record height of 5 ft. 5 in. 4 Finland's Lauri Lehtinen just holds off America's Ralph Hill in the 5,000 metres. Some people thought that the Finn had impeded the American, and demanded his disqualification, but the result was allowed to stand.

Official Report of the 1932 Olympics

Official Report of the 1932 Olympics

Central Press

34

5 A well judged race by Britain's Tom Hampson gave him the 800 metres title by 0.2 sec from Canada's Alex Wilson in a world record of 1 min 49.8 sec. **6** The American yacht *Angelita* had only one opponent, Canada's *Santa Maria*, in the 8-metre class.

Central Press

Official Report of the 1932 Olympics

5 Carr and Ben Eastman (the world 440 and 880 yards record holder). Carr won by 0.2 sec, setting a world record of 46.2 sec, with Eastman second, a second ahead of Canada's Alex Wilson. Eastman did not feature in his country's 4 by 400 metres relay team, but the Americans still won, beating Great Britain by 3 seconds in 3 min 8.2 sec—a world record.

Three days before the 400 metres final, Wilson had been even closer to a gold medal. Britain's Tom Hampson, who was fifth at the half-way stage, won his country's fourth consecutive 800 metres title after a tremendous battle with Wilson down the home straight. His time of 1 min 49.7 sec was officially rounded off to 1 min 49.8 sec—a world record and the first time a man had broken 1 min 50 sec.

The 5,000 metres produced a controversial finish between Finland's Lauri Lehtinen and the American champion Ralph Hill. In a desperate last lap Hill tried to pass his opponent, and there can be no doubt that Lehtinen, albeit

6 unintentionally, impeded the American. Some of the judges and a section of the crowd thought that the Finn should have been disqualified, but the chief judge ruled otherwise and the announcer settled the crowd with the words 'Remember, please, these people are our guests'.

The '3,000 metres' steeplechase was an extraordinary race on account of a strange error on the part of the officials. Finland's Volmari Iso-Hollo had won his heat in an Olympic record time of 9 min 14.6 sec, but in the final he recorded 10 min 33.4 sec. It was later discovered that the official responsible for counting the laps had been taken ill and his substitute had failed to record one of the laps—in all a distance of 3,460 metres was run.

The finish of the marathon was one of the closest in history, with just 65 seconds covering the first four men. Argentina's Juan Zabala beat Britain's Sam Ferris by 19 seconds for the gold medal. Another close finish came in the 110 metres hurdles. The movie film of the race was instrumental in clarifying the placings. The race was clearly won by America's George Saling, with his team-mate Percy Beard in second place. The bronze medal was at first awarded to another American Jack Keller, but the film showed that he had been beaten by Britain's Don Finlay, and Keller went to the British team's quarters personally to give Finlay the medal.

For the first time, the United States failed to win the high jump, which crossed the border into Canada. Duncan McNaughton won the jump-off against Robert van Osdel and Cornelius Johnson of the United States and Simeon Toribio of Argentina. Two other jumping events—the

pole vault and long jump—went to American competitors, but Japan won the triple jump through Chuhei Nambu, whose 51 ft. 7 in. clearance was over a foot better than the silver-medal-winning effort of Sweden's Erik Svensson.

The outstanding female athlete of the Games was Mildred 'Babe' Didrikson, who won the 80 metres hurdles and the javelin, and was second in the high jump, in which she shared a new world record with the winner Jean Shiley.

Swimming

Japan, inspired by the victory of Yoshiyuki Tsuruta in the 200 metres breaststroke at the 1928 Games, set off for America with the firm belief that what one could do, they could all do. And how right they were. They won five of the six men's swimming titles, and even won their first women's Olympic swimming medal through Hideko Maehata who was second in the 200 metres breaststroke.

Yoshiyuki Tsuruta retained his breaststroke crown, with his team-mate Reizo Koike second. Kusuo Kitamura, at 14 years old the youngest man to win an Olympic swimming title, was first in the 1,500 metres freestyle and was followed home by Shozo Makino. And in the 100 metres freestyle, an American preserve since 1908, they took first and second places. They won all three medals in the 100 metres backstroke, and beat the United States by 12.1 sec to win the 4 by 200 metres relay in a world record time of 8 min 58.4 sec. Japan's tally of medals was 11 out of a possible 16, and they got all three of their permitted competitors through to the last six of every men's race.

American pride was salvaged in the diving where they took all 12 medals and in the women's swimming, in which the host country won four of the five events. Helene Madison won both the 100 and 400 metres freestyle (setting a world record in the latter) and took a third gold as a member of the winning American relay team. The only non-American women's winner was Australia's Clare Dennis, who set a world record in the 200 metres breaststroke. Her time of 3 min 6.3 sec was 0.1 sec faster than Miss Maehata. Britain's only medallist was Valerie Davies of Wales, third in the 100 metres backstroke.

Hungary, with 35 goals in their favour and only 2 scored against them, were conclusive winners of the water polo tournament for the first time. They beat the Japanese team 18-0.

Other sports

The gymnastics events saw the great Italian Romeo Neri in action. He was the most successful gymnast on show, winning three gold medals, in the combined exercises individual and team events and on the parallel bars. The United States team was much in evidence, with victories in the horizontal bar and the rings (both 'regular' gymnastic events) and in three more unusual competitions, rope climbing, tumbling, and Indian club swinging.

The rowing course at Long Beach could accommodate four crews abreast, but was made difficult by a tricky cross wind which made some of the times slower than usual. The United States were understandably the most successful team, with three victories—in the double sculls, coxed pairs, and eights. Great Britain's small team, which contested only four races and reached the final of each, won two golds, in the coxless pairs and the coxless fours. 'Jumbo' Edwards created something of a record by being a member of both winning crews. Australia's Henry Pearce retained the single sculls title he had won in Amsterdam in 1928, the first man to do so,

Shooting, omitted from the 1928 programme, returned with two events, the free pistol and small bore rifle. Both events were won by European marksmen, Renzo Morigi of Italy taking the pistol gold, and Bertil Ronnmark of Sweden the rifle.

The Swedish team was the most successful in the wrestling events, winning two freestyle and four Graeco-Roman golds. Ivar Johansson was their most outstanding competitor, winning the freestyle middleweight and the Graeco-Roman welterweight titles.

Although the relative isolation of California from the main population centres of the world had cut down the number of participants at the 1932 Olympics, the Games themselves were a success. It would be more than 20 years before the Olympics were again held outside Europe but the Los Angeles Games had shown that the Olympics could move from continent to continent.

LOS ANGELES OLYMPIC GAMES, 1932 Gold Medallists

Athletics—Men				Parallel bars	Romeo Neri	Italy	
100 metres	Eddie Tolan	USA	10.3 sec	Pommell horse	Istvan Pelle	Hungary	
200 metres	Eddie Tolan	USA	21.2 sec	Vault	Savino Guglielmetti	Italy	
400 metres	Bill Carr	USA	46.2 sec	Rings	George Gulack	USA	
800 metres	Tommy Hampson	Great Britain	1 min 49.8 sec	Rope climbing	Raymond Bass	USA	
1,500 metres	Luigi Beccali	Italy	3 min 51.2 sec	Tumbling	Rowland Wolfe	USA	
5,000 metres	Lauri Lehtinen	Finland	14 min 30.0 sec	Indian club swinging	George Roth	USA	
10,000 metres	Janusz Kusocinski	Poland	30 min 11.4 sec	**Modern Pentathlon**	Johan Oxenstierna	Sweden	
Marathon	Juan Zabala	Argentina	2 hr 31 min 36 sec	**Rowing**			
4 x 100 metres relay		USA	40.0 sec	Single sculls	Henry Pearce	Australia	7 min 44.4 sec
4 x 400 metres relay		USA	3 min 8.2 sec	Double sculls	William Garrett-Gilmore,		
110 metres hurdles	George Saling	USA	14.6 sec		Kenneth Myers	USA	7 min 17.4 sec
400 metres hurdles	Bob Tisdall	Eire	51.8 sec	Coxless pairs	'Jumbo' Edwards,		
Steeplechase*	Volmari Iso-Hollo	Finland	10 min 33.4 sec		Lewis Clive	Great Britain	8 min 0.0 sec
50 kilometres walk	Thomas Green	Great Britain	4 hr 50 min 10 sec	Coxed pairs	Charles Kieffer,		
High jump	Duncan McNaughton	Canada	6 ft 5½ in		Joseph Schauers,		
Pole vault	William Miller	USA	14 ft 1⅞ in		Edward Jennings (cox)	USA	8 min 25.8 sec
Long jump	Edward Gordon	USA	25 ft 0¾ in	Coxless fours		Great Britain	6 min 58.2 sec
Triple jump	Chuhei Nambu	Japan	51 ft 7 in	Coxed fours		Germany	7 min 19.0 sec
Shot	Leo Sexton	USA	52 ft 6 in	Eights		USA	6 min 37.6 sec
Discus	John Anderson	USA	162 ft 4½ in	**Shooting**			
Hammer	Patrick O'Callaghan	Eire	176 ft 11 in	Free pistol	Renzo Morigi	Italy	
Javelin	Matti Jarvinen	Finland	238 ft 6½ in	Small bore rifle	Bertil Ronnmark	Sweden	
Decathlon	James Bausch	USA	8,462.23 pts	**Swimming—Men**			
			(6,588 pts by 1962 tables)	100 metres freestyle	Yasuji Miyazaki	Japan	58.2 sec
				400 metres freestyle	Clarence Crabbe	USA	4 min 48.4 sec
Athletics—Women				1,500 metres freestyle	Kusuo Kitamura	Japan	19 min 12.4 sec
100 metres	Stanislawa Walasiewicz	Poland	11.9 sec	200 metres breaststroke	Yoshiyuki Tsurata	Japan	2 min 45.4 sec
4 x 100 metres relay		USA	47.0 sec	100 metres backstroke	Masaji Kiyokawa	Japan	1 min 8.6 sec
80 metres hurdles	Mildred Didrikson	USA	11.7 sec	4 x 200 metres freestyle relay		Japan	8 min 58.4 sec
High jump	Jean Shiley	USA	5 ft 5 in	Springboard diving	Michael Galitzen	USA	
Discus	Lilian Copeland	USA	133 ft 1⅞ in	Highboard diving	Harold Smith	USA	
Javelin	Mildred Didrikson	USA	143 ft 4 in	**Swimming—Women**			
Boxing				100 metres freestyle	Helene Madison	USA	1 min 6.8 sec
Flyweight	Istvan Enekes	Hungary		400 metres freestyle	Helene Madison	USA	5 min 28.5 sec
Bantamweight	Horace Gwynne	Canada		200 metres breaststroke	Clare Dennis	Australia	3 min 6.3 sec
Featherweight	Carmelo Robledo	Argentina		100 metres backstroke	Eleanor Holm	USA	1 min 19.4 sec
Lightweight	Lawrence Stevens	South Africa		4 x 100 metres freestyle relay		USA	4 min 38.0 sec
Welterweight	Edward Flynn	USA		Springboard diving	Georgia Coleman	USA	
Middleweight	Carmen Barth	USA		Highboard diving	Dorothy Poynton	USA	
Light-heavyweight	David Carstens	South Africa		**Water Polo**		Hungary	
Heavyweight	Alberto Lovell	Argentina		**Weightlifting**			
Cycling				Featherweight	Raymond Suvigny	France	633¼ lb
1,000 metres sprint	Jacobus van Egmond	Netherlands		Lightweight	Rene Duverger	France	716¼ lb
1,000 metres time trial	Edgar Gray	Australia	1 min 13.0 sec	Middleweight	Rudolf Ismayr	Germany	760½ lb
2,000 metres tandem	Maurice Perrin,			Light-heavyweight	Louis Hostin	France	804½ lb
	Louis Chaillot	France		Heavyweight	Jaroslav Skobla	Czechoslovakia	837¼ lb
4,000 metres team pursuit		Italy	4 min 52.9 sec	**Wrestling**			
Road race	Attilio Pavesi	Italy	2 hr 28 min 5.6 sec	*Freestyle*			
Equestrian				Bantamweight	Robert Pearce	USA	
Dressage—individual	Francois Lesage	France		Featherweight	Hermanni Pihlajamaki	Finland	
—team		France		Lightweight	Charles Pacome	France	
Show jumping —individual	Takeichi Nishi	Japan		Welterweight	Jack van Bebber	USA	
—team		No complete team finished		Middleweight	Ivar Johansson	Sweden	
Three day event—individual	Ferdinand de Mortanges	Netherlands		Light-heavyweight	Peter Mehringer	USA	
—team		USA		Heavyweight	Johan Richtoff	Sweden	
Fencing—Men				*Graeco-Roman*			
Foil—individual	Gustavo Marzi	Italy		Bantamweight	Jakob Brendel	Germany	
—team		France		Featherweight	Giovanni Gozzi	Italy	
Epee—individual	Giancarlo Medici	Italy		Lightweight	Erik Malmberg	Sweden	
—team		France		Welterweight	Ivar Johansson	Sweden	
Sabre—individual	Gyorgy Piller	Hungary		Middleweight	Vaino Kokkinen	Finland	
—team		Hungary		Light-heavyweight	Rudolf Svensson	Sweden	
Fencing—Women				Heavyweight	Carl Westergren	Sweden	
Foil—individual	Ellen Preis	Austria		**Yachting**			
Hockey		India		Monotype	Jacques Lebrun	France	
Gymnastics				Star	Gilbert Gray,		
Combined exercises—individual	Romeo Neri	Italy			Andrew Libano	USA	
—team		Italy		6-metre		Sweden	
Floor exercises	Istvan Pelle	Hungary		8-metre		USA	
Horizontal bar	Dallas Bixler	USA					

* An extra lap was run through 'official error', and the distance run in the final was 3,460 metres.

Eddie Tolan (left) winning the 100 metres from Ralph Metcalfe. Tolan followed this victory with another in the 200 metres.

Ireland's Bob Tisdall (right) wins the 400 metres hurdles. Fourth (second from left) was the 1928 champion, Lord Burghley.

Berlin Olympic Games (1936)

An 'infamous festival dominated by Jews' was the first published Nazi verdict on the Olympic Games when it was learned in 1931 that the games of the XIth Olympiad would be held in Berlin four years later. It was hardly an auspicious start to a pageant designed to foment international amity through sport. But at that time Hitler was not yet undisputed master of Germany. As the deadline for the Games approached, he awoke to their immense propaganda value, and spared no expense to make the occasion the best organized and the most efficiently equipped in the history of the Olympics.

Many nations were beginning to flex their muscles before plunging into the maelstrom of World War II, and a number of private scraps broke out in the months preceding the Berlin Olympics, any one of which might have persuaded the organizers to call the whole thing off. Russia was making threatening gestures at China and Japan. France, Greece, and Austria were riven with political dissension. Japan invaded Manchuria, and Italy helped herself to Ethiopia. Spain exploded into civil war, and over all hung the brooding shadow of the swastika.

In 1913 the Kaiser had dedicated a 60,000-seat stadium at Grunewald, a suburb of Berlin, in preparation for the 1916 Games, which had been awarded to Germany, but which never took place. When Hitler came to power in 1933 the Germans extended the site to produce a magnificent stadium holding 100,000 spectators, and a sumptuous Olympic village to house 4,000 competitors — and conveniently adaptable to military needs. State money was poured out to make the Berlin Games the best ever, for the glory of sport—and of the Third Reich.

1 Lit by Greek virgins from the light of the sun, the first Olympic flame to burn in the modern Olympics nears the brazier at Berlin. 2 Czechoslovakia's Alois Hudec, strongman of the rings and gold medallist at Berlin. 3 Bespectacled Godfrey Brown, baton in hand, wins the 4 x 400 metres for Britain. Frederick Wolff, Godfrey Rampling, and William Roberts had built up a 5-yard lead and Brown made no mistake.

Germany, as expected, won most gold medals at the Olympics in Berlin. They took **33** golds to America's **24**, but most of them were in the more esoteric events. **1** There was a close finish in the eights, with the USA crew from Washington University winning by 0.2 sec from Italy (2nd) and Germany. German oarsmen won medals in all the Berlin rowing events. **2** Ken Carpenter of America broke the German monopoly of throwing events to beat the German world record holder Willie Schroeder with a throw of 50.48 metres, an Olympic record. **3** Britain won only two gold medals in track and field at Berlin. One of them, came from Harold Whitlock in the 50 km walk. **4** Winner of three gold medals, Karl Schwarzmann shows his technique on the parallel bars. Germany dominated the gymnastic events and won **6** out of the **8** golds at stake in this sport.

Pictorial Press

Popperfoto

Nazi ideology inevitably produced problems in the realm of sport. In Britain, and more particularly the United States, there was widespread agitation to boycott the Games. Assurances were sought, and glibly given, that there would be no racial discrimination against the selection of non-Aryans to represent Germany, if they reached the required athletic standard.

But official anti-Jewish sentiment soon made itself evident. Dr Lewald, the head of the German organizing committee at that time, was of partly Jewish descent. The Nazis began by forcing him to resign from the national athletic committee; they then tried to remove him from the German and International Olympic committees. They did everything they

could to take over the jurisdiction of the Games. Count Baillet Latour, president of the IOC, and his fellow members refused to kowtow to the Fuehrer's demands and stood courageously behind Dr Lewald. They insisted that the Games must be presented in the spirit of the Olympic ideal; that the preparations for the Games were to be carried out by the organizing committee, supervised by the IOC; and that the whole tournament must be entirely non-political in character. Finally they threatened that if these conditions were not met, they would cancel the 1936 Olympic Games. Hitler reluctantly acquiesced.

A gigantic bell, some 9 feet in diameter and weighing more than 14 tons, summoned the youth of

the world to Berlin. It was hung in a special tower at the Olympic Stadium. Swastikas outnumbered Olympic flags in this great Nazi showpiece. The torch relay was instituted for the first time. On July 30 a torch was lit by the rays of the sun at Olympia, in Greece, and carried by nearly 3,000 athletes who each ran one kilometre, through Greece, Bulgaria, Yugoslavia, Hungary, Austria, Czechoslovakia, and Germany to reach the Olympic Stadium on August 1.

On the opening day 110,000 spectators squeezed into the huge stadium to watch the march-past. A military band perched on the top of the towers that flanked the Marathon Gate heralded the arrival of the Fuehrer. The Germans sang 'Deutschland Uber Alles' and the 'Horst Wessel'

song, the flags of the competing nations fluttered to the mastheads, and the Olympic bell tolled its message.

The 50-nation march-past began. Hitler took the salute—which was revealing in its variety. The French team favoured the Olympic salute, similar to the Nazi salute, and were given a tremendous reception. The British immediately behind, gave a curt 'eyes right' and were greeted with stony silence. The political implications could not be disguised.

The German team, nearly 500 strong, brought up the rear of the procession, marching with military precision. Thousands of doves soared skywards to signal the arrival of a beautifully proportioned, flaxen-haired athlete holding the Olympic torch in his right hand. He came down a long flight of steps, ran halfway round the track looking for all the world like some athlete from the pages of Greek mythology, then plunged the torch into a brazier. The Olympic flame burst forth, to thunderous applause from the delighted multitude. Spiridon Louis, winner of the first marathon, in 1896, impressively attired in Greek national costume, presented Hitler with an olive branch; the Olympic oath was taken; a message from Baron de Coubertin was relayed over the loudspeakers; the crowd joined in the singing of the 'Hallelujah' chorus—and the opening ceremony was over.

There were 130 gold medals to be won (counting each of the team events as one medal) in the 19 sports.

Athletics
Track and field events consisted of 23 events for men (nowadays there are 24—there is a 20 km as well as a 50 km walk), and six for women. More than 700 men from 42 nations, and just over 100 women competitors from 20 nations, competed.

The outstanding athlete of the Berlin Games was the American Negro Jesse Owens. He gained three individual gold medals and was the first runner of the American quartet in the sprint relay, which they won by a good three yards in a new world record time. In both the 100 metres and the 200 metres he stormed through four rounds to head the field easily on each occasion. His times in the 100 metres were 10.3, 10.2, 10.4, and 10.3 sec. His 10.2 sec was disallowed as a world record because of a following wind of slightly more than two metres a second. In the 200 metres he produced times of 21.1, 21.1, 21.3, and 20.7 sec. He thus equalled the Olympic record for the 100 metres and beat the previous record for the 200 metres by half a second.

The long jump turned out to be one of the most exciting contests of all time. Owens, to the dismay of his fans, started with two foul jumps and faced elimination. It was then, according to Owens, that the German champion Luz Long (later killed on the Eastern Front) almost certainly saved him by pointing out that his run-up mark was wrong. With three final jumps to go, Owens led Long by just over an inch, but with his fifth leap the German equalled Owen's best effort of 25 ft 9¾ in. Methodically, almost casually, Owens sprinted down the track and cleared 26 ft 0½ in. The jump was immortalized in Leni Riefenstahl's historic film of the 1936 Games, which shows Owens jumping and Long watching. In the final jumps, Long fouled and Owens, with the pressure off, did 26 ft 5¼ in, more than a foot further than the previous Olympic record.

There was hardly an event during the eight full days of competition that did not excite the crowd. The stadium was always full, even for the heats. In the 400 metres, the duel between the two Americans, Archie Williams and Jimmy Luvalle, and Godfrey Brown and Bill Roberts from Britain was magnificent. Williams, running in lane 5, beat Brown in lane 6 by a very short yard, while Luvalle in lane 3 was inches ahead of Roberts in lane 4. Brown and Roberts gained their revenge in the relay team which pushed the Americans into second place in the 4 by 400 metres relay. The only other British gold medal was won by Harold Whitlock in the 50 km walk.

The 1,500 metres was a triumph for Jack Lovelock from New Zealand, who defeated the finest field of middle distance runners to date. Glenn Cunningham, the great American miler, was in the lead 400 metres from home, when suddenly a wispy figure in black streaked past him and stayed in front all the way to the tape. The fair-haired New Zealand medical student covered

1 Cyclists from 27 nations contested the 100 km race which was eventually won by Robert Charpentier of France. The French cyclists also took the team medals for the best overall result in the event. Germans were never famous for their cycling prowess, but the competitors from the host country won two of the six cycling titles at Berlin. 2 One of the most touching moments in Olympic history was when Spiridon Louis, who was the first Olympic marathon champion when he ran from Marathon to Athens in 1896, presented the German Chancellor with the age-old symbol of peace, an olive branch. The Berlin Games were full of incidents of this kind, most of them arranged by the German stage managers to make the Games the most successful ever. Germany's sportsmen were trained for the Games so that they would not be disgraced by the 'black auxiliaries' included in other countries' teams. The opening ceremony was marked by the release of thousands of doves; there was a special performance of a festival play, *Olympic Youth,* written by Dr Carl Diem, one of the Olympic committee; and a performance of Beethoven's Ninth Symphony, the choral movement of which was used as an anthem for all-German teams until the 1964 Games, when the combined German team was split into East/West.

Pictorial Press

Fox Photos

BERLIN OLYMPIC GAMES, 1936 Gold Medallists

Athletics—Men			
100 metres	Jesse C. Owens	USA	10.3 sec
200 metres	Jesse C. Owens	USA	20.7 sec
400 metres	Archie F. Williams	USA	46.5 sec
800 metres	John Woodruff	USA	1 min 52.9 sec
1,500 metres	John E. Lovelock	New Zealand	3 min 47.8 sec
5,000 metres	Gunnar Hoeckert	Finland	14 min 22.2 sec
10,000 metres	Ilmari Salminen	Finland	30 min 15.4 sec
3,000 metres Steeplechase	Volmari Iso-Hollo	Finland	9 min 03.8 sec
110 metres Hurdles	Forrest G. Towns	USA	14.2 sec
400 metres Hurdles	Glenn F. Hardin	USA	52.4 sec
50 kilometres Walk	Harold H. Whitlock	GB	4 hr 30 min 41.4 sec
Marathon	Kitei Son	Japan	2 hr 29 min 19.2 sec
4 x 100 metres Relay		USA	39.8 sec
4 x 400 metres Relay		GB	3 min 09.0 sec
High Jump	Cornelius C. Johnson	USA	6 ft 8 in
Pole Vault	Earle Meadows	USA	14 ft 3¼ in
Long Jump	Jesse C. Owens	USA	26 ft 5¼ in
Triple Jump	Naoto Tajima	Japan	52 ft 6 in
Shot	Hans Woellke	Germany	53 ft 1¾ in
Discus	Kenneth Carpenter	USA	165 ft 7½ in
Hammer	Karl Hein	Germany	185 ft 5 in
Javelin	Gerhard Stoeck	Germany	235 ft 8½ in
Decathlon	Glenn Morris	USA	
Athletics—Women			
100 metres	Helen H. Stephens	USA	11.5 sec
80 metres Hurdles	Trebisonda Valla	Italy	11.7 sec
4 x 100 metres Relay		USA	46.9 sec
High Jump	Ibolya Csak	Hungary	5 ft 3 in
Discus	Gisela Mauermeyer	Germany	156 ft 3¼ in
Javelin	Tilly Fleischer	Germany	148 ft 2¾ in
Basketball		USA	
Boxing			
Flyweight	Willi Kaiser	Germany	
Bantamweight	Ulderico Sergo	Italy	
Featherweight	Oscar Casanovas	Argentina	
Lightweight	Imre Harangi	Hungary	
Welterweight	Sten Suvio	Finland	
Middleweight	Jean Despeaux	France	
Light-Heavyweight	Roger Michelot	France	
Heavyweight	Herbert Runge	Germany	
Canoe Racing			
10,000 metres			
One seater collapsable	Gregor Hradetzky	Austria	50 min 01.2 sec
Two seater collapsable	Sven Johansson, Eric Blandstroem	Sweden	45 min 48.9 sec
One seater Kayak	Ernst Krebs	Germany	46 min 01.7 sec
Two seater Kayak	Paul Wevers, Ludwig Landen	Germany	41 min 45.0 sec
Two seater Canadian	Vaclav Mottl, Zdenek Skrdlant	Czechoslovakia	50 min 33.8 sec
1,000 metres			
One seater Kayak	Gregor Hradetzky	Austria	4 min 22.9 sec
Two seater Kayak	Adolph Kainz, Alfonz Dorfner	Austria	4 min 03.8 sec
One seater Canadian	Francis Amyot	Canada	5 min 32.1 sec
Two seater Canadian	R. Vladimir Syrovatka, Felix J. Brzak	Czechoslovakia	4 min 50.1 sec
Cycling			
1,000 metres Scratch	Toni Merkens	Germany	
1,000 metres Time Trial	Arie G. van Vliet	Netherlands	1 min 12.0 sec
2,000 metres Tandem	Ernst Ihbe, Carl Lorenz	Germany	
4,000 metres Team Pursuit		France	4 min 45.0 sec
Road Race—Individual	Robert Charpentier	France	2 hr 33 min 05.0 sec
—Team		France	7 hr 39 min 16.2 sec
Equestrian Sports			
Dressage—Individual	Heinrich Pollay	Germany	
—Team		Germany	
Three Day Event			
—Individual	Ludwig Stubbendorff	Germany	
—Team		Germany	
Jumping Prix de Nations			
—Individual	Kurt Hasse	Germany	
—Team		Germany	
Fencing			
Foil—Individual	Giulio Gaudini	Italy	
—Team		Italy	
Foil (Ladies)	Ilona Schacherer-Elek	Hungary	
Epee—Individual	Franco Riccardi	Italy	
—Team		Italy	
Sabre—Individual	Endre Kabos	Hungary	
—Team		Hungary	
Football		Italy	
Gymnastics			
Individual championship—Men	Karl A. M. Schwarzmann	Germany	
Team championship—Men		Germany	
Women		Germany	
Apparatus championship—men			
Horizontal Bar	Aleksanteri Saarvala	Finland	
Rings	Alois Hudec	Czechoslovakia	
Pommelled Horse	Konrad Frey	Germany	
Free Exercises	Georges Miez	Switzerland	
Parallel Bars	Konrad Frey	Germany	
Long Horse	Karl A. M. Schwarzmann	Germany	
Handball		Germany	
Hockey		India	
Modern Pentathlon			
Individual	Gotthardt Handrick	Germany	
Team		USA	
Polo		Argentina	
Rowing			
Single Sculls	Gustav Schaefer	Germany	8 min 21.5 sec
Double Sculls	Jack Beresford, Leslie F. Southwood	GB	7 min 20.8 sec
Coxless Pairs	Willi Eichhorn, Hugo Strauss	Germany	8 min 16.1 sec
Coxed Pairs	Gerhard Gustmann, Herbert Adamski, Dieter Arend (Cox)	Germany	8 min 36.9 sec
Coxless Fours		Germany	7 min 01.8 sec
Coxed Fours		Germany	7 min 16.2 sec
Eights		USA	6 min 25.4 sec
Shooting			
Automatic pistol or revolver (25 metres)	Cornelius M. van Oyen	Germany	
Target—pistol (50 metres)	Torsten Ullman	Sweden	
Miniature rifle (50 metres)	Willy Roegeberg	Norway	
Swimming and Diving—Men			
100 metres Freestyle	Ferenc Czik	Hungary	57.6 sec
400 metres Freestyle	Jack Medica	USA	4 min 44.5 sec
1,500 metres Freestyle	Noboru Terada	Japan	19 min 13.7 sec
200 metres Breaststroke	Tetsuo Hamuro	Japan	2 min 42.5 sec
100 metres Backstroke	Adolph Keifer	USA	1 min 5.9 sec
4 x 200 metres Freestyle Relay		Japan	8 min 51.5 sec
Springboard Diving	Richard Degener	USA	
High Diving	Marshall Wayne	USA	
Swimming and Diving—Women			
100 metres Freestyle	Hendrika Mastenbroek	Netherlands	1 min 5.9 sec
400 metres Freestyle	Hendrika Mastenbroek	Netherlands	5 min 26.4 sec
200 metres Breaststroke	Hideko Maehata	Japan	3 min 3.6 sec
100 metres Backstroke	Dina Senff	Netherlands	1 min 18.9 sec
4 x 100 metres Freestyle Relay		Netherlands	4 min 36.0 sec
Springboard Diving	Marjorie Gestring	USA	
High Diving	Dorothy Poynton Hill	USA	
Water Polo		Hungary	
Weight lifting			
Featherweight	Anthony Terlazzo	USA	688½ lb
Lightweight	Mohammed Ahmed Mesbah	Egypt	754½ lb
Middleweight	Khadr el Touni	Egypt	854 lb
Light-Heavyweight	Louis Hostin	France	821 lb
Heavyweight	Josef Manger	Germany	903½ lb
Wrestling			
Catch as Catch Can			
Bantamweight	Odon Zombori	Hungary	
Featherweight	Kustaa Pihlajamaeki	Finland	
Lightweight	Karoly Karpati	Hungary	
Welterweight	Frank W. Lewis	USA	
Middleweight	Emile Poilve	France	
Light-Heavyweight	Knut Fridell	Sweden	
Heavyweight	Kristjan Palusalu	Estonia	
Greco-Roman Style			
Bantamweight	Marton Loerincz	Hungary	
Featherweight	Yasar Erkan	Turkey	
Lightweight	Lauri Koskela	Finland	
Welterweight	Rudolph Suedberg	Sweden	
Middleweight	Ivar Johansson	Sweden	
Light-Heavyweight	Axel Cadier	Sweden	
Heavyweight	Kristjan Palusalu	Estonia	
Yachting			
6-metre class		GB	
8-metre class		Italy	
International Star class		Germany	
Olympic Monotype	Daniel Kabchelland	Netherlands	

'Storm-troopers march with a steady, quiet tread . . .' sang the Germans, but their dreams of athletic supremacy were shattered by the 'Tan Streak from Ohio State'—Jesse Owens. Legend has it that Hitler, who met and congratulated the Aryan winners of the first three finals, deliberately snubbed Owens. If he snubbed anyone it was Cornelius Johnson and David Allbritton, American negroes who were first and second in the high jump, the fourth event. In fact Hitler had overstayed his intended visit and, by design or not, had left the stadium before the result was announced. The IOC

1 the last lap in an amazing 55.7 sec and won by five yards in a world record time of 3 min 47.8 sec. Cunningham also finished inside the old world record, and the next three runners broke the Olympic record.

Finland won the 5,000 metres, 10,000 metres, and steeplechase, but were rather surprisingly defeated in the javelin by the German Gerhard Stoeck. Another surprise German victory was in the shot, which went to Hansje Woellke, with Stoeck third. The world record holder Jack Torrance of the United States who in 1934 had put up a remarkable world record of 57 ft 1 in, was more than six feet below his best, and nearly three feet behind the winning put of 53 ft 1¾ in. The third German men's victory came in the hammer. Carpenter Karl Hein, in the presence of the Fuehrer, achieved a tremendous throw of 185 ft 5 in, beating the 24-year-old Olympic record by nearly six feet. But in the discus, world record holder Willie Schroeder of Germany was nearly 20 feet below his best, and Americans finished first and second.

The pole vault produced a duel that continued into the night. In the glare of the floodlights, the American Earl Meadows soared to a victorious 14 ft 3¼ in, within three inches of the world record. His two Japanese rivals were beaten by four inches. World and Olympic records were shattered in the decathlon, that awe-inspiring 10-event contest decided over two days, with Americans in the three first places. In the marathon, the brash Argentine newsboy Juan Carlos Zabala, defending his title, collapsed exhausted, and Korean-born Kitei Son of Japan romped home by a clear two minutes.

The American women won the sprint relay by default—the German women dropped the baton when yards ahead. The American sprinter Helen Stephens beat Stella Walsh of Poland, the 1932 winner, by two yards in the 100 metres. Tribisonda Valla of Italy equalled the world record of 11.6 sec in the 80 metres hurdles, and Ibolya Csak of Hungary took the high jump. In that event Britain's Dorothy Odam, just 16 years old, cleared the same height as the winner, but lost the jump-off. When the next Games took place in London 12 years later, Dorothy, then Mrs Tyler and the mother of two children, again cleared the same height as the winner, but had to be content with second place because of the rule for deciding ties. This rule was changed after the 1936 Games. Had the new rule been in operation in 1936, Dorothy would have won the gold, while had the old rule been in existence in 1948 she would also have won the gold.

The United States won 12 of the 23 men's track and field events,

told Hitler it was not his job to congratulate anyone—but if he did he should not discriminate. Thereafter Hitler did not congratulate anyone—in public at least. 1 Owens wins the long jump with a leap of 26 ft 5¼ in, an Olympic record that stood until 1960. 2 In the heat of the 100 metres Owens equalled the Olympic record of 10.3 sec. 3 Germany's Anny Steuer (right) and Italy's Trebisonda Valla (far left) were second and first in a blanket finish of the hurdles.
4 German girls set a world record in the heat of the 400 metres relay but dropped the baton in the final.

thanks largely to their 'black auxiliaries', as they were described in the Nazi press. These 10 negroes, headed by Jesse Owens, won a total of six gold, three silver, and two bronze medals—a score superior to that of any other single nation, including the rest of the American team. They were the victors in every flat race from 100 to 800 metres.

Swimming and diving
In the 18,000-seat swimming pool, next to the athletics stadium, Japan ruled the ripples. The Japanese splashed their way to 10 out of a possible 17 medals in the men's events, and took another in the women's events. But the Netherlands dominated the women's races, winning the other four titles.

In the diving, the United States were supreme. They made a clean sweep of the medals in the men's and women's springboard and were first and second in both highboard events—Germany won the bronzes—for a total of 10 out of 12 medals. Thirteen-year-old Marjorie Gestring, who won the springboard title, became the youngest champion of the modern Olympic Games.

One of the surprises was the victory of Hungary's Ferenc Csik in the 100 metres freestyle race. With all eyes on the favoured Americans and Japanese in the centre lanes, Csik crept forward on the outside to gain a shock first place.

The men's breaststroke set a new style. For the first time in the Olympics, the over-water arm recovery, the 'high sail' (later to become the butterfly), was used by some swimmers for part of the race. Despite this display of power, particularly by Germany's Erwin Sietas, little Tetsuo

Hamuro of Japan, using a neat, orthodox, underwater recovery throughout, was victorious.

Dina Senff from the Netherlands created a sensation in the 100 metres backstroke. She missed her touch at the turn and had to swim back to the wall again. Astonishingly, she still won. Another great Dutch girl, Ria Mastenbroek, took the 100 and 400 metres freestyle—the only woman yet to achieve this double —and won the silver in the backstroke. Hideko Maehata became Japan's first and only woman Olympic swimming champion in taking the 200 metres breaststroke, with Denmark's tiny 13-year-old Inge Sorensen, third.

Rowing
Rowing was a triumph for the Germans. They won five of the seven events, and a silver and a bronze medal in the other two. Their only defeats occurred in the double sculls, where Jack Beresford (competing in his fifth successive Olympics) and Leslie Southwood of Britain won a brilliant victory over the Germans who had defeated them in the heats; and in the eights, in which the first three crews finished within a second of each other, the United States defeating Italy by three-fifths of a second.

Other events
In the boxing events, although the continental judges appeared to favour attack unduly when awarding points, there was next to no criticism of the decisions. France and Germany each won two gold medals.

A new event was canoe racing —in which Austria won three golds, and Germany and Czechoslovakia two each.

France gained three of the six

gold medals for cycling, finishing first and second in the 100 km road race, which was held for the first time under massed-start conditions. All six equestrian events—three individual and three team—were won by Germany, and the seven gold medals for fencing were shared by Italy (four) and Hungary (three).

In securing their hockey title, India played five matches, scoring 39 goals and conceding only one —to Germany in the final.

Among the gymnasts, two magnificent German athletes, Karl Sdhwarzmann and Konrad Frey, won three gold medals each; and such was the appeal of the weightlifters that more than 20,000 people crammed into the arena to watch their hero, Joseph Manger of Germany, win the heavyweight crown.

The Germans scooped a total of 35 gold, 23 silver, and 29 bronze medals in the summer Olympics of 1936. Equestrian events, gymnastics, and rowing— for which they had prepared massively—accounted for 16 of their golds. The United States, who came next overall, were consoled with their 12 golds in men's track and field events—one more than all the other nations put together. In those events, five world records had been broken and one equalled and 17 new Olympic records set.

On the final day the Olympic fire flickered out and the five-ringed flag was struck in the Berlin twilight. The best organized, and for that reason possibly least truly Olympian Games, had come to an end. It was to be 12 years in time, and a whole lifetime in experience, before the world would awake to the austerity Games in the battle-weary, bomb-scarred London of 1948.

1 Ernst Krebs from Munich won the 10,000 metres single kayak event from 15 other competitors. This is one of the events no longer included in the Games.
2 Germany's first ever track and field gold medal was won by Hans Wollke in the shot put. Like all other winners in the Games he received his medal and a potted oak tree.
3 One of the last of the flying Finns, Gunnar Hoeckert, won the 5,000 metres in an Olympic record time. His win was helped by the collision of his compatriots, Lauri Lehtinen and Ilmari Salminen, who lost valuable ground and could finish only second and fourth. Henry Jonsson of Sweden picked up the bronze.
4 The podgy, 150-lb Dutch girl Hendrika Mastenbroek (lane 5) won the 100 metres freestyle in an Olympic record time—65.9 sec. Her medal collection at the Games amounted to three golds (two individual and one team) and a silver in the backstroke.

Diving has been an Olympic sport since 1904, at St Louis, when a competition for men, with dives from both highboard and springboard, was held. A women's diving competition was held at Stockholm in 1912, but it was not until 1928 that the Olympic diving programme was limited to its present four-event formula—highboard and springboard for men and women.

London Olympic Games (1948)

After six years in which most of the world had been locked in World War II, the Olympic Games were revived after a 12-year gap. The war had caused the scheduled Games of 1940 and 1944 to be cancelled, but in October 1945 London applied to stage the Games of 1948. This privilege was granted in March 1946, and in a little over two years the Games were planned and carried out.

The economic situation in the post-war years did not make things easy for the organizing committee. They were fortunate in having in London—at Wembley—the buildings of the 1924 British Empire Exhibition, which were more suitable than the White City site of the 1908 Olympics. The Empire Stadium was the scene of the athletics, the soccer semi-finals and final, hockey semi-finals and final, and the equestrian show jumping. The Empire Pool, close by, accommodated the swimming and boxing (a special bridge was built across the pool). The basketball was held at Harringay Arena, cycling at Herne Hill in South London, and the yachting at Tor Bay in Devon. It had originally been decided to hold the gymnastics in the stadium, but the inclement weather forced the gymnasts to go indoors, to the Empress Hall in the Earl's Court exhibition complex, where the weightlifting and wrestling events had already been held.

Fifty-nine countries sent 4,030 men and 438 women to compete in the Games. They were housed in special centres around London, as there was insufficient capital to provide an Olympic Village as at Los Angeles and Berlin. Notable absentees were, not surprisingly, the Germans and Japanese, while the USSR were not affiliated to the International Olympic Committee and thus could not compete.

Athletics

The original running track in the Empire Stadium had not been used for over 20 years, and had been covered with a greyhound track. Laying a special cinder track and other 'temporary works' cost the organizing committee nearly £80,000, while compensation paid to the proprietors of the stadium for loss of revenue from greyhound racing amounted to £90,000. There was intensive press, radio, and—for the first time—television coverage of the track events. Belgium, Czechoslovakia, and Jamaica won their first Olympic athletics gold medals.

The track and field events in which there were 600 men and nearly 150 women entrants, got off to an inauspicious start when the first event, the heats of the 400

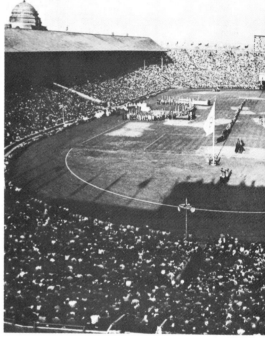

metres hurdles, was delayed for a good half-hour because the marks for spacing the hurdles had not been laid down. The one track final that day—the 10,000 metres—more than made up for any organizational chaos. Viljo Heino of Finland, the world record holder, was the favourite, although he was threatened by a new name, Emil Zatopek of Czechoslovakia who had recently come within a few seconds of the Finn's time. For the first eight laps Heino was in front, but after 10 laps Zatopek took the lead and never relinquished it. Heino tried to follow the Czech, but with 9 laps to go, to everyone's astonishment, he left the track. Thereafter Zatopek went farther and farther ahead, winning by over three-quarters of a minute, and becoming the first man to beat the half-hour in an Olympic Games. Three days later, Zatopek was involved in another race, the final of the 5,000 metres. He had qualified for that final the day after the 10,000 metres in a peculiar heat, in which he and Sweden's Erik Ahlden had raced

neck and neck for the tape—an unnecessary duel as the third man was over 80 yards behind. The track for the final was sodden by heavy rain. Zatopek set a fast pace, and by the half-distance only he, Ahlden, Gaston Reiff of Belgium, and the Dutchman Willem Slykhuis were in the hunt. In the tenth lap, Reiff 'jumped' the opposition and at the bell was 20 yards ahead of Slykhuis, with Zatopek another 50 yards behind. With 300 yards left Zatopek made one of those apparently mad rushes which were to be such a feature of his performances in years to come. First he caught and passed the Dutchman, and then he cut into Reiff's lead at an alarming rate. The Belgian seemed to be on his last legs, and a victory for Zatopek appeared certain, but half-a-dozen yards from the tape Reiff glanced over his shoulder, and hung on grimly to win by 0.2 sec. Zatopek seemed to have misjudged his race, but years later claimed he was very tired three laps from home, and then found a new lease of life at the bell.

The last running event was the marathon. At half-way, a former Belgian paratrooper, 21-year-old Etienne Gailly, was over half-a-minute clear of the field, and nearly two minutes ahead of the British favourite, Jack Holden, who later dropped out. With 12 kilometres to go, Gailly was still half-a-minute in front, but in the next 5,000 metres was passed by Choi of Korea and Delfo Cabrera of Argentina. Gailly, hardly able to drag one foot after the other, somehow regained the lead, while Choi dropped out. He entered the stadium a few yards ahead of Cabrera and Welshman Tommy Richards. In the final circuit of the track, Gailly was passed by Cabrera, the winner, and Richards, both still full of running. The marathon had once again produced a dramatic finish.

At the other end of the distance scale, the 100 metres produced an upset of form. The United States were represented in the final by Mel Patton, the world 100 yards record holder, Barney Ewell, who held the world 100 metres record,

6

1 Australia's John Winter won the high jump with a leap of 6 ft. 6 in. He was the last eastern cut-off jumper to win an Olympic gold medal.
2 Although Belgium's Etienne Gailly (left) was the first marathon runner to enter the stadium, he was overtaken in the last yards by Argentina's Delfo Cabrera (right) and Britain's Tom Richards.
3 Cycling at Herne Hill. Italy (white shirts) beating Britain in the tandem final.
4 America's mighty John Davis won the first of his two Olympic heavyweight titles with a total of 996½lb.
5 The Empire Stadium laid out for the show jumping. The hockey and soccer finals were also held there.
6 The 17-year-old American Bob Mathias caused a shock in the decathlon. After being in the stadium for over 12 hours on the second day, he won by 165 points.

Official Report of 1948 Olympics

Sport & General

Sport & General

and Harrison Dillard, world record holder for the 120 yards hurdles who had failed to make the team in the hurdles and had scraped into third place in the American trials for the 100 metres. Dillard—the dark horse—won clearly from Ewell. And Ewell was to gain a second silver, in the 200 metres, which was won by Mel Patton, who had been pushed into fifth place in the 100.

Another world record holder, Jamaica's Herb McKenley, was relegated to second place, in the 400 metres. McKenley, the first man to beat 46 seconds for the distance, was beaten by his fellow-Jamaican Arthur Wint. Jamaica were, not surprisingly, favourites for the 4 by 400 metres relay, but their chances of winning were obliterated on the third leg when Arthur Wint collapsed with cramp. Wint also featured in the 800 metres final, in which he was beaten by three yards by America's Mal Whitfield.

The two hurdles events produced some outstanding performances. The 110 metres saw

William Porter lead home the American trio of medal winners in an Olympic record 13.9 sec. And in the 400 metres 29-year-old Roy Cochran—who had won the American championship in 1939—gained a six-yard victory over Duncan White of Ceylon, who thus became the first Ceylonese to win an Olympic athletics medal.

The United States won three of the eight field events—the pole vault, long jump (Willie Steele won by nearly a foot from Australia's Thomas Bruce), and the shot. Australia won her first high jump title through John Winter (with a modest 6 ft. 6 in. clearance), and Adolfo Consolini and Giuseppe Tosi took first and second places in the discus for Italy. The real surprise was a 17-year-old American, Bob Mathias. He gained a brilliant victory in the decathlon, winning by 165 points from France's Ignace Heinrich. The Americans also won the 4 by 100 metres relay. At first it was announced that they had been disqualified, and the gold medals were to be awarded to the British

quartet. The crowd did not relish a home victory being earned in this way, and they were very relieved when the initial decision was reversed and the medals awarded to the Americans.

Fanny Blankers-Koen dominated the women's events, winning four gold medals in the nine-event programme. She won the 100 and 200 metres with some ease, was pushed all the way in the 80 metres hurdles by Britain's Maureen Gardner, and ran a fine anchor leg for the Netherlands in the 4 by 100 metres relay to pull up from fourth to first place. Mrs Blankers-Koen held the world records for the high and long jump, but did not compete in those events at London.

The high jump produced a great struggle between Britain's Dorothy Tyler, who as Dorothy Odam had been second at Berlin in 1936, and America's Alice Coachman. Both girls cleared 5 ft. 6⅛ in. and the gold medal went to the American because she had cleared the final height at her first attempt while Mrs Tyler needed a second jump.

Micheline Ostermeyer of France gained a shot-discus double, and Austria's Hermine Bauma gained her country's first Olympic athletics title, in the javelin. She had missed a bronze medal at Berlin in 1936 by a mere 6 inches.

Despite the bad weather—it was rainy and cold on several days—the track and field events were conducted in front of a very interested crowd, and there was no 'incident' that soured the happy atmosphere of this first Olympic Games for 12 years.

Swimming
The Empire Pool, built for the 1934 British Empire Games but closed to aquatic activities since World War II, was reopened for the Olympics and proved to be a magnificent arena.

The absence of Germany, and more particularly Japan, opened the way to American pre-eminence in the men's events. American swimmers won all the swimming events—five individual titles and the 4 by 200 metres relay (which produced the only swimming

45

world record of the Games)—and took 5 of the other 10 medals open to them.

But Japan had the last laugh on their wartime enemies. On the days that Bill Smith won the 400 metres freestyle in 4 min 41.0 sec and Jim McLane the 1,500 metres in 19 min 18.5 sec, Hironashin Furuhashi was demonstrating just what those two medals were worth. In Tokyo, in the Japanese championships which were timed to coincide with the Olympic programme, he swam 400 metres in 4 min 33.0 sec, and 1,500 metres in 18 min 37.0 sec—world best times which were never ratified as world records as Japan had not then been readmitted to the International Swimming Federation.

The Americans did not have it all their own way in the five women's swimming events, winning two titles—the 400 metres freestyle (through Ann Curtis) and the 4 by 100 metres relay. Denmark challenged strongly for Olympic honours, with Greta Andersen taking the 100 metres freestyle, Karen Harup the 100 metres backstroke, and this pair helping their country to silver medals in the freestyle relay.

There were signs of an Australian revival in both men's and women's events. John Marshall took a bronze in the 400 metres and a silver in the 1,500 metres; Nancy Lyons was second in the 200 metres breaststroke (behind Nel van Vliet of the Netherlands), and Judy Joy Davies was third in the backstroke. Britain's only medal—a bronze—went to Cathie Gibson in the 400 metres. She closed right up on backstroke champion Karen Harup to miss the silver medal by 1.3 sec.

The Americans achieved a clean sweep of diving gold medals. Victoria Draves became the first woman to win both highboard and springboard titles at the same Games, and Sammy Lee and Bruce Harlan took the men's crowns. American divers, in fact, won 10 of the 12 medals, and only Mexico's Joaquin Capilla and the Danish girl Birte Christoffersen intervened, both with bronze medals in the highboard.

European champions in 1947, Italy won the water polo gold medals for the first time, in a tournament which was criticized—as all water polo tournaments tend to be—for the amount of fouling and inefficient refereeing.

Other Sports

When Sweden were announced as winners of the dressage team event, few people could have guessed that they would be stripped of their medals. It was subsequently discovered, however, that one of their team—Gehnall Persson, who finished 6th—was not an officer, and thus ineligible to compete. The gold medals were therefore belatedly awarded to France.

In the team sports, the United States retained their basketball title, and India beat Great Britain 4-0 to win their fourth successive hockey gold medals. Sweden, with their brilliant inside-forward trio of Gunnar Gren, Gunnar Nordahl, and Nils Liedholm, beat Yugoslavia 3-1 in a splendid soccer final.

Henley was the scene of the canoeing and rowing events. Gert Fredriksson won both individual kayak titles—over 1,000 and 10,000 metres—while his fellow Swedes took both K-2 events. British oarsmen won two of the seven rowing golds—the double sculls and the coxless pairs. John Wilson and Stanley Laurie, the 1938 Silver Goblets winners back from 10 years service in the Sudan, won the coxless pairs, and Herbert Bushnell and Richard Burnell won the double sculls. Mervyn Wood gave Australia her third single sculls title when he beat Uruguay's Eduardo Risso by a 14-second margin.

On the fencing *piste*, the most remarkable performance came from 41-year-old Ilona Elek of Hungary who retained the women's foil title she had won 12 years before, with Ellen Muller-Preiss, the 1932 champion, adding another bronze to the one she gained in 1936. Finnish gymnasts were supreme, winning four of the eight titles, including a unique triple tie for the pommel horse gold medal. The women's team event, the only women's gymnastic event on the programme, went to Czechoslovakia.

Of the 59 competing nations, 17 failed to place a competitor in the first six in any event. The United States were by far the most successful team, winning 35 gold medals, while Sweden were next with 13. The significance of the Games of the XIV Olympiad, however, was not to be gauged in terms of world records or gold medals, or even in national domination, but in the way that countries of the world had come together to compete in London in a friendly way. The scars of the war—many of the belligerents in which came face to face again at Wembley—were hardly healed, but the Olympics did do something towards restoring a shattered world to the sanity it so badly needed.

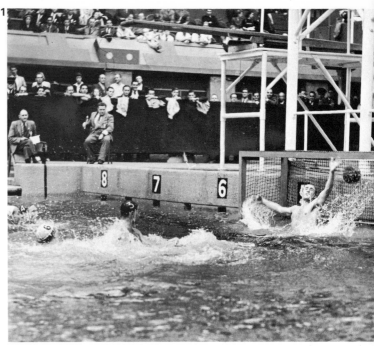

1 The Dutch goalkeeper gropes helplessly as the Italians score their second goal in a 4-2 victory. Italy won the gold medals in the water polo tournament, and the Netherlands the bronzes.
2 A happier moment for the Dutch—Fanny Blankers-Koen wins the 100 metres from Britain's Dorothy Manley (691)—one of the Flying Dutchwoman's four gold medals. **3** Richard Burnell and Herbert Bushnell winning the double sculls for Britain by 4 seconds from the Danish pair.

LONDON OLYMPIC GAMES, 1948 Gold Medallists

Athletics—Men			
100 metres	Harrison Dillard	USA	10.3 sec
200 metres	Mel Patton	USA	21.1 sec
400 metres	Arthur Wint	Jamaica	46.2 sec
800 metres	Mal Whitfield	USA	1 min 49.2 sec
1,500 metres	Henry Eriksson	Sweden	3 min 49.8 sec
5,000 metres	Gaston Rieff	Belgium	14 min 17.6 sec
10,000 metres	Emil Zatopek	Czechoslovakia	29 min 59.6 sec
Marathon	Delfo Cabrera	Argentina	2 hr 34 min 51.6 sec
4 x 100 metres relay		USA	40.6 sec
4 x 400 metres relay		USA	3 min 10.4 sec
110 metres hurdles	William Porter	USA	13.9 sec
400 metres hurdles	Roy Cochran	USA	51.1 sec
3,000 metres steeplechase	Tore Sjostrand	Sweden	9 min 4.6 sec
10 kilometres walk	John Mikaelsson	Sweden	45 min 13.2 sec
50 kilometres walk	John Ljunggren	Sweden	4 hr 41 min 52 sec
High jump	John Winter	Australia	6 ft 6 in
Pole vault	Guinn Smith	USA	14 ft 1¼ in
Long jump	Willie Steele	USA	25 ft 8 in
Triple jump	Arne Ahman	Sweden	50 ft 6¼ in
Shot	Wilbur Thompson	USA	56 ft 2 in
Discus	Adolfo Consolini	Italy	172 ft 2 in
Hammer	Imre Nemeth	Hungary	183 ft 11½ in
Javelin	Tapio Rautavaara	Finland	228 ft 11 in
Dacathlon	Bob Mathias	USA	7,139 pts (1934 tables)
Athletics—Women			
100 metres	Fanny Blankers-Koen	Netherlands	11.9 sec
200 metres	Fanny Blankers-Koen	Netherlands	24.4 sec
4 x 100 metres relay		Netherlands	47.5 sec
80 metres hurdles	Fanny Blankers-Koen	Netherlands	11.2 sec
High jump	Alice Coachman	USA	5 ft 6⅛in
Long jump	Olga Gyarmati	Hungary	18 ft 8¾ in
Shot	Micheline Ostermeyer	France	45 ft 1½ in
Discus	Micheline Ostermeyer	France	137 ft 6 in
Javelin	Hermine Bauma	Austria	149 ft 6 in
Basketball		USA	
Boxing			
Flyweight	Pascual Perez	Argentina	
Bantamweight	Tibor Csik	Hungary	
Featherweight	Ernesto Formenti	Italy	
Lightweight	Gerald Dreyer	South Africa	
Welterweight	Julius Torma	Czechoslovakia	
Middleweight	Laszlo Papp	Hungary	
Light-heavyweight	George Hunter	South Africa	
Heavyweight	Rafael Iglesias	Argentina	
Canoeing			
1,000 metres—Men			
Kayak singles	Gert Fredriksson	Sweden	4 min 33.2 sec
Kayak pairs	Hans Berglund, Lennart Klingstrom	Sweden	4 min 7.3 sec
Canadian singles	Josef Holecek	Czechoslovakia	5 min 42 sec
Canadian pairs	Jan Brzak, Bohumil Kudrna	Czechoslovakia	5 min 7.1 sec
10,000 metres—Men			
Kayak singles	Gert Fredriksson	Sweden	50 min 47.7 sec
Kayak pairs	Gunnar Akerlund, Hans Wetterstrom	Sweden	46 min 9.4 sec
Canadian singles	F. Capek	Czechoslovakia	62 min 5.2 sec
Canadian pairs	Stephen Lysak, Stephen Macknowski	USA	55 min 55.4 sec
500 metres—Women			
Kayak singles	K. Hoff	Denmark	2 min 31.9 sec
Cycling			
1,000 metres sprint	Mario Ghella	Italy	
1,000 metres time trial	Jacques Dupont	France	1 min 13.5 sec
2,000 metres tandem	Renato Perona, Ferdinando Teruzzi	Italy	
4,000 metres team pursuit		France	4 min 57.8 sec
Road race—individual	Jose Beyaert	France	5 hr 18 min 12.6 sec
Road race—team		Belgium	15 hr 58 min 17.4 sec
Equestrian			
Dressage—individual	Hans Moser	Switzerland	
Dressage—team		France	
Show jumping—individual	Humberto Mariles	Mexico	6.25 pts
Show jumping—team		Mexico	34.25 pts
Three day event—individual	Bernard Chevalier	France	
Three day event—team		USA	
Fencing—Men			
Foil—individual	Jean Buhan	France	
Foil—team		France	
Epee—individual	Luigi Cantone	Italy	
Epee—team		France	
Sabre—individual	Aladar Gerevich	Hungary	
Sabre—team		Hungary	
Fencing—Women			
Foil—individual	Ilona Elek	Hungary	

Football		Sweden	
Gymnastics—Men			
Combined exercises—Individual	Veikko Huhtanen	Finland	
Combined exercises—team		Finland	
Floor exercises	Ferenc Pataki	Hungary	
Horizontal bar	Josef Stalder	Switzerland	
Parallel bars	Michael Reusch	Switzerland	
Pommel horse	Paavo Aaltonen	Finland	
	Veikko Huhtanen	Finland	
	Heikki Savolainen	Finland	
Vault	Paavo Aaltonen	Finland	
Rings	Karl Frei	Switzerland	
Gymnastics—Women			
Combined exercises—team		Czechoslovakia	
Hockey		India	
Modern Pentathlon	William Grut	Sweden	
Rowing			
Single sculls	Mervyn Wood	Australia	7 min 24.4 sec
Double sculls	Herbert Bushnell, Richard Burnell	Great Britain	6 min 51.3 sec
Coxless pairs	John Wilson, Stanley Laurie	Great Britain	7 min 21.1 sec
Coxed pairs	T. Henriksen, F. Pedersen, C. Andersen (cox)	Denmark	8 min 0.5 sec
Coxless fours		Italy	6 min 39.0 sec
Coxed fours		USA	6 min 50.3 sec
Eights		USA	5 min 56.7 sec
Shooting			
Free pistol	E. Vasquez	Peru	
Automatic pistol	Karoly Takacs	Hungary	
Free rifle	Émil Grunig	Switzerland	
Small-bore rifle	Arthur Cook	USA	
Swimming—Men			
100 metres freestyle	Walter Ris	USA	57.3 sec
400 metres freestyle	Bill Smith	USA	4 min 41.0 sec
1,500 metres freestyle	Jim McLane	USA	19 min 18.5 sec
200 metres breaststroke	Joe Verdeur	USA	2 min 39.3 sec
100 metres backstroke	Allan Stack	USA	1 min 6.4 sec
4 x 200 metres freestyle relay		USA	8 min 46.0 sec
Springboard diving	Bruce Harlan	USA	
Highboard diving	Sammy Lee	USA	
Swimming—Women			
100 metres freestyle	Greta Andersen	Denmark	1 min 6.3 sec
400 metres freestyle	Ann Curtis	USA	5 min 17.8 sec
200 metres breaststroke	Petronella van Vliet	Netherlands	2 min 57.2 sec
100 metres backstroke	Karen Harup	Denmark	1 min 14.4 sec
4 x 100 metres freestyle relay		USA	4 min 29.2 sec
Springboard diving	Victoria Draves	USA	
Highboard diving	Victoria Draves	USA	
Water Polo		Italy	
Weightlifting			
Bantamweight	Joseph de Pietro	USA	678 lb
Featherweight	Mahmoud Fayad	Egypt	733 lb
Lightweight	Ibrahim Shams	Egypt	793½ lb
Middleweight	Frank Spellman	USA	860 lb
Light-heavyweight	Stanley Stanczyk	USA	920½ lb
Heavyweight	John Davis	USA	996½ lb
Wrestling			
Freestyle			
Flyweight	Lennart Viitala	Finland	
Bantamweight	Nasuk Akkar	Turkey	
Featherweight	Gazanfer Bilge	Turkey	
Lightweight	Cedal Atik	Turkey	
Welterweight	Yasar Dogu	Turkey	
Middleweight	Glen Brand	USA	
Light-heavyweight	Henry Wittenberg	USA	
Heavyweight	Gyula Bobis	Hungary	
Graeco-Roman			
Flyweight	Pietro Lombardi	Italy	
Bantamweight	Kurt Petterson	Sweden	
Featherweight	Mohammed Oktav	Turkey	
Lightweight	Karl Freij	Sweden	
Welterweight	Gosta Andersson	Sweden	
Middleweight	Axel Gronberg	Sweden	
Light-heavyweight	Karl Nilsson	Sweden	
Heavyweight	Ahmed Kirecco	Turkey	
Yachting			
6-metres		USA	
Dragon		Norway	
Star	Hilary Smart, Paul Smart	USA	
Swallow	S. Morris, D. Bond	Great Britain	
Firefly	Paul Elvstrom	Denmark	

Helsinki Olympic Games (1952)

One of the closest secrets at any Olympic Games is the name of the runner who carries the flame on the last leg of its journey from Olympia to light the fire that burns for the duration of the Games. When the runner appeared in the Helsinki stadium in 1952 there was a mighty shout from the 70,500 crowd. He was a balding 55-year-old whose athletics feats had thrilled the world 30 years before—Paavo Nurmi. With his characteristic upright gait he completed nearly a lap and lit the flame. Then he handed the torch to Hannes Kolehmainen, the first of the Flying Finns, winner of the 5,000 and 10,000 metres at Stockholm in 1912—who was taken by a lift to the top of a 250-ft. tower to light another flame.

Heavy downpours of rain could not quench the Finns' enthusiasm, but one incident was out of place. Soon after the lighting of the flame, a woman dressed in white entered the stadium, ran gracefully round the track, and tried to address the crowd from the rostrum where the oath had been taken minutes before. Gripping the microphone, she started to speak, but was cut off and hustled out of the arena. She was, it transpired, a 23-year-old student from Stuttgart, and a fanatical peace enthusiast. Her entrance was perfectly timed, and most of the crowd, though puzzled, did not really resent the intrusion.

The Olympics were 12 years late arriving in Helsinki. Tokyo and Helsinki were the two applicants for the 1940 Games, which were awarded to Tokyo. In 1938, Japan, because of her military commitments in Asia, abandoned the project, and Helsinki offered to stage them. The outbreak of World War Two put paid to the idea, and it was not until 1952 that the Games were staged in their country.

As was generally expected, the Finns' organization was superb in every way. Sixty-nine nations sent more than 6,000 men and nearly 800 women to take part in 17 different sports. Men from 61 nations were housed in an Olympic Village (new blocks of flats afterwards let to the public) at Kapyla, about 1½ miles from the stadium. Other teams both male and female, including the USSR, Bulgaria, Hungary, and Poland, were quartered at Otaniemi, 5 miles from Helsinki, while the main women's village was a nurses training college half-a-mile from the stadium, accommodating more than 600 competitors. Over 1,800 journalists, broadcasters, and photographers were catered for.

The main stadium was full to capacity for the opening ceremony, and nearly so for many of the track and field events. The football matches attracted a total of about 370,000, and swimming 110,000.

Athletics

In 19 of the 24 men's events the Olympic record was beaten, and in two others it was equalled, while in the nine women's events, seven new Olympic records were set. Six world records, three men's and three women's, were established. Unhappily for the Finns, there were no gold medals for them, while the Russians, competing in

Central Press

1 Finland's athletics hero Paavo Nurmi lights the flame.
2 Wilf White, on Nizefela, clears an obstacle during the show jumping, thus helping to win Britain's only gold medal.
3 Nina Romashkova won the women's discus—one of the USSR's two gold medals in the track and field events.
4 Werner Lueg leads the 1,500 metres field into the home straight. Josy Barthel (406) sprinted past him to win a surprise gold for Luxembourg, while Bob McMillen (992) pipped the German on the tape for the silver medal. Roger Bannister (177) was 4th.

U.P.I.

Official Report of the 1952 Olympics

Keystone

their first Olympics since 1912, had to rely on their women to win their two golds for athletics.

The outstanding competitor of the entire Games was seen in action in the long-distance running events—all three of them. He was Emil Zatopek, a Czechoslovakian army officer who ran as if every step would be his last, apparently in agony. This remarkable man retained the 10,000 metres title he had won in London four years previously, and improved from second to first in the 5,000 metres—setting Olympic records in both.

The 5,000 metres was Zatopek's severest test. With one lap left there were four men left in contention—Zatopek, Britain's Chris Chataway, Herbert Schade of Germany, and Alain Mimoun of France. Along the back straight Chataway made a burst, but was closely followed by the Czech. Around the final turn Chataway tripped on the kerb and fell, while Schade was visibly fading. Only Mimoun held on to the flying Zatopek, but he finally had to concede first place, just as he had a few days earlier in the 10,000 metres. On the same day as Zatopek's 5,000 metres triumph, his wife, Dana, won the javelin.

Three days after that gruelling 5,000 metres, Zatopek lined up for what was—officially—the first marathon of his career. Though tiring towards the end, he won by over $2\frac{1}{2}$ minutes from Reinaldo Gorno of Argentina. His time was yet another Olympic record, and he had completed a unique treble that few men even attempt.

Athletes from the United States won 14 of the 24 men's events, and their victories were evenly split between track and field. Lindy Remigino's win in the 100 metres was an extremely close affair. Many people thought that Herb McKenley of Jamaica, the world record holder for 440 yards who had entered the 100 for a kind of training spin, should have had the verdict, but the photo-finish camera showed that Remigino had won by inches. McKenley won another silver medal in the 400 metres, where his fast finish was not quite good enough to catch his team-mate George Rhoden although they were both credited with an Olympic record time of 45.9 sec. Arthur Wint—another Jamaican—made a game bid to retain his 1948 title, but he lapsed into fifth place. These three West Indians teamed up with Leslie Laing to win the 4 by 400 metres relay, beating the world record by over 4 seconds in 3 min 3.9 sec.

Mal Whitfield retained his 800 metres title in 1 min 49.2 sec, the same time as at Wembley four years previously, with Arthur Wint again occupying second place. But in the 1,500 metres there was an unexpected win for Josy Barthel of Luxembourg, who beat another 'outsider', Bob McMillen of the United States, by inches, with the world record holder, Werner Lueg of Germany, 0.2 sec behind, third.

Apart from Zatopek and Whitfield, two other champions retained their titles, the American Bob Mathias in the decathlon and John Mikaelsson of Sweden in the 10 kilometres track walk. Harrison Dillard, who won the 100 metres in London, won his favourite event, the 100 metres hurdles, from his fellow-American Jack Davis, both being timed at 13.5 sec.

While the USSR did not secure a single victory in the men's events,

5 André Noyelle of Belgium is the triumphant winner of the 190.4-km cycling road race. Noyelle also led home the winning team in the event.
6 The 1948 champion, Bob Mathias, in the second event of the decathlon—the long jump. Mathias retained his title with a world record score of 7,887 points—912 more than the runner-up, Milton Campbell.
7 Australia's Marjorie Jackson wins the 100 metres in 11.5 sec, a world record.
8 Valeria Gyenge—one of the all-conquering Hungarian women's swimming team—won the 400 metres freestyle in an Olympic record time of 5 min 12.1 sec, just 1.6 sec in front of her team rival Eva Novak, the runner-up in the 200 metres breaststroke.

Associated Press

5

Central Press

Official Report of the 1952 Olympics

8

U.P.I.

their women excelled, winning the shot and discus with new Olympic records. The United States, in contrast, had only one victory, and a lucky one at that. At the last changeover of the 4 by 100 metres relay the Australian team fumbled while in the lead, Marjorie Jackson and Winsome Cripps contriving to drop the baton. The team recovered, but the time lost in the adventure was too great and the Australian girls did not even win a medal. In the 80 metres hurdles, Shirley Strickland, the bronze medallist in London, beat a field including defending champion Fanny Blankers-Koen who struck a hurdle and failed to finish.

Swimming

The swimming events were dominated by the Hungarian women's team who won four out of the five events. They were given a special award for the greatest achievement of the swimming section of the Games for their world record winning time of 4 min 24.4 sec in the 4 by 100 metres relay.

Three members of this team also won individual medals. Katalin Szoke was first, and Judit Temes third, in the 100 metres freestyle. It was a remarkable final in which only 0.3 sec covered the first five swimmers, while the lead changed

Official Report of the 1952 Olympics

1

HELSINKI OLYMPIC GAMES, 1952 Gold Medallists

Athletics—Men

Event	Name	Country	Result
100 metres	Lindy Remigino	USA	10.4 sec
200 metres	Andy Stanfield	USA	20.7 sec
400 metres	George Rhoden	Jamaica	45.9 sec
800 metres	Malvin Whitfield	USA	1 min 49.2 sec
1,500 metres	Josef Barthel	Luxembourg	3 min 45.2 sec
5,000 metres	Emil Zatopek	Czechoslovakia	14 min 6.6 sec
10,000 metres	Emil Zatopek	Czechoslovakia	29 min 17.0 sec
Marathon	Emil Zatopek	Czechoslovakia	2 hr 23 min 3.2 sec
110 metres hurdles	Harrison Dillard	USA	13.7 sec
400 metres hurdles	Charles Moore	USA	50.8 sec
3,000 metres steeplechase	Horace Ashenfelter	USA	8 min 45.4 sec
10 kilometres walk	John Mikaelsson	Sweden	45 min 2.8 sec
50 kilometres walk	Giuseppe Dordoni	Italy	4 hr 28 min 7.8 sec
4 x 100 metres relay		USA	40.1 sec
4 x 400 metres relay		Jamaica	3 min 3.9 sec
High Jump	Walter Davis	USA	6 ft 8½ in
Pole Vault	Robert Richards	USA	14 ft 11¼ in
Long Jump	Willie Steele	USA	25 ft 8 in
Triple Jump	Adhemar da Silva	Brazil	53 ft 2½ in
Shot	Wilbur Thompson	USA	56 ft 2 in
Discus	Sim Iness	USA	180 ft 6½ in
Hammer	Josef Csermak	Hungary	197 ft 11½ in
Javelin	Cyrus Young	USA	240 ft 0½ in
Decathlon	Robert Mathias	USA	8,887 pts

Athletics—Women

Event	Name	Country	Result
100 metres	Marjorie Jackson	Australia	11.5 sec
200 metres	Marjorie Jackson	Australia	23.7 sec
80 metres hurdles	Shirley Strickland	Australia	10.9 sec
4 x 100 metres relay		USA	45.9 sec
High Jump	Esther Brand	South Africa	5 ft 5½ in
Long Jump	Yvette Williams	New Zealand	20 ft 5¾ in
Shot	Galina Zybina	USSR	50 ft 1½ in
Discus	Nina Romashkova	USSR	168 ft 8½ in
Javelin	Dana Zatopkova	Czechoslovakia	165 ft 7 in

Basketball

USA

Boxing

Event	Name	Country
Flyweight	Nathan Brooks	USA
Bantamweight	Pentti Hamalainen	Finland
Featherweight	Jan Zachara	Czechoslovakia
Lightweight	Aureliano Bolognesi	Italy
Light-welterweight	Charles Adkins	USA
Welterweight	Zygmunt Chychla	Poland
Light-middleweight	Laszlo Papp	Hungary
Middleweight	Floyd Patterson	USA
Light-heavyweight	Norvel Lee	USA
Heavyweight	Edward Sanders	USA

Canoeing

Event	Name	Country	Result
1,000 metres—Men			
Kayak singles	Gert Fredriksson	Sweden	4 min 7.9 sec
Kayak pairs	Kurt Wires, Yrjo Hietanen	Finland	3 min 51.1 sec
Canadian singles	Josef Holecek	Czechoslovakia	4 min 53.6 sec
Canadian doubles	Bent Rasch, Finn Haunstoft	Czechoslovakia	4 min 38.3 sec
500 metres—Women			
Kayak singles	Sylvi Saimo	Finland	2 min 18.4 sec

Cycling

Event	Name	Country	Result
1,000 metres sprint	Enzo Sacchi	Italy	
1,000 metres time trial	Russell Mockridge	Australia	1 min 11.1 sec
2,000 metres tandem	Russell Mockridge, Lionel Cox	Australia	
4,000 metres team pursuit		Italy	4 min 46.1 sec
Road race—individual	Andre Noyelle	Belgium	5 hr 6 min 3.4 sec
Road race—team		Belgium	15 hr 20 min 46.6 sec

Equestrian

Event	Name	Country
Dressage—individual	Henri St Cyr	Sweden
—team		Sweden
Show jumping		
—individual	Pierre d'Oriola	France
—team		Great Britain
Three day event		
—individual	Hans von Blixen-Finecke	Sweden
—team		Sweden

Fencing—Men

Event	Name	Country
Foil—individual	Christian d'Oriola	France
—team		France
Epee—individual	Edoardo Mangiarotti	Italy
—team		Italy
Sabre—individual	Pal Kovacs	Hungary
—team		Hungary

Fencing—Women

Event	Name	Country
Foil—individual	Irene Camber	Italy

Football

Hungary

Gymnastics—Men

Event	Name	Country
Combined exercises		
—individual	Viktor Chukarin	USSR
—team		USSR
Floor exercises	Karl Thoresson	Sweden
Horizontal bar	Jack Gunthard	Switzerland
Parallel bars	Hans Eugster	Switzerland
Pommel Horse	Viktor Chukarin	USSR
Vault	Viktor Chukarin	USSR
Rings	Grant Shaginyan	USSR

Gymnastics—Women

Event	Name	Country
Combined exercises		
—individual	Maria Gorokhovskaya	USSR
—team		USSR
Floor exercises	Agnes Keleti	Hungary
Asymmetrical bars	Margit Korondi	Hungary
Beam	Nina Bocharyova	USSR
Vault	Yekaterina Kalinchuk	USSR

Hockey

India

Modern Pentathlon

Event	Name	Country
Individual	Lars Hall	Sweden
Team		Hungary

Rowing

Event	Name	Country	Result
Single sculls	Yuri Tyukalov	USSR	8 min 12.8 sec
Double sculls	Tranquilo Copozzo, Eduardo Guerrero	Argentina	7 min 32.2 sec
Coxless pairs	Charles Logg, Thomas Price	USA	8 min 20.7 sec
Coxed pairs	Raymond Salles, Gaston Mercier, Bernard Malivoire (Cox)	France	8 min 28.6 sec
Coxless fours		Yugoslavia	7 min 16.0 sec
Coxed fours		Czechoslovakia	7 min 33.4 sec
Eights		USA	6 min 25.9 sec

Shooting

Event	Name	Country
Sport pistol	Huelet Benner	USA
Rapid fire pistol	Karoly Takacs	Hungary
Free rifle	Anatoliy Bogdanov	USSR
Small-bore rifle, prone	Josif Sarbu	Romania
Small-bore rifle, three positions	Erling Kongshaug	Norway
Clay pigeon	Georges Genereux	Canada

Swimming and Diving—Men

100 metres freestyle	Clarke Scholes	USA	57.4 sec
400 metres freestyle	Jean Boiteux	France	4 min 30.7 sec
1,500 metres freestyle	Ford Konno	USA	18 min 30.0 sec
200 metres breaststroke	John Davies	Australia	2 min 34.4 sec
100 metres backstroke	Yoshi Oyakawa	USA	1 min 5.4 sec
4 x 200 metres freestyle relay		USA	8 min 31.1 sec
Springboard diving	David Browning	USA	
Highboard diving	Sammy Lee	USA	

Swimming and Diving—Women

Event	Name	Country	Result
100 metres freestyle	Katalin Szoke	Hungary	1 min 6.8 sec
400 metres freestyle	Valeria Gyenge	Hungary	5 min 12.1 sec
200 metres breaststroke	Eva Szekely	Hungary	2 min 51.7 sec
100 metres backstroke	Joan Harrison	South Africa	1 min 14.3 sec
4 x 100 metres freestyle relay		Hungary	4 min 24.4 sec
Springboard diving	Pat McCormick	USA	
Highboard diving	Pat McCormick	USA	

Water Polo

Hungary

Weightlifting

Event	Name	Country	Result
Bantamweight	Ivan Udodov	USSR	694.5 lb
Featherweight	Rafael Chimiskyan	USSR	774 lb
Lightweight	Thomas Kono	USA	799 lb
Middleweight	Peter George	USA	882 lb
Light-heavyweight	Trofim Lomakin	USSR	920.5 lb
Middle-heavyweight	Norbert Schemansky	USA	903.75 lb
Heavyweight	John Davis	USA	1,014 lb

Wrestling

Freestyle

Event	Name	Country
Flyweight	Hasan Gemici	Turkey
Bantamweight	Schoohachi Ishii	Japan
Featherweight	Bayram Sit	Turkey
Lightweight	Olle Anderberg	Sweden
Welterweight	William Smith	USA
Middleweight	David Cimakuridze	USSR
Light-heavyweight	Wiking Palm	Sweden
Heavyweight	Arsen Mekokishvili	USSR

Graeco-Roman

Event	Name	Country
Flyweight	Boris Gurevich	USSR
Bantamweight	Imre Hodos	Hungary
Featherweight	Yakov Punkin	USSR
Lightweight	Khasame Safin	USSR
Welterweight	Miklos Szilvasi	Hungary
Middleweight	Axel Gronberg	Sweden
Light-heavyweight	Kaelpo Grondhal	Finland
Heavyweight	Johannes Kotkas	USSR

Yachting

Event	Name	Country
Single-handed	Paul Elvstrom	Denmark
Star	Agostino Straulino, Nicole Rode	Italy
Dragon		Norway
5.5 metres		USA
6.0 metres		USA

1 New Zealand's Yvette Williams won the long jump by clearing 20 ft 5¾ in. 2 Jean Boiteux led from start to finish to win the 400 metres freestyle. His victory so excited his father that he jumped into the water to congratulate him. 3 Emil Zatopek leads Alain Mimoun of France and Herbert Schade of Germany into the home straight of the 5,000 metres. They finished in that order, and the fallen Chris Chataway came fifth.
4 Hungary's goalkeeper, Gyula Grosics, plucks a cross out of the air during the final against Yugoslavia. Hungary won 2-0, and in five matches scored 20 goals, conceding only 2. 5 The photo-finish of the men's 100 metres shows Lindy Remigino (third from top) nosing Herb McKenley (second from top) out of the gold medal spot, while Britain's McDonald Bailey (second from bottom) clinches the bronze medal. 6 A baton mix-up between Winsome Cripps (left) and Marjorie Jackson left the Australians floundering in the women's relay, but they still managed to finish fifth. 7 Viktor Chukarin—the winner of the combined exercises, pommel horse, and vault—in action on the parallel bars, in which he was placed second.

2

hands three times in the last 10 metres. The versatile Eva Novak added two silvers—in the 400 metres freestyle and the 200 metres breaststroke—to her relay gold. Other Hungarians beat her in both races, Valeria Gyenge in the 400 metres, and Eva Szekely in the breaststroke. In 1952, breaststroke and butterfly had not been made separate strokes and Eva (whose husband Deszo Gyarmati won a water polo gold at these games) used the 'butterfly' recovery while Miss Novak kept to the classic orthodox underwater breaststroke arm action. Britain's Elenor Gordon, also an orthodox breaststroke swimmer, was third.

The men's events were not without their surprises and incidents. Clarke Scholes of the United States took the 100 metres freestyle after his team-mate Dick Cleveland, the world record holder, had failed to reach the final. Jean Boiteux became, in the 400 metres freestyle, France's first Olympic swimming champion. As soon as the race was over his father, fully clothed, jumped into the water to embrace his son.

There were protests galore in the water polo tournament. Russia got FINA secretary Max Ritter out of bed at six in the morning to protest over the draw—and a re-

draw was made. And Yugoslavia protested over the Belgian referee who handled their match against the Netherlands, which they lost. They had no grounds for complaint, yet were given a replay, which they won. The Yugoslavs went on to win the silver medals, while the Netherlands, one of the best teams at Helsinki, failed to get into the last four.

Equestrianism
Great Britain won her only gold medal of the Games in the Grand Prix show jumping team event. Sixteen teams, comprising 48 riders, lined up for the big equestrian test, which started at 8 a.m. Britain's hero was Fox-

hunter, the horse that had helped Britain to win the bronze medals in London at the previous Games. The crucial round was Foxhunter's final trial: Britain were five points clear of Chile, so Foxhunter and Harry Llewellyn could afford just one fence down. But they did not even need that. A clear round made sure of the golds.

There was a five-way jump-off for the individual medals. Pierre d'Oriola of France on Ali Baba went first and set such a hot pace that nobody could match him. He went round clear in 40 seconds. The nearest challenger to his supremacy was Oscar Christi of Chile on Bambi who collected four faults in a 44 second round.

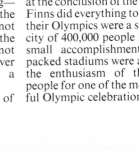

Germany's Fritz Thiedemann on Meteor went round in 38.5 seconds, but had two fences down for eight faults and finished third.

Other Sports
A total of 27 nations claimed gold medals at Helsinki, and the honours were fairly widely distributed. Australia's Russell Mockridge won two golds in cycling—the 1,000 metres time trial and the 2,000 metres tandem. He was not entered in his favourite event, the 1,000 metres sprint, and had not partnered Lionel Cox (the silver medallist in the sprint) on a tandem before the Games.

The United States won five of

the 10 boxing championships, including the newly introduced light-welterweight. Two future world heavyweight champions were on show. Floyd Patterson, aged 17, won the middleweight crown, and turned professional on returning to America. Some four years later he became the youngest ever world heavyweight champion. Ingemar Johansson—who beat Patterson to win the world heavyweight championship in 1959—found himself disqualified in the heavyweight final for not trying.

The outstanding woman fencer of the Games was the silver medallist Hungary's Ilona Elek, champion in 1936 and 1948. A 45-year-old, she fought her way through a fiercely contested competition to tie for first place in the final—only to lose in the fight-off to Irene Camber of Italy, a girl she had already beaten twice on the way. In the men's foil Christian d'Oriola, the 1948 silver medallist, won all his eight bouts in the final pool to clinch the title, and he was a member of the winning foil team.

The Hungarian soccer team won their first Olympic tournament, and in the team were such outstanding names as Ferenc Puskas, Josef Bozsik, Sandor Kocsis, Zoltan Czibor, and Nandor Hidegkuti. They beat Yugoslavia 2-0 in the final.

The USSR made a great impact on the gymnastics world, winning 22 medals in all, including eight golds. It was the first time that Russia had been prominent in this sport.

The masters of the hockey field, however, were still India, who gained their fifth successive title and conceded only two goals in the competition, and scored 13.

Six nations won rowing gold medals, the United States winning two—the coxless pairs and the eights. Russia's team were outstanding in this sport as well, claiming one gold and two silver medals. They excelled in weightlifting, too, winning three gold medals. The United States claimed four. Forty nations took part in the weightlifting, and seven world records were set up and five equalled, while Olympic bests were equalled 16 times and beaten 18 times. John Davis, the 1948 heavyweight champion, was the only man to repeat his success. Wrestling was also a sport contested by many nations—37—but this time the honours were more widespread. The USSR won four Greco-Roman and two free-style titles, but 14 countries won medals of some sort.

From the moment Nurmi set foot in the stadium with the torch, until the flame was allowed to die at the conclusion of the Games, the Finns did everything to ensure that their Olympics were a success. In a city of 400,000 people this was no small accomplishment, and the packed stadiums were a witness to the enthusiasm of the Finnish people for one of the most successful Olympic celebrations ever

Melbourne Olympic Games (1956)

In 1956, for the first time, the Olympic Games were celebrated in the Southern Hemisphere. And for the first time, too, they were held as late in the year as November and December. Ten of the previous 12 Games had been held in July and August. Nevertheless, 67 nations sent some 2,800 men and 370 women to compete in the 16 sports. The suppression of the Hungarian uprising by the Russians and the British and French adventure in the Middle East had resulted in the withdrawal of Egypt, Iraq, Lebanon, the Netherlands, and Spain. But Ethiopia, Kenya, and Malaya were represented for the first time.

More than 88,000 people were present for the opening ceremony, which the Duke of Edinburgh performed. The final lap of the Olympic torch relay was run by the young Ron Clarke, Australia's junior mile record holder. World mile record holder John Landy took the Olympic Oath.

Athletics

The Melbourne Cricket Ground, with a newly laid track, provided a fine setting for the athletics events, as well as for the hockey and soccer finals and the opening and closing ceremonies.

The outstanding competitor in the track events was the Russian Vladimir Kuts, who won the 5,000 and 10,000 metres gold medals, the former in a Games record which stood for the next three Olympiads. His 10,000 metres victory on the first day of the athletics was Russia's first ever gold medal in Olympic track and field events. He had set a world record of 28 min 30.4 sec in Moscow some 10 weeks earlier, and in Melbourne set out to burn up the field with a fast early pace. By the 5,000 metres mark, Kuts had disposed of all his rivals except Britain's Gordon Pirie. Pirie was weakened by the Russian's constant variations of pace, and after 8,000 metres dropped

back, eventually to finish in eighth position. This left Kuts out on his own, and he won easily.

The second leg of Kuts' double came five days later, in the 5,000 metres final. Although he was trailed for much of the way by two Englishmen, Pirie and Derek Ibbotson, he was never in much danger, and 1,000 metres from home was in complete command. He won by 11 seconds from Pirie in 13 min 39.6 sec, thus beating the Olympic record by 27 seconds.

Bobby Morrow's 100-200 metres double was the first by a man in the Olympics since 1936. In each event he was followed home by other Americans. It was in the 100 metres that 'hustling' Hec Hogan won Australia's first men's sprint medal since 1900, a bronze. America's depth of sprinters made the result of the 4 by 100 metres relay a foregone conclusion, and Bobby Morrow thus gained his third gold of the Games in anchoring his country's winning squad in world record time. The United States also took the first three places in the 110 metres hurdles. Lee Calhoun won by a whisker from Jack Davis, who thus gained his second successive silver medal in this event.

Whereas only one European reached a sprint final, three got through to the 400 metres final. America's Lou Jones, the world record holder, was an early leader in the outside lane, but faded to fifth place, at least 15 yards behind the winner, his team-mate Charles Jenkins. Tying for third place—the only instance of such an occurrence on the track—were Russia's Ardalion Ignatyev and Finland's Voitto Hellsten, both timed at 47.0 sec.

For the fourth Olympics in succession, the United States provided the winner of the 800 metres. But Tom Courtney won only after a fierce battle down the finishing straight with Britain's Derek Johnson.

The 1,500 metres lived up to its reputation as one of the Games' most exciting races, and produced a surprise winner in Ireland's Ron Delany, whose searing burst over the last 300 metres was too good for the others, including the Australian John Landy who came third. The first nine finishers beat Josy Barthel's 1952 Olympic record.

The longest running event— the marathon—enabled Alain Mimoun of France to win, at last, an Olympic gold medal. Three times an Olympic runner-up behind Emil Zatopek, the determined French-Algerian won by over half a minute. Zatopek, a pale shadow of his former self, was 4½ minutes behind Mimoun in sixth place.

The 3,000 metres steeplechase provided the most controversial event of the Games. Britain's unfancied third string Chris Brasher surprised the field with a last-lap burst to win by nearly 20

1 America's Hal Connolly won the gold medal in the hammer with a throw of 207 ft. 3½ in. It was over 17 ft. below his three-week old world record of 224 ft. 10 in.
2 Britain's Gillian Sheen (left) takes on Renée Garilhe of France in the women's foil event. Miss Sheen won the gold medal—Britain's first Olympic fencing title—and Mlle Garilhe the bronze.
3 Vladimir Kuts breaks away from the British trio of Gordon Pirie (189—2nd), Derek Ibbotson (188—3rd) and Chris Chataway (11th) in the final of the 5,000 metres.

yards. But he had to survive a disqualification for obstruction and a long wait before the jury of appeal allowed him to call the gold medal his own. It was Britain's only athletics gold at Melbourne and their first individual track title since the 1932 Olympics.

Of the nine field events (including the decathlon), the United States won seven. Charles Dumas, the first man to clear 7 feet, beat Australia's Charles Porter by $\frac{3}{4}$ in., with an Olympic record of 6 ft. $11\frac{1}{2}$ in. In the pole vault Bob Richards successfully defended his title, but not without a couple of missed heart beats when he took three tries to get over 13 ft. $1\frac{1}{2}$ in. in the qualifying competition. In the final, however, he set an Olympic record of 14 ft. $11\frac{1}{2}$ in. to beat his compariot Bob Gutowski by $1\frac{1}{4}$ in.

Conditions for record breaking in the long jump were non-existent, with a wind veering from not far short of 30 mph against to 20 mph in favour of the jumpers. Only 2 of the 13 finalists exceeded 25 feet —the winner Gregory Bell (25 ft. $8\frac{1}{4}$ in.) and his fellow-American, silver medallist John Bennett (25 ft. $2\frac{1}{4}$ in.). Further United States successes came through Parry O'Brien in the shot, the 20-year-old Al Oerter in the discus, Harold Connolly in the hammer, and Milton Campbell in the decathlon.

Brazilian triple jump specialist Adhemar Ferreira da Silva retained his title with an Olympic record combination jump of 53 ft. $7\frac{3}{4}$ in., though he was hard pressed by Iceland's Vilhjálmur Einarsson (53 ft. $4\frac{1}{4}$ in.). In the javelin, Egil Danielsen of Norway deprived Poland's Janusz Sidlo of both the Olympic title and his world record with a throw of 281 ft. $2\frac{1}{2}$ in.—more than 40 feet farther than his own next best throw in the competition.

The heroine of the women's events was the 18-year-old Betty Cuthbert who won the 100 and 200 metres, and anchored Australia to a world record and a close victory over Great Britain in the 4 by 100 metres relay. Shirley De la Hunty, competing in her third Olympic Games, retained her 80 metres hurdles title and was also a member of Australia's winning relay team. Of the other Australians, Marlene Mathews was third in both the 100 and the 200 metres, and Norma Thrower was third in the hurdles.

America's Mildred McDaniel was a clear winner of the high jump with a world record of 5 ft. $9\frac{1}{4}$ in., $3\frac{1}{2}$ inches better than Thelma Hopkins of Britain and Maria Pisaryeva of Russia, who were both awarded silver medals. In the long jump Elzbieta Krzesinka of Poland equalled her own world record of 20 ft. 10 in. to win by nearly a foot.

Czechoslovakia's Olga Fikotova won the discus gold medal with a throw of 176 ft. $1\frac{1}{2}$ in., but while at Melbourne she also gained a

husband, the American hammer thrower Harold Connolly. The pair were married in 1957, only after much diplomatic dithering, and the Connollys continued to compete, though without repeating their Melbourne successes, in the next three Olympic Games.

Russia's contribution to the women's athletics events came through two throwers. The massive, 17-stone Tamara Tyshkyevich won the shot with her last throw to beat defending champion Galina Zybina by $2\frac{1}{4}$ inches. And in the javelin Inese Jaunzeme won by over 11 feet from Chile's Marlene Ahrens with Russia's world record holder Nadyezhda Konyayeva third.

Swimming

In the new 5,500-seat swimming pool in Olympic Park, the Games were an unqualified triumph for Australia, and equally disastrous for the United States, although the absence of the Dutch girls affected the outcome somewhat.

Australia's Jon Henricks, John Devitt, and Gary Chapman took first, second, and third places respectively in the 100 metres freestyle, and Murray Rose won both the 400 and 1,500 metres freestyle. In both of these events Japan's Tsuyoshi Yamanaka was second and America's George Breen (who set a world 1,500 metres record of 17 min 52.9 sec in his heat) third. Rose, Devitt, and Henricks were joined by Kevin O'Halloran in the 4 by 200 metres relay which they won in a world record of 8 min 23.6 sec, 7.9 sec in front of the Americans.

The Australian girls emulated their men in the 100 metres freestyle, with Dawn Fraser first, Lorraine Crapp second, and Faith Leech third. Sandra Morgan helped these three to win the 4 by 100 metres relay. America's only individual women's freestyle medal came through Sylvia Ruuska, third in the 400 metres. She was well beaten by Lorraine Crapp and Dawn Fraser, who thus claimed two gold and one silver medal each.

Britain claimed her first Olympic swimming champion in 32 years through Judy Grinham in the 100 metres backstroke, and had the added pleasure of Margaret

4 Norman Read of New Zealand (No. 10) leads the field at the start of the 50-km walk. He stayed in front to win the gold medal from Russia's Yevgeniy Maskinskov with over two minutes to spare. **5** Women's 100 metres final: Betty Cuthbert of Australia (466) was first, Christa Stubnick of Germany (right) second, and Australia's Marlene Mathews (470) third. **6** Chris Brasher takes the final water jump on his way to a surprise gold medal in the 3,000 metres steeplechase. Though at first disqualified, he was later reinstated.

Keystone

Keystone

H. M. Abrahams

Edwards and Julie Hoyle coming third and sixth, respectively. American wins came through Bill Yorzyk in the men's butterfly, and Shelley Mann in the women's butterfly.

America won three of the four diving titles, with Pat McCormick retaining the springboard and highboard crowns she had won at Helsinki in 1952—the first diver of either sex to achieve this feat. But the men's highboard went to Mexico's Joaquin Capilla—who had been third in 1948 and second in 1952—by 0.03 of a point.

Hungary, whose team had got out of Budapest only days after the rebellion in their country, retained the water polo title, but not without a real blood battle with the Soviet Union, who tried to match technical and tactical excellence with rough play. It required police assistance to calm infuriated spectators and players alike after Hungary's Ervin Zador had his eyebrow split. But Hungary beat the Russians 4-0 and won their final game 2-1, against runners-up Yugoslavia, to emerge undefeated champions.

Other Sports

If the United States had claimed the lion's share of honours in athletics and Australia in swimming, it was the turn of Russia to come good in the other sports. It was in shooting, wrestling, and gymnastics that the Russians showed their prowess to the full.

The gymnastics events were very closely contested, but Russia's well balanced men's team came away with six outright wins, and one shared. Viktor Chukarin won three gold medals—in the team, individual combined exercises, and parallel bars. He won the combined title from Japan's Takashi Ono by 0.05 of a point. The gold medals in the women's events were shared evenly between Russia and Hungary. Hungary's Agnes Keleti and Russia's Larissa Latynina were joint champions in the floor exercises, and won two individual and one team title each.

Two sons of famous fathers competed for the United States in the rowing events, John B. Kelly Jr and Bernard Costello Jr. John Kelly and Paul Costello had won

1 British flyweight Terry Spinks lays into René Libeer of France during their semi-final bout. Spinks won, and went on to beat Romania's Mircea Dobrescu in the final.
2 The American Yale crew (top) won the eights gold from Canada (bottom). 3 A thrilling 1,500 metres final saw Ron Delany of Eire come through with a well-timed burst to take the gold medal in front of Germany's Klaus Richtzenhain (134—2nd) and Australia's John Landy. 4 The 800 metres was equally exciting. America's Tom Courtney had to fight right to the end to hold off the challenge of Britain's Derek Johnson. Courtney's winning time— 1 min 47.7 sec—beat the Olympic record by 1½ sec.

MELBOURNE OLYMPIC GAMES, 1956 Gold Medallists

Athletics—Men			
100 metres	Bobby Morrow	USA	10.5 sec
200 metres	Bobby Morrow	USA	20.6 sec
400 metres	Charles Jenkins	USA	46.7 sec
800 metres	Tom Courtney	USA	1 min 47.7 sec
1,500 metres	Ron Delany	Eire	3 min 41.2 sec
5,000 metres	Vladimir Kuts	USSR	13 min 39.6 sec
10,000 metres	Vladimir Kuts	USSR	28 min 45.6 sec
Marathon	Alain Mimoun	France	2 hr 25 min 0.0 sec
4 x 100 metres relay		USA	39.5 sec
4 x 400 metres relay		USA	3 min 4.8 sec
110 metres hurdles	Lee Calhoun	USA	13.5 sec
400 metres hurdles	Glenn Davis	USA	50.1 sec
3,000 metres steeplechase	Chris Brasher	Great Britain	8 min 41.2 sec
20 kilometres walk	Leonid Spirin	USSR	1 hr 31 min 27.4 sec
50 kilometres walk	Norman Read	New Zealand	4 hr 30 min 42.8 sec
High jump	Charles Dumas	USA	6 ft 11¼ in
Pole vault	Bob Richards	USA	14 ft 11½ in
Long jump	Gregory Bell	USA	25 ft 8¼ in
Triple jump	Adhemar da Silva	Brazil	53 ft 7½ in
Shot	Parry O'Brien	USA	60 ft 11 in
Discus	Al Oerter	USA	184 ft 10½ in
Hammer	Hal Connolly	USA	207 ft 3½ in
Javelin	Egil Danielsen	Norway	281 ft 2 in
Decathlon	Milton Campbell	USA	7,937 pts
Athletics—Women			
100 metres	Betty Cuthbert	Australia	11.5 sec
200 metres	Betty Cuthbert	Australia	23.4 sec
4 x 100 metres relay		Australia	44.5 sec
80 metres hurdles	Shirley De la Hunty	Australia	10.7 sec
High jump	Mildred McDaniel	USA	5 ft 9¼ in
Long jump	Elzbieta Krzesinka	Poland	20 ft 10 in
Shot	Tamara Tyshkyevich	USSR	54 ft 5 in
Discus	Olga Fikotova	Czechoslovakia	176 ft 1½ in
Javelin	Inese Jaunzeme	USSR	176 ft 8½ in
Basketball		USA	
Boxing			
Flyweight	Terry Spinks	Great Britain	
Bantamweight	Wolfgang Behrandt	Germany	
Featherweight	Vladimir Safranov	USSR	
Lightweight	Dick McTaggart	Great Britain	
Light-welterweight	Vladimir Enguibarian	USSR	
Welterweight	Necolae Linca	Romania	
Light-middleweight	Laszlo Papp	Hungary	
Middleweight	Genadiy Schatkov	USSR	
Light-heavyweight	James Boyd	USA	
Heavyweight	Peter Rademacher	USA	
Canoeing			
1,000 metres—Men			
Kayak singles	Gert Fredriksson	Sweden	4 min 12.8 sec
Kayak pairs	Michel Scheuer, Meinrad Miltenberger	Germany	3 min 49.6 sec
Canadian singles	Leon Rottman	Romania	5 min 5.3 sec
Canadian pairs	Alexe Dumitru, Simion Ismailciuc	Romania	4 min 47.4 sec
10,000 metres—Men			
Kayak singles	Gert Fredriksson	Sweden	47 min 43.4 sec
Kayak pairs	Janos Uranyi, Laszlo Fabian	Hungary	43 min 37.0 sec
Canadian singles	Leon Rottman	Romania	56 min 41.0 sec
Canadian pairs	Pavel Kharine, Gratsian Botev	USSR	54 min 2.4 sec
500 metres—Women			
Kayak singles	Elisaveta Dementieva	USSR	2 min 18.9 sec
Cycling			
1,000 metres sprint	Michel Rousseau	France	
1,000 metres time trial	Leandro Faggin	Italy	1 min 9.8 sec
2,000 metres tandem	Ian Browne, Anthony Marchant	Australia	
4,000 metres team pursuit		Italy	4 min 37.4 sec
Road race (116 miles, 1,144 yards)			
—individual	Ercole Baldini	Italy	5 hr 21 min 17 sec
—team		France	
Fencing—Men			
Foil—individual	Christian d'Oriola	France	
—team		Italy	
Epee—individual	Carlo Pavesi	Italy	
—team		Italy	
Sabre—individual	Rudolf Karpati	Hungary	
—team		Hungary	
Fencing—Women			
Foil—individual	Gillian Sheen	Great Britain	
Football		USSR	
Gymnastics—Men			
Combined exercises			
—individual	Viktor Chukarin	USSR	
—team		USSR	
Floor exercises	Valentin Muratov	USSR	
Horizontal bar	Takashi Ono	Japan	
Parallel bars	Viktor Chukarin	USSR	
Pommel horse	Boris Shakhlin	USSR	
Vault	Helmuth Bantz	Germany	
	Valentin Muratov	USSR	
Rings	Albert Azarian	USSR	

Gymnastics—Women			
Combined exercises team		USSR	
Team drill		Hungary	
Combined exercises individual	Larissa Latynina	USSR	
Floor exercises	Agnes Keleti	Hungary	
	Larissa Latynina	USSR	
Asymmetrical bars	Agnes Keleti	Hungary	
Beam	Agnes Keleti	Hungary	
Vault	Larissa Latynina	USSR	
Hockey		India	
Modern Pentathlon			
Individual	Lars Hall	Sweden	
Team		USSR	
Rowing			
Single sculls	Vyacheslav Ivanov	USSR	8 min 2.5 sec
Double sculls	Aleksandr Berkutov, Yuri Tyukalov	USSR	7 min 24.0 sec
Coxless pairs	James Fifer, Duvall Hecht	USA	7 min 55.4 sec
Coxed pairs	Arthur Ayrault, Conn Findlay, Kurt Seiffert (cox)	USA	8 min 26.1 sec
Coxless fours		Canada	7 min 8.8 sec
Coxed fours		Italy	7 min 19.4 sec
Eights		USA	6 min 35.2 sec
Shooting			
Free pistol	Pentti Linnosvuo	Finland	
Silhouette pistol	Stefan Petrescu	Romania	
Free rifle	Vasiliy Borissov	USSR	
Running deer	Vitalii Romanenko	USSR	
Small bore rifle			
—three positions	Anatoliy Bogdanov	USSR	
—prone	Gerald Ouellette	Canada	
Clay pigeon	Galliano Rossini	Italy	
Swimming—Men			
100 metres freestyle	Jon Henricks	Australia	55.4 sec
400 metres freestyle	Murray Rose	Australia	4 min 27.3 sec
1,500 metres freestyle	Murray Rose	Australia	17 min 58.9 sec
200 metres breaststroke	Masaru Furukawa	Japan	2 min 34.7 sec
200 metres butterfly	Bill Yorzyk	USA	2 min 19.3 sec
100 metres backstroke	David Theile	Australia	1 min 2.2 sec
4 x 200 metres freestyle relay		Australia	8 min 23.6 sec
Springboard diving	Robert Clotworthy	USA	
Highboard diving	Joaquin Capilla	Mexico	
Swimming—Women			
100 metres freestyle	Dawn Fraser	Australia	1 min 2.0 sec
400 metres freestyle	Lorraine Crapp	Australia	4 min 54.6 sec
200 metres breaststroke	Ursula Happe	Germany	2 min 53.1 sec
100 metres butterfly	Shelley Mann	USA	1 min 11.0 sec
100 metres backstroke	Judy Grinham	Great Britain	1 min 12.9 sec
4 x 100 metres freestyle relay		Australia	4 min 17.1 sec
Springboard diving	Pat McCormick	USA	
Highboard diving	Pat McCormick	USA	
Water Polo		Hungary	
Weightlifting			
Bantamweight	Charles Vinci	USA	759 lb
Featherweight	Isaac Berger	USA	776½ lb
Lightweight	Igor Rybak	USSR	837½ lb
Middleweight	Fyeodor Bogdanovskiy	USSR	925¾ lb
Light-heavyweight	Tommy Kono	USA	986¼ lb
Mid-heavyweight	Arkhadiy Vorobiev	USSR	1,019¼ lb
Heavyweight	Paul Anderson	USA	1,102 lb
Wrestling			
Freestyle			
Flyweight	Mirian Tsalkalamanidze	USSR	
Bantamweight	Mustafa Dagistanli	Turkey	
Featherweight	Shozo Sasahara	Japan	
Lightweight	Emamali Habibi	Iran	
Welterweight	Mitsuo Ikeda	Japan	
Middleweight	Nikola Nikolov	Bulgaria	
Light-heavyweight	Gholam-Reza Takhti	Iran	
Heavyweight	Hamit Kaplan	Turkey	
Graeco-Roman			
Flyweight	Nikolay Solovyev	USSR	
Bantamweight	Konstantin Vyroupaev	USSR	
Featherweight	Rauno Makinen	Finland	
Lightweight	Kyosto Lehtonen	Finland	
Welterweight	Mithat Bayrak	Turkey	
Middleweight	Guivi Kartosia	USSR	
Light-heavyweight	Valentin Nikolaev	USSR	
Heavyweight	Anatoliy Parfenov	USSR	
Yachting			
Finn	Paul Elvstrom	Denmark	
Star	Herbert Williams, Lawrence Low	USA	
12 square metres	Peter Mander, John Cropp	New Zealand	
5.5 metres		Sweden	
Dragon		Sweden	

the double sculls together in 1920 and 1924, but their sons were less successful. Kelly Jr was third in the single sculls, and Costello Jr second in the double sculls.

Yale University achieved America's eighth successive victory in the eights—but first had to fight their way through the repechage, having been beaten into third place in their heat. They won the final by a small margin from Canada.

All thoughts of Budapest and the Gaza Strip were dispelled from the Olympic arena during the closing ceremony. On the suggestion of a Chinese-Australian

4

Official Report of the 1956 Olympics

17-stone Tamara Tyshkyevich won the women's shot with a throw of 54 ft. 5 in.

schoolboy, the competitors in the Games marched together in a single body for the first time—possibly an omen of better things to come in the world outside sport.

Equestrian Sports
Because of Australia's strict quarantine regulations, the equestrian events were held in July 1956 in Stockholm—the first instance of an individual sport being held in a different country from the main summer Games.

The Swedish dressage ace Henri St Cyr brought his tally of Olympic titles to four by retaining his individual title and gaining a gold medal as a member of the Swedish team, who won the dressage team title for the third successive time. Hans Winkler of Germany won two golds in the show jumping, one individual and one team. He collected 4 faults, with the Italian

5

Associated Press

Opposite page: The winner of the silver medal in the decathlon at Melbourne was the American Rafer Johnson. At Rome four years later in 1960, he was to beat the Formosan Yang to take the gold medal.
1 The long jump was one of Johnson's best events. Although he did not compete, he was selected for the long jump for the United States in the 1956 Olympic Games.
2 An ungainly high jump landing during the AAU decathlon championships in 1960. Johnson cleared 5 ft 10 in to help him take yet another world record.
3 The final event of the decathlon at Rome was the 1500 metres. Yang had to beat Johnson by more than 11 seconds to win the gold medal, but Johnson held on to keep the margin down to 1.2 seconds and thus success.
4 Vyacheslav Ivanov, the world's leading sculler of the 1950s and 1960s, won the first of his three Olympic Golds at Melbourne.
5 Just 20 and little known outside the United States, Al Oerter won the first of a record consecutive discus golds at Melbourne with a first throw distance of 184 ft 11 in.

Associated Press

1

2

Associated Press

3

Armin Hary, specialist of the
blitz start, appears confident on
the blocks before the start of
the 1960 Olympic 100 metres.

Rome Olympic Games

(1960)

A record number of 5,337 competitors—4,800 men and 537 women—gathered in Rome in late August and early September 1960 to contest 150 separate events in 18 different sports. The total number of competitors exceeded the previous record—4,925 at Helsinki in 1952—by over 400.

The Olympics were over 50 years late in arriving at 'the Eternal City.' The 1908 Games were originally scheduled for Rome. But some two years earlier the Italians had to stand down, and Britain stepped into the breach to organize what is generally recognised as the first of the great modern Games. But the 50-year wait did not affect the Italians' enthusiasm. Cash from football pool profits supported the Olympic movement financially, and in the city new sports stadiums had been built to accommodate the biggest sporting occasion to grace the Italian capital since the fall of the Roman Empire.

Athletics

In the men's track and field events, only four countries won more than one gold medal—the United States (nine), the USSR (five), New Zealand (two), and Poland (two). The Russians dominated the women's events, with 6 wins in 10 events; America won three titles, and Romania one.

For the first time since 1928 the men's sprint title eluded the Americans. The 100 metres went to the newly crowned world record holder, Armin Hary, who thus proved that his 10.0 sec world record in Zurich three months earlier was no fluke. He

1 Armin Hary blazes through the tape to win the 100 metres title from Dave Sime of the United States (far right).
2 New Zealand's Peter Snell pips Belgium's Roger Moens to win the 800 metres title.
3 A second gold for New Zealand came from Murray Halberg, 5,000 metres winner.
4 Herb Elliott (9) won the 1,500 metres in record time.

was Germany's first ever male track gold medallist, and he also won a second gold medal. In the 4 by 100 metres relay Germany finished second to the United States but the Americans were disqualified for a faulty take-over. The discomfiture of American sprinters was completed by the result of the 200 metres. Despite the competition from no fewer than three co-holders of the world record, Italy's Livio Berruti himself equalled the record in the semi-final and final to win the country's first athletics gold since 1936. The Roman crowd celebrated by lighting hundreds of paper torches as Berruti, who always

ran in dark glasses, acknowledged the cheers by removing them.

New Zealand's two gold medals came on a single afternoon, September 2. The first came in the 800 metres. The 21-year-old Peter Snell had come to the Games with a personal best time of 1 min 49.2 sec for 880 yards. But he improved to 1 min 46.3 sec to win the final by inches from the Belgian world record holder Roger Moens. An hour later came the 5,000 metres final, and New Zealand's hope in this race was 27-year-old Murray Halberg. He ran the race of a lifetime, breaking away boldly 1,000 metres from the finish with a 61.5 sec lap to open up a 30-yard lead before the rest of the field were aware of it. Though his last lap took 73.0 sec and he collapsed at the end of it, he still won by 1.2 sec from Hans Grodotzki of Germany who was 0.2 sec in front of the bronze medallist Kazimierz Zimny of Poland. Six days later Grodotzki won a second silver medal, in the 10,000 metres. In that race he was second to Russia's Pyotr Bolotnikov, who beat Vladimir Kuts's

1956 Olympic record by 13 seconds with 28 min 32.2 sec.

But the showpiece of the track events was the 1,500 metres. Australia's Herb Elliott, the world record holder, was the favourite, and he made winning in world record time look almost simple. He took the lead soon after passing the 800-metre mark, and surged majestically away from the others to finish in 3 min 35.6 sec. A distant second was the young Frenchman Michel Jazy in 3 min 38.4 sec: the first six to finish beat the previous Olympic record of 3 min 41.2 sec.

If Elliott's victory was sweeping, the finish of the 400 metres was desperately close. The final resolved into a battle between America's Otis Davis and Carl Kaufmann, representing Germany but born in New York. The early leader was South Africa's Malcolm Spence, but he faded to finish third, and in the home straight it was Davis who led by about 5 yards. Kaufmann produced a tremendous finish and it took a photograph to decide that Davis had just held him off. Both

shared a new world record of 44.9 sec.

Otis Davis teamed up with Glenn Davis, Jack Yerman, and Earl Young to win the 4 by 400 metres relay in a world record 3 min 0.7 sec, with Kaufmann anchoring the German team to the silver medals. Glenn Davis was the first champion ever to retain the 400 metres hurdles title, and the same thing happened in the 110 metres, which Lee Calhoun retained. Americans took all three medals in both hurdles events.

The steeplechase, on the other hand, was an all-European affair. The 1958 European 5,000 and 10,000 metres champion Zdzislaw Krzyszkowiak took the title in 8 min 34.2 sec—less than 3 seconds outside his world record—and two Russians, Nikolai Sokolov and Semyon Rzhishchin, the silver and bronze respectively.

Honours were evenly divided between the United States and Europe in the jumps, with Don

record throw of 194 ft. 2 in., nearly 4 feet better than Rink Babka's silver medal throw of 190 ft. 4¼ in. In the shot, the gold went to a late addition to the American team, Bill Nieder, and the silver to twice-winner Parry O'Brien.

The javelin and hammer went to the Soviet Union. Defending champion Hal Connolly could do no better than place eighth in the hammer although he had only three weeks earlier set a world record of 230 ft. 9 in. He threw only 208 ft. 7½ in., whereas the winner, Vasiliy Rudenkov, managed 220 ft. 1¾ in. and the runner-up Gyula Zsivotsky of Hungary, 215 ft. 10¼ in. In the javelin it was a case of third time lucky for Viktor Tsibulenko, fourth in 1952 and third in 1956, who won with 277 ft. 8¼ in. The 1956 champion, Egil Danielsen of Norway, failed to qualify for the final rounds.

The two-day battle for the decathlon honours was one of the closest in Olympic history. There

was never more than 144 points between America's Rafer Johnson and Formosa's Yang Chuankwang, and the result was in doubt until the final event, the 1,500 metres. Yang tried to run away from Johnson, but the American hung on to win the competition.

Two days after the last track and field event came the marathon, an event that heralded the arrival of African runners into the Olympic honours list. Two men, Abebe Bikila from Ethiopia and Rhadi Ben Abdesselm of Morocco broke away from the field, and Abebe went into a lead—narrow but decisive—only in the last kilometre. Abebe won, in a world best time of 2 hr 15 min 16.2 sec; Rhadi was second and Barry Magee of New Zealand was third.

The outstanding woman athlete of the Games was 20-year-old Wilma Rudolph from Tennessee, who became the third woman since World War II to win

1 Britain's Don Thompson steps out towards a gold medal in the 50 kilometres walk.
2 Abebe Bikila of Ethiopia won the marathon—barefoot—in the fastest time ever recorded for the distance.
3 Tennessee State's Wilma Rudolph wins the 200 metres. She collected two more gold medals, in the 100 metres and the 4 x 100 metres relay.
4 Russia's Irina Press just outpaced Britain's Carole Quinton to win the 80 metres hurdles. Britain's Mary Rand (left) came home fourth.
5 A statuesque encounter in the freestyle wrestling, a sport in which the United States, uncharacteristically, were extremely successful. But Turkey, with seven gold and two silver medals, were the dominant wrestling team.
6 Future world heavyweight champion Cassius Clay stands at the top of the Olympic light-heavyweight boxing tree.

Bragg winning the States' fourteenth successive pole vault title and Ralph Boston taking the long jump with a historic 26 ft. 7¾ in.—thus beating Jesse Owen's 24-year-old Olympic record set at Berlin by 2½ inches. The favourite for the high jump, world record holder John Thomas, was relegated to third place by two Russians, Robert Shavlakadze and Valeriy Brumel. Thomas was more than 3 inches below his world record, while Shavlakadze won the gold medal on the fewer misses rule after clearing 7 ft. 1 in. In the triple jump five men beat Ferreira da Silva's 1956 Olympic record, with world record holder Jozef Schmidt of Poland beating them all with 55 ft. 1¾ in. Da Silva, in his fourth Olympic Games, finished a sad 14th.

Russia and the United States divided the gold medals in the throwing events. But America won all three discus and shot medals. Al Oerter retained his discus title with an Olympic

Olympic golds in the 100 and 200 metres and the 4 by 100 metres relay. In the two individual events she was in a class of her own, winning each by at least three yards. In her semi-final of the 100 metres she equalled the world record of 11.3 sec, and in the final—with a following wind just over the maximum allowed—she returned 11.0 sec. In the 200 metres, after coming within 0.3 sec of her own world record (22.9 sec) in her heat, she won the final in 24.0 sec (against a strong headwind) by 0.4 sec from Germany's Jutta Heine. And in the relay final, after sharing in a new world record in the heat, she took over some yards behind Miss Heine but still managed to finish in front.

After a gap of 32 years, the women's programme included an 800 metres again, and unlike the race at Amsterdam in 1928 this one produced no undue distress in any of the finalists. Ludmilla Shevtsova of the USSR had to equal her world record of 2 min 4.3 sec to hold off the challenge of Australia's Brenda Jones. Another win for Russia on the track came through Irina Press in the 80 metres hurdles. She was closely challenged by Britain's Carole Quinton who hurdled better than the Russian holder of the world pentathlon record, but Miss Press was the more powerful and won by 0.1 sec.

Four field events fell to athletes from Russia. The 'strong woman' of the Games was Tamara Press, elder sister of Irina: she took the gold medal in the shot with 56 ft. 10 in., an Olympic record, and the silver medal in the discus, over 8 feet behind the winner, Nina Ponomaryeva, another Russian. Mrs. Ponomaryeva thus regained the title she had won in 1952 and lost in 1956, when she was third. The 1956 discus winner—Olga Fikotova of Czechoslovakia, but by now Mrs. Hal Connolly of the United States—was seventh. The javelin title went to 20-year-old Elvira Ozolina, the world record holder, and the long jump to Vyera Krepkina who beat the defending champion Elzbieta Krzesinska of Poland into second place by 4 inches. Mrs. Krepkina's winning jump, 20 ft. 10¾ in., was only one inch below the world record.

The only field event not won by a Russian was the high jump, and somewhat inevitably the winner was Iolanda Balas from Romania, whose winning 6 ft. 0¾ in. jump was more than 5 inches better than the joint silver medallist— Dorothy Shirley of Britain and Jaroslawa Jozwiakowska of Poland.

Swimming

The magnificent Stadio del Nuoto was the scene of an American comeback in Olympic swimming. Smarting from their trouncing at Melbourne, the Americans made amends by winning 9 of the 15 swimming events and both men's diving titles. Their gold medals tally could have been one more but for the disputed decision in the 100 metres freestyle in which Australia's John Devitt was given the victory over Lance Larson of the United States.

Australians were first home in four men's events: Murray Rose became the first man to retain the Olympic 400 metres title, and David Theile also retained his 1956 title, in the 100 metres backstroke. Devitt took the 100 metres, and John Konrads edged Murray Rose out of first place in the 1,500 metres. The only Australian woman to win was Dawn Fraser, who retained her 100 metres freestyle title. But for Australia this was a poor return: bad weather spoilt the team's training, their plane was held up for 24 hours in the steamy heat of Bahrein on the way to Rome, and in Rome a number of the team—including Melbourne 100 metres winner Jon Henricks—went down with 'Roman tummy' (gastroenteritis).

The British team had their best Games since 1924. Anita Lons-

brough won the 200 metres breaststroke in world record time —the only title that did not go to Australia or America, Natalie Steward won a silver in the backstroke and a bronze in the 100 metres freestyle, and to their surprise the men's 4 by 200 metres squad set a European record in coming fourth.

In the diving, Ingrid Kramer of Germany became the first non-American to win both women's titles. Bronze medals for Britain came through Liz Ferris in the women's springboard and Brian Phelps in the men's highboard. And for the hosts, Italy, gold medals came from victory in the water polo.

Other Sports

Traditionally a strong cycling nation, Italy missed only one gold medal in the six-event programme. Italians won the first event, the newly instituted road team time trial by over two minutes from Germany, and proceeded to monopolize the honours until the very last race, the individual road race. Sante Gaiardoni won the 1,000 metres sprint and the 1,000 metres time trial, the first time this particular double had been accomplished in the Olympics. But a historic clean sweep eluded

5

6

the host country: Viktor Kapitonov **1**
of Russia beat Livio Trape of
Italy in a sprint finish to the road
race with the pursuing 'bunch'
some 20 seconds in arrears. It was
Russia's first Olympic cycling
gold. One unfortunate incident
soured this part of the Games:
Denmark's Knud Jensen died in
hospital after collapsing during the
team trial. Autopsy reports suggested that his death may have
been due to the effects of drugs,
but his collapse was later officially
ascribed to sunstroke.

Another traditional winner to
triumph—yet again—was the
United States basketball team who
won their fifth Olympic tournament. But some favourites who
failed were India, winners since
1928 of the hockey. A goal
scored after 13 minutes in the
final was sufficient for Pakistan to
defeat them.

The perennial Gert Fredriksson
added two more Olympic canoeing medals to his collection which
began with two golds in 1948. At
Rome he was third in the kayak
singles, less then 3 seconds
behind the winner, and first, with
Sven Sjodelius, in the kayak
doubles. Rome proved to be his
last Olympics, and his tally stood
at six Olympic golds, one silver,
and one bronze. But in another
water sport, rowing, a new name
began to become known—the
Ratzeburg Ruder Club. Coached
by Karl Adam, the German eight,
composed of Ratzeburg members,
broke the 40-year-old American
hold on this title: it was also
Germany's first win in the event.

The soccer title went again to
eastern Europe, and this time it
was the turn of Yugoslavia who
defeated Denmark 3-1 in the
final. This victory came despite
the dismissal of captain Milan
Galic after only 39 minutes when
Yugoslavia were leading 2-0.
Hungary won the bronze medals
by beating Italy 2-1 in their play-
off.

The outstanding part of the
equestrian events was the success
of Australia in the three-day
competition. Not only did the
Australian team of Laurie Morgan, Neale Lavis, and Bill Roy-
croft win the team event with only
128.18 penalty points (against
runners-up Switzerland's 386.02),
but Morgan took the individual
gold and Lavis the silver. And
they were Australia's first equestrian medallists in Olympic competition.

Far away in the Bay of Naples,
the heir to the Greek throne,
Prince Constantine, was at the
helm of the winning Dragon class
vessel. The Prince, a better sailor
than politician, had been sailing a
Dragon for less than 18 months.
One very experienced competitor
whose victory was less of a surprise
was Paul Elvstrom, who won his
fourth successive gold medal in
single-handed events and his third
successive gold in the Finn
category.

1 Russia's first Olympic gold **2**
in cycling went to Viktor
Kapitonov (left) who held off
a strong challenge from
Italy's Livio Trape to win
the 109-mile road race.
2 Gert Fredriksson (left)
took his collection of Olympic
canoeing gold medals to six.
3 Laurie Morgan won the three-
day event title with a rare
'plus' score, and added a
second gold as a member of
Australia's winning team.
4 Prince Constantine of
Greece helmed his Dragon class
yacht to win an Olympic gold
medal. It was the only medal
of any colour won by Greece
at these Olympic Games.

3

4

Keystone

Italy's Raimondo d'Inzeo, gold medallist at Rome ahead of his brother, Piero. The brothers completed a family set of medals by collecting a bronze in the team event.

The great Herb Elliott (2), whose greatest race was undoubtedly the 1960 Olympic 1,500 metres final. Into the last 400 metres, Elliott had opened up a 10-yard lead, and at the finish was almost 3 seconds ahead, winning his gold medal in world-record time.

ROME OLYMPIC GAMES, 1960 Gold Medallists

Athletics—Men

Event	Name	Country	Result
100 metres	Armin Hary	Germany	10.2 sec
200 metres	Livio Berruti	Italy	20.5 sec
400 metres	Otis Davis	USA	44.9 sec
800 metres	Peter Snell	New Zealand	1 min 46.3 sec
1,500 metres	Herb Elliott	Australia	3 min 35.6 sec
5,000 metres	Murray Halberg	New Zealand	13 min 43.4 sec
10,000 metres	Pyetor Bolotnikov	USSR	28 min 32.2 sec
Marathon	Abebe Bikila	Ethiopia	2 hr 15 min 16.2 sec
4 x 100 metres relay		Germany	39.5 sec
4 x 400 metres relay		USA	3 min 2.2 sec
110 metres hurdles	Lee Calhoun	USA	13.8 sec
400 metres hurdles	Glenn Davis	USA	49.3 sec
3,000 metres steeplechase	Zdzislaw Krzyszkowiak	Poland	8 min 34.2 sec
20 kilometres walk	Vladimir Golubnichiy	USSR	1 hr 34 min 7.2 sec
50 kilometres walk	Don Thompson	Great Britain	4 hr 25 min 30.0 sec
High jump	Robert Shavlakadze	USSR	7 ft 1 in
Pole vault	Don Bragg	USA	15 ft 5 in
Long jump	Ralph Boston	USA	26 ft 7$\frac{3}{4}$ in
Triple jump	Jozef Schmidt	Poland	55 ft 1$\frac{3}{4}$ in
Shot	Bill Nieder	USA	64 ft 6$\frac{3}{4}$ in
Discus	Al Oerter	USA	194 ft 2 in
Hammer	Vasiliy Rudenkov	USSR	220 ft 1$\frac{3}{4}$ in
Javelin	Viktor Tsibulenko	USSR	277 ft 8$\frac{1}{4}$ in
Decathlon	Rafer Johnson	USA	8,392 points

Athletics—Women

Event	Name	Country	Result
100 metres	Wilma Rudolph	USA	11.0 sec
200 metres	Wilma Rudolph	USA	24.0 sec
800 metres	Ludmilla Shevtsova	USSR	2 min 4.3 sec
4 x 100 metres relay		USA	44.5 sec
80 metres hurdles	Irina Press	USSR	10.8 sec
High Jump	Iolanda Balas	Romania	6 ft 0$\frac{3}{4}$ in
Long jump	Vyera Krepkina	USSR	20 ft 10$\frac{3}{4}$ in
Shot	Tamara Press	USSR	56 ft 10 in
Discus	Nina Ponomaryeva	USSR	180 ft 9$\frac{1}{4}$ in
Javelin	Elvira Ozolina	USSR	183 ft 8 in

Basketball

USA

Boxing

Event	Name	Country
Flyweight	Gyula Torok	Hungary
Bantamweight	Oleg Grigoryev	USSR
Featherweight	Francesco Musso	Italy
Lightweight	Kazimierz Pazdzior	Poland
Light-welterweight	Bohumil Nemecek	Czechoslovakia
Welterweight	Giovanni Benvenuti	Italy
Light-middleweight	Wilbert McClure	USA
Middleweight	Edward Crook	USA
Light-heavyweight	Cassius Clay	USA
Heavyweight	Franco de Piccoli	Italy

Canoeing—Men

Event	Name	Country	Result
1,000 metres K-1	Erik Hansen	Denmark	3 min 53.00 sec
1,000 metres K-2	Gert Fredriksson, Sven Sjodelius	Sweden	3 min 34.73 sec
4 x 500 metres K-1 relay		Germany	7 min 39.43 sec
1,000 metres C-1	Janos Parti	Hungary	4 min 33.03 sec
1,000 metres C-2	Leonid Geyshter, Stephan Makarenko	USSR	4 min 17.04 sec

Canoeing Women

Event	Name	Country	Result
500 metres K-1	Antonina Seredina	USSR	2 min 8.08 sec
500 metres K-2	Maria Shubina, Antonina Seredina	USSR	1 min 54.76 sec

Cycling

Event	Name	Country	Result
1,000 metres sprint	Sante Gaiardoni	Italy	
1,000 metres time trial	Sante Gaiardoni	Italy	1 min 7.27 sec
2,000 metres tandem	Sergio Bianchetto, Giuseppe Beghetto	Italy	
4,000 metres team pursuit		Italy	4 min 38.41 sec
Road team time trial (100 km)		Italy	2 hr 14 min 33.53 sec
Road race (175.38 km)	Viktor Kapitonov	USSR	4 hr 20 min 37 sec

Equestrian

Event	Name	Country
Dressage—Individual	Sergey Filatov	USSR
Show jumping —individual	Raimondo d'Inzeo	Italy
—team		Germany
Three day event —individual	Laurie Morgan	Australia
—team		Australia

Fencing—Men

Foil—individual	Viktor Zhdanovich	USSR
—team		USSR
Epee—individual	Giuseppe Delfino	Italy
—team		Italy
Sabre—individual	Rudolph Karpati	Hungary
—team		Hungary

Fencing—Women

Event	Name	Country
Foil individual	Heidi Schmid	Germany
—team		USSR

Football

Yugoslavia

Gymnastics—Men

Combined exercises —individual	Boris Shakhlin	USSR
—team		Japan
Floor exercises	Nobuyuki Aihara	Japan
Horizontal bar	Takashi Ono	Japan
Parallel bars	Boris Shakhlin	USSR
Pommell horse	Boris Shakhlin	USSR
	Eugen Ekman	Finland
Vault	Takashi Ono	Japan
	Boris Shakhlin	USSR
Rings	Albert Azaryan	USSR

Gymnastics—Women

Event	Name	Country
Combined exercises —individual	Larissa Latynina	USSR
—team		USSR
Floor exercises	Larissa Latynina	USSR
Asymmetrical bars	Polina Astakhova	USSR
Beam	Eva Bosakova	Czechoslovakia
Vault	Margarita Nikolayeva	USSR

Hockey

Pakistan

Modern Pentathlon

Event	Name	Country
Individual	Ferenc Nemeth	Hungary
Team		Hungary

Rowing

Event	Name	Country	Result
Singe sculls	Vyacheslav Ivanov	USSR	7 min 13.96 sec
Double sculls	Vaclav Kozak, Pavel Schmidt	Czechoslovakia	6 min 47.50 sec
Coxless pairs	Valentin Boreyko, Oleg Golovanov	USSR	7 min 2.01 sec
Coxed pairs	Bernhard Knubel, Heinz Renneburg, Klaus Zerta (cox)	Germany	7 min 29.14 sec
Coxless fours		USA	6 min 26.26 sec
Coxed fours		Germany	6 min 39.12 sec
Eights		Germany	5 min 57.18 sec

Shooting

Event	Name	Country
Free pistol	Alexei Gustchin	USSR
Rapid fire pistol	William McMillan	USA
Free rifle	H. Hammerer	Austria
Small bore rifle —three positions	Vicktor Shamburkin	USSR
—prone	Peter Kohnke	Germany
Clay pigeon	Ion Dumitrescu	Romania

Swimming—Men

Event	Name	Country	Result
100 metres freestyle	John Devitt	Australia	55.2 sec
400 metres freestyle	Murray Rose	Australia	4 min 18.3 sec
1,500 metres freestyle	John Konrads	Australia	17 min 19.6 sec
200 metres breaststroke	Bill Mulliken	USA	2 min 37.4 sec
200 metres butterfly	Mike Troy	USA	2 min 12.8 sec
100 metres backstroke	David Theile	Australia	1 min 1.9 sec
4 x 200 metres freestyle relay		USA	8 min 10.2 sec
4 x 100 metres medley relay		USA	4 min 5.4 sec
Springboard diving	Gary Tobian	USA	
Highboard diving	Bob Webster	USA	

Swimming—Women

Event	Name	Country	Result
100 metres freestyle	Dawn Fraser	Australia	1 min 1.2 sec
400 metres freestyle	Chris von Saltza	USA	4 min 50.6 sec
200 metres breaststroke	Anita Lonsbrough	Great Britain	2 min 49.5 sec
100 metres butterfly	Carolyn Schuler	USA	1 min 9.5 sec
100 metres backstroke	Lynn Burke	USA	1 min 9.3 sec
4 x 100 metres freestyle relay		USA	4 min 8.9 sec
4 x 100 metres medley relay		USA	4 min 41.1 sec
Springboard diving	Ingrid Kramer	Germany	
Highboard diving	Ingrid Kramer	Germany	

Water Polo

Italy

Weightlifting

Event	Name	Country	Result
Bantamweight	Charles Vinci	USA	760 lb
Featherweight	Evgeniy Minayev	USSR	821 lb
Lightweight	Viktor Bushuyev	USSR	876 lb
Middleweight	Aleksandr Kurynov	USSR	964$\frac{1}{4}$ lb
Light-heavyweight	Ireneusz Palinski	Poland	975$\frac{1}{4}$ lb
Mid-heavyweight	Arkhadiy Vorobyev	USSR	1,014$\frac{1}{4}$ lb
Heavyweight	Yuri Vlasov	USSR	1,184$\frac{1}{2}$ lb

Wrestling

FREESTYLE

Flyweight	A. Bilek	Turkey
Bantamweight	Terrence McCann	USA
Featherweight	Mustafa Dagistanli	Turkey
Lightweight	Shelby Wilson	USA
Welterweight	Douglas Blubaugh	USA
Middleweight	Hassan Gungor	Turkey
Light-heavyweight	Ismet Atli	Turkey
Heavyweight	Wilfred Dietrich	Germany

GRAECO-ROMAN

Event	Name	Country
Flyweight	Dumitru Pirvulescu	Romania
Bantamweight	Oleg Karavayev	USSR
Featherweight	Muzanir Sille	Turkey
Lightweight	Avtandil Koridze	USSR
Welterweight	Mithat Bayrak	Turkey
Middleweight	Dimitar Dobrev	Bulgaria
Light-heavyweight	Trofim Kis	Turkey
Heavyweight	Ivan Bogdan	USSR

Yachting

Event	Name	Country
Finn	Paul Elvstrom	Denmark
Flying Dutchman	Peter Lunde, Bjorn Bergvall	Norway
Star	Timir Pinegin, Fyedor Shutkov	USSR
Dragon	Prince Constantine, Odysseus Eskidjoglou, Georges Zaimis	Greece
5.5 metres	George O'Day, James Hunt, David Smith	USA

Britain's golden girl at the Tokyo Olympics, Mary Rand. Her victory in the long jump, together with Lynn Davies's success in the men's event, brought Britain a memorable 'double'.

Tokyo Olympic Games

(1964)

In the afternoon of October 10, 1964, Yoshinoro Sakai performed an act of dual significance in the Olympic stadium in Tokyo. By running the last lap of the Olympic torch relay and lighting the flame, he formed an integral part of the opening ceremony of the Games of the XVIIIth Olympiad. But, more important perhaps, this young man, born under the shadow of the mushroom cloud of the atomic bomb dropped on Hiroshima in 1946, was a symbol of his country's acceptance of a new role in the world, and the world's acceptance of Japan.

An age had passed since 1940, when Japan was originally due to host the Games, the first of two

Olympic celebrations which were cancelled as a result of the various wars taking place around the world. Japan, as a defeated nation, had not even been invited to the London Games of 1948, but Japanese sportsmen had competed at Helsinki in 1952. And despite inclement weather ` all concerned agreed that the 1964 Games were, as the latest Games always seem to be, the biggest and the best. They were not quite the biggest, as travelling distances had cut down on the number of competitors, but the stadiums, almost all built new for the Games, made them the costliest—more than £200,000,000.

The magnificent venues certainly inspired the competitors to reach new heights, and four of them claimed their third successive gold medals: Al Oerter in athletics, Dawn Fraser in swimming, Vyacheslav Ivanov in sculling, and Hans Winkler in the equestrian show jumping team event.

Athletics—Men

Twice a winner of the discus already, Al Oerter became the second man in Olympic athletics history to win an individual event for the third time (the first being John Flanagan in the hammer in 1900, 1904, and 1908). But this time he was not only opposed by stiff opposition, including the new world record holder Ludvik Danek of Czechoslovakia, but handicapped by the effects of a dislocated neck sustained earlier in the year and a strained cartilage of the trunk incurred just before the Games opened. Oerter, however, was not going to let mere

Left, **Symbolizing Japan's rebirth as a world power, Yoshinoro Sakai lights the flame of the Tokyo Olympics.** *Below,* **American unknown Billy Mills streaks past world record holder Ron Clarke to win the 10,000 metres title.**

U.P.I.

injury stop him. He discarded his surgical collar and took cortizone to allay the pain in his body. But as Danek went into the lead in the first round of the final with 195 ft. 11½ in. and improved with his fourth throw to 198 ft. 6½ in., it looked all over for the champion. Yet with his fifth effort, Oerter sent the discus flying beyond the 200-ft. mark, to 200 ft. 1½ in., to earn him his third consecutive gold medal. Danek won the silver medal, and Oerter's team-mate, David Weill, the bronze.

The previous day, the first of the athletics events, the United States had had an unexpected triumph in the 10,000 metres. The favourite was Australia's Ron Clarke, holder of the world record for this distance and many others, and he led the field of 38 through the first few laps. By half-way he had dropped most of the others, but with a lap to go he was being pressed by Mohamed Gammoudi of Tunisia and Billy Mills of the

United States. As they moved over the track to pass lapped runners, it was first Clarke in the lead, and then Mills appeared on his shoulder. But Gammoudi suddenly burst between them, opening up a 10-yard gap with 250 yards to go, a lead that lasted until 50 yards from the tape. Clarke came up to challenge first, and then Mills stormed past to win his country's first Olympic title in the longer track events. Gammoudi held on for the silver, and Clarke had to be content with the bronze.

Clarke had even less reward in the 5,000 metres. He made much of the pace, but when it came to the last lap he could not match the fast finishing of the others and wound up ninth. The winner, after a 54.8 sec last 400 metres, was America's Bob Schul, with his team-mate, 30-year-old Bill Dellinger, third.

Matching Oerter's achievement was Peter Snell's complete domination of the 800 and 1,500 metres. A surprise winner of the 800 metres at Rome in 1960, he had since developed into one of the finest middle-distance talents ever, with world records for 800 metres, 880 yards, and one mile. In the 800 metres he came through the preliminary rounds untroubled, although in other heats George Kerr of Jamaica and Wilson Kiprugut of Kenya reduced the Olympic record to 1 min 46.1 sec. In the final Kiprugut led the eight finalists round the first lap, with Snell in seventh position. But moving with unmistakable power, the black-vested New Zealander simply ran round his opponents to take the lead with 200 metres to go and won unpressed in 1 min 45.1 sec—the second fastest time ever recorded for the distance. In the 1,500 metres he was opposed by his team-mate John Davies, whose pre-Games performances had been better than Snell's. But once again the big figure of Snell was dominant in the final, and he won by 1½ seconds from Josef Odlozil of Czechoslovakia in 3 min 38.1 sec. Davies, who had made much of the early pace, was third.

The traditional domination of the United States in the sprint events, somewhat eroded at the Rome Olympics, was reasserted in no uncertain way. Powerful Bob Hayes, who looked menacing enough in qualifying, simply destroyed his rivals in the final, which he won in a world-record-equalling 10.0 sec, after recording a wind-assisted 9.9 sec in the semi-final. Enrique Figuerola of Cuba took the silver, and erratic Harry Jerome of Canada the bronze. Hayes's amazing speed stood the United States in good stead in the 4 by 100 metres relay. Running the last leg in the final he received the baton in fifth position. Not only did he make up lost ground, but he exploded into action to win by three yards to make the team's final time 39.0 sec—a world record. Seven of the eight teams in the final broke the 1960 Olympic record.

In contrast to Hayes's almost animal power, grace and technique triumphed in the 200 metres in the person of Henry Carr. He glided round the bend to win the gold medal by 0.2 sec from his team-mate Paul Drayton in an Olympic record of 20.3 sec.

Britain's best hopes for a gold medal on the track appeared to be vested in team captain Robbie Brightwell in the 400 metres. But the opposition was too strong for him and he came home a disappointed man in fourth place, behind the American winner, 30-year-old Mike Larrabee (45.1 sec), Wendell Mottley of Trinidad and Tobago (45.2 sec), and the Pole Andrzej Badenski (45.6 sec). However Brightwell had his revenge on the place-medallists when it came to the 4 by 400 metres relay. Britain had a useful quartet entered—including Tim Graham, sixth in the 400 metres; John Cooper, silver medallist in the 400 metres hurdles; Adrian Metcalfe, Britain's joint-fastest ever man over 400 metres, and Brightwell. Larrabee, running second for America, put his team well in front and as Brightwell took over for the last leg he was third, behind Henry Carr of the United States and Mottley, Trinidad and Tobago's last man. Running with the same style that had taken him to the 200 metres gold, Henry Carr swept on to his second gold medal. Behind him Brightwell was running the race of a lifetime to oust Mottley from second place. The United States (3 min 0.7 sec), Britain (3 min 1.6 sec) and Trinidad and Tobago (3 min 1.7 sec) all beat the existing world record.

This race capped a most successful Games for Britain's men,

their best since 1908. In the marathon, behind Abebe Bikila, Basil Heatley won the silver medal. Abebe, only recently having had his appendix removed, was never in danger and won by over 4 minutes in a world best time of 2 hr 12 min 11.2 sec, and when he had finished treated the crowd to an impromptu display of limbering down exercises. Heatley, third as he entered the stadium, mortified the Japanese fans by overtaking their champion Kokichi Tsuburaya within sight of the tape. It was Britain's fourth silver medal in this Olympic event. In the 3,000 metres steeplechase Maurice Herriott picked up a well deserved silver behind the Belgian Gaston Roelants. And in the 50 kilometres walk, Paul Nihill pressed the great Italian Abdon Pamich almost all the way to claim his reward of a silver.

Britain's male heroes, however, were Ken Matthews and Lynn Davies. Matthews, who had col-

Europeans. In the high jump the world record holder Valeriy Brumel, second at the Rome Olympics, improved to take the gold medal with an Olympic record of 7 ft. 1¾ in., the same height as runner-up John Thomas of the United States. But Brumel was a safe winner on the fewer failures rule. In the pole vault the supremacy of the United States was sorely put to the test during a competition which lasted 13 hours and finished under floodlights. The lone American during the final stages of the contest was Fred Hansen. He had passed at 16 ft. 6¾ in., a height cleared first time by Germany's Wolfgang Reinhardt, so Hansen, a dental student from Texas, had to clear 16 ft. 8¾ in. to win. This he did at his third attempt, and in a tense atmosphere he watched Reinhardt fail. America's run of wins, unbroken since 1896, was safe, although Germans were placed second, third, and fourth.

The first eight places in the triple jump were filled by Europeans. The winner, almost inevitably, was the incomparable Pole Jozef Schmidt, the champion in Rome. He went into the lead in the second round with 54 ft. 7½ in., and with his final effort reached out to 55 ft. 3½ in. Russians were second and third, while Britain's Fred Alsop was fourth.

The throwing events were equally divided between the Old World and the New. American giants Dallas Long and Randy Matson were first and second in the shot, with veteran Parry O'Brien relegated to fourth place behind Vilmos Varju of Hungary. And Oerter took the discus gold. The hammer final was held in the rain, and was a complete triumph for the Eastern Europeans. The gold medallist was the 31-year-old Russian Romuald Klim, who threw over 2 feet farther than his perennial rival Gyula Zsivotsky of Hungary (228 ft. 10½ in. to

226 ft. 8 in.). Finland's Pauli Nevala revived memories of his country's greatness by winning the javelin. Once again, this event was hampered by rain, which accounted for his relatively modest winning distance of 271 ft. 2½ in.

Athletics—Women

American women won only two events in track and field—the sprints—and once again they had their long-striding negro girls to thank. In the 100 metres Wyomia Tyus beat her team-mate Edith McGuire by 0.2 sec to take the gold medal, with Poland's Ewa Klobukowska in third place. Miss McGuire took the 200 metres title in 23.0 sec, only 0.1 sec away from the world record. Miss Klobukowska (later to have world records but not her Olympic medals taken away from her after failing a 'sex test') and Irene Kirszenstein, the 200 metres silver medallist, were both members of Poland's winning 4 by 100 metres relay team who set a world record of 43.6 sec.

There was a new event on the women's programme, the 400 metres, which provided Australia's 'golden girl' of the 1956 Olympics, Betty Cuthbert, with an opportunity to win her fourth Olympic gold. Miss Cuthbert, starting very fast and taking a breather down the back straight, made no mistake in beating Britain's Ann Packer by 0.2 sec in 52.0 sec. Miss Packer had been a pre-Games favourite for this event, but she had a second chance in the 800 metres, in which she had not had much experience. But running a more relaxed race, the British girl used her speed well to come through in the final straight to take a surprise gold medal and set an even more surprising world record of 2 min 1.1 sec, which was not beaten until 1968.

Miss Packer's gold medal was, in fact, Britain's second ever women's athletics title. The first had come only six days previously—in the long jump. And the winner of this event, in another world record, was Mary Rand. As Mary Bignal in 1960, she had had the mortifying experience of failing to qualify for the final six, but she was now a far more mature athlete. In the qualifying round this time Mrs Rand cleared an Olympic record of 21 ft. 4½ in., and in the final she improved to the world record distance of 22 ft. 2¼ in. Mrs Rand collected a full set of Olympic medals at these games. She was runner-up to Russia's Irina Press in the pentathlon although she put up better performances than Miss Press in four of the five events. And her bronze came in the 4 by 100 metres relay.

Irina Press's sister, Tamara, was an impressive winner of the shot and discus gold medals, improving on her Rome performances in both events. But

1 **Veteran Mike Larrabee (709) pips Wendell Mottley (613) for the 400 metres gold, as Britain's Robbie Brightwell (153) comes home fourth.**
2 **Master of the marathon Abebe Bikila was head and shoulders above his rivals, winning for the second time in a world's best performance.**
3 **Another champion who dominated his opponents was Belgium's Gaston Roelants in the 3,000 metres steeplechase.**
4 **A gripping struggle in the 50 kilometres walk resulted in a win for Italy's Abdon Pamich (left) over Britain's Paul Nihill. The margin of victory was a mere 18.8 sec in over 4 hours walking.**
5 **Familiar conditions of rain and wind hampered Welsh long jumper Lynn Davies less than the redoubtable Ter-Ovanesyan and Boston as he soared to win Britain's first field event gold medal since 1908.**

lapsed while in the lead in the 20 kilometres walk at Rome four years before, made no mistakes this time in adding the Olympic gold medal to his European championship of 1962 by a margin of over 1½ minutes. But the man who captured the imagination of the British public was long-jumper Lynn Davies. Faced by men whose best performances were as much as a foot longer than his, he responded better than anyone else to the challenge of competing in rainy and windy conditions. With his penultimate effort in the final he made the best of a lull in the wind to reach 26 ft. 5¾ in. and claim Britain's first Olympic field event gold medal since 1908, with America's world record holder and 1960 Olympic champion Ralph Boston relegated to second place and Russia's European champion Igor Ter-Ovanesyan third.

The medals in the other jumping events also went mostly to

69

the javelin was a surprise win for Mihaela Penes of Romania. At 17 years and 2 months she became the youngest Olympic athletics champion ever. The high jump, in contrast, was a complete triumph for 27-year-old Iolanda Balas, another Romanian, whose winning height of 6 ft. 2¾ in. was almost 4 inches better than that of the runner-up, Michele Brown of Australia.

Swimming
The superb, brand new swimming pool brought out the best in the competitors. World records were set in all but 2 of the 10 men's races, and 4 of the 8 women's. But overshadowing even this aggregate of achievement were the feats of Dawn Fraser and Don Schollander.

Australia's Miss Fraser became the first woman in any Olympic sport to win three successive gold medals in the same event—in her case the 100 metres freestyle which she had previously won at Melbourne in 1956 and Rome in 1960. America's Don Schollander became the first swimmer to win four gold medals at the same Games, in the 100 and 400 metres freestyle and both freestyle relays. He took the 100 metres freestyle by 0.1 sec from Britain's Bobby McGregor, and in the longer event he swam both 200 metres at almost even pace and broke the world record with 4 min 12.2 sec, finishing 2.7 sec ahead of the East German Frank Wiegand, who swam for the combined German team.

The United States took 13 of the 18 swimming titles, but Australians won 3 of the 6 individual men's races. Bob Windle (1,500 metres freestyle), Ian O'Brien (200 metres breaststroke), and Kevin Berry (200 metres butterfly) saved Australia from a total rout, and Berry and O'Brien also set world records in winning.

The only European to win a gold medal was Galina Prosumenschikova from Moscow, who won Russia's first Olympic swimming gold, by leading the 200 metres breaststroke finalists home with a world record. And East Germany's Ingrid Engel-Kramer successfully defended her springboard diving title (Europe's only success in this field), but lost the highboard by 1.35 points to America's Lesley Bush.

In the water polo, Hungary won the gold medals for the third time in four games, but this time their victory came only as a result of their having a superior goal average to Yugoslavia. Completing a customary European sweep of the medals, the USSR were third.

Other Sports
Dominating the rowing on the Toda course, some 15 miles from Tokyo, was the Russian sculler Vyacheslav Ivanov. Champion in 1956 and 1960, he caused a sen-

1 Wyomia Tyus (217) leads the way in the 100 metres, but Ewa Klobukowska (166) had revenge in the relay, 2, in which she anchored Poland to victory with the USA second.
3 Mary Rand won a rare set of gold, silver, and bronze medals at the Tokyo Games.
4 Long-legged Iolanda Balas won the high jump by a 3¾-in. margin to win one of Romania's two athletics golds.
5 Triple gold medallist Dawn Fraser (left) and challenger Sharon Stouder pose after the 100 metres freestyle final.

sation in the heats by being beaten by America's Don Spero. But he fought back to win his repechage easily, and then in the final he finished nearly 4 seconds ahead of Germany's Achim Hill (as he had also done in 1960) to take his third straight gold medal. In the eights, the classic rowing event, Germany's crew, defending the title won by Ratzeburg at Rome, were beaten in a storming finish by America's Vesper Boat Club. Another man who won a third

gold medal was Hans Winkler, in Germany's grand prix show jumping team. In 1956 (when he also won the individual title) and 1960, Winkler had ridden Halla, but this time his gold medal was won on a new horse, Fidelitas. Even Winkler's achievement was overshadowed by that of the French veteran, Pierre d'Oriola. Olympic show jumping champion in 1952, he found a touch of genius to produce a clear round when it really mattered to take a second gold medal after a 12-year gap and also take his team into second place.

The Tokyo Olympics saw judo assume a place in the Olympic programme. It was suited to the Games not only because of the fact that Japan gave this sport to the world, but also because the sporting conventions of this combat make it ideal for the Olympic Games. And of course the Japanese were hoping that their champions would win them justly deserved gold medals. Although the home team won gold medals in the three restricted categories, they failed in their real objective—

to beat the giant Dutch world **5** champion Anton Geesink. The Japanese hope, Kaminaga, had been drawn against Geesink in the preliminaries, and lost. But he fought his way through four more eliminations to enter the final. There, after 9 min 22 sec, the Japanese was pinned to the mat and Geesink took the gold medal to add to the world title he had won in 1961—again at Japan's expense.

But the Japanese enjoyed their share of success in, for them, other traditionally successful sports. In gymnastics, led by Yukio Endo, the Japanese won five out of the eight events—the team, combined exercises and parallel bars (Endo), rings (Takuji Hayata), and vault (Haruhiro Yamashita). Pushing the Japanese were the Russians, led by their veteran champion Boris Shakhlin who won the horizontal bar. The women's events were divided between the Russian girls and Czechoslovakia's Vera Caslavska. Vera won golds in the combined exercises, vault, and beam to be the Games outstanding individual

Central Press

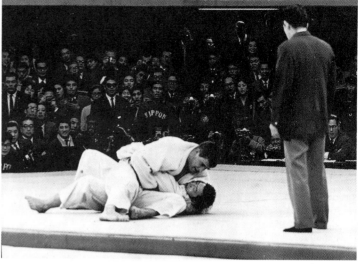

Central Press

1 Pierre d'Oriola, champion in 1952, claimed his second individual show jumping gold medal and helped the French to win their first ever team medals—silvers—behind a German squad which included Hans Winkler, who was winning his third successive gold in the competition.

2 Giant Dutchman Anton Geesink mortified the Japanese by beating their judo champion Akio Kaminaga to win the unlimited category gold.
3 A new Olympic sport, volleyball, resulted in the USSR winning the men's competition and the highly trained Japanese the women's.

Central Press

gymnast, but Russia won the team event for the fourth consecutive time.

In the wrestling events Japan's Osamu Watanbe won his 186th consecutive victory to take the freestyle featherweight title. Japan won four other gold medals, two freestyle and two Graeco-Roman, to emerge as the world's top wrestling nation.

For controversy, the boxing events took first prize. Two boxers were suspended (one for life) for assaulting, or trying to assault, referees who—they thought—did not come up to their own standards of judging. Another man sat in his corner for 51 minutes after being disqualified and would not be moved. In national terms, Poland and the USSR tied with three gold medals each. America's one gold medal winner was rather more significant: six years later Joe Frazier won the world's professional heavyweight title as well.

In the team sports the *status quo* prevailed. The United States once again went through the basketball tournament without losing a game, and Russia were second for the fourth consecutive Olympics, while Brazil were third, as they had been in Rome. In hockey, India regained the title they had lost in Rome, beating Pakistan 1-0 in the final. In Rome, Pakistan had won 1-0. Hungary, champions in 1952 won their second Olympic soccer title in grand style, with their ace forward Ferenc Bene scoring 12 goals to head the list of goalscorers. Hungary beat Czechoslovakia 2-1 in the final, and a combined Germany beat the United Arab Republic 3-1 in the play-off for third place.

Taking all sport into consideration, the USSR headed the medal table with 30 golds, 31 silver, and 35 bronze—a total of 96. The United States were relegated to second place with 90—no fewer than 37 of which had come in swimming. But as 41 countries won a medal of one sort or another, perhaps it was not such a 'two-horse race' after all.

TOKYO OLYMPIC GAMES, 1964 Gold Medallists

Athletics—Men			
100 metres	Bob Hayes	USA	10.0 sec
200 metres	Henry Carr	USA	20.3 sec
400 metres	Mike Larrabee	USA	45.1 sec
800 metres	Peter Snell	New Zealand	1 min 45.1 sec
1,500 metres	Peter Snell	New Zealand	3 min 38.1 sec
5,000 metres	Bob Schul	USA	13 min 48.8 sec
10,000 metres	Billy Mills	USA	28 min 24.4 sec
Marathon	Abebe Bikila	Ethiopia	2 hr 12 min 11.2 sec
4 x 100 metres relay		USA	39.0 sec
4 x 400 metres relay		USA	3 min 0.7 sec
110 metres hurdles	Hayes Jones	USA	13.6 sec
400 metres hurdles	Warren Cawley	USA	49.6 sec
3,000 metres steeplechase	Gaston Roelants	Belgium	8 min 30.8 sec
20 kilometres walk	Ken Matthews	Great Britain	1 hr 29 min 34.0 sec
50 kilometres walk	Abdon Pamich	Italy	4 hr 11 min 12.4 sec
High jump	Valeriy Brumel	USSR	7 ft $1\frac{3}{4}$ in
Pole vault	Fred Hansen	USA	16 ft $8\frac{3}{4}$ in
Long jump	Lynn Davies	Great Britain	26 ft $5\frac{3}{4}$ in
Triple jump	Jozef Schmidt	Poland	55 ft $3\frac{1}{2}$ in
Shot	Dallas Long	USA	66 ft $8\frac{1}{2}$ in
Discus	Al Oerter	USA	200 ft $1\frac{1}{2}$ in
Hammer	Romuald Klim	USSR	228 ft $10\frac{1}{2}$ in
Javelin	Pauli Nevala	Finland	271 ft $2\frac{1}{2}$ in
Decathlon	Willi Holdorf	Germany	7,887 pts
Athletics—Women			
100 metres	Wyomia Tyus	USA	11.4 sec
200 metres	Edith McGuire	USA	23.0 sec
400 metres	Betty Cuthbert	Australia	52.0 sec
800 metres	Ann Packer	Great Britain	2 min 1.1 sec
4 x 100 metres relay		Poland	43.6 sec
80 metres hurdles	Karin Balzer	Germany	10.5 sec
High jump	Iolanda Balas	Romania	6 ft $2\frac{3}{4}$ in
Long jump	Mary Rand	Great Britain	22 ft $2\frac{1}{4}$ in
Shot	Tamara Press	USSR	59 ft 6 in
Discus	Tamara Press	USSR	187 ft $10\frac{1}{2}$ in
Javelin	Mihaela Penes	Romania	198 ft $7\frac{1}{2}$ in
Pentathlon	Irina Press	USSR	5,246 pts
Basketball		USA	
Boxing			
Flyweight	Fernando Otzori	Italy	
Bantamweight	Takao Sakurai	Japan	
Featherweight	Stanislav Stepashkin	USSR	
Lightweight	Jozef Grudzien	Poland	
Light-welterweight	Jerzy Kulej	Poland	
Welterweight	Marian Kasprzyk	Poland	
Light-middleweight	Boris Lagutin	USSR	
Middleweight	Valeriy Popenchenko	USSR	
Light-heavyweight	Cosimo Pinto	Italy	
Heavyweight	Joe Frazier	USA	
Canoeing			
1,000 metres—Men			
Kayak singles	Rolf Peterson	Sweden	3 min 57.13 sec
Kayak pairs	Sven Sjodelius, Gunnar Utterberg	Sweden	3 min 38.54 sec
Kayak fours		USSR	3 min 14.67 sec
Canadian singles	Jurgen Eschert	Germany	4 min 35.14 sec
Canadian pairs	Andrei Khimich, Stepan Oschepkov	USSR	4 min 4.65 sec
500 metres—Women			
Kayak singles	Ludmilla Khvedosink	USSR	2 min 12.87 sec
Kayak pairs	Roswitha Esser, Annemie Zimmermann	Germany	1 min 56.95 sec
Cycling			
1,000 metres sprint	Giovanni Pettenella	Italy	
1,000 metres time trial	Patrick Sercu	Belgium	1 min 9.59 sec
2,000 metres tandem	Sergio Bianchetto, Angelo Damanio	Italy	
4,000 metres pursuit	Jiri Daler	Czechoslovakia	5 min 4.75 sec
4,000 metres team pursuit		Germany	4 min 35.67 sec
Road team time trial (109.89 km)		Netherlands	2 hr 26 min 31.19 sec
Road race (194.83 km)	Mario Zanin	Italy	4 hr 39 min 51.63 sec
Equestrian			
Dressage—individual	Henri Chammartin	Switzerland	
—team		Germany	
Show jumping—individual	Pierre d'Oriola	France	
—team		Germany	
Three day event —individual	Mauro Checcoli	Italy	
—team		Italy	
Fencing—Men			
Foil —individual	Egon Franke	Poland	
—team		USSR	
Epee —individual	Grigory Kriss	USSR	
—team		Hungary	
Sabre —individual	Tibor Pezsa	Hungary	
—team		USSR	
Fencing—Women			
Foil —individual	Ildko Rejto	Hungary	
—team		Hungary	
Gymnastics—Men			
Combined exercises —individual	Yukio Endo	Japan	
—team		Japan	
Floor exercises	Franco Menicelli	Italy	
Horizontal bar	Boris Shakhlin	USSR	
Parallel bars	Yukio Endo	Japan	
Pommell horse	Miroslav Cerar	Yugoslavia	
Vault	Haruhiro Yamashita	Japan	
Rings	Takuji Hayata	Japan	
Gymnastics—Women			
Combined exercises —individual	Vera Caslavska	Czechoslovakia	
—team		USSR	
Floor exercises	Larissa Latynina	USSR	
Asymmetrical bars	Polina Astakhova	USSR	
Beam	Vera Caslavska	Czechoslovakia	
Vault	Vera Caslavska	Czechoslovakia	
Hockey		India	
Judo			
Lightweight	Takehide Nakatani	Japan	
Middleweight	Isao Okanao	Japan	
Heavyweight	Isao Inokuma	Japan	
Open division	Anton Geesink	Netherlands	
Modern Pentathlon			
Individual	Ferenc Toerek	Hungary	
Team		USSR	
Rowing			
Single sculls	Vyacheslav Ivanov	USSR	8 min 22.51 sec
Double sculls	Oleg Tyurin, Boris Dubrovsky	USSR	7 min 10.66 sec
Coxless pairs	George Hungerford, Roger Jackson	Canada	7 min 32.94 sec
Coxed pairs	Edward Ferry, Conn Findlay, Kent Mitchell (cox)	USA	8 min 21.33 sec
Coxless fours		Denmark	6 min 59.30 sec
Coxed fours		Germany	7 min 0.44 sec
Eights		USA	6 min 18.23 sec
Shooting			
Small bore rifle —three positions	Lones Wigger	USA	
—prone	Laszlo Hammerl		
Free pistol	Vaino Markkanen	Finland	
Free rifle	Gary Anderson	USA	
Rapid fire pistol	Pentti Linnosvuop	Finland	
Clay pigeon	Ennio Mattarelli	Italy	
Soccer		Hungary	
Swimming—Men			
100 metres freestyle	Don Schollander	USA	53.4 sec
400 metres freestyle	Don Schollander	USA	4 min 12.2 sec
1,500 metres freestyle	Bob Windle	Australia	17 min 1.7 sec
200 metres breaststroke	Ian O'Brien	Australia	2 min 27.8 sec
200 metres butterfly	Kevin Berry	Australia	2 min 6.6 sec
200 metres backstroke	Jed Graef	USA	2 min 10.3 sec
400 metres individual medley	Dick Roth	USA	4 min 45.4 sec
4 x 100 metres freestyle relay		USA	3 min 33.2 sec
4 x 200 metres freestyle relay		USA	7 min 52.1 sec
4 x 100 metres medley relay		USA	3 min 58.4 sec
Springboard diving	Ken Sitzberger	USA	
Highboard diving	Bob Webster	USA	
Swimming—Women			
100 metres freestyle	Dawn Fraser	Australia	59.5 sec
400 metres freestyle	Ginny Duenkel	USA	4 min 43.3 sec
200 metres breaststroke	Galina Prozumenschikova	USSR	2 min 46.4 sec
100 metres butterfly	Sharon Stouder	USA	1 min 4.7 sec
100 metres backstroke	Cathie Ferguson	USA	1 min 7.7 sec
400 metres individual medley	Donna de Varona	USA	5 min 18.7 sec
4 x 100 metres freestyle relay		USA	4 min 3.8 sec
4 x 100 metres medley relay		USA	4 min 33.9 sec
Springboard diving	Ingrid Engel-Kramer	Germany	
Highboard diving	Lesley Bush	USA	
Volleyball—Men		USSR	
Volleyball—Women		Japan	
Water Polo		Hungary	
Weightlifting			
Bantamweight	Alexey Vakhonin	USSR	$787\frac{3}{4}$ lb
Featherweight	Yoshinobu Miyake	Japan	876 lb
Lightweight	Waldemar Baszanowski	Poland	$953\frac{1}{4}$ lb
Middleweight	Hans Zdrazila	Czechoslovakia	$980\frac{3}{4}$ lb
Light-heavyweight	Rudolf Plyukeider	USSR	1,046 lb
Mid-heavyweight	Vladimir Golovanov	USSR	$1,074\frac{1}{2}$ lb
Heavyweight	Leonid Zhabotinsky	USSR	1,262 lb
Wrestling			
Freestyle			
Flyweight	Yoshikatsu Yoshida	Japan	
Bantamweight	Yojiro Uetake	Japan	
Featherweight	Osamu Watanabe	Japan	
Lightweight	Enio Dimor	Bulgaria	
Welterweight	Ismail Ogan	Turkey	
Middleweight	Prodan Gardjer	Bulgaria	
Light-heavyweight	Alexandr Medved	USSR	
Heavyweight	Alexandr Wanitsky	USSR	
Graeco-Roman			
Flyweight	Tsutomu Hanahara	Japan	
Bantamweight	Masamitsu Ichiguchi	Japan	
Featherweight	Imre Polyak	Hungary	
Lightweight	Kazim Ayvaz	Turkey	
Welterweight	Anatoly Koleslav	USSR	
Middleweight	Branislav Simic	Yugoslavia	
Light-heavyweight	Boyan Alexandrov	Bulgaria	
Heavyweight	Istvan Kozma	Hungary	
Yachting			
Finn	Willi Kuhweide	Germany	
Star	D. Knowles, C. Cook	Bahamas	
Flying Dutchman	Helman Pederson, E. Wells	New Zealand	
5.5 metres		Australia	
Dragon		Denmark	

One of the truly outstanding sports photos captures the power and determination that won America's Willie Davenport his gold medal in the 110 metres hurdles at Mexico City.

Mexico City Olympic Games (1968)

Politics, sex, commercialism . . . and sport—these four topics dominated the Games of the XIXth Olympiad held in Mexico City in October 1968, the most controversial Olympics ever.

The most argued-about decision was to hold the Games in Mexico City at all. The capital of Mexico is situated some 7,347 feet above sea level, a height at which the air is so rarefied that a man normally living at sea level may take more than a month to become used simply to living there. For an athlete, the time required to acclimatize for events lasting more than one and a half minutes is longer than a month.

The decision to award the Games to Mexico City was made at the 1963 meeting of the IOC in Baden-Baden. It excited no special comment at first and the IOC must have thought it a progressive step to hold the Games in one of the more developed Latin-American countries. But in 1964, Onni Niskanen, the Swedish coach to Abebe Bikila, brought the issue to a head when he stated quite bluntly: 'There will be those who will die.'

The altitude issue was quite straightforward. Lowland athletes in any endurance event would have to get used to competing in a rarified atmosphere. Some athletes, such as Mexicans, Kenyans, and Ethiopians, already lived in such conditions. For the rest of the

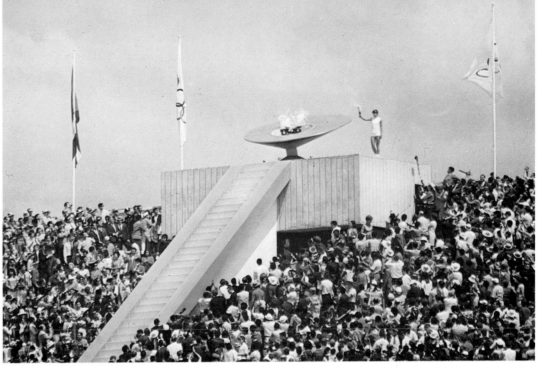

world there was the choice between competing at a grave disadvantage or breaking the IOC's rule that no competitor could train at high altitudes for more than four weeks in the three months preceding the Games. The French built a high-altitude sports centre at Font Romeu in the Pyrenees. The town of South Lake Tahoe built the United States team a training centre at a height of 6,000 feet in Nevada, where the team trained as part of the 'South Lake Tahoe United States Olympic Medical and Testing Program'.

In addition to the altitude controversy, there was another cloud on the Olympic scene—the world of power politics. In August 1968, the invasion of Czechoslo-

Enriqueta Basilio holds the Olympic torch aloft after igniting the flame—the first woman in the history of the Olympic Games to do so.

vakia by the armies of the Warsaw Pact countries to suppress the liberal Dubcek regime cast a dark shadow over the Games.

The IOC was itself very concerned with the increasing commercialization of the Olympic movement. In Mexico, the markings on running shoes was their chief cause for concern, mainly because some athletes were known to wear the distinctively marked shoes of two German companies only if they were paid to do so. But there was nothing the IAAF or the

IOC could do about it.

Even the internal conditions in Mexico did not augur well. Violent riots broke out before the Games opened, and were ruthlessly repressed. The state of public order made it uncertain that the Games would take place at all. But eventually, and in time for the Olympics to begin, Mexico City was quiet again.

The Games were formally opened on October 12, with troops arranged in force outside the new Olympic Stadium. Diaz Ordaz, the Mexican President, and IOC president Avery Brundage made the speeches, and for the first time, a woman—Enriqueta Basilio, who ran for Mexico in the 400 metres—lit the Olympic flame.

Athletics—Men

By tradition, the men's 10,000 metres was held as a final on the first day of the athletics events, and the fears of the world's lowland distance runners were confirmed in this event. The winner's time— 29 min 27.4 sec—was 1 min 48 sec slower than Ron Clarke's world record, and a slow time for even the most tactical of races. The early pace was easy, sensibly so at this altitude, but it would have been funereal at sea level. And so it continued for the first 8,400 metres. Then, with four laps to go, the pace suddenly hotted up. Seven men broke away—Kenya's Naftali Temu and Kipchoge Keino, Australia's Ron Clarke, Tunisia's Mohamed Gammoudi, the hero of the Mexico crowd Juan Martinez, Russia's Nikolai Sviridov, and Mamo Wolde of Ethiopia. Of these, only Ron Clarke was not born or domiciled at a high altitude but he had lived for some time at Font Romeu. Wolde, Temu, Keino, and Martinez actually live at altitude, and Gammoudi and Sviridov were known to have trained for months in the highlands.

Clarke himself was eventually dropped by the other six, and Keino dropped out, suffering from a stomach complaint. With only two laps left Temu and Wolde accelerated, dragging Gammoudi with them, Wolde leading this sudden rush because of his lack of a finishing sprint. But Temu held on and sprinted ahead in the straight to win by 0.6 sec from Wolde, with a well-beaten Gammoudi just holding off Martinez for third place. It was a gripping struggle between great runners, none of whom was prepared to let up for a moment, and yet it lost much of its meaning because of the effects of the altitude. Ron Clarke collapsed after finishing 6th and was given oxygen by the Australian team doctor. Jurgen Haase, the European champion, finished 15th. Even Russia's Leonid Mikityenko, the fifth fastest man in the world in 1968, was relegated to 17th position. Their times were, of course, much slower than their best performances at a lower altitude. The only lowlander who was at all prominent was Britain's Ron Hill, who had for a moment led the field to show that he was not in Mexico just for a ride, and he finished 7th.

It was the same story in the 5,000 metres and the steeplechase. The first four men in the 5,000 metres—Gammoudi, Keino, Temu, and Martinez—and the first two in the steeplechase— Amos Biwott and Benjamin Kogo (both of Kenya)—were altitude men. The 5,000 metres was won by Gammoudi from Keino in a desperate sprint finish. Gammoudi's last 400-metre lap took him only 54.8 sec, an indication of the overall slowness of the race. Eight of the first nine places were filled by men with experience of high altitudes, gained either at home or in

special training camps.

In the 3,000 metres steeplechase, runners whose performances before the Games would have made them hot favourites for medals were unceremoniously eliminated in the heats, while less experienced — and slower — 'highlanders' qualified. The Tokyo silver medallist, Britain's Maurice Herriott, was put out with a heat time of 9 min 33.0 sec, over a minute slower than his best sea-level time. And the final was perhaps one of the most bizarre Olympic races ever. The Kenyan team included a peculiar runner named Amos Biwott. He had the most rudimentary style of hurdling, and would make every effort to avoid putting his feet in the water jump. He had little idea of tactics, and with a lap to go was 30 yards behind the leaders. As his team-mate Ben Kogo, America's George Young,

Australia's Kerry O'Brien, the defending champion from Belgium, Gaston Roelants, and Russia's Viktor Kudinskiy battled for the major prizes—or so they thought—Biwott suddenly tore past them all to win by five yards in 8 min 51.0 sec.

The marked advantages of the highlanders were not so apparent in the other endurance events on the track and road. True, Mamo Wolde won the marathon, but he was followed by other men without vast altitude experience. Second to Wolde was Kenji Kimihara of Japan, 3rd New Zealand's Mike Ryan, 4th Ismail Akcay of Turkey, 5th Britain's Bill Adcocks, and 6th Merawi Gebru of Ethiopia. But what of the great Abebe Bikila, who had threatened to win his third Olympic marathon? He had been suffering from a leg injury and in fact retired after 17 of the

42 kilometres. In the walks, the 'highland' countries had never been a force to be reckoned with, and their only medal came through José Padraza of Mexico in the 20 kilometres. He entered the stadium third, close behind two Russians— Vladimir Golubnichiy and Nikolai Smaga. Experienced commentators were unanimous in their view that if ever a man ran in a walking race, Pedraza did on the last hectic lap of the Olympic stadium. First he cut down Smaga in the back straight, and then he went after Golubnichiy. But the experienced

Mexico's Juan Martinez leads the 10,000 metres field. Ron Clarke is second, with the eventual winner Naftali Temu of Kenya (No. 575) on his shoulder. 'High-altitude men' dominated the 5,000 and 10,000 metres events.

Rex Features

76

Britain's only athletics gold at Mexico City came in the 400 metres hurdles, when David Hemery, here working out over the high hurdles, simply annihilated his opposition to win in a world record 48.1 sec, 0.7 sec faster than the previous record.

Kenya's Kipchoge Keino, gold medallist in the Mexico City 1,500 metres and the torch-bearer of black Africa's dramatic entry on to the sports fields of the world.

Russian held him off to claim his second Olympic title in this event. The 50 kilometres was won, as expected, by East Germany's Christoph Hohne—by over 10 minutes from Hungary's Antal Kiss.

In the 1,500 metres, the front-running tactics of Kenya's Kip Keino and the finishing burst of world record holder Jim Ryun were expected to produce the Games' greatest race. Ryun had been suffering from glandular fever early in the year, but he expected to be able to win with a time in the region of 3 min 38 sec. He did not reckon with the form of Keino, who ran one of his best races despite having already run in the 10,000 and 5,000 metres. Keino's team-mate Ben Jipcho set a fast early pace, passing 400 metres in 56.0 sec, and Keino then took over to pass 800 metres in 1 min 55.3 sec, a fast pace even at sea level. Keino continued to pour on the pressure and was well ahead at 1,200 metres. Ryun then, at last, began to move, but despite his last 400 metres in 55.7 sec was never a danger to the brave Kenyan who eventually beat him by about 20 yards. Here was a case of the highland runner beating the sea level man entirely on merits. Keino's time—3 min 34.9 sec—was the second fastest ever.

A Kenyan also took second place in the 800 metres, which was the real meeting point between the highland and lowland runner. The winner here was Australia's Ralph Doubell, and he equalled the world record of 1 min 44.3 sec in beating Kenya's Wilson Kiprugut by 0.2 sec.

If the distance runners suffered from the altitude, whatever their origin, the sprinters came into their own in the thin air. And the United States, whose only middle- and long-distance honours had been bronzes in the 800 metres and 50-kilometre walk, swept up 9 of the 11 medals open to them in the 100, 200, and 400 metres, and the two relays. Jim Hines equalled the world record of 9.9 sec in the 100 metres, and Lee Evans chopped 0.3 sec off the world record in the 400 metres. American quartets set new world marks in both relays, and averaged just over 44 sec apiece in the 4 by 400 metres.

The talking point of the sprints was the victory of Tommie Smith in the 200 metres. He won easily in 19.8 sec—a world record—from Australia's Peter Norman and his fellow-American Negro John Carlos. It was a beautiful run, with no inhibitions, and once the long-legged Smith had got into his stride he was clearly the only man in the race. But the aftermath of the race was the victory ceremony, which is the most notorious incident of its kind in the history of the Games. Smith and Carlos walked to the rostrum clad in official United States tracksuits, embellished with

a badge of the Olympic Project for Human Rights. Smith wore a black leather glove on his right hand, Carlos one on his left. Both carried an easily identified running shoe. They received their medals with dignity from Lord Burghley, and turned to face the flags of their country as the national anthem was played. Then they raised their gloved hands in the 'black power' salute and bowed their heads. The crowd was taken aback, and some elements began booing and whistling. Smith explained his motive simply and succinctly: it was only through running that he could approach the prestige of any white American. 'If I win I am an American, not a black American. But if I did something bad then they would say a Negro.' Both Smith and Carlos were sent home.

The United States retained their grip on the high hurdles title, which American athletes had won in 13 of the 15 previous Games. Willie Davenport more than made up for his disappointing showing in the 1964 Games (when eliminated in his semi-final) by winning in an Olympic record of 13.3 sec. The 400 metres hurdles title was expected to go to the United States, where it had remained since 1936. But the Americans had played host to Britain's Dave Hemery at Boston University since 1964, and during his stay there he had matured from being a fair 110 metres hurdler to a good 400 metres man —just how good had to be put to the test. And although the Americans had been prominent in the preliminary rounds, British observers could see Hemery holding himself back. In the final, Hemery appeared to be in the lead from the first barrier onwards, and won by seven yards in a world and Olympic record of 48.1 sec, 0.7 sec faster than Geoff Vanderstock's world record set in the United States trials at Lake Tahoe. Second in 49.0 sec, was West Germany's Gerhard Hennige, and third—in the same time—Britain's John Sherwood.

In the tense, but less immediate, world of the field events some remarkable happenings were taking place, including perhaps the most amazing single performance in the history of athletics. In the long jump, Bob Beamon, with his first effort—and the first 'legal' jump of the final rounds—soared to a world record of 29 ft. 2½ in., 21 inches farther than the previous best. It killed the event as a competition, but provided a talking point for years to come. And if the triple jump record was not improved by such a vast margin, the fact that no fewer than five improvements were made in the world mark is a testimony to the keen competition and the helpful effects of the thin air. Giuseppe Gentile of Italy started the ball rolling with the first world mark—56 ft. 1¼ in.— in the qualifying rounds. And in

the final the next day, his first jump was another world record— 56 ft. 6 in. It was short-lived, however, as in the third round Viktor Saneyev of the USSR added a centimetre to Gentile's mark (56 ft. 6¼ in.). The title looked set to go to Brazil after the fifth round, in which Nelson Prudencio reached 56 ft. 8 in. Yet Saneyev reacted to the Brazilian's effort with a hop, step, and jump of 57 ft. 0¾ in. with his final jump to snatch the gold.

If no records fell in the pole vault, this did not stop the event being one of the most exciting ever held, with the United States desperately close to losing their record of having won every Olympic pole vault. The first three men, Bob Seagren (United States), Claus Schiprowski (West Germany) and Wolfgang Nordwig (East Germany), tied, each with a clearance of 17 ft. 8½ in. They were placed in that order on the 'count-back' rule. The competition lasted 7½ hours, and was continually interrupted by victory ceremonies, including that of the 200 metres.

For sheer individualism, the winner of the high jump, Dick Fosbury of the United States, took the prize. Using his personal back lay-out style, he would run flat out up to the bar, turn onto his back, and land on his shoulders on the inflated mattress in the pit. He delighted the capacity crowd with his display, and emerged a clear winner: he was the only man to jump 2.24 metres (7 ft. 4¼ in.).

The most acclaimed feat in the throwing events was the victory of Al Oerter in the discus.

Champion three times before—in 1956, 1960, and 1964—this remarkable man, whose best throw before the Games in 1968 was 205 ft. 10 in.—far inferior to his compatriot Jay Silvester's world record of 224 ft. 5 in.—unleashed his best ever throw of 212 ft. 6½ in. to win the title from men who before the Games had been his superiors.

Silvester was completely unnerved by Oerter's competitiveness, and finished fifth with 202 ft. 8 in., and nobody else could rival the veteran Long Islander.

Randy Matson duly added the Mexico City gold to his Tokyo silver in the shot. And in the hammer, Gyula Zsivotsky brought his career to a wonderful climax by adding a gold to the silvers he had won in Rome and Tokyo. After a ding-dong battle with his perennial rival Romuald Klim, Zsivotsky reached his winning distance of 240 ft. 8 in. in the fifth round to win by 3 inches.

Janis Lusis, Russia's world record holder, added the Olympic javelin gold to his two European championships with a winning effort of 295 ft. 7 in. In the decathlon, Bill Toomey of the United States beat West Germany's Hans Joachim Walde by 82 points with a total score of 8,193 pts. Toomey dominated the first day's events— his 400 metres of 45.6 sec earned him 1,021 pts—to lead at the halfway stage by 4,499 pts to 4,384 over East Germany's Joachim Kirst, and held on to his advantage to beat the fast-finishing Walde by a relatively scant margin.

MEXICO CITY OLYMPIC GAMES, 1968 Gold Medallists—Athletics			
Men			
100 metres	Jim Hines	USA	9.9 sec
200 metres	Tommie Smith	USA	19.8 sec
400 metres	Lee Evans	USA	43.8 sec
800 metres	Ralph Doubell	Australia	1 min 44.3 sec
1,500 metres	Kipchoge Keino	Kenya	3 min 34.9 sec
5,000 metres	Mohamed Gammoudi	Tunisia	14 min 5.0 sec
10,000 metres	Naftali Temu	Kenya	29 min 27.4 sec
Marathon	Mamo Wolde	Ethiopia	2 hr 20 min 26.4 sec
4 x 100 metres relay		USA	38.2 sec
4 x 400 metres relay		USA	2 min 56.1 sec
110 metres hurdles	Willie Davenport	USA	13.3 sec
400 metres hurdles	David Hemery	Great Britain	48.1 sec
3,000 metres steeplechase	Amos Biwott	Kenya	8 min 51.0 sec
20 kilometres walk	Viktor Golubnichiy	USSR	1 hr 33 min 58.4 sec
50 kilometres walk	Christoph Hohne	East Germany	4 hr 20 min 13.6 sec
High jump	Dick Fosbury	USA	7 ft 4¼ in
Pole vault	Bob Seagren	USA	17 ft 8½ in
Long jump	Bob Beamon	USA	29 ft 2½ in
Triple jump	Viktor Saneyev	USSR	57 ft 0¾ in
Shot	Randy Matson	USA	67 ft 4¾ in
Discus	Al Oerter	USA	212 ft 6½ in
Hammer	Gyula Zsivotsky	Hungary	240 ft 8 in
Javelin	Janis Lusis	USSR	295 ft 7 in
Decathlon	Bill Toomey	USA	8,193 pts
Women			
100 metres	Wyomia Tyus	USA	11.0 sec
200 metres	Irena Szewinska	Poland	22.5 sec
400 metres	Colette Besson	France	52.0 sec
800 metres	Madeline Manning	USA	2 min 0.9 sec
4 x 100 metres relay		USA	42.8 sec
80 metres hurdles	Maureen Caird	Australia	10.3 sec
High jump	Miroslava Rezkova	Czechoslovakia	5 ft 11¾ in
Long jump	Viorica Viscopoleanu	Romania	22 ft 4½ in
Shot	Margit Gummel	East Germany	64 ft 4 in
Discus	Lia Manoliu	Romania	191 ft 2½ in
Javelin	Angela Nemeth	Hungary	198 ft 0½ in
Pentathlon	Ingrid Becker	West Germany	5,098 pts

1 What the Olympics are about: eight men start the second semi-final of the 100 metres. Charlie Green has the strapped thigh, and the leader is lusciously named Ravelmonantsoa of Madagascar. **2** Tommie Smith and John Carlos show the world what they think of their country. **3** Bob Seagren—the United States' sixteenth successive Olympic pole vault champion. **4** David Hemery clears the penultimate hurdle well ahead of the field. **5** Poland (left), Britain (centre) and the Ivory Coast contest the minor placings in the first 4 x 100 metres relay semi-final. **6** His lungs burning from lack of air, an exhausted runner breathes in much needed oxygen after competing—a familiar sight in the athletics area at Mexico City. **7** Tommie Smith (in the black socks) strides to victory in the second heat of the 200 metres. **8** Individualism triumphs yet again—Dick Fosbury 'flops' in the high jump. **9** Even the lowliest finisher gave his all—Perera of Ceylon, after coming 51st in the marathon. **10** Heat 1 of the 400 metres hurdles: West Germany's Gerhard Hennige (16) leads Geoff Vanderstock of America (312), and Russia's deaf-mute Vyacheslav Skomorokhov (828). **11** Thirty-seven men started the 50-km walk, and 28 finished. Paul Nihill (centre) was one of those forced to drop out.

Athletics—Women

For the first time, sex tests for women were held at an Olympic Games. And although they had been used in the Asian and Commonwealth Games and in the 1966 European athletics championships, with embarrassing results for some, there was no such incident in Mexico City. This, at least, was a happy omen for world sport.

Three 1964 champions defended their titles—Wyomia Tyus in the 100 metres, Karin Balzer in the 80 metres hurdles, and Mihaela Penes in the javelin. Of these, only Miss Tyus was successful, and she thus became the first sprinter—man or woman—to retain the 100 metres crown. She won by 0.1 sec from her compatriot Barbara Ferrell in a world record of 11.0 sec. Third was Irena Kirszenstein-Szewinska, who had equalled the old world record of 11.1 sec in the second round.

Mrs Szewinska claimed the 200 metres gold medal with a world record run of 22.5 sec, 0.2 faster than her own existing record. She was a clear winner from two young Australian girls, Raelene Boyle and Jennifer Lamy. The American team won the 4 by 100 metres relay, and set two world records in that event during the Games. They won their heat in a record 43.4 sec, and saw it equalled by the Netherlands in the second heat. But in the final they improved to 42.8 sec, with a well-drilled Cuban quartet second in 43.3 sec.

There had been no hotter favourite before the Games than Britain's Lillian Board in the 400 metres. This burden—foisted on her largely by the British press—undoubtedly affected her running. She was warned by the judges for not having her feet in contact with the ground at the start, but led by a few yards as the field entered the home straight. She was visibly tiring, and was caught on the line by a little-known French girl, Colette Besson, who equalled the Olympic record of 52.0 sec. Miss Board, aged only 19, set a national record of 52.1 sec to take the silver medal.

In the 800 metres, the world record holder Vera Nikolic of Yugoslavia had impressed observers in training, but when she competed it was clear she was not in the peak of condition. She won her heat easily enough in 2 min 5.7 sec, but in her semi-final she ran off the track after 300 metres. The girl was certainly upset, and it was said she tried to commit suicide after the race. But what was more certain was that she had been called upon to carry too great a burden, mentally and physically. She was training even on the morning of her semi-final. The absence of this fine runner who had set her world record of 2 min 0.5 sec in the British championships earlier in the year rendered the final a little anti-climatic, but this could not detract from the fine running of Madeline

Above, **Wyomia Tyus is well ahead as she receives the baton from Mildrette Netter and takes the United States to victory in the women's relay, with Cuba (third from outside) second.**

Ed Lacey

1 Margitta Lange claimed the silver medal in the women's shot behind her team-mate Margit Gummel. 2 Madeline Manning wins the 800 metres from Ileana Silai of Romania (215—2nd) and the Netherland's Mia Gommers (148—3rd) in 2 min 0.9 sec.

Manning of the United States. After Romania's Ileana Silai had set the pace through the first lap (59.1 sec), Miss Manning broke away around the final bend to win in 2 min 0.9 sec—the third fastest time ever recorded.

The hurdles, too, provided an upset of form. Russia's new world record holder, Vera Korsakova, did not even reach the final, and the defending champion, Karin Balzer, was placed fifth. Maureen Caird, a 17-year-old from New South Wales, led from start to finish to defeat her more experienced team-mate Pam Kilborn. Miss Caird thus became the youngest Olympic athletics champion ever.

With recent memories of the Russian invasion of Czechoslovakia still fresh, there was no more popular winner than Milena Rezkova in the high jump. Miss Rezkova had to clear the final height—5 ft. 11¾ in.—to win, because her opponents, Russia's Antonina Okorokova had a sup-

erior record at lower heights. But the Czech girl, 18 years old and 5 ft. 6½ in. tall, went over to the delight of the crowd with her final try, leaving the two Russians to pick up the place medals.

Mexico City must have been the favourite venue of long jumpers. The world record was broken in the women's event as well, by Romania's Viorica Viscopoleanu. She cleared 22 ft. 4½ in. with her first jump in the final rounds to clinch the title. Britain gained a silver medal in this event through Sheila Sherwood, wife of the 400 metres hurdles bronze medallist.

The gold medals in the three throwing events went behind the Iron Curtain. The shot was a complete triumph for the East Germans Margit Gummel and Margitta Lange. Miss Gummel set two world records in Mexico City, 62 ft. 6¾ in. and 64 ft. 4 in., and won by a clear margin from her team-mate, whose best effort was 61 ft. 7½ in. Mihaela Penes,

the defending champion, lost her javelin title to Hungary's Angela Nemeth. Miss Penes started well with a throw of 196 ft. 7 in., but the Hungarian girl came through in the second round with 198 ft. 0½ in. to make sure of the gold. The win of Lia Manoliu in the discus was a triumph for perseverance. This 36-year-old engineer from Bucharest was competing in her fifth Olympic Games, and had been third twice, in 1960 and 1964. She was the only thrower to overcome the wet conditions, and although her winning throw of 191 ft. 2½ in. was over 10 feet less than the world record, it was more than her rivals, better throwers on paper, could manage.

West German Ingrid Becker's score of 5,098 points in the pentathlon could not match the Olympic and world record of 5,246 set by Irina Press in the Tokyo Olympics, but it was enough to beat Austria's Liese Prokop by 132 points. Miss Becker overtook her rival on the last event, the 200 metres, which she ran in 23.5 sec, worth 1,077 points, while the Austrian could achieve only 25.1 sec (923 points).

London Express News & Feature Service

1 Debbie Meyer was hailed as Olympic champion three times in the swimming events—in the 200, 400, and 800 metres freestyle.
2 The start of the men's 100 metres freestyle. Winner Mike Wenden of Australia (in 52.2 sec—a world record) is in lane 4. Zac Zorn of America (lane 5) took an early lead, but made his effort too soon and finished 8th. Britain's Bobby McGregor, the only survivor from the Tokyo final, is in lane 6 and came 4th.
3 All action in the water polo, won by Yugoslavia.

Swimming

The pre-Olympic spotlight was not focused on the problems of altitude in relation to swimming. Yet it was in the pool that there were many collapses, in a sport for which post-racing distress is the exception and not the rule. The most dramatic incident concerned America's John Ferris, the bronze medallist in the 200 metres individual medley. He had to be supported during the medal presentation ceremony by the winner, his team-mate Charles Hickcox, and fell to the ground at the foot of the rostrum as soon as the presentations were over. Oxygen was needed to revive him, and he later fainted again during the medal winners' interview and had to have more oxygen.

It was not only the altitude

Mexico City, and his apparently effortless successes were among the highlights of the Games. Three other men won two individual titles—Mike Wenden the 100 and 200 metres freestyle, Mike Burton the 400 and 1,500 metres freestyle, and Charles Hickcox the 200 and 400 metres individual medley.

But the swimmer who won most gold medals was America's Debbie Meyer. Helped by the introduction of two new events in the programme, she became the first swimmer to win three individual titles—all for freestyle—at the same Games. She took 11½ seconds off the 1964 Olympic record in the 400 metres and also won the newly instituted 200 and 800 metres. Her team-mate Claudia Kolb won two titles, the

Ed Lacey

that affected the results. A stomach virus infection—'Montezuma's revenge'—also claimed many victims. They included America's Catie Ball, holder of all the world breaststroke records. She lost 10 lb in weight, was relegated to fifth place in the 100 metres breaststroke, and was too ill even to start in the heats of the 200 metres. But others — including Djurdjica Bjedov, the shock winner of the 100 metres breaststroke and Yugoslavia's first individual swimming medallist—were completely unaffected by the conditions.

The combination of these factors affected the general level of performance, and only three individual world records were broken during the 29-event swimming programme. Australia's Mike Wenden claimed one, in winning the 100 metres freestyle in 52.2 sec. Kaye Hall of the United States trimmed the women's 100 metres backstroke mark to 66.2 sec. And Roland Matthes swam the first leg—100 metres backstroke— in East Germany's medley relay squad in 58.0 sec.

Backstroker Matthes, who won both individual battles, was one of the outstanding competitors in

200 and 400 metres individual medley, to add two golds to the silver she had won in the Tokyo 200 metres breaststroke.

The United States, in fact, dominated the swimming section of the Games, winning 10 of a possible 15 men's titles, and 11 of a possible 14 women's. Don Schollander, the quadruple gold medallist at Tokyo in 1964, could not qualify for the American team to defend his 100 and 400 metres titles, but was in the 200 metres, and finished second behind Wenden. Britain's only medal in the pool came through Martyn Woodroffe, who shocked everyone by splitting America's Carl Robie and John Ferris to win the silver in the 200 metres butterfly.

Both the springboard diving titles went to America, but the highboard crowns went to countries who had never before claimed an individual title in the pool. Italy's Klaus Dibiasi won the men's, and Czechoslovakia's Milena Duchkova beat her Russian rival Natalia Lobanova by 4.45 marks in the women's, only two months after Russian troops had entered her home city of Prague.

Other Sports 1

The Russian invasion of Czechoslovakia had meant that many Czechoslovak sportsmen and women had to curtail their preparation for the Games, none more than Vera Caslavska, the blonde gymnast who had gathered three gold medals at the 1964 Olympic Games. But once she arrived in Mexico the stresses of the invasion were behind her. Miss Caslavska turned on immaculate performances to win the combined exercises title by 1.40 points and two of the four individual events—the vault and the asymmetrical bars—outright, tie for first place in the floor exercises and gain silver medals in the beam and the team events. After the Games she married the Czech middle-distance runner Josef Odlozil, the 1,500 metres silver medallist in 1964.

There was no such outstanding performer in the men's events, but Miroslav Cerar, the Yugoslav pommel horse expert, staked a claim as one of the most consistent gymnasts ever. He maintained an unbeaten record in world and Olympic events on this apparatus which had lasted from 1962. In national terms, the Japanese challenge to the supremacy of the Russians was the outstanding feature. They won five of the eight titles at stake, tied for another, and won 12 of a possible 22 medals.

It was expected that the United States might, after taking all six previous titles, lose the basketball event at last. But despite losing many of their top college players to the professional ranks, the Americans proved to be unbeatable. The Russians, four times winners of the silver medals, went down narrowly to the Yugoslavs—63-62—and had to settle for the bronzes.

India, who had never failed to finish first or second in the hockey, were surprisingly beaten 2-1 by Australia in the semi-finals. Australia met Pakistan in the final, and despite at one stage holding the Asians to 1-1, they were eventually beaten 2-1. India beat West Germany 2-1 for the bronze medals, but must have been far from satisfied with their performance.

The Japanese women, who had been so outstanding in winning the volleyball golds in Tokyo, were this time without the services of their legendary coach Hirofumi Daimatsu, and they succumbed to the power of the Russian women, whose men also won their event. But Japan, not a traditional power in the sport, won the bronze medals in soccer, thanks largely to the efforts of their tall striker Kunigishe Kamamoto. They beat Mexico 2-0 in the third place match, both goals coming from Kamamoto. In the final Hungary beat Bulgaria 4-1. No fewer than four players were sent off in this game by the referee, three

Bulgarians and one Hungarian, and the Mexican fans showed their disapproval by showering the field with cushions. This tournament, the customary blooding ground of many Iron Curtain players for the harsher tests of the World Cup, was played in the venues of the 1970 World Cup tournament, and the success of the World Cup organization was in no small way due to the Olympic competition.

The Mexican organization was much in evidence at the Xochimilco rowing course, and only the altitude prevented it from being one of the best meetings in Olympic history. Rowing events normally last about 6 minutes for the 2,000 metres course, and this period of exertion proved too much even for these tough, highly trained athletes. Martin Studach, the Swiss sculler, unbeaten in major events since 1965, collapsed in his heat and was carried away on a stretcher. The United States, for the first time, failed to win a single gold medal, and their tally amounted to just one silver and one bronze. East Germany won two of the seven events and also a silver medal. New Zealand's coxed four led from start to finish to win their event by nearly three

seconds from the East Germans, but despite a good effort in the eights final New Zealand had to be content with fourth place. The gold medals, almost as a matter of course, went to the West German team coached by the redoubtable Karl Adam. Russia, normally a force to be reckoned with in the world of rowing, won two medals, a gold and a bronze. The canoeing events were held over the same course and, as usual, were dominated by European paddlers of both sexes. No 'high-altitude' country won medals of any sort in rowing or canoeing.

It was the same story in the

Morley L. Pecker

3

Associated Press

1 The Olympic flame still burns, but was extinguished soon after the team show jumping—the final event of the Games. **2** Waldemar Baszanowski of Poland successfully defended his lightweight title with a total of 964¼ lb. **3** Rodney Pattisson and Iain Macdonald-Smith (K 163) were convincing winners of the Flying Dutchman gold medals. **4** The modernistic basketball arena dominated the hockey field: Australia (white) beat India 2-1 in the semi-final to reach their first-ever final.

Ed Lacey

4

cycling, in which all the medals were claimed by European riders. The most bemedalled cyclist was the Frenchman Pierre Trentin, who won golds in the 1,000 metres time trial and tandem sprint, and was third in the 1,000 metres sprint. But the talking point of the meeting was the disqualification of the West German quartet in the 4,000 metres team pursuit. In the final race, between Denmark and West Germany, the Germans seemed to have an easy victory, but one of their team appeared to receive assistance on the last lap, an illegal procedure in this form of racing. The Danes protested, and

the Germans were disqualified. Denmark were thus awarded the gold medals, and the silvers were withheld. West Germany, by virtue of reaching the final, did get the silver medals some weeks after the end of the Games.

Britain's heroes were few and far between in Mexico, but Rodney Pattisson and Iain Macdonald-Smith were out on their own in the Flying Dutchman yachting event held on the beautiful waters of Acapulco Bay. After being disqualified in the first race, they won five races in succession and were a careful second in the last to win the gold medal with 3.0 penalty points

to runner-up West Germany's 43.7. Paul Elvström, four times an Olympic winner, was fourth in the Star class.

In the equestrian events, the gold medals in the three-day event went to Britain. The bad weather and tough cross-country course suited the British riders, and 54-year-old Major Derek Allhusen, Sergeant Ben Jones, Richard Meade, and Jane Bullen (the first woman to feature in a winning Olympic three-day team) collected 175.93 penalty points to win by nearly 70 points from the United States. Britain's chances of team medals in the show jumping

disappeared when Marion Coakes, winner of the silver medal in the individual competition, crashed into one of the bigger fences with her tiny pony Stroller. Winners of this team prize were Canada, relative newcomers to this type of competition, thanks to a careful last round by Jim Elder.

The show jumping team event was the last competition of the Games, held in the Olympic stadium just before the closing ceremony. It brought to an end an Olympic Games filled with controversy but in which the Olympic ideals, if sorely tried, tested, and tempted, had at least survived.

MEXICO CITY OLYMPIC GAMES, 1968 Gold Medallists

Basketball		USA	
Boxing			
Light-flyweight	Francisco Rodriguez	Venezuela	
Flyweight	Ricardo Delgado	Mexico	
Bantamweight	Valeriy Sokolov	USSR	
Featherweight	Antonio Roldan	Mexico	
Lightweight	Ronnie Harris	USA	
Light-welterweight	Jerzy Kulej	Poland	
Welterweight	Manfred Wolke	East Germany	
Light-middleweight	Boris Lagutin	USSR	
Middleweight	Chris Finnegan	Great Britain	
Light-heavyweight	Dan Pozdniak	USSR	
Heavyweight	George Foreman	USA	
Canoeing			
1,000 metres—Men			
Kayak singles	Mihaly Hesz	Hungary	4 min 2.63 sec
Kayak pairs	Alexander Shaparenko, V. Morosov	USSR	3 min 37.54 sec
Kayak fours		Norway	3 min 14.38 sec
Canadian singles	Tibor Tatai	Hungary	4 min 36.14 sec
Canadian pairs	Ivan Patazichin, S. Covakiov	Romania	4 min 7.18 sec
500 metres—Women			
Kayak singles	Ludmilla Pinaeva	USSR	2 min 11.09 sec
Kayak pairs	A. Zimmermann, R. Esser	West Germany	1 min 56.44 sec
Cycling			
1,000 metres sprint	Daniel Morelon	France	
1,000 metres time trial	Pierre Trentin	France	
2,000 metres tandem	Daniel Morelon, Pierre Trentin	France	
4,000 metres team pursuit		Denmark	4 min 22.44 sec
Road team time trial (104 km)		Netherlands	2 hr 7 min 49.06 sec
Road race (196.2 km)	Pierfranco Vianelli	Italy	4 hr 41 min 25.24 sec
Equestrian			
Dressage —individual	Ivan Kizimov	USSR	
—team		West Germany	
Show jumping—individual	Bill Steinkraus	USA	
—team		Canada	
Three day event—individual	Jean Guyon	France	
—team		Great Britain	
Fencing—Men			
Foil —individual	Ion Drimba	Romania	
—team		France	
Epee —individual	Gyozo Kulcsar	Hungary	
—team		Hungary	
Sabre —individual	Jerzy Pawlowski	Poland	
—team		USSR	
Fencing—Women			
Foil —individual	Elena Novikova	USSR	
—team		USSR	
Football		Hungary	
Gymnastics—Men			
Combined exercises			
—individual	Sawao Kato	Japan	
—team		Japan	
Floor exercises	Sawao Kato	Japan	
Horizontal bar	Mikhail Voronin, Akinari Nakayama	USSR, Japan	
Parallel bars	Akinari Nakayama	Japan	
Pommell horse	Miroslav Cerar	Yugoslavia	
Vault	Mikhail Voronin	USSR	
Rings	Akinari Nakayama	Jaapn	
Gymnastics—Women			
Combined exercises			
—individual	Vera Caslavska	Czechoslovakia	
—team		USSR	

Floor exercises	Larissa Petrik, Vera Caslavska	USSR, Czechoslovakia	
Asymmetrical bars	Vera Caslavska	Czechoslovakia	
Beam	Natalia Kuchinskaya	USSR	
Vault	Vera Caslavska	Czechoslovakia	
Hockey		Pakistan	
Modern Pentathlon			
Individual	Bjorn Ferm	Sweden	
Team		Hungary	
Rowing			
Single sculls	Henri Wienese	Netherlands	7 min 47.80 sec
Double sculls	Anatoly Sass, Alexander Timoshinin	USSR	6 min 51.82 sec
Coxless pairs	Jorg Lucke, Heinz Bothe	East Germany	7 min 26.56 sec
Coxed pairs	P. Baran, R. Sambo, B. Cipolla (cox)	Italy	8 min 4.81 sec
Coxed fours		New Zealand	6 min 45.62 sec
Coxless fours		East Germany	6 min 39.18 sec
Eights		West Germany	6 min 7.00 sec
Shooting			
Small bore rifle			
—three positions	Bernd Klingner	West Germany	
—prone	Jan Kurka	Czechoslovakia	
Free pistol	Gregory Kosyth	USSR	
Free rifle	Gary Anderson	USA	
Rapid fire pistol	Jozef Zapedzki	Poland	
Clay pigeon	Bob Braithwaite	Great Britain	
Skeet	Evgeny Petrov	USSR	
Volleyball—Men		USSR	
Volleyball—Women		USSR	
Weightlifting			
Bantamweight	Mohamed Nassiri	Iran	809¾ lb
Featherweight	Yoshinobu Miyake	Japan	865 lb
Lightweight	Waldemar Baszanowski	Poland	964½ lb
Middleweight	Viktor Kurentsov	USSR	1,046¾ lb
Light-heavyweight	Boris Selitsky	USSR	1,068¼ lb
Mid-heavyweight	Kaarlo Kangasniemi	Finland	1,140½ lb
Heavyweight	Leonid Zhabotinsky	USSR	1,261¾ lb
Wrestling			
Freestyle			
Flyweight	Shigeo Nakata	Japan	
Bantamweight	Yojiro Uetake	Japan	
Featherweight	Masaaki Kaneko	Japan	
Lightweight	Abdollah Mohaved	Iran	
Welterweight	Mahmut Atalay	Turkey	
Middleweight	Boris Gurevitch	USSR	
Light-heavyweight	Ahmed Ayuk	Turkey	
Heavyweight	Alexandr Medved	USSR	
Graeco-Roman			
Flyweight	Petar Kirov	Bulgaria	
Bantamweight	Janos Varga	Hungary	
Featherweight	Roman Rurua	USSR	
Lightweight	Muneji Munemura	Japan	
Welterweight	Rudolf Vesper	East Germany	
Middleweight	Lothar Metz	East Germany	
Light-heavyweight	Boyan Radev	Bulgaria	
Heavyweight	Istvan Kozma	Hungary	
Yachting			
Finn	Valentin Mankin	USSR	
Star	Lowel North, Peter Barrett	USA	
Flying Dutchman	Rodney Pattisson, Iain Macdonald-Smith	Great Britain	
5.5 metres		Sweden	
Dragon		USA	

No fewer than 144 ambitious cyclists set out on the 122-mile road race, won by 22-year-old Pierfranco Vianelli of Italy.

Rex Features

Munich Olympic Games (1972)

On September 5 1972, the Olympic Games finally lost the battle to disassociate itself from the pernicious influence of world politics on sport. In the early hours of that fateful day, war came to the XXth Olympiad, and in those moments the considerable efforts of the West German organisers to present the largest, the most smoothly run, and the most costly Games were completely tarnished.

The Olympic Village became the platform for political propaganda of the most cold-blooded variety. A squad of Palestinian guerrillas invaded the Israeli team headquarters, claimed hostages in a violent struggle during which two members of the Israeli team received fatal injuries, and demanded the release of 200 Arab political prisoners. The intensive world-wide interest in the Games afforded them the very maximum publicity for their grievance.

All athletic activity immediately ceased and for several hours a complete cancellation appeared possible. The Olympic Games stood still and watched with the rest of the world as the West German Government and its security forces grappled with the problem. After a day of impasse their first positive move was directed at removing the conflict out of its sporting setting. Around 10.00 pm, three helicopters flew out of the Village, two containing the guerrillas with their hostages; the third had government officials aboard.

Their destination was the airbase at Fuerstenfeldbruck. Here the tragedy was compounded. Shortly after 11.30 pm, news bulletins around the world carried the story that, after an exchange of gunfire at the airfield, the hostages had all been safely recovered. It was a story without substance, and within four hours came the bitter retraction. True, there had been shots fired, but the tactics of local police had turned sour.

A troop of crack marksmen had been delegated to shoot down the Arabs the moment that they disembarked from the helicopters to transfer to the jet which they had demanded for a safe passage to Cairo. Four of the eight guerrillas moved forward to inspect the jet; as they returned to their comrades the police opened fire. Three were hit but the fourth reached the sanctuary of the helicopters. And then there was silence—for over an hour.

In that time the police prepared for an assault with armoured cars. It took too long. For, just after

midnight, the hostages were murdered, some as a result of a hand-grenade tossed into one helicopter by a fleeing guerrilla, the rest shot. In all, 11 Israelis had been killed; five Arabs also died while three were taken into custody; another victim was a policeman slain by a terrorist bullet.

While the initial post-mortem centred on a security system that allowed any person wearing a track-suit, as the guerrillas had done, to enter the Olympic Village without a pass, and on the housing of the athletes, which had put the Israelis in a vulnerable station near the perimeter rather than in a more easily guarded and central post, the value of the Olympic Games and its uneasy tendency to arouse nationalism was also questioned.

Its cause was not helped on that Wednesday morning when a memorial service was held for the dead Israelis. Avery Brundage, at 84 in his last few days as chairman of the International Olympic Congress, appeared to lack any sensitivity when, in his address, he compared the killings to the problems over the inclusion of Rhodesia in the Games as 'commercial, political and now criminal pressure'. And there seemed a hurry which was almost indecent about the resumption of competition.

The Rhodesian question had ensured that politics was never far from the mind at the outset of these sumptuous Olympics which cost £300 million to stage. The IOC in 1971 had consented to the Rhodesian application for entry, on the grounds that they competed as a British colony, and duly a team of 30 athletes had arrived in Munich. But the African nations, surprised that Rhodesia had for sporting purposes rejected her independence, protested and threatened a boycott if Rhodesia took part. This was tantamount to 'blackmail', the word used by Avery Brundage after the event, but the IOC were forced to retract and the Rhodesian team were expelled.

Nor did the tragedy of the Israelis bring an end to nationalist overtones. The very day after the memorial service, two black Americans, Vince Matthews and Wayne Collett, stood relaxed, hands on hips and holding a conversation while the American national anthem was being played at their victory ceremony for the 400 metres final. It was every bit

Colorsport

Associated Press

Munich's day of mourning: the Israeli flag, along with the flags of all the competing nations, flies at half mast; a small group of Israelis, with a crepe covered flag, sit in silence during the memorial service to the 11 Israeli team members killed by Palestinian terrorists.

as much a demonstration for Black Power as the raised fists of Tommie Smith and Juan Carlos four years earlier, and the IOC duly banned the two athletes from any further Olympic competition, though they were allowed to retain their gold and silver medals.

Though the competition in all sports was of the usual elevated standards, the XXth Olympiad seemed even further removed from the original ideal. Even at the outset, amateurism was far removed when it was learned that the West German athlete, Heidi Schuller, who took the Olympic oath at the opening ceremony, had charged photographers for taking her picture in the preceding days. It provided an appropriate beginning for the fortnight.

Athletics—Men

Though world records were not achieved with the ease of the Mexican Games and its rarified air, the athletics stadium was the scene of intense and often spectacular competition. And on the track the extreme competition in the 10,000 metres and the 400 metres hurdles did stimulate the winners to exceed the previous world's best times.

Both races provided distinct disappointments for British hopes. In the 10,000 metres, 22-year-old David Bedford entered the final as the holder of the world record. But Bedford had endured an unhappy preparation for the Games. A week before Munich, he had been disastrously defeated in a two-mile race in Sweden; a stomach bug had been sapping his strength throughout that week; and when he arrived in Germany he was charged with infringing his amateur status through advertising—charges that were eventually dropped.

Yet he performed well enough in his heat, coming second to Emile Puttemans of Belgium by a fifth of a second, both running half a minute inside the previous Olympic record. They were the fastest qualifiers, but only the Belgian could recreate that form in the final. Bedford, without the security of a finishing sprint, had to set the pace from the front if he was to win; but he never freed himself from the pack.

By the end of the 14th lap his challenge was finished. The race was left for the sprinters and the fastest finish belonged to a 23-year-old policeman from Finland, Lasse Viren. Viren had good fortune when, in colliding with

The Soviet Union's Valeri Borzov (932) cruises to a comfortable win over Roberts of Trinidad and Jamaica's Hardware in his first-round heat of the 200 metres. In the two sprint finals, Borzov eclipsed his opposition to complete the first men's 100-200 double since 1956.

the Tunisian, Mohamed Gammoudi, the Finn stumbled to the ground but recovered, while Gammoudi tumbled out of the race. Only Puttemans could match Viren, but not for long enough, and the Finn won easily in the world record time of 27 min 38.4 sec.

In the 400 metres hurdles, David Hemery was bidding to retain the Olympic title he had gained so worthily in Mexico. He might have done so but for the emergence of a remarkable and relatively unknown athlete. The Ugandan, John Akii-Bua, one of a family of 43 children, completely rewrote the standard for the event with a breathtaking win in 47.8 sec. Hemery lost second place to the American, Ralph Mann, almost at the tape, but took the bronze medal; there was little despondency from him when he said: 'I'm glad that my medal and world record have gone in this way. I'd have hated it to have gone in a slow time.'

Mann's silver medal was one consolation for the United States men's team which experienced a series of disasters, some of them of their own design. First, their two leading 100 metres men, Eddie Hart and Rey Robinson, failed to appear on the blocks for the second round of the heats, a complete misunderstanding of the schedule for the events. And Robert Taylor, who just arrived in time to qualify for the final, was completely outclassed by the powerful Russian, Valeri Borzov, who won the gold medal in 10.14 sec, only the second non-American victor in this event since 1932.

The Americans have shown even greater dominance in the pole vault—they had provided winners since 1896—but now Bob Seagren, gold medallist in Mexico, found his 'Catapult' style vaulting pole banned and lost his title to Wolfgang Nordwig of East Germany. The shot, too, escaped the Americans, George Woods being unable to match the winning effort of Komar of Poland, who achieved 69 ft 6 in. And then came the ignominious behaviour of Matthews and Collett, whose subsequent ban destroyed the USA 4 x 400 metres relay team.

The final disaster came in a 1,500 metres heat in which, by some strange quirk of the computer which controlled the composition of the heats, Mexico silver medallist Jim Ryun was drawn with the reigning champion Kip Keino. All might have been well, with Ryun comfortably placed to make his bid for qualification with 500 metres left, but as he moved out to step up his pace he collided with another runner and crashed on to the track. Though he bravely pursued the field his chance had disintegrated in that desperate moment.

Apart from Matthews' 400

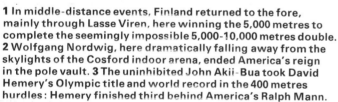

1 In middle-distance events, Finland returned to the fore, mainly through Lasse Viren, here winning the 5,000 metres to complete the seemingly impossible 5,000-10,000 metres double. 2 Wolfgang Nordwig, here dramatically falling away from the skylights of the Cosford indoor arena, ended America's reign in the pole vault. 3 The uninhibited John Akii-Bua took David Hemery's Olympic title and world record in the 400 metres hurdles: Hemery finished third behind America's Ralph Mann.

Colorsport

metres success, the United States men were limited to athletics golds from Rod Milburn in the 110 metres hurdles, Frank Shorter in the marathon, Randy Williams in the long jump (with a frantic effort in his first jump after straining a leg while warming-up), the 4 x 100 metres relay, and Dave Wottle in the 800 metres. And Wottle embarrassed himself considerably by forgetting to remove his trademark, a peaked cap, during the national anthem on the victors rostrum.

If the Americans struggled it was Finland who made the advance. The success of Viren in the 10,000 metres was compounded

within a few hours on Sunday, September 10. In the 5,000 metres David Bedford again took up the challenge with Viren, and again could not match him. On the final lap the Finn was left to duel with Gammoudi, the reigning champion, and it was the younger man who came home more than five yards clear. Behind Gammoudi, Ian Stewart outlasted the field to win a bronze medal for Great Britain. Viren's winning time, 13 min 26.4 sec, was an Olympic record.

A British runner, Brendan Foster, played an influential part in the 1,500 metres. He acted as pacemaker for the opening two

laps, until Keino, gold medallist in Mexico, eased his way to the front. With him went Finland's Pekka Vasala, and it was Vasala who kicked off the final bend to make the day belong entirely to Finland. Foster finished gallantly in fifth place.

Keino had been forced to withdraw from the 5,000 metres, his other main event, because of a clash in the timings of the heats with those of the 1,500 metres. But he had trained hard for the 3,000 metres steeplechase, a completely new event to him. And though he had run the race only four times before in his career, his sheer pace brought

him Olympic gold, though his style made the purists shudder. He won in an Olympic record time of 8 min 23.6 sec, beating his team-mate Ben Jipcho, with Kantanen giving the Finns further joy with a bronze medal.

Valeri Borzov duly completed the sprint double for Russia; his smooth, powerful stride beating three Americans and the Italian, Mennea, in a time of 20 sec dead. Sadly, the greatness of his dual triumph may always be open to question because he never had the opportunity to beat Hart and Robinson, the Americans who missed their heats. That criticism probably does disservice to an

Colorsport

athlete who seemed a class above all his rivals, particularly when many judges felt that Taylor, who took the silver in the 100 metres, was the most effective of the United States entrants.

For the USSR—the satisfaction of the only athlete who retained his title. Viktor Saneyev took his second successive gold medal in the triple jump, though his winning leap of 56 ft 11 in was 13 inches less than he achieved in Mexico. The Russians also took gold in the high jump, where no one could match the 7 ft 4¼ in leap with which Dick Fosbury flopped to fame in 1968, but Tarmak won the Olympic title

with a jump of just half an inch less. They also won the hammer competition, where Bondarchuk broke the Olympic record, and the decathlon, in which Avilov's 8454 pts was a world record.

Jay Silvester could not succeed to the crown handed down by the great Al Oerter, and he could only finish second in the discus to Danek of Czechoslovakia, while Klaus Wolfermann of West Germany raised the Olympic javelin standard with a winning throw of 296 ft 10 in. In the walking event there was a gold medal for Frenkel of East Germany in the 20 km, and for Kannenberg of West Germany in the 50 km.

The performance of the fancied Paul Nihill in the former event highlighted a problem in the approach of many of the British team to the competition.

Nihill, like many others, had trained at altitude to improve his performance when he came to compete at the lower level of Munich. But during the 20 km walk he complained that his legs had never felt as tired before; he felt that he had returned from altitude too late and that the benefits of this type of training had been slightly misunderstood by the doctors who had recommended the idea. It was perhaps a partial explanation of the poor showing

of the British team.

Nevertheless, the last male track event did provide some consolation, when the 4 x 400 metres relay team of Martin Reynolds, Alan Pascoe, David Hemery and David Jenkins came second behind Kenya. Hemery, running third, produced an inspired lap of 44.9 sec to hand over to Jenkins in fourth place. The West German leader tied up in sight of home, and Sang of Kenya took the lead while Jenkins showed all his promising power to overtake both German and French runners; the silver medal came in a new British record of 3 min 0.5 sec.

Athletics—Women

It was a new Olympic event for women, the 1,500 metres, which provided perhaps the most outstanding performance in a series of excellent contests. At the start of 1972, the world record for the event stood at 4 min 9.6 sec, but throughout the Games, Ludmilla Bragina of the USSR clinically made such a time seem increasingly archaic. In her first round heat, this 5 ft 7 in girl, who weighs a mere 110 lb, was a winner in 4 min 6.5 sec; in her semi-final she sliced that time down to 4 min 5.1 sec.

Then in the final she produced an even better performance. After two fast opening laps, the 29-year-old Russian took over chased by Sheila Carey from Coventry. The English girl held her own on lap three, but understandably faded over the last 250 yards, nevertheless finishing fifth in a new British record. But Bragina raced home, slaughtering her own previous best of a few days earlier with yet another world record of 4 min 1.4 sec, and really placing the four minute mile for women within reach.

For Great Britain, an athletics gold medal became reality when 33-year-old Mary Peters of Belfast won the pentathlon. Her triumph was based on a tre-

mendous effort on the first day of this two-day event; it was then that she established a strong lead with her performances in three of the five events. By sprinting the 100 metres hurdles in 13.29 sec; by putting the shot 53 ft 1¼ in, and by high jumping a personal best of 5 ft 10½ in, she totalled 2969 points, the best ever first day score in the women's pentathlon. As she battled to get some sleep that night, she must have reflected on the proximity of the world record holder Pollak of East Germany, just 97 points behind, and the West German, Heidi Rosendahl, then in fifth place, but with her two strongest events, the long jump and the 200 metres, Mary's weakest, to follow.

The drama took its predictable course. Rosendahl, who had already won the gold medal in the women's long jump, even improved on that winning leap; her 22 ft 5 in was nearly two feet in front of Mary Peters' best jump. And to add further bite to the tension, the two girls were drawn in the same heat of the 200 metres. Again the West German girl responded to the occasion; her 22.9 sec was a career best, but the 11 stone Irish girl clung on to record 24.08, and to win the gold medal by

2 just 10 points!

Apart from that success for Great Britain, the women's events were shared between three nations, USSR and East and West Germany. In the short sprints, Renate Stecher of East Germany, a strongly built girl, emulated the achievement of Borzov in the men's events with a double in the 100 and 200 metres, her 22.40 sec in the latter equalling the world record; both silvers went to the Australian, Raelene Boyle. East Germany, an increasing force in the Games, also won the 400 metres with M. Zehrt, the 110 metres hurdles through A. Ehrhardt, the 4 x 400 metres relay, while Ruth Fuchs set a new Olympic record in winning the javelin.

The West German success belonged almost exclusively to Heidi Rosendahl, who came back in the most decisive fashion from the disappointment of an injury in Mexico which cost her the gold medal in the pentathlon. After her long jump win and her second place to Mary Peters, she played the vital part in a thrilling 4 x 100 metres relay. In front of a packed and intensely partisan crowd she took the last leg, and in a frenzy of excitement held off the great Renate Stecher and East Germany by .14 of a second; the winning time of 42.81 equalled the world and Olympic record.

But there was even more of the fairytale about the triumph of 16-year-old Ulrike Meyfarth in the high jump. Before the Games began, her best jump was just ¾ in over 6 ft, but she took the gold medal by equalling the world record of 6 ft 3½ in, and above all she showed remarkable composure and maturity in withstanding the pressure of a competition which lasted four and a half hours. Britain's Barbara Inkpen finished a creditable fourth with a jump of 6 ft 0½ in.

There was a victory, too, for the home team in the 800 metres, an Olympic record run from Hildergard Falck, while the Russian team, without a gold in the women's track and field in Mexico City, responded to the example set by Ludmila Bragina and were victorious in both discus and shot. Faina Melnik took the discus title by over five feet with another Olympic record, 218 ft 7 in, and the giant Nadizhda Chizhova set new world standards in the shot putt. She pushed her own world record up to 69 ft an advance of over a foot, and she won by the impressive margin of 3 ft 8 in.

For Great Britain there was Mary Peters to remember . . . and very little else.

1 Penthathlon gold medallist Mary Peters in a moment of intense concentration.
2 Heidi Rosendahl—darling of the German supporters.

Gerry Cranham

Swimming

The 1972 Olympic swimming competition will be remembered entirely for the performance of one man whose phenomenal success is unlikely to ever be equalled. Mark Spitz, a 22-year-old Californian, won seven gold medals; he accomplished this feat over a period of just eight days, and in each event a world record was broken.

His haul comprised four golds for individual races and three for relays, and in most cases he won with great ease. He took the 100 metres and 200 metres free-style titles, and also the 100 and 200 metres butterfly, and was a key figure in the USA successes in all three relay events. In the individual races his narrowest success came in the 100 metres freestyle, when another American, Jerry Heidenreich, finished four tenths of a second behind him, but even that represented a comfortable margin for the supremely talented and confident Spitz.

Fifteen-year-old Shane Gould from Australia made a creditable effort to emulate Spitz in the women's competition. She had three golds—and world records—in the 200 and 400 metres free-style and in the 200 metres medley relay, winning the 400 metres freestyle in the most impressive

fashion by 3.4 seconds; in an event in which the United States had traditionally excelled, they were out of the medals when Novella Calligaris of Italy and Gudrun Wegner of East Germany followed Miss Gould home. The young Australian, however, could only manage a well-beaten second in the 800 metres and a bronze medal in the 100 metres freestyle.

Undoubtedly the saddest saga of the swimming tournament concerned the young American Rick Demont, who failed a dope test after he had won the 400 metres freestyle. He admitted to using the drug ephedrine as a prescribed aid to an asthmatic condition, but had been unaware that it could also be construed as a stimulant. After a lengthy debate, Brad Cooper of Australia, who had come second by one hundredth of a second to Demont, was finally awarded the gold medal, and as further punishment the 16-year-old from California was barred from competing in the final of the 1,500 metres freestyle.

That race turned out to be one of the most exciting of the Games, and the United States had some consolation for Demont's absence by winning the gold medal. Mike Burton, the gold medallist in Mexico City, became engaged in

Tony Duffy

1 If Mark Spitz's was the supreme performance, Shane Gould's was the one that drew the public to her. The 15-year-old Australian won three golds (200m freestyle, 400m freestyle, and 200m medley), a silver (800m freestyle) and a bronze (100m freestyle)—the most medals by a woman swimmer in a single Games. 2 Medley king at Munich was Sweden's Gunnar Larsson, who did most of his training in the United States. However, his gold medal victory in the 400 metres medley could not have been closer: the electronic timing separated him from America's Tim McKee by a mere 1/500th of a second. 3 'Golden Boy' was an apt description of Mark Spitz; for after his unparalleled performance in the Munich pool—seven gold medals, seven world records—he turned professional as the million-dollar offers poured in. 4 The distinguished style of East Germany's Roland Matthes. Arguably the best backstroke exponent the swimming world has known, he retained both his Mexico City Olympic titles in Munich.

3

Colorsport

4

Ed Lacey

MUNICH OLYMPIC GAMES, 1972 Gold Medallists—Swimming			
Men			
100 metres freestyle	Mark Spitz	USA	51.22 sec
200 metres freestyle	Mark Spitz	USA	1 min 52.78 sec
400 metres freestyle	Rick Demont	USA	4 min 00.26 sec
disqualified for taking a banned drug – gold medal went to			
	Brad Cooper	Australia	4 min 00.27 sec
1500 metres freestyle	Mike Burton	USA	15 min 52.58 sec
100 metres breaststroke	Nabutaka Taguchi	Japan	1 min 04.94 sec
200 metres breaststroke	John Hencken	USA	2 min 21.55 sec
100 metres butterfly	Mark Spitz	USA	54.27 sec
200 metres butterfly	Mark Spitz	USA	2 min 00.70 sec
100 metres backstroke	Roland Matthes	East Germany	56.58 sec
200 metres backstroke	Roland Matthes	East Germany	2 min 02.82 sec
200 metres individual medley	Gunnar Larsson	Sweden	2 min 07.17 sec
400 metres individual medley	Gunnar Larsson	Sweden	4 min 31.98 sec
4 x 100 metres freestyle relay		USA	3 min 26.42 sec
4 x 200 metres freestyle relay		USA	7 min 35.78 sec
4 x 100 metres medley relay		USA	3 min 48.16 sec
Springboard diving	Vlademir Vasin	USSR	594.09 pts
Highboard diving	Klaus Dibiasi	Italy	504.12 pts
Women			
100 metres freestyle	Sandra Neilson	USA	58.59 sec
200 metres freestyle	Shane Gould	Australia	2 min 03.56 sec
400 metres freestyle	Shane Gould	Australia	4 min 19.04 sec
800 metres freestyle	Keena Rothammer	USA	8 min 53.68 sec
100 metres breaststroke	Catharine Carr	USA	1 min 13.58 sec
200 metres breaststroke	Beverley Whitfield	Australia	2 min 41.71 sec
100 metres butterfly	Mayumi Aoki	Japan	1 min 03.34 sec
200 metres butterfly	Karen Moe	USA	2 min 15.57 sec
100 metres backstroke	Melissa Belote	USA	1 min 5.78 sec
200 metres backstroke	Melissa Belote	USA	2 min 19.19 sec
200 metres individual medley	Shane Gould	Australia	2 min 23.07 sec
400 metres individual medley	Gail Neall	Australia	5 min 02.97 sec
4 x 100 metres freestyle relay		USA	3 min 55.19 sec
4 x 100 metres medley relay		USA	4 min 20.75 sec
Springboard diving	Micki King	USA	450.03 pts
Highboard diving	Ulrika Knape	Sweden	390.00 pts
Water Polo		USSR	

an enthralling duel with an enthralling duel with Australia's Graham Windeatt. First Burton led, then, at the halfway mark, Windeatt took such a lead that the contest seemed to be over. But in the last quarter mile, Burton reduced the margin and stormed to the front and finally won in the world record time of 15 minutes 52.58 seconds. Such had been the competition between the two men that Burton's winning time had been pushed to an incredible 46.3 sec greater than in his winning race in 1968.

The British team again disappointed by winning, for the third successive Olympics, only one single medal. This time it was a success for Scotland, with David Wilkie from Edinburgh coming second to John Hencken of the United States in the 200 metres breaststroke. Wilkie, who had prepared in America, also broke the European and Commonwealth records with his time of 2 min 23.67 sec. Wilkie also won a final place in the 100 metres breaststroke final, a race won by Taguchi of Japan, but his performance could scarcely compensate for the failure of a British squad which had had the benefit of more pre-Games training than those of former years.

In the diving, Micki King of the United States, who had seemed certain of a medal in 1968 until she broke a wrist in the competition, took the women's springboard title, but again the Americans, for so long the most influential diving nation, faltered. Ulrike Knape, of Sweden, second to the King in the springboard, took the highboard title with the American girls fourth and fifth. Klaus Dibiasi retained his men's highboard diving title for Italy, who also won a bronze and silver through Cagnotto in the two competitions. The springboard title went to a Russian for the first time in Olympic history, when Vladimir Vasin edged the Italian out of first place.

And the drama of the Olympic pool extended into the water polo competition. The successful Hungary team, who have claimed medals in every Olympics since 1928, met Russia in the last match knowing that a win would give them the gold medal again. But in a thrilling game Russia held out for a 3-3 draw and thereby took the title for themselves, for the first time.

1 Akinori Nakayama, winner of three gold medals in Mexico City, collected two (on the rings and team), plus a silver and bronze at Munich.
2 The incomparable Olga, the 17-year-old Russian whose charisma charmed the watching world as her captivating routines brought her three golds and a silver.

Alan E. Burrows.

Colorsport

Other Sports

In the 18 other sports outside the main athletic and swimming events, the most enchanting performance came from perhaps the smallest competitor. The delightful Russian gymnast, Olga Korbut, 17 years old, under five feet tall and weighing around six stone, possessed all the precocious appeal of a young child, and her genuine charisma charmed both spectators and judges—and she was in the Russian team as a late replacement only. Her phenomenal agility and the captivating manner in which she performed her routines brought her gold medals in the individual floor exercises and beam, and also a team gold in the combined exercises.

The boxing arena provided heroes of different stature, and three bronze medals for Britain. Ralph Evans, in the light-flyweight division, George Turpin, bantamweight, and Alan Minter, light-middleweight, were all losing semi-finallists in a very popular sport at the Games—all the seats in the hall were sold out for every night of the tournament. But though Britain achieved more than might have been expected, the surprise nation was Cuba who provided three gold medallists and the biggest puncher of the competition in Teofilo Stevenson. Among a series of spectacular wins during his progress to the heavyweight final there was included the destruction of a much-praised white American, Duane Bobeck, who many experts had predicted would break the coloured domination of professional heavyweight boxing. But there was no sensational final performance from the Cuban; his Romanian opponent rather wisely withdrew through injury.

Wrestling and weightlifting provided two strongmen, both Russians. Alex Medved won a third successive Olympic medal with his winning performance in the super-heavyweight freestyle class, while Alexeyev earned his title as the strongest man in the Games by recording a total of 1409¼ lb in the super-heavyweight lifting contest.

If Britain achieved their expected success in the equestrian events—Richard Meade took the gold medal in the individual three-day event, with Meade, Mary Gordon-Watson, Bridget Parker and Mark Phillips winning the team gold, and Anne Moore earning the silver in the individual show jumping—medals came from an unexpected source in the judo competition. David Starbrook won Britain's first ever Olympic medal in this sport when he took the second place in the middle-heavyweight division, and later Brian Jacks, middleweight, and Angelo Parisi, open, won bronze medals. Their success was part

97

of the breaking of the traditional Japanese domination of this sport. In the six judo events, the Japanese claimed only three golds and one bronze medal.

A more expected success for Great Britain came at Kiel, where the yachting competition was held. Rodney Pattison, who won the Flying Dutchman gold medal in Mexico with Iain Macdonald-Smith, triumphed again with a new partner, Chris Davies. Pattison's total dedication in his preparation for the Olympics typified the overriding approach of the successful competitors in the Games. Britain had a silver medal to enjoy, too, as Alan Warren and David Hunt sailed in second to the Russian yacht in the Tempest Class. Another medal, a bronze, came in the cycling team pursuit race when the British team of Mick Bennett, Ian Hallam, Ronald Keeble and Willie Moore came in behind West Germany and East Germany, whilst John Kynoch also took a bronze medal in the moving target shooting event, improving 11 points on his previous personal best.

The ball sports provided moments of drama and controversy. Russia ended the American domination of the basketball, scoring the winning points in the very last second of the final, stunning the holders who had, at one time, been cruising to victory. Not even lengthy post-match protests from the United States' squad, who claimed that time had run out, could reverse what was, perhaps, the most sensational finish in the entire games. Hockey had its controversy when the whole of the Pakistan team were banned from further Olympic competition for their behaviour while losing their title to West Germany. Football brought success again to an Eastern European nation, this time Poland, whose footballers are as near full-time as professionals in the West. The volleyball golds went to Japan in the men's competition, and the Russian women's team; the latter defeated Japan in the final, which was perhaps only just, as a Munich observer had taken out a law suit against the coach of the Japanese squad for brutal training methods!

1 Russia's Vasili Alexeyev, super-heavyweight gold medallist with an Olympic record total of 1,410¾ lb.
2 For Britain there was double gold in the three-day event, with Richard Meade, on Major Derek Allhusen's Laurieston, taking the individual title and leading the team—Mary Gordon-Watson, Bridget Parker and Mark Phillips.
3 Dave Starbrook won a surprise bronze for Britain in the light-heavy judo.

Keystone

In the inevitable though un-official, medal table that intro-duces nationalistic feeling to a competition which is essentially between individuals, Russia were the most successful country with 50 golds and a total of 99 medals, five more than the United States. But East Germany, third in the table with 20 gold medals and 66 medals in all, made the most decisive steps forward since Mexico City, and had the two Germanys competed as one nation, they would have been the most successful, totalling 106 medals between them. Britain equalled their Mexico City total with 18 medals, but of the four gold, only that won by Mary Peters was a pure athletic success; the other three victories had either horse or yacht to aid the competitor.

But for all the improvement in competition, the 1972 Olympic Games will always leave a taste that is tainted. Commercialism, professionalism and nationalism had all been threats to an insti-tution which had at least been peaceable if not wholly resistable. Munich must now be remem-bered for its violence, and the death of 11 members of a team. That is a cross that the Olympic Games, in the lavish, expensive and enormous form expressed by the XXth Olympiad, will find very hard to bear.

1 Rodney Pattison, this time with Chris Davies crewing, retained his title in the Flying Dutchman class.
2 New Zealand, East Germany, Denmark, Romania, USSR, and West Germany battle out the coxless fours.

Popperfoto

MUNICH OLYMPIC GAMES, 1972 Gold Medallists

Archery			
Men	John Williams	USA	2,538 pts
Women	Doreen Wilber	USA	2,424 pts
Basketball		USSR	
Boxing			
Light-flyweight	Gyoergy Gedo	Hungary	
Flyweight	Gheorgi Kostadinov	Bulgaria	
Bantamweight	Orlando Martinez	Cuba	
Featherweight	Boris Kousnetsov	USSR	
Lightweight	Jan Sczcepanski	Poland	
Light-welterweight	Ray Seales	USA	
Welterweight	Emilio Correa	Cuba	
Light-middleweight	Dieter Kottysch	West Germany	
Middleweight	Viatchesian Lemenchev	USSR	
Light-heavyweight	Mate Parlov	Yugoslavia	
Heavyweight	Teofilo Stevenson	Cuba	
Canoeing—Slalom			
Men			
Kayak singles	Siegbert Horn	East Germany	4 min 28.56 sec
Canadian singles	Reinhard Eiben	East Germany	5 min 15.84 sec
Canadian pairs	Walter Hoffman Rolf-Dieter Amend	East Germany	310.68 pts
Women			
Kayak singles	Angelika Bahmann	East Germany	364.50 pts
Canoeing—Straight Races			
Men			
Kayak singles	Aleksandr Shaparenko	USSR	3 min 48.06 sec
Kayak pairs	Nikolai Gorbachev Viktor Kratassyuk	USSR	3 min 31.23 sec
Kayak fours		USSR	3 min 14.02 sec
Canadian singles	Ivan Patzaichin	Romania	4 min 08.94 sec
Canadian Pairs	Vladas Chessyunas Yuri Lobanov	USSR	3 min 52.60 sec
Women			
Kayak singles	Yulia Ryabchinskaya	USSR	2 min 03.17 sec
Kayak pairs	Ludmila Pinayeva Ekaterina Kuryshko	USSR	1 min 53.50 sec

Cycling			
1000 metres time trial	Niels Fredborg	Denmark	1 min 06.44 sec
1000 metres sprint	Daniel Morelon	France	
Tandem sprint		USSR	
4000 metres individual pursuit	Knut Knudsen	Norway	4 min 45.74 sec
Team pursuit		West Germany	4 min 22.14 sec
100 kilometres team time trial		USSR	2 hr 11 min 17.8 sec
Individual road race	Henry Kuyper	Netherlands	4 hr 14 min 37.0 sec
Equestrian			
Three-day event—individual	Richard Meade	GB	
—team		GB	
Show jumping —individual	Graziano Mancinelli	Italy	
—team		West Germany	
Dressage —individual	Liselott Linsenhoff	West Germany	
—team		USSR	
Fencing			
Men			
Foil —individual	Witold Woyda	Poland	
—team		Poland	
Epee —individual	Csaba Fenyvesi	Hungary	
—team		Hungary	
Sabre —individual	Viktor Sidiak	USSR	
—team		Italy	
Women			
Foil —individual	Antonella Ragno Lonzi	Italy	
—team		USSR	
Football		Poland	
Gymnastics			
Men			
Combined exercises —individual	Sawao Kato	Japan	
—team		Japan	
Floor exercises	Nikolai Andrianov	USSR	
Horizontal bar	Mitsuo Tsukahara	Japan	
Parallel bars	Sawao Kato	Japan	
Pommell horse	Viktor Klimenko	USSR	
Long horse	Klaus Koeste	East Germany	
Rings	Akinori Nakayama	Japan	
Women			
Combined exercises —individual	Ludmilla Tourischeva	USSR	
—team		USSR	

Floor exercises	Olga Korbut	USSR
Asymmetrical bars	Karin Janz	East Germany
Beam	Olga Korbut	USSR
Long Horse	Karin Janz	East Germany
Handball		Yugoslavia
Hockey		West Germany
Judo		
Lightweight	Takeo Kawaguchi	Japan
Welterweight	Kazutoyo Nomura	Japan
Middleweight	Shinobu Sekine	Japan
Light-heavy	Shota Chochoshvili	USSR
Heavyweight	Willem Ruska	Netherlands
Open	Willem Ruska	Netherlands
Modern Pentathlon		
Individual	Andras Balczo	Hungary
Team		USSR
Rowing		
Single sculls	Yuri Malishev	USSR
Double sculls	Aleksandr Timoshinin	} USSR
	Gennadi Korshikov	
Coxless pairs	Siegfried Brietzke	} East Germany
	Wolfgang Mager	
Coxed pairs	Wolfgang Gunkel	} East Germany
	Joerg Lucke	
Coxed fours		West Germany
Coxless fours		East Germany
Eights		New Zealand
Shooting		
Small bore rifle		
—3 positions	John Writer	USA
—prone	Ho Jun Li	North Korea
Free pistol	Ragnar Skanaker	Sweden
Free rifle	Lones Wigger	USA
Rapid fire pistol	Josef Zapedzki	Poland
Clay pigeon	Angelo Scalzone	Italy
Skeet	Konrad Wirnhier	West Germany
Moving target	Lakov Zhelezniak	USSR
Volleyball		
Men		Japan
Women		USSR

Weightlifting			
Flyweight	Zygmunt Smalcerz	Poland	743¾ lb
Bantamweight	Imre Foeldi	Hungary	831¾ lb
Featherweight	Norair Nurikyan	Bulgaria	887 lb
Lightweight	Mukharbi Kirzhinov	USSR	1013¾ lb
Middleweight	Yordan Bikov	Bulgaria	1068¾ lb
Light-heavyweight	Leif Jensen	Norway	1118¾ lb
Middle-heavyweight	Andon Nikolov	Bulgaria	1157 lb
Heavyweight	Yan Talts	USSR	1278¼ lb
Super-heavyweight	Vasili Alexeyev	USSR	1409¼ lb
Wrestling			
Freestyle			
Light-flyweight	Roman Dmitriev	USSR	
Flyweight	Kiyomi Kato	Japan	
Bantamweight	Hideaki Yanagida	Japan	
Featherweight	Zagalav Abdulbekov	USSR	
Lightweight	Dan Gable	USA	
Welterweight	Wayne Wells	USA	
Middleweight	Levan Tedioshvili	USSR	
Light-heavyweight	Ben Peterson	USA	
Heavyweight	Ivan Yarygin	USSR	
Super-heavyweight	Alexandr Medved	USSR	
Graeco-Roman			
Light-flyweight	Gheorghe Berceanu	Romania	
Flyweight	Petar Kirov	Bulgaria	
Bantamweight	Rustem Kazakov	USSR	
Featherweight	Gheorghi Markov	Bulgaria	
Lightweight	Shamil Khisamutdinov	USSR	
Welterweight	Vitezspav Macha	Czechoslovakia	
Middleweight	Csaba Hegedus	Hungary	
Light-heavyweight	Valeri Rezantsev	USSR	
Heavyweight	Nicolae Martinescu	Romania	
Super-heavyweight	Anotoly Roshin	USSR	
Yachting			
Finn	Serge Maury	France	
Star	David Forbes	Australia	
Flying Dutchman	Rodney Pattison	} GB	
	Chris Davies		
Soling	Harry Melges	USA	
Tempest	Valentin Mankin	USSR	
Dragon	John Cuneo	Australia	

Olympic Football

As regular as the Olympic tournament itself is the well-worn controversy about the 'shamateurism' of the East Europeans in Olympic football. Munich and 1972 were no different. This time it was the turn of Stanley Rous to right the wrongs. His answer was to ban all World Cup players from the Olympics, thereby seriously weakening the strength of the Eastern European countries and, hopefully, allowing the emerging soccer nations to compete on more equal terms.

Excellent as it seemed, Rous' proposal was greeted with predictable hostility by anyone who felt that it affected their interests for the worse. And so the 1972 Olympics went as almost everyone predicted they would, Eastern European countries dominating the qualifying groups and monopolizing the semi-finals. It was left to Poland, who had never before won a major honour, to provide the one real surprise of the tournament when they, and not Hungary, won the final to take the gold medal.

There was a trace of irony in Rous' proposal, for without the success of Olympic football in the 1920s, the World Cup would have taken a longer time to materialize. Football had been introduced to the Olympics at Paris in 1900, but only as an exhibition, when Upton Park (representing Britain) beat France 4-0. It was eventually adopted in London in 1908, though only six teams took part and two were from France. The British side (all English) beat Sweden 12-1, the Netherlands 4-0, and Denmark 2-0 (in front of 8,000 people at the White City) to take the gold medal.

The 1912 tournament at Stockholm produced 11 entrants, all from Europe, but the same finalists. In intense heat Britain defeated Hungary 7-0 and Finland 4-0 before overcoming by 4-2 an injury-hit Danish side, who had eliminated Norway and the Netherlands.

Britain's dominance ended ignominiously when the Olympics were resumed at Antwerp in 1920. The FA stormed out of the Games, claiming that they had been playing against professionals. Professionalism was indeed already seeping through in the form of lavish expenses and broken-time payments (for time lost from work), but a more likely explanation for Britain's chagrin was their 3-1 defeat at the hands of Norway, one of the few amateur sides present. Czechoslovakia emerged as new stars, beating Yugoslavia 7-0, Norway 4-0, and France 4-1 to reach the final where they met Belgium—the home side. The

Czechs, however, were to go home without reward. They disagreed strongly with many decisions, some justifiably, and when the referee awarded Belgium their second goal, and let it stand after furious protest, they left the pitch and were disqualified. After a complicated play-off system Spain, beaten by Belgium 3-1 in the second round, took the silver medal, while the Dutch had to be content with the bronze for the third successive time, despite having won the match for third place before the disqualification of Czechoslovakia.

Soon after the Antwerp Games several European nations legalized various forms of broken-time payments for amateurs. In 1923 FIFA refused to accept the British definition of the term, and both Britain and Denmark did not compete in 1924. The four British associations finally withdrew from FIFA after that body had insisted the Olympic committee legalize broken-time payments for their members during the Amsterdam tournament, and did not rejoin until 1946. Football was dropped from the 1932 Games at Los Angeles, and in 1936 there was a return to the strict definition of the amateur: Britain and Denmark reappeared, but Uruguay, Argentina, Belgium, and Switzerland refused to participate.

With the emergence of government-assisted athletes from the Eastern European bloc, the FA attitude softened after the Second World War and in 1948 the FA gave tentative approval to broken-time payments for representative matches.

At Paris in 1924 football had really made its mark. A quarter of a million people saw the 21 games, including 41,000 for the final, and soccer contributed over a third of the total Olympic revenue. The entry (22) was considerably broadended, and one of the two major surprises was Egypt's 3-0 win over Hungary, the favourites. The other was Sweden's elimination of the holders, Belgium, by 8-1. But attention fixed on the South American champions Uruguay, who defeated Yugoslavia 7-0, USA 3-0, France 5-1, and the Netherlands 2-1 to make the final, where after an even first half they put three goals past Switzerland.

The 1928 competition endorsed the New World's success with an all-South American final. Argentina scored 23 goals against USA, Belgium, and Egypt, while Uruguay, if less spectacular statistically, had little trouble with greater opposition in the Netherlands, Germany, and Italy. Uruguay overcame their neighbours and old rivals after a replay in a foretaste of the first World Cup final two years later.

When soccer returned to the Olympic agenda at Berlin in 1936, the competition was organized with Teutonic thoroughness and efficiency.

The 16 teams were seeded—8 strong ones playing 8 weaker ones in the first round—but there were plenty of surprises to upset the officials' calculations. Newcomers Japan upset the ratings by beating Sweden 3-2, before losing 8-0 to Vittorio Pozzo's Italy. Norway held out against the meticulously prepared Germans—who were sent away in disgrace—and Britain, who had beaten China 2-0 in the first round, went down 5-4 to Poland after trailing 5-1 at one stage. Italy and Austria, coached by Jimmy Hogan, beat Norway and Poland respectively to reach the final, where the Italians needed extra time and a lucky goal to win the gold medal.

The London Olympics of 1948 were won in grand style by Sweden, coached by George Raynor and full of players later to make their mark with European clubs. They beat Austria 3-0, Korea 12-0, Denmark 4-2 and, in the final, Yugoslavia, who had beaten Great Britain (managed by Matt Busby), 3-1 in the semi-final. Britain had earlier beaten the Netherlands and France, who in turn had struggled in beating India, who had nine players competing without boots.

If 1948 belonged to Sweden, 1952 and Helsinki was the story of Hungary. They eliminated Romania, Italy, Turkey, and Sweden (6-0) before meeting Yugoslavia, who had scored 26 goals in their five matches. The Hungarians—10 of whom were to be in the side that shattered England at Wembley the following year—brought that run to an abrupt end in the final and won 2-0, despite Puskas missing a penalty. The shock of the competition was provided by Luxembourg with a 5-3 win over Britain in the preliminary round.

The 1956 series in Melbourne was a dull affair. Many countries, including Hungary, stayed out because of the travelling expense, and the entry went down from the 25 of 1952 to 11—the lowest since 1912. England were invited after being eliminated in the qualifiers by Bulgaria—who promptly beat them 6-1 in the second round. The Russians, fielding their full international side, beat Yugoslavia, and the luckless Yugoslavs thus took their third successive silver medal.

Yugoslavia's turn was to come at Rome in 1960 when—with the help of five full caps—they beat Denmark in the final. It was unfortunate that their success was clouded by the situation in the semi-final, when they won through on the drawing of lots after fruitless extra time with Italy. For the first time the competition employed groups, with the top club from each qualifying for the semi-finals. There the series produced its one upset, with Denmark beating a star-studded Hungarian side 2-0.

Eastern Europe again provided

Colorsport

3

Above: Great Britain, Olympic champions in 1908 and 1912, got close to the honours at the second London Olympics, in 1948. But in the semi-final, Britain (white) lost 1-3 to Yugoslavia and then went down 3-5 to Denmark in the third-place match. **1** Sweden (dark shirts), with their famed Grenoli trio, took the gold medals at London. **2** Hungary's Lajos Szucs scores against Japan in their **1968** semi-final in Mexico City. Japan, surprisingly, won the bronze medals. Less of a shock was the east European final between Hungary and Bulgaria. Unfortunately, the game developed into a brawl, with four players being sent off and the officials being bombarded with cushions (**3**). **4** The magnificent setting for the 1972 Olympic football final in Munich.

OLYMPIC GOLD MEDAL SIDES

Britain (1908): Bailey; Corbett, Smith; Hunt, Chapman, Hawkes; Berry, Woodward, Stapley, Purnell, Hardman
Britain (1912): Brebner; Burn, Knight; Littlewort, Hanney, Dines; Berry, Woodward, Walden, Hoare, Sharpe
Belgium (1920): De Bie; Swartenbroecks, Verbeek; Masch, Hause, Fierens; van Hegge, Coppee, Bragard, Larnoe, Bastin
Uruguay (1924): Mazzali: Nasazzi, Arispe; Andrade, Vidal, Ghierra; A. Urdinaran, Scarone, Petrone, Cea, Romano
Uruguay (1928): Mazzali; Nasazzi, Arispe; Andrade, Fernandez, Gestido; S. Urdinaran, Scarone, Petrone, Cea, Castro
Italy (1936): Venturini; Foni, Rava; Baldo, Piccini, Locatelli; Frossi, Marchini, Bertoni, Biagi, Gabriotti
Sweden (1948): Lindberg; K. Nordahl, Nilsson; Rosengren, B. Nordahl, Andersson; Rosen, Gren, G. Nordahl, Carlsson, Liedholm
Hungary (1952): Grosics; Buzansky, Lantos; Bozsik, Lorant, Zakarias; Hidegkuti, Kocsics, Palotas, Puskas, Czibor
USSR (1956): Yachin; Kuznetsov, Ogonkinov; Maslenkin, Bachachkin, Netto; Tatouchkin; Issaev, Simonian, Salnikov, Ilyin
Yugoslavia (1960): Vidinic; Durkovic, Jusufi; Zanetic, Roganovic, Perusic; Ankovic, Matous, Galic, Knez, Kostic
Hungary (1964): Szentmihalyi; Novak, Iliasz; Szepesi, Orban, Nogradi; Farkas, Csernai, Bene, Komora, Katona
Hungary (1968): Fater; Novak, Drestyak; Pancsics, Menczel, Szucs; Fazekas, A. Dunai, Nagy, Nosko, Juhasz
Poland (1972): Kostka; Gut, Gorgon; Cmikiewicz, Anczok, Szoltysik; Masczyk, Kraska, Deyna, (s. Szynczak), Lubanski, Godocha

1 the winner at Tokyo in 1964, with Hungary beating Czechoslovakia. East Germany took third place, but there was no other European opposition. The 14 sides were arranged in two groups of four and two of three, with the top eight forming the quarter-finalists. Hungary, having beaten Morocco and Yugoslavia (6-5) in their group, then eliminated Romania and the UAR to reach the final.

For 1968 in Mexico two genuinely amateur European countries, France and Spain, returned to the fray and both won their sections. The relatively unadvanced soccer nations of Asia, Africa, and Central America provided nine entrants, but it was two of the three state-sponsored teams—Hungary and Bulgaria, again using the Olympics as a practice for the subsequent World Cup—who provided the finalists. The final, however, was ruined by a mixture of violent play and over-zealous refereeing, and four players were sent off. Conduct was to improve, but abuse of the system was not, in 1972.

1 The Hungarians celebrate Varadi's goal in the usual manner, but it was the Poles, with two goals by Deyna, who took the football gold medals at Munich.
2 Quick thinking by Gunnar Nordahl brought Sweden a goal in the 1948 semi-final with Denmark. Realizing he could be off-side, he stepped into the net—and out of play—and Carlsson's goal stood.

OLYMPIC SOCCER

Year	Venue	Teams	First		Second		Third		Fourth	
1908	London	†6	Great Britain	2	Denmark	0	Netherlands	2	Sweden	1
1912	Stockholm	11	Great Britain	4	Denmark	2	Netherlands	9	Finland	0
1920	Antwerp	14	‡Belgium		‡Spain		‡Netherlands		‡France	
1924	Paris	22	Uruguay	3	Switzerland	0	Sweden	1:3	Netherlands	1:1
1928	Amsterdam	17	Uruguay	1:2	Argentina	1:1	Italy	11	Egypt	3
1936	Berlin	16	*Italy	2	Austria	1	*Norway	3	Poland	2
1948	London	18	Sweden	3	Yugoslavia	1	Denmark	5	Great Britain	3
1952	Helsinki	25	Hungary	2	Yugoslavia	0	Sweden	3	Germany	0
1956	Melbourne	11	USSR	1	Yugoslavia	0	Bulgaria	3	India	0
1960	Rome	16	Yugoslavia	3	Denmark	1	Hungary	2	Italy	1
1964	Tokyo	14	Hungary	2	Czechoslovakia	1	East Germany	3	UAR	1
1968	Mexico City	16	Hungary	4	Bulgaria	1	Japan	2	Mexico	0
1972	Munich	16	Poland	2	Hungary	1	*§East Germany	2	§USSR	2

* after extra time † including two French sides. ‡ Czechoslovakia, losing 2-0 to Belgium in the final, walked off the field and were disqualified. Spain, Sweden, Italy, and Norway played off for the right to meet the Netherlands (beaten by Belgium in the semi-final) for second place, and Spain then beat the Netherlands 3-1. France had earlier lost to the Netherlands in the play-off between the losing semi-finalists. § East Germany and USSR shared third place.

104

The Winter Olympic Games

Tony Nash and Robin Dixon
overcame tremendous
handicaps to become Britain's
first ever bobsleigh Olympic
champions, at Igls in 1964.

Sports Illustrated – Time Life/James Drake

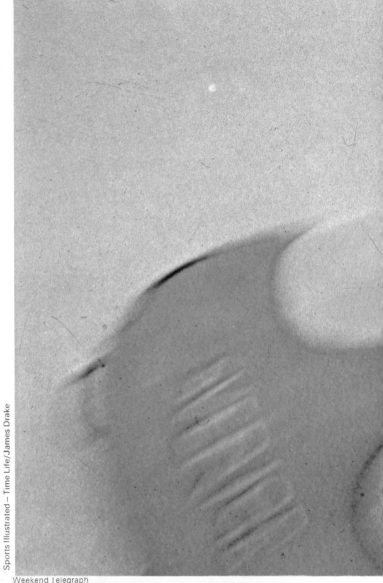

Weekend Telegraph

Colorsport

Syndication International

The speed skater striving for the extra yard of pace; the ski jumper defying gravity to the utmost; the bobsleigh crew hurtling down a funnel of ice; the figure skater entrancing with breathtaking spins and jumps; the skier twisting and weaving downhill through the slalom poles . . . all contribute to making the Winter Olympics an absorbing spectacle of speed and grace, courage and self-expression.

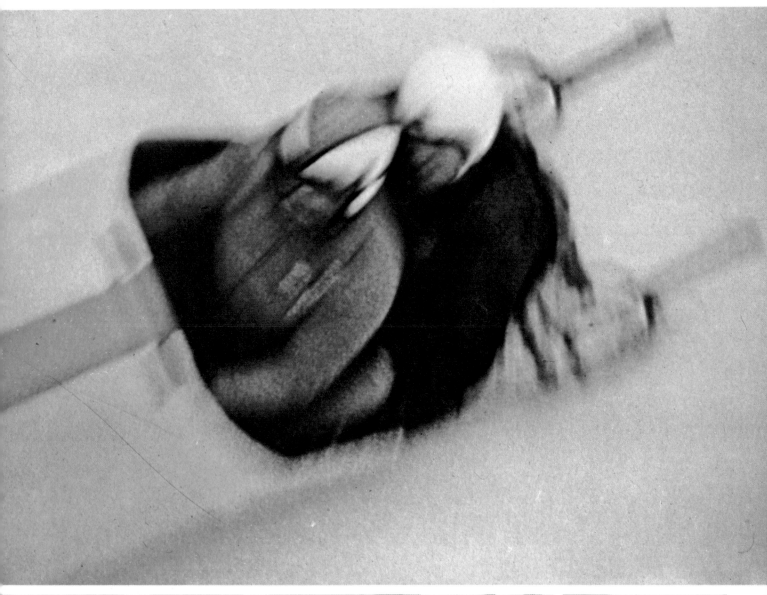

Above: **Jean-Claude Killy, sex symbol of the slopes and the second Alpine skier, after Austria's Toni Sailer, to win three gold medals in one Winter Olympics. Soon after achieving this, at Grenoble, Killy turned professional.**

107

1

2

3

Left: **The Special Jump, which has been a largely Scandinavian preserve since its Olympic inception in 1924. It was first practised in Norway as early as 1866.**

Although ice figure skating competitions were included in the original list of proposed Olympic events drawn up at the first Olympic conference, at Paris on June 23, 1894, which led to the revival of the Olympic Games, skating had to wait until 1908 and the first London Olympics to make its debut in the Games.

But from this belated beginning arose the Winter Olympic Games, officially the 'Olympic Winter Games', held quadrennially since 1924 as a separate celebration. The early listing of skating was due to its being one of the earliest sports to be organized internationally, and its delayed appearance in the Games was due only to the difficulty of finding a suitable rink in the host cities. London was the first able to provide it.

The second Olympic contest in figure skating, together with the first Olympic ice hockey tournament, took place at the Antwerp

Games of 1920. And although such events could have continued to form part of the summer Games, the growing popularity of Nordic skiing prompted the logical setting up of a separate winter programme. Thus the first Winter Olympic Games were held at Chamonix in 1924. There, Nordic ski racers and jumpers, four-man bobsledders, and speed skaters joined the figure skaters and ice hockey players in a self-contained schedule.

For the second Winter Olympics, at St Moritz in 1928, skeleton tobogganing was included on the Cresta Run. (This competition was revived in 1948 at the same venue, but was not held at any other Winter Olympics.) In other fields, too, the programme expanded. For the third meeting, at Lake Placid, New York, two-man bobsledding was added. Alpine skiing was included at the 1936 Games at Garmisch-Partenkirchen, and the popularity of the Winter Games was such that they were revived immediately after World War II, at St Moritz in 1948.

The 1952 events were the first to be staged near a capital city, Oslo, and this factor considerably boosted the attendance figures. By this time the Games were an integral feature of the winter sports calendar, and the three gold medals won by Toni Sailer at Cortina in 1956 made his name as well known throughout the world as those of the heroes of the summer Olympics.

For the Squaw Valley Games of 1960, the second to be held in the United States, the programme was strengthened by the inclusion of women's speed skating and the men's biathlon—a combination cross-country skiing and shooting event—though bobsleigh was temporarily excluded. And though the number of entrants may have been reduced because of the distance of Squaw Valley from Europe, when the 1964 Games were staged in Innsbruck they attracted over 1,000 competitors from a record 36 countries. These Games also saw the introduction of luge tobogganing. Further records were broken at Grenoble in 1968, when 1,293 competitors from 37 nations attended.

The Winter Olympic Games are the one occasion every four years when all the major snow and ice sports are being staged in one

Above, **The opening ceremony of the 1968 Winter Olympics at Grenoble, the 10th to be held since 1924, when 293 men and women met at Chamonix. At Grenoble there were 1,293 competitors. 1 Bobsleigh was an Olympic sport from the very start, but 2 alpine skiing, perhaps the most publicized of winter sports, did not join the list until 1936. 3 Ice hockey, for a long time the domain of the Canadians, and 4 figure skating preceded the Winter Olympics by appearing in earlier Olympic Games.**

area. Even so, because of the disparate nature of many of the sports involved, which require differing facilities, the competitions tend to be rather dispersed. This, however, is true of any major event, and is a reflection of the difficulty of staging the winter Games. Consequently, the cost to the host city is enormous, and it may be indicative that Denver, in Colorado, USA, withdrew as the venue for the 1976 Winter Olympics; and it was decided to hold them at Innsbruck, where winter sport facilities were available without the burden of unnecessary expense.

WINTER OLYMPIC GAMES

Year	Venue	Date	Competitors		
			Men	Women	Total
1924	Chamonix	25 Jan—4 Feb	280	13	293
1928	St Moritz	11-19 Feb	464	27	491
1932	Lake Placid	4-13 Feb	277	30	307
1936	Garmisch	6-16 Feb	680	76	756
1948	St Moritz	30 Jan—8 Feb	636	77	713
1952	Oslo	14-25 Feb	624	108	732
1956	Cortina	26 Jan—5 Feb	778	146	924
1960	Squaw Valley	18-28 Feb	521	144	665
1964	Innsbruck	29 Jan—9 Feb	914	197	1,111
1968	Grenoble	6-18 Feb	1,065	228	1,293
1972	Sapporo	3-13 Feb	911	217	1,128

Figure skating events were also held in 1908 and 1920 as part of the main Olympic celebrations.

Chamonix Winter Olympic Games (1924)

Nobody knew it then, but a competitor who finished last at the Chamonix Winter Olympics was later to become the most famous of all Winter Olympics entrants. These first Winter Olympics marked the international debut of a tiny, 11-year-old Norwegian schoolgirl —Sonja Henie—who was later to reign as queen of the ice with three Olympic and 10 world championship crowns.

But in these early days of Winter Olympics, the big talking point was whether they would take place at all. Despite Chamonix's favourable climatic record, there was at first no snow; and when it did snow on the French Alpine resort, 36,000 cubic metres of it had to be cleared from the ice rink. With only a week to go, rain transformed the speed-skating rink into a lake. Fortunately, frosts returned, and conditions were ideal when Monsieur Gaston Vidal, French Undersecretary of State, declared the Games open.

Although figure skating had already formed part of the 1908 London Olympic Games, and was again contested, along with ice hockey, at Antwerp in 1920, the Chamonix Games were the first occasion on which other snow and ice sports gained Olympic status. And so Nordic skiers, bobsledders, and speed skaters joined figure skaters and ice hockey players at Chamonix for the first self-contained, separate Winter Olympics.

One hundred and two skiers, 82 ice hockey players, 39 bobsledders, 31 speed skaters, and 29 figure skaters representing 16 nations contested the 14 titles. The only women competitors were the 13 figure skaters, 5 of whom took part in the pairs as well as the solo event. Norway and Finland finished the most successful countries, winning 4 gold medals each, followed by Austria with 2, and the United States, Switzerland, Canada, and Sweden with 1 each.

The outstanding individuals were the Norwegian skier Thorleif Haug and the Finnish skater Clas Thunberg, both winning three gold

1 Sonja Henie made her debut at Chamonix, placing last in a field of eight: an inauspicious start to a remarkable career.
2 The jumping was won by Jacob Tham, and the other three Nordic events by his compatriot, Thorleif Haug (3).

Competitors gather in the French Alpine resort of Chamonix for the opening of the first Winter Olympics.

medals each. In addition, Thunberg collected a silver and a bronze, and Haug also won a bronze. In a sense, one of Thunberg's gold medals was complimentary because it was awarded to the best overall performer in the four speed-skating events, the only time a combination award has been made for Olympic speed skating.

Haug led a strong team of Norwegian skiers who, in the 1920s, were acknowledged world masters both of cross-country and jumping events. His superiority was most marked in the gruelling 50 kilometres cross-country, in which only 21 of the 33 contestants finished a course made hazardous by several frozen downhill slopes. Haug's three team-mates followed him to take the next places and little more than five minutes separated the four. The fifth-placed competitor, however, was more than 21 minutes slower than Haug.

The story was much the same in the 18 kilometres, except that a Finn took the bronze. And by winning the Nordic combination, a challenging test of overall cross-country and jumping skill, Haug illustrated his versatility and collected his third gold.

The Norwegian skiers completed the grand slam when Jacob Thams won the specialized jump event. It was held on a hill erected with possible leaps of 60 metres in mind, but the jury shortened the in-run and so lessened the distance potential. Thams took the title with two leaps of 49 metres in the adjudged best style. The longest clearance, 50 metres, was made by an American Anders Haugen, who eventually finished fourth.

Successful though the Norwegians were in skiing, their eclipse in all the speed-skating events was a major surprise, for this was another sport in which the nation had distinguished traditions. Thunberg convincingly won the two middle distances, 1,500 metres and 5,000 metres, finished second in the 10,000 to his fellow Finn Julius Skutnabb, and tied for third place

1 American runner-up, was followed by Britain's Ethel Muckelt, with an endearingly diminutive Sonja Henie last in the field of eight. In the pairs, Alfred Berger and Helene Engelmann struck another blow for the Viennese school by outpointing the Finns, Walter and Ludovika Jakobsson.

Bobsledding at Chamonix was confined to one event, for crews of four or five riders. The bob run at the time was considered pretty hazardous and technically below the top international standards, and there were some nasty incidents. Although the Swiss won the gold medal, they had mixed fortunes. Their number one sled had to withdraw after a serious crash, and it was left to their second crew, driven by Eduard Scherrer, to clock the fastest times in each of the first three runs to take the title.

The ice hockey was, as it has been since, the big spectator draw, and Europeans were dazzled by the consistently high standard of the Canadian and American teams, which they were unable to match. Goals galore in uneven games seldom failed to mesmerize onlookers, who admired and respected a brand of play they had not been accustomed to.

The transatlantic teams overwhelmed the best Europe could offer, Canada running up scores of 30-0 against Czechoslovakia and 22-0 against Sweden. Their least one-sided game was their 6-1 victory over the United States, America's only defeat. Great Britain, though losing 2-19, were the only side to score more than once against the champions, and by beating Sweden 4-3 they earned the bronze medal.

It is an Olympic tradition that the host country may present in the programme two additional sports as demonstration events. At Chamonix, the chosen demonstration events were curling and a military patrol race. Three nations contested the curling—the more widely practised rules of Scottish origin were used—which was won by a British team led by T. S. Aikman, with Sweden runners-up.

The military patrol race, combining skiing and rifle marksmanship over a difficult 30 kilometres course, was a forerunner of the modern biathlon. The earlier sport had a more military appearance than its successor, and was especially popular in Switzerland whose team narrowly defeated Finland.

The Chamonix Games had made a great start for separate Winter Olympics. Other events have been added since then, and at Grenoble in 1968, more than double the nations represented at Chamonix sent over five times the number of competitors to contest more than twice the events.

1 Herma Plank-Szabo, five times world champion, was a convincing winner of the women's figure skating.
2 A goalmouth incident in the ice hockey final between the United States (dark shirts) and Canada, who won 6-1.

Presse Sports

CHAMONIX WINTER OLYMPIC GAMES, 1924 Gold Medallists

Nordic Skiing			
18 kilometres	Thorleif Haug	Norway	1 hr 14 min 31.0 sec
50 kilometres	Thorleif Haug	Norway	3 hr 44 min 32.0 sec
Jumping	Jacob Thams	Norway	
Combination	Thorleif Haug	Norway	
Figure Skating			
Men	Gillis Grafstrom	Sweden	
Women	Herma Plank-Szabo	Austria	
Pairs	Alfred Berger, Helene Engelmann	Austria	
Speed Skating			
500 metres	Charles Jewtraw	USA	44.0 sec
1,500	Clas Thunberg	Finland	2 min 20.8 sec
5,000 metres	Clas Thunberg	Finland	8 min 39.0 sec
10,000 metres	Julius Skutnabb	Finland	18 min 4.8 sec
Combined	Clas Thunberg	Finland	
Bobsleigh		Switzerland	
Ice Hockey		Canada	

in the 500 metres sprint, won by the American Charles Jewtraw.

All the ice events were held in a stadium that was admirable by the standards of the time. A complex arena, capable of holding more than 10,000 spectators, it included a 400 metres speed-skating perimeter around two ice hockey rinks, with the end semicircles used by figure skaters.

The individual figure-skating golds each went to the respected greats in the sport's history. Sweden's Gillis Grafström gained a narrow verdict over his Austrian rival Willy Böckl, being placed first by only four of the seven judges. And Herma Plank-Szabó, one of the early exponents of the Viennese school of technique and world champion for five consecutive years from 1922, took the women's title by a unanimous vote. Beatrix Loughran, the

Radio Times Hulton Picture Library

St Moritz Winter Olympic Games (1928)

A sharp increase in the number of entries for the second Winter Olympics, at the Swiss glamour resort of St Moritz in 1928, reflected the substantial rise in popularity of snow and ice sports during the four years since the first Winter Games at Chamonix, France. The 491 competitors—464 men and 27 women—numbered almost 200 more than in 1924, and represented 25 participating nations, an increase of 9.

Despite the high altitude of 6,066 feet, an unseasonably mild westerly *fohn* wind caused a dramatic thaw which affected many performances and caused the 10,000 metres speed skating to be cancelled. In fact a deluge of rain, almost unheard of in this area during February, caused one completely blank day in the middle of the meeting. Fortunately, a rapid freeze followed in time to save the programme. One new event on the programme was skeleton tobogganing on the challenging Cresta Run.

In unusually heavy conditions, Per Erik Hedlund's victory for Sweden in the 50 kilometres cross-country ski marathon took 68

Official Report of 1928 Olympics

minutes longer than Thorleif Haug's in 1924. This underlined the difficulty of comparing the times in cross-country ski races at different dates or venues, with weather conditions variable enough to make the going more than an hour slower. Swedes took all the medals in this event but it was Norway's turn for a grand

Above. **An ice-hockey match in the picturesque setting of St Moritz during the 1928 Winter Olympics. Canada won the second of four successive gold medals in this event.**
Below. **Per Erik Hedlund led a clean sweep for Sweden in the 50 kilometres cross-country Nordic skiing event.**

slam in the 18 kilometres. On a contrasting course, crackling with frost, Johan Grottumsbraaten finished a full two minutes ahead of two compatriots. In convincing style, Grottumsbraaten also won the Nordic combination (18 kilometres cross-country and ski jumping) in which Norwegians once more monopolized the medals.

Although hampered by a short in-run for the take-off, Alf Andersen clinched another gold for Norway in the jumping, after Jacob Tullin-Thams, the defending champion, crashed when landing what would have been a winning leap. Sigmund Ruud took the silver for Norway but third place went surprisingly to a Czech, Rudolf Burkert, the only Central European to win a medal in this event before World War II.

The Finnish speed skater Clas Thunberg, although nearly 35 years old, proved still a master by winning two gold medals for the two shorter distances, the 500 and 1,500 metres. But in the 500 metres sprint, Norwegian Bernt Evensen also took a gold with an equal time, the first winter Olympic occasion when two golds were awarded for an individual event. A triple dead heat for third place meant the award of three bronze medals.

The 5,000 metres revealed the early word-beating class of yet another Norwegian, Ivar Ballangrud, who was almost 9 seconds in

Official Report of 1928 Olympics

front of Julius Skutnabb of Finland, the runner-up. The cancellation of the 10,000 metres was a bitter disappointment to the United States because, at the time of curtailment, the American racer Irving Jaffee had been leading the Norwegian favourite Evensen.

The figure skating saw the last of Gillis Granstrom's three men's victories for Sweden and the first of Sonja Henie's three women's wins for Norway—a master at his peak and a prodigy on her way up. The elegant Grafstrom, 30, skated a freestyle programme clearly better than his previous performances, appreciably superior to that of the young fourth-placed Austrian Karl Schafer, who was to be Grafstrom's successor four years later. But the runner-up was another Austrian, Willy Bockl, who closely challenged Grafstrom all the way.

Miss Henie, already the world champion but not quite 16, enjoyed a more comfortable passage and introduced a refreshingly more athletic element into women's freestyle. In the pairs event, the French partnership of Pierre Brunet and Andree Joly set a high standard in well timed lifts.

Despite their home course advantage, the Swiss were disappointing in the five-man bobsleigh event, contested by 23 teams from 14 countries. The thawing course allowed only two runs instead of the usual four. The American sleds took the first two places, with William Fiske ably piloting the winner. Jennison Heaton, who drove the second bob, won the first Olympic skeleton toboggan event on the separate Cresta Run, with his brother John in second place, ahead of Britain's Earl of Northesk.

The ice hockey tournament emphasized that a wide gulf still existed between the Canadians and the 10 other competing nations. The United States did not enter and, because of their obvious superiority, the Canadians were granted exemption until the semi-finals, a stage also reached by Sweden, Swizerland,

1 Alpine forests form a scenic backdrop to the ski jumping.
2 The great Nordic skier Johan Grottumsbraaten won the 18-km cross-country and the Nordic combined competitions for Norway.
3 Norway also came home first in the Military Ski Patrol: this demonstration event was the forerunner of the skiing-shooting biathlon which was included in the 1960 Olympics.

and Great Britain.

Scoring double figures without conceding a goal against each of the other three (an aggregate of 38-0), Canada displayed complete mastery, while the Swedes proved best of the rest by defeating third placed Switzerland 4-0 and Great Britain 3-1. The Swiss beat the British 4-0 to take the bronze medals.

A military patrol ski event was demonstrated at these Games, and this was a basic forerunner of the shooting/cross-country-skiing biathlon, which gained full Olympic status in 1960. But perhaps the most significant development at St Moritz really took place at the conference table, for it was there that Arnold Lunn seized an opportunity to persuade the then Nordic-biased International Ski Federation to agree in principle on the future Olympic inclusion of Alpine skiing, even though the motion took another eight years to reach reality. As someone observed at the time, Lunn's achievement was comparable to a Norwegian's getting the rules of cricket changed.

ST MORITZ WINTER OLYMPIC GAMES, 1928 Gold Medallists			
Nordic Skiing			
18 kilometres	Johan Grottumsbraaten	Norway	1 hr 37 min 1.0 sec
50 kilometres	Per Hedlund	Sweden	4 hr 52 min 3.0 sec
Combination	Johan Grottumsbraaten	Norway	17.8 pts
Jumping	Alf Andersen	Norway	19.2 pts
Figure Skating			
Men	Gillis Grafstrom	Sweden	2,698.2 pts
Women	Sonja Henie	Norway	1,455.8 pts
Pairs	Pierre Brunet, Andree Joly	France	100.5 pts
Speed Skating			
500 metres	Clas Thunberg	Finland	43.4 sec
	Bernt Evensen	Norway	43.4 sec
1,500 metres	Clas Thunberg	Finland	2 min 21.1 sec
5,000 metres	Ivar Ballangrud	Norway	8 min 50.5 sec
Bobsleigh			
5 man		USA	3 min 20.5 sec
Skeleton Tobogganing			
	Jennison Heaton	USA	3 min 1.8 sec
Ice Hockey		Canada	

Lake Placid Winter Olympic Games (1932)

In 1932, both summer and winter Olympic Games were held in the United States, the Winter Olympics at Lake Placid in northern New York State, and the summer Games at Los Angeles, 3,000 miles away in California. Only once previously, in 1904, had an Olympic celebration been held outside Europe, and the long travelling distances and enormous expenses involved kept the number of participants at Lake Placid down to a total of 262 competitors from 17 nations, compared with the 1928 total of 494 entrants from 25 nations.

Scandinavians dominated the four Nordic skiing events, held at an altitude of 1,860 ft. There were, in fact, Norwegian clean sweeps in both the jumping and the combination contests. Norway's Hans Beck jumped 5 metres farther than his team-mate Birger Ruud with his first attempt in the ski jump. But in the second round Beck played for safety—as he thought—and Ruud, possibly the best ski-jumper of all time, out-jumped him by 5½ metres to snatch the gold medal. Ruud was to add a second gold and a silver

19-year-old Norwegian ski jumper Birger Ruud soars through the American air to a narrow Olympic victory at Lake Placid in 1932.

in the two subsequent Winter Games in 1936 and 1948. In the Nordic combination event the versatile Johan Gröttumsbraaten, another of Norway's giants, crowned a glorious career by winning the gold for the second time running, having been second at Chamonix in the first Winter Games in 1924 behind fellow-Norwegian Thorleif Haug.

The 50 kilometres cross-country marathon provided a close and exciting duel between two Finns, Veli Saarinen and Väinö Liikkanen. After nearly 4½ hours of gruelling skiing, Saarinen finished just 20 seconds clear of his compatriot, with the third-placed man, Norway's Arne Rustadstuen, 3 minutes behind them. But the 18-kilometres event was a clear win for Sweden's Sven Utterström, who came in a clear two minutes ahead of fellow-Swede Axel Wikström.

In 1932 Sonja Henie was at the zenith of her career, and it came as no surprise when she won her second Olympic figure skating gold medal with a unanimous judges' verdict over Fritzi Burger of Austria. But even the popular Norwegian's magnificent display was overshadowed by the interest taken in the men's event. The

question was, could the remarkable Swedish skater Gillis Grafström, who had won gold medals in this event at Antwerp in 1920 (when figure skating was included in the Summer Games), at Chamonix in 1924, and at St Moritz in 1928, win for a fourth successive time at the remarkable age of 38? The rising star of men's figure skating was the Austrian Karl Schäfer, a youngster of 22, and he won a thrilling tussle by a 5-2 decision and went on to retain the title in 1936. In fairness to Grafström it must be recorded that he was suffering from a knee injury, and this probably cost him the chance of becoming the first man to win four successive Olympic titles. He still finished an easy second, 66.2 points ahead of the bronze medallist, Montgomery Wilson of Canada.

The pairs title was retained by the French couple, Pierre and Andrée Brunet, who had married since their 1928 victory. Their nearest challengers, Sherwin Badger and Beatrix Loughran from the United States, came close enough to take better marks from two of the seven judges.

American skaters won all four of the men's speed skating events, John Shea winning the 500 and 1,500 metres, and Irving Jaffee the 5,000 and 10,000 metres. Their successes were gained with more than the usual home advantages. For the only time in an Olympic Games or world championship event, the customary international rules of skating in pairs were suspended, and the races were run according to the American rules of 'pack' starts with heats and finals. This meant a complete revolution in tactics for the European competitors, who were more used to the international format, the strategy of spurting and the use of 'elbowing' techniques being completely new to them. The redoubtable Finn Clas Thunberg (co-champion in 1928) declined to take part in these controversial circumstances, and the only two Europeans able to gain medals were the Norwegians Ivar Ballangrud (second in the 10,000 metres) and Bernt Evensen (second in the 500 metres). John Shea equalled the Olympic record for the 500 metres with 43.4 sec, but his victory in the 1,500 metres and both of Irving Jaffee's wins in the longer distances were the slowest Olympic successes ever recorded. The Americans were conclusively outpaced during the annual world championships held later that year on the same track under normal two-at-a-time rules. Ivar Ballangrud won all four events.

Only four nations—the United States, Canada, Germany, and Poland—contested the ice hockey, and each played the other teams twice. The United States, with a much-improved side, came close to toppling the Canadians (champions in 1920, 1924, and 1928). The

two Canada v USA matches decided the issue: in the first Canada won 2-1 in extra time, and drew the other 2-2 after three additional periods.

The bobsleigh course, at Mount Van Hoevenberg, was long and dangerous. It measured 1½ miles instead of the generally accepted 1 mile, and was a challenging, snaking ice chute demanding special care at the now famous Shady Corner and Zigzag turns. A crash in training put one German sled and crew out of action, and it was replaced by an American bob and a new crew hastily recruited from German residents in the United States. American bobs won both the events, and the status of bobsledding was enhanced by the introduction of 2-man bobs, only a 4-man event being contested at the two previous Winter Games. William Fiske steered cleverly to win his second 4-man bob title in successive Games, while one of the crew, Clifford Gray, had also shared in the 1928 triumph. Fiske and Gray thus became the first men to win two Olympic bobsleigh gold medals. The American No. 2 crew, led by Henry Homburger, were 2.2 sec slower, but they won the silvers, and in the 2-man event the American brothers Hubert and Curtis Stevens had just 1.44 sec in hand over the runners-up, Switzerland's Reto Capadrutt and Oscar Geier.

Supporting the official Olympic programme at Lake Placid were demonstration events, contested by Americans and Canadians alone, in curling, dogsleigh races, and women's speed skating. Of these, the women's speed skating found a place on the Olympic schedule in 1960.

Associated Press

1 Sven Utterström of Sweden easily won the 18-kilometre cross-country skiing race. **2** Ice hockey has drawn large crowds in post-war years, but in 1932 few spectators were on hand to watch Canada crush Germany 4-1 in the Olympic series at Lake Placid. The Canadian team won the gold medal. **3** Two Lake Placid brothers, Hubert and Curtis Stevens, won the first 2-man Olympic bob sled event over 1½ slippery miles. Americans also won the 4-man race. **4** Irving Jaffee, winner of the 5,000 and 10,000 speed-skating races. **5** Jack Shea won the 500 and 1,500 metres to give the United States a clean sweep. **6** Norway's Johan Gröttumsbraaten recorded his second Olympic triumph in the Nordic combination event.

International Newsreel

Wide World

Wide World

LAKE PLACID WINTER OLYMPIC GAMES, 1932 Gold Medallists

Nordic Skiing—Men

18 kilometres	Sven Utterstrom	Sweden	1 hr 23 min 7.0 sec
50 kilometres	Veli Saarinen	Finland	4 hr 28 min 0.0 sec
Combination event	Johan Grottumsbraaten	Norway	446.0 pts
Jumping	Birger Ruud	Norway	228.1 pts

Figure Skating

Men	Karl Schafer	Austria	2,602.0 pts
Women	Sonja Henie	Norway	2,302.5 pts
Pairs	Pierre Brunet, Andree Brunet	France	76.7 pts

Speed Skating—Men

500 metres	John Shea	USA	43.4 sec
1,500 metres	John Shea	USA	2 min 57.5 sec
5,000 metres	Irving Jaffee	USA	9 min 40.8 sec
10,000 metres	Irving Jaffee	USA	19 min 13.6 sec

Bobsleigh

2-man	Hubert Stevens, Curtis Stevens	USA	8 min 14.74 sec
4-man		USA	7 min 53.68 sec

Ice Hockey

		Canada	

Garmisch Winter Olympic Games (1936)

Fourteen thousand incredulous spectators packed the elaborate new Olympic Ice Stadium at Garmisch as Carl Erhardt led Britain's ice hockey team in a historic victory over Canada, the acknowledged masters of the game who had won every previous Olympic contest. Yet Britain beat them 2-1 and by holding the United States to a goal-less draw in the final game, they not only won the gold medal but showed that the North American teams were not invincible.

Fewer reserves were carried then than there are today, and just 12 players—Sandy Archer, James Borland, Ed Brenchley, Jimmy Chappell, John Coward, Gordon Dailley, John Davey, Carl Erhardt, Jimmy Foster, John Kilpatrick, Archie Stinchcombe, and Bob Wyman—accomplished this once seemingly impossible task to provide the surprise result of the fourth Winter Olympics.

Staged in and around the picturesque Bavarian resort of Garmisch-Partenkirchen, these Games attracted a then record entry of 755 competitors from 28 nations. Australia, Bulgaria, Greece, Liechtenstein, Spain, and Turkey all participated for the first time.

Separate winter Olympic meetings were, by this time, an undoubted success, and, with the host country intent on prestige, money was available to organize a meeting on a scale hitherto unparalleled. And the easily accessible location, midway between Munich and Innsbruck, enabled half a million spectators to attend the 17 events.

For the first time, Baron Pierre de Coubertin, founder of the modern Olympic series, excused himself from attending the opening ceremony. It was Hitler's turn to inaugurate the Games, and though no serious political incident occurred, the swastika's appearance ominously heralded the eclipse of the Winter Olympics for 12 years.

Alpine skiing was included for the first time and, when a crowd of 70,000 turned up to see the men's slalom, the sport's pioneer Arnold Lunn, who was referee, must have been proud to see his brainchild so enthusiastically acclaimed. Men's and women's downhill slalom contests were held, but medals were awarded only to the best overall performers, Franz Pfnür and Christel Cranz, both Germans. Fraulein Cranz's victory gave her the distinction of being the first women's skiing gold medallist. But because women were not yet represented in nordic

1 The ice hockey gold medal at Garmisch was won by Great Britain who created the sensation of the Games when they beat previous champions Canada by two goals to one.
2 Christel Cranz fell in the downhill race but overcame a loss of 19 seconds to win the ladies' Alpine combination.
3 The bobsleigh gold medals were won by the United States (two-man) and Switzerland (four-man), so ending hopes of a home success on the new, steeply banked Riessersee course. 4 The jumping event saw Norway's Birger Ruud keep the title he won in 1932.

Fox Photos

Fox Photos

skiing or speed skating, the extremely versatile Norwegian girl Schou Nilsen was deprived of even greater fame. Only 16, she dominated the downhill and took the bronze medal in the alpine combination — a sensational achievement for one of the prominent tennis players of the day who also held no fewer than five world speed skating records.

Not surprisingly, Scandinavians monopolized the nordic skiing honours. Swedes won both the individual cross-country races—the gruelling 50 kilometres test of endurance going to Elis Wiklund and the relatively short 18 kilometres to Erik Larsson. A Finnish quartet took the first Olympic relay title to be contested but they beat the Norwegians by only 6 seconds, a small margin after four legs of 10 kilometres each.

Oddbjörn Hagen retained the nordic combination for Norway. And thanks to his stylish compatriot, Birger Ruud, who with leaps of 75 and 77.5 metres, withstood a spirited challenge from the Swede Sven Eriksson in the special ski jumping, Norway remained undefeated in the event after four Olympics. For this event 150,000 awe-struck onlookers clustered around the 'horse-shoe' below the impressive Olympic jump tower.

But it was another Norwegian, speed skater Ivar Ballangrud, who was the real star of the Garmisch Games. In his third Olympics and less than a month from his 32nd birthday, Ballangrud won three gold medals, in the 500, 5,000 and 10,000 metres, and also took the silver in the 1,500 metres, finishing just one second slower than his fellow countryman Charles Mathiesen.

Inevitably the figure skating will be remembered most for Sonja Henie's third Olympic victory. But whereas she had clearly dominated the event previously, the gap between her and her rivals had now decreased. Though eight years Sonja's junior, Bri-

tain's Cecilia Colledge, who was to become world champion the following season, proved a dangerous challenger. No longer did the Norwegian star enjoy a unanimous verdict—one judge placed the two girls equal—and she was perhaps wise to turn professional soon afterwards.

Karl Schäfer, a star pupil of the Vienna Skating School's most glorious era, comfortably retained the men's crown he had captured in 1932. His nearest challenger, Ernst Baier, was compensated with a hard-earned victory for Germany in the pairs contest, partnered by his future wife, Maxi Herber. The pairs was something of a cliff-hanger, with a young Viennese brother and sister, Erik and Ilse Pausin, stealing the spectators' hearts with a skilful interpretation of a lilting Strauss waltz. But the Germans' more experienced technique split the judges voting 7-2 in their favour.

In the bobsleigh, a home success had been expected on the new, steeply banked Riessersee course, but it was not to be. In the two-man event, Ivan Brown, with Alan Washbond as brakeman, piloted the United States boblet to victory, just half a second clear of the Swiss sled driven by Fritz Feierabend. The Swiss made no mistake, however, in the four-man event. Their second and first crews—led by Pierre Musy and Reto Capadrutt respectively—took the gold and silver medals in that order, with Fred McEvoy guiding the British sled home for the bronze.

As had now become a customary feature of the Winter Olympics, there were two demonstration events—a ski military patrol race, forerunner of the present-day biathlon, and German-style curling. No medals are awarded for these supporting contests, but the skiing and shooting, over a 25-km course, produced an unexpected victory for Italy, led by Captain Silvestri, and the curling honours went to Austria.

GARMISCH WINTER OLYMPIC GAMES, 1936 Gold Medallists

Nordic Skiing

18 kilometres	Erik Larsson	Sweden	1 hr 14 min 38.0 sec
50 kilometres	Elis Wiklund	Sweden	3 hr 30 min 11.0 sec
4 x 10 km relay		Finland	2 hr 41 min 33.0 sec
Jumping	Birger Ruud	Norway	
Combination	Oddbjorn Hagen	Norway	

Alpine Skiing—Men

Combination	Franz Pfnur	Germany	

Alpine Skiing—Women

Combination	Christel Cranz	Germany	

Figure Skating

Men	Karl Schafer	Austria	
Women	Sonja Henie	Norway	
Pairs	Ernst Baier	} Germany	
	Maxi Herber		

Speed Skating

500 metres	Ivar Ballangrud	Norway	43.4 sec
1,500 metres	Charles Mathiesen	Norway	2 min 19.2 sec
5,000 metres	Ivar Ballangrud	Norway	8 min 19.6 sec
10,000 metres	Ivar Ballangrud	Norway	17 min 24.3 sec

Bobsleigh

2-man	Ivan Brown	USA	5 min 29.29 sec
	Alan Washbond		
4-man		Switzerland	5 min 19.85 sec

Ice Hockey

		Great Britain	

Encyclopedia of the Olympic Winter Games

4

Alpine skiing consists of three different disciplines—downhill, slalom, and giant slalom. Downhill courses usually have a vertical descent of between 2,500 metres and 3,000 feet and vary between 1½ to 3 miles according to the terrain. Slalom courses are considerably shorter and comprise a series of 'gates' through which the skier must pass. The giant slalom blends characteristics of the downhill and slalom in one event.

St Moritz Winter Olympic Games (1948)

After 20 years and a world war, the Winter Olympic Games returned to St Moritz in 1948. Lack of training facilities and the paltry allowance of only five Swiss francs a day for the members of some teams made participation in these Games a truly remarkable achievement. The Germans and Japanese were excluded from this bold revival. The Americans appeared monetarily unfettered, staying at the best hotels in a resort famous for luxurious living. In striking contrast, their wartime British allies suffered the humility of appearing the poor relations through having to economize drastically with regard to accommodation and everything that had to be paid for in foreign currency.

For a nation that had contributed so much towards Europe's liberation, the situation was ludicrous enough to inspire a *Daily Express* Giles cartoon which showed the British team encamped under canvas in the snow beside a five-star hotel and one of the competitors calling to a dignified waiter: 'Garcon, would you mind fetching us a can of water for our cocoa?'

This humorous exaggeration bore a strong element of truth. Several European nations were severely handicapped financially, but their admirable determination to overcome this difficulty did much to put the Olympic movement unsteadily back on its feet. The International Olympic Committee somehow rode a multiplicity of administrative problems which reached a climax when separate icy hockey teams claimed to represent the same nation.

Even this early, the pseudo-amateur controversy was rearing its head. Critics on the spot had harsh words to say about the supplanting of true sporting traditions by purely commercial interests, and some eminent observers made no attempt to disguise their opinions that certain competitors were as good as committing perjury by signing the Olympic oath.

Petty squabbles—and they were mostly petty—were numerous enough to inspire one reporter to comment: 'In an assembly of feuding factions whose dogmatic attitude sometimes reduced the Games to a farcical level, it was a pity that some organisations did not settle their domestic differences at home beforehand instead of airing their grievances in public while the Olympics were on.'

The fifth Winter Olympic meeting was originally scheduled for 1940 at Sapporo, Japan, but World War II intervened and

Sapporo has had to wait until 1972. The selection of St Moritz for a second time was the result of the resort's suitability in almost every respect, especially its facilities, and Switzerland's central location and political stability. The atmosphere throughout the programme appeared to be that of a brave front being put on by Europeans still suffering in many respects from the aftermath of war, but the important thing was that the Olympic flame could be rekindled despite countless frustrations.

In the circumstances, the entry of 28 nations was encouraging, equal to that of 1936, though the total number of competitors, 636

men and 77 women, fell 40 short of the Garmisch figures—understandably, in view of various travel and financial problems which also greatly reduced the numbers of spectators. But for the first time there were Chilean, Danish, Icelandic, Korean, and Lebanese competitors.

The development of Alpine skiing since 1936 justified the extension of medals for these competitions to include separate awards for downhill, slalom, and combined. Significantly, 25 nations were represented in the downhill—10 more than in any Nordic ski event. Ideal weather was temporarily interrupted by a thawing *fohn* wind, less severe

1 France's Henri Oreiller was the most successful Alpine skier at St Moritz, with wins in the downhill and combined events, and a slalom bronze.
2 Switzerland's Edi Reinalter wins a slalom event.
3 Gretchen Frazer of the United States won her country's only Alpine skiing medals at St Moritz—a slalom gold and a combined silver.

than 20 years previously, but sufficient to affect the 10,000 metres speed skating and some of the ice hockey matches. Fortunately, this time no event had to be cancelled.

The Swedes proved supreme in

the cross-country skiing, taking all three medals in the 18 kilometres, the first two places in the 50 kilometres, and leading the Finnish runners-up by 9 seconds in the team relay.

Martin Lundstrom, victor in the 18 kilometres, got his second gold medal in the relay, but the Swedish strength in depth was underlined by the ability to win the latter without the services of Nils Karlsson, an impressive 50 kilometres champion despite being more troubled than most by an altitude to which he was unaccustomed.

The all-round ability of two Finns earned gold and silver in the Nordic combination for Heikki Hasu and Martti Huhtala. Switzerland's Niklaus Stump, fourth, achieved the highest place in this event yet by a central European, with the best Norwegian sixth.

The Norwegians reasserted their traditional supremacy in the jumping, taking all the medals for an event in which they had yet to concede first place. The winner, Petter Hugsted, owed his victory more to near-perfect posture than to sheer distance. His longest jump was 3 metres shorter than the 138 metres covered by the fourth placed Matti Pietikainen from Finland, whose style cannot have pleased the judges. At 36 years of age, Birger Ruud gained a noteworthy bronze medal—16 years after his first gold for the same event.

In the men's Alpine skiing, a downhill triumph with more than four seconds in hand and third place in the slalom gave Frenchman Henri Oreiller the academic combined title to total two gold medals and a bronze. Edi Reinalter won the slalom for Switzerland with an aggregate for the two runs just half a second faster than another Frenchman, James Couttet.

The women's honours were shared by three nations. Hedy Schlunegger took the downhill for Switzerland. Gretchen Frazer, at 29, was a surprise American slalom winner—the first skiing medal to be won by the United States. Austrian Trude Beiser, second in the downhill, was unplaced in the slalom but her overall performance was just good enough to pip Miss Frazer for the combined title.

The figure skating saw the American continent take the top honours through the United States' Dick Button and Canada's Barbara Ann Scott who gave Europe a first glimpse of the new American school of theatrical athleticism in jumps. Displaying a new degree of physical strength and suppleness, Button was the forerunner of a revolutionary trend that was to characterize future men's free-skating. The more orthodox Swiss, Hans Gerschwiler, held second place only by virtue of his figures, having been outpointed in free-style by another American, John

Lettengarver. Miss Scott serenely withstood hard pressure from Britain's Jeannette Altwegg in the figures and from Austrian's Eva Pawlik in the free-skating. The Belgians Pierre Baugniet and Micheline Lannoy, a gracefully authentic partnership, clinched the pairs title after a resolute Hungarian bid from Ede Kiraly and Adrea Kekessy.

Norwegians won three of the four speed skating events. Finn Helgesen snatched the 500 metres by a tenth of a second from his compatriot Thomas Byberg and two Americans, Ken Bartholomew and Robert Fitzgerald, whose equal times earned the first Winter Olympic triple tie for silver medals. Sverre Farstad won the 1,500 metres and Reidar Liaklev the 5,000. But a Swede, Ake Seyffarth, was the most noteworthy speed skater on view. A decisive winner of the 10,000 metres with nearly 10 seconds to spare, he was also runner-up in the 1,500; he was a powerful racer who had passed his peak form, after establishing world records over two distances during the war years.

An intimate knowledge of their home course enabled the Swiss to secure gold and silver medals in the two-man bobsleigh event. The Americans took first and third places in their four-man sleds, separated by a Belgian crew in second spot.

Skeleton tobogganing made its second Olympic appearance on

the Cresta Run. The event provided Italy's first gold medal in winter sports, thanks to the rare skill of Nino Bibbia, the cleverest exponent the course had known, no doubt due largely to his being a St Moritz resident. Another man who was familiar with the course, American John Heaton, gained a notable silver medal—repeating his achievement of 20 years previously, when runner-up to his brother Jennison.

The Canadians recaptured the ice hockey title, avenging their unexpected defeat by the British in 1936, but only by a goal-average verdict over the Czechs. Each won seven of their eight matches, their direct encounter ending in a rare goalless stalemate. The Czech line-up included a player who gained greater fame as a tennis star—Jaroslav Drobny.

There was confusion and embarrassment concerning the American ice hockey entry. Two United States teams arrived at St Moritz and the one eventually allowed to compete finished fourth, only to be disqualified by the IOC because it was not affiliated to the American Olympic Association.

Two supporting demonstration events were a military patrol ski race, won by the host nation in a field of eight teams, and an enterprising winter pentathlon, comprising cross-country skiing, pistol shooting, a downhill race, fencing, and horse-riding. In this widely varied combination the Swedes proved best.

This second St Moritz Winter Olympic presentation determinedly overcame unenviable difficulties and emphasized the compactness and easy access of all the sites, in very favourable comparison to some of the subsequent venues. The palpable will to revive the Games was the most heartening element of all.

Fox Photos

1 The two-man bobsleigh contest proved to be a triumph for the
Swiss hosts: their No. 2 bob won first place, and the No. 1 bob
was second, with the United States pair third, 5 seconds behind.
2 Nino Bibbia negotiates Church Leap on his way to a gold medal
in the skeleton tobogganing on the Cresta Run—an event held
twice and only when the Olympic Games have been at St Moritz.
3 Not many spectators watch this speed skating event. Norway,
Finland, Sweden, and the United States won all the medals
in this sport, with Norway's skaters winning three titles.
4 The Olympic flame burns in the ice stadium. The mere fact
that these Games were held at all was a sign of hope for a
world only just at peace and beset with political worries.

ST MORITZ WINTER OLYMPIC GAMES, 1948 Gold Medallists

Nordic Skiing

18 kilometres	Martin Lundstrom	Sweden	1 hr 13 min 50.0 sec
50 kilometres	Nils Karlsson	Sweden	3 hr 47 min 48.0 sec
4 x 10 km relay		Sweden	2 hr 32 min 8.0 sec
Combination	Heikki Hasu	Finland	448.8 pts
Jumping	Petter Hugsted	Norway	228.1 pts
Alpine Skiing—Men			
Downhill	Henri Oreiller	France	2 min 55.0 sec
Slalom	Edi Reinalter	Switzerland	2 min 10.3 sec
Combined	Henri Oreiller	France	3.2 pts
Alpine Skiing—Women			
Downhill	Hedy Schlunegger	Switzerland	2 min 28.3 sec
Slalom	Gretchen Frazer	USA	1 min 57.2 sec
Combined	Trude Beiser	Austria	6.5 pts
Figure Skating			
Men	Dick Button	USA	1,720.6 pts
Women	Barbara Ann Scott	Canada	1,467.7 pts
Pairs	Pierre Baugniet,		
	Micheline Lannoy	Belgium	123.5 pts
Speed Skating			
500 metres	Finn Helgesen	Norway	43.1 sec
1,500 metres	Sverre Farstad	Norway	2 min 17.6 sec
5,000 metres	Reidar Liaklev	Norway	8 min 29.4 sec
10,000 metres	Ake Seyffarth	Sweden	17 min 26.3 sec
Bobsleigh			
2 man	Felix Endrich,		
	Fritz Waller	Switzerland	5 min 29.2 sec
4 man		USA	5 min 20.1 sec
Skeleton Tobogganing			
	Nino Bibbia	Italy	5 min 23.2 sec
Ice Hockey		Canada	

Above: **A well-nigh perfect performance in the compulsory figures gave Britain's Jeanette Altwegg a valuable start in the figure skating at Oslo, for though she was bettered by Tenley Albright in the free skating, she held her overall lead to add a gold medal to the bronze she had won four years earlier in London.** *Below:* **Another 1948 medallist was America's Dick Button. His medal, however, was a gold, and he won another at Oslo, where his skating spearheaded a new athleticism in jumping on skates. His *tour de force* was the triple jump—three mid-air revolutions before landing, and at Oslo he unleashed the first real triple loop.**

Oslo Winter Olympic Games (1952)

The first Winter Olympics to be held in a capital city, the Oslo Games of 1952 drew a record entry of 30 nations. Germany and Japan made their first post-World War II appearances in the Olympic arena, and New Zealand and Portugal made their Winter Games debuts. Even so, the total number of competitors—624 men and 108 women—fell slightly short of the record 1936 figures.

The siting of the events was relatively compact for a Winter Games. The cross-country and ski jumping were held at Holmenkollen, only a few miles from the city centre, and the slalom events took place on the nearby Rodkleiva slope. All the ice sports were located within the Oslo area, and only the downhill and giant slalom contests were any distance from the city—at Norefjell, some 75 miles to the north-west.

It was the first time that the Games had gone to the country that pioneered sport on skis, and appropriately the Olympic flame was lit not in Greece, as is the custom, but in Morgedal, the village in the Norwegian province of Telemark where Sondre Nordheim, the 'father of skiing', had been born in 1825. The torch was carried by 94 skiers along the 137 miles to Oslo, where Eigil Nansen, grandson of the famous explorer Fridtjof Nansen, ran the final lap in the Bislet Stadium. In the opening ceremony, a minute's silence was observed to mark the death of Britain's King George VI.

Attendances were very high. Over half a million people paid to see the events: 130,000 witnessed the four speed skating competitions, and a similar number watched the ski jumping finale.

Hallgeir Brenden took the 18 kilometres cross-country ski sprint title to Norway for the first time since Johnn Grottumsbraaten's success at St Moritz in 1928. Another home triumph came in the Nordic combination event, consisting of 18 kilometres cross-country and ski jumping. Simon Slattvik's 1 hr 5 min 40 sec and three jumps of 67.5, 67, and 66.5 metres gave him 451.6 points, 4 more than the runner-up, Heikki Hasu of Finland. Hasu was a member of Finland's winning

Popperfoto

Keystone

4 by 10 kilometres relay team who beat Norway by nearly 3 minutes. Further success for Finland came in the 50 kilometres cross-country, won by Veikko Hakulinen with team-mate Eero Kolehmainen second. Finland's women cross-country skiers won all three medals in their 10-kilometre event, the first held in an Olympic Games. The winner was the robust and well-schooled Lydia Wideman.

The Scandinavian monopoly in the Nordic events was not as surprising as the significant success of Stein Eriksen in the giant slalom, and his silver, and Gutterm Berge's bronze, in the slalom. The other Alpine events went to true Alpine skiers. Othmar Schneider of Austria won the slalom, and was runner-up to Zeno Colo of Italy in the downhill.

1 Norway's Stein Eriksen was a surprise winner of the giant slalom—an alpine event. 2 Another Norwegian to shine before his home audience was triple gold medallist speed skater Hjalmar Andersen.

Twenty-seven of the 30 competing nations were represented in the men's downhill and slalom—more than in any other events.

America's Andrea Mead-Lawrence was a double winner in the women's Alpine skiing. She took the gold medals in the slalom and giant slalom, but a crash put paid to her chances in the downhill, which was won by Austria's Trude Jochum-Beiser.

The outstanding individual of the Games was the Norwegian speed skater Hjalmar Andersen, who won three events—the 1,500,

5,000, and 10,000 metres, setting Olympic records in the two longer distances. Only a week previously he had set a world record for 10,000 metres that was not beaten until 1960. Ken Henry won the 500 metres, America's third gold medal in this event in six Winter Games, with his team-mate Donald McDermott second. Norway's Arne Johansen and Canada's Gordon Audley dead-heated for the bronze medals.

The figure skating audience saw America's Dick Button retain his title. As a result of arduous practice he made the first ever triple loop jump in winning comfortably for a second time. In the women's figures Jeanette Altwegg made well-nigh perfect compulsory figures to add the Olympic gold to her bronze of 1948 and the world championship she had won

the previous year. Even so, she was surpassed in free skating by the American Tenley Albright who won the silver medal and Jacqueline du Bief of France who was third. The pairs gold medals went to the German husband and wife team, Paul and Ria Falk, whose precision timing in lifts and skilful 'shadow' jumps and spins were quite unusual.

Germany also excelled in the bobsleigh events. Cashing in on what was then a legitimate weight advantage, German crews won both 2-man and 4-man events. Andreas Ostler (driver) and Lorenz Nieberl (brakeman) were in both winning crews, and in each case they won by more than two seconds. The advantage the Germans gained by having heavy crews prompted the International Bobsleigh Federation to amend

123

the rules, setting maximum combined weights of sleds and riders to create fairer conditions.

Canada won the ice hockey for the sixth time in seven Games. In eight matches they conceded only one point—in a tie with the United States, who were runners-up. In a play-off for third place Sweden beat Czechoslovakia after the Czechs had established a 3-0 lead. By way of a contrast, bandy—a form of hockey on ice, with rules similar to soccer's—was the official demonstration sport, and in this Sweden won a three-way contest against Norway and Finland.

The final event, and the climax of the Games, was the ski jumping at Holmenkollen. A vast crowd in festive mood assembled to watch, and they were not disappointed when local hero Arnfinn Bergmann retained the title for Norway.

OSLO WINTER OLYMPIC GAMES, 1952 Gold Medallists			
Nordic Skiing—Men			
18 Kilometres	Hallgeir Brenden	Norway	1 hr 1 min 34.0 sec
50 kilometres	Veikko Hakulinen	Finland	3 hr 33 min 33.0 sec
4 x 10 km relay		Finland	2 hr 20 min 16.0 sec
Combination	Simon Slattvik	Norway	451.6 pts
Jumping	Arnfinn Bergmann	Norway	226.0 pts
Nordic Skiiing—Women			
10 kilometres	Lydia Wideman	Finland	41 min 40.0 sec
Alpine Skiing—Men			
Downhill	Zeno Colo	Italy	2 min 30.8 sec
Slalom	Othmar Schneider	Austria	2 min 0.0 sec
Giant slalom	Stein Eriksen	Norway	2 min 25.0 sec
Alpine Skiing—Women			
Downhill	Trude Jochum-Beiser	Austria	1 min 47.1 sec
Slalom	Andrea Mead-Lawrence	USA	2 min 10.6 sec
Giant slalom	Andrea Mead-Lawrence	USA	2 min 6.8 sec
Figure Skating			
Men	Dick Button	USA	1,730.3 pts
Women	Jeannette Altwegg	Great Britain	1,455.8 pts
Pairs	Paul Falk & Ria Falk	Germany	102.6 pts
Speed Skating			
500 metres	Ken Henry	USA	43.2 sec
1,500 metres	Hjalmar Andersen	Norway	2 min 20.4 sec
5,000 metres	Hjalmar Andersen	Norway	8 min 10.6 sec
10,000 metres	Hjalmar Andersen	Norway	16 min 45.8 sec
Bobsleigh			
2-man	Andreas Ostler, Lorenz Nieberl	Germany	5 min 22.54 sec
4-man		Germany	5 min 7.84 sec
Ice Hockey		Canada	

1 Dick Button of the United States, who retained his Olympic figure skating title at Oslo with comparative ease.
2 Norway's Arnfinn Bergmann collected 226 points to take first place in the ski-jumping. Altogether the host country won seven gold medals—almost a third of the total. **3** Like all the other teams in the two-man bobsleigh, Guillard and Chatelus of France found that German combination of Andreas Ostler and Lorenz Nieberl too powerful.

Cortina Winter Olympic Games (1956)

Millions of people watched on television, and 13,000 gaily expectant onlookers packed the newly built stands of the £750,000 Olympic Ice Stadium for the opening of the seventh Winter Olympics, at the picturesque Italian resort of Cortina d'Ampezzo. And after the speech by President Giovanni Gronchi, Italian ice racer Guido Caroli skated the final lap with the Olympic Flame, which had been brought 500 miles in relay from Rome's ruined Temple of Jupiter. Then, diminutive Italian skier Juliana Minuzzo took the Olympic oath on behalf of the others.

The Cortina Olympics were one of the most colourful and lavish ever. Profits from Italy's nationalized football pools had largely subsidized the elaborately erected sites, and it mattered little that the 231 million lire netted from the 157,000 admission tickets repaid only a proportion of the £2½ million promotional costs.

In addition, as these were the first Winter Olympics to be internationally televised, world-wide publicity brought substantial long-term commercial benefits to both Italy in general and Cortina in particular, as well as to winter sports. Such obvious assets ensured no shortage of applicants to stage subsequent Olympics.

At least one outstanding performer emerges from most Olympic meetings and Cortina was no exception. The big name on this occasion was the Austrian Alpine skier, Toni Sailer, a 20-year-old plumber from Kitzbühel.

Sailer was hailed as the most brilliant and daring Alpine skier yet seen, not just because he won all of his events, but because of his impressive, hip-swinging style and the decisive time margins that quite outclassed the opposition.

His giant slalom time was 6.2 seconds better than that of the runner-up, fellow Austrian Anderl Molterer. And in the slalom, 4 clear seconds separated him from the American-based Chiharu Igaya, the first Japanese to win an Olympic Winter Games medal. Finally, the icy, windswept downhill gave Sailer a 3.5 seconds lead over the second-placed Swiss, Raymond Fellay, and brought him his third gold medal.

But the Swiss had more glory in the women's events. Dairymaid Madeleine Berthod was the most successful, winning the downhill and coming fifth in the slalom. Her compatriot, Renée Collard, triumphed in the slalom, but Ossi Reichert, a German hotelier's daughter, took the giant slalom.

Competing for the first time in the Winter Olympics, the Russians took the lion's share of medals and earned respect as an obviously increasing force. Their well-balanced Nordic ski team earned a convincing team relay win, but the individual cross-country stars were the seemingly indefatigable Swede Sixten Jernberg and the never-flagging Finn Heikko Hakulinen. Jernberg's medal tally—a gold, two silver, and a bronze—was one more than even Sailer's. In all six previous Winter Olympics Norway had won each jumping gold, but their dominance was at last cracked at Cortina, by a Finn, Antti Hyvärinen, who won with a new aerodynamic drop style.

An unprecedented spate of speed-skating records on the outdoor circuit at Lake Misurina was due to rapidly improving techniques at high altitude. In the four events, three skaters set new world records, while 73 competitors were inside the previous best Olympic times for their distances.

Soviet racers gained four gold medals for winning three events, because compatriots Jurij Mikailov and Eugenij Grischin tied in the 1,500 metres, both clocking a new world-record time. Grischin, the outstanding ice sprinter of his day, also established a new world time to win the 500 metres. For the

Right, **Ossi Reichert shows the form that won her a gold medal in the giant slalom.** *Below,* **Toni Sailer, skiing star of the Cortina Olympics.**

Presse Sports

first time since 1932, Norway failed to get a speed-skating gold.

The technical and spectacular highlight of the figure skating was the freestyle of the dominant American men's trio, Hayes Jenkins, Ronnie Robertson, and David Jenkins, Hayes' younger brother, who finished in that order. Hayes Jenkins won by virtue of a slender lead gained in the figures, and though his free-skating was excellent, its contents were not quite as difficult as those displayed by Robertson.

Robertson was a sensational, at times almost acrobatic, free-skater, and he gave everything he had on this occasion. He touched a hand down when landing in a triple loop jump, then completed a triple salchow to perfection, and concluded with a fast cross-toe spin, altogether a thrilling programme for the mesmerized audience.

In the women's contest, Tenley Albright, runner-up in the previous Winter Olympics to Britain's Jeannette Altwegg, presented a wonderfully delicate programme, dramatically timed to *Tales of Hoffman* in a seemingly effortless, graceful style, ending splendidly with a rapid cross-foot spin.

But if a miracle were needed by Carol Heiss to overtake her brilliant compatriot, this she nearly achieved. Very speedy and impressive, she not only scored almost as many marks as Tenley, but was actually placed first in the freestyle by 5 of the 11 judges.

In the pairs event, the elegant Viennese partnership of Kurt Oppelt and Sissy Schwartz gained a controversial verdict over Canada's Norris Bowden and Frances Dafoe, both couples synchronizing superbly.

The ice hockey, as usual, drew the greatest number of spectators. At their first attempt, the Russians emerged victorious and unbeaten in their five final pool matches against the previously fancied United States, who were second, and Canada, Sweden, Czechoslovakia, and Germany.

Scoring 25 goals and conceding only 5, the Russian players never looked unduly ruffled. Their clever stick-handling and superior skating, in both defence and attack, decided the issue in the two games that mattered most, and they defeated the United States 4-0, and Canada, who finished third, 2-0.

Forty-six-year-old Franz Kapus became the oldest gold medallist in any Winter Olympics when he cannily piloted the Swiss sled to victory in the four-man bobsleigh event, 1.26 seconds ahead of the Italian ace Eugenio Monti. Monti was pipped again in the two-man boblet, but this time by his fellow Italian Dalla Costa—a popular home success and a triumph for the new Podar-designed sleds, which were subsequently adopted by nearly every nation.

1 Hayes Jenkins, gold medallist in the men's figure skating.
2 Soviet speed skating star Boris Schilkov won the 5,000 metres in Olympic record time.
3 The Italian boblet, piloted by Lamberto Dalla Costa.
4 Toni Sailer swings into action in the giant slalom.

CORTINA WINTER OLYMPIC GAMES, 1956 Gold Medallists

Nordic Skiing—Men

15 kilometres	Hallgeir Brendan	Norway		49 min	39.0 sec
30 kilometres	Veikko Hakulinen	Finland	1 hr	44 min	6.0 sec
50 kilometres	Sixten Jernberg	Sweden	2 hr	50 min	27.0 sec
4 x 10 km relay		USSR	2 hr	15 min	30.0 sec
Jumping	Antti Hyvärinen	Finland			
Combination	Sverre Stenersen	Norway			

Nordic Skiing—Women

10 kilometres	Ljubov Kozyreva	USSR		38 min	11.0 sec
3 x 5 km relay		Finland	1 hr	9 min	1.0 sec

Alpine Skiing—Men

Downhill	Toni Sailer	Austria
Slalom	Toni Sailer	Austria
Giant Slalom	Toni Sailer	Austria

Alpine Skiing—Women

Downhill	Madeleine Berthod	Switzerland
Slalom	Renee Colliard	Switzerland
Giant Slalom	Ossi Reichert	Germany

Figure Skating

Men	Hayes Jenkins	USA
Women	Tenley Albright	USA
Pairs	Kurt Oppelt	Austria
	Elisabeth Schwarz	

Speed Skating

500 metres	Eugenyi Grischin	USSR			40.2 sec
1,500 metres {	Eugenyi Grischin	USSR	2 min	8.6 sec
	Jurij Mikailov	USSR			
5,000 metres	Boris Schilkov	USSR		7 min	48.7 sec
10,000 metres	Sigvard Ericsson	Sweden		16 min	35.9 sec

Bobsleigh

2-man	Lamberto Dalla Costa	Italy
	Giacomo Conti	
4-man		Switzerland

Ice Hockey | | USSR |

Squaw Valley Winter Olympic Games

(1960)

'The gamble that came off' is a phrase aptly describing the choice of venue for the eighth Winter Olympics. In face of keen competition from three well-established European resorts, Squaw Valley, an empty, scarcely known Californian site where everything had to be built from scratch, won the International Olympic Committee vote. On the eastern side of the Sierra Nevada, 200 miles from San Francisco, and at an altitude of 6,230 feet, this location seemed like a risky throw of the dice. But Alexander Cushing, who owned the land, insisted with oratorial conviction that the compactness would be a key feature—and so it proved.

As pageantry committee chairman, filmdom's Walt Disney supervised all the ceremonial arrangements, and he did not miss a trick. But the miracle of these Games was the weather. After weeks of rain had threatened to wash away the courses, snow and wind threatened to ruin the elaborately planned opening by Vice-President Nixon. Then, with only 15 minutes to go, as if by magic, the clouds cleared and the sun shone, and only the humorist attributed this dramatic effect to Disney.

Throughout the entire 11-day meeting, warm Californian sunshine on incongruous-looking snow and ice dominated the proceedings. The great asset of Squaw Valley, and a boon to the spectators, was that, except for the cross-country ski courses 17 miles away on the McKinney Creek, everything was within short walking distance. Sometimes it was possible to watch speed skating, figure skating, ice hockey, downhill skiing, and ski jumping simultaneously from the same spot—something that could not be done anywhere else in the world.

The entry for these Games, the second to be held outside Europe, totalled 521 men and 144 women from 30 countries, which was not quite as good as Cortina because many nations pruned their numbers to reduce travel costs. But an increase of 13 countries since the Lake Placid Games in 1932 reflected the widening of winter sports interest through three decades.

There was some dissension because no bobsleigh or tobogganing runs were built, but this was the only real shortcoming, and it was somewhat atoned for by the friendly spirit so prevalent among competitors and spectators. Andrea Mead-Lawrence, an alpine skier from the United

States, carried the torch, lit at Morgedal, Norway, as in 1952, on its last ski-borne relay, and the American ice racer Ken Henry skated a final lap with it before igniting the sacred flame.

Five inside the world record, 8 inside the Olympic record, and 12 inside their national records—all in one event: that, in the history-making 10,000 metres, was the speed skating highlight. Norwegian Knut Johannesen fairly whistled through to chop 46 seconds off the 1952 record established by the great Hjalmar Andersen, and even Britain's Terence Monaghan, who came fifth, was a full second faster than Andersen's previous world best.

· Eugenii Grischin equalled his own world record time of 40.2 sec in winning the 500 metres for the USSR, emphasizing that, at 28, he still had no peers as a sprinter. He also tied with the Norwegian Roald Aas to share the 1,500 metres gold medal award. In the

Czech Karol Divin. Jenkins's compatriot and future sister-in-law, Carol Heiss, won the women's event by a comfortable margin, and the Canadian combination Robert Paul and Barbara Wagner were equally convincing in the pairs.

The United States really clinched the ice hockey issue with a 2-1 upset of form-favoured Canada. It was their first win over Canada in any major international competition since 1956, and only their third since 1920. Both the Canadians and the Americans defeated the Russians, the Soviet side suffering a clear setback after their 1956 triumph.

The general atmosphere of goodwill during these Games was exemplified by a Russian suggestion to the American ice hockey team to take oxygen during second intervals. At this altitude, the tip paid handsome dividends. Never before had United States ice hockey players

shadowed by less publicized team colleagues.

Canadian Anne Heggtveit, victor of the women's slalom, did well enough in the other races to register the best all-round performance, but Yvonne Ruegg, a downhill specialist, confounded the experts by winning the giant slalom for Switzerland. Heidi Biebl took the downhill for Germany and Americans came second in all three events. Penny Pitou got silvers for the downhill and giant slalom—pipped in the latter by a mere tenth of a second—and Betsy Snite was runner-up in the slalom.

Nobody ever did discover why the mountain used for the men's slalom and women's downhill was called KT-22, but there was no lack of suggestions—ranging from that of the 22 kick-turns it took the first skier to get down it to that of a historic fight with red-skins that resulted in these words being carved on a tree: 'Killed by

5,000 metres, Russian Viktor Kosichkin was nearly 10 sec faster than Johannesen.

Women's speed skating was included for the first time, and another Russian, Lidia Skoblikova, had the distinction of being the only contestant in the Games to win two outright individual golds, for the 1,500 metres and the 3,000 metres, setting a new world record in the former. The 500 metres was won by Helga Haase of Germany, and the 1,000 by Klara Guseva of the USSR.

In the men's figure skating at the architectural prize-winning Blyth Arena, American David Jenkins included in his free-skating high triple and double jumps of a standard no European could match, to overhaul a lead in the compulsory figures by the

won Olympic gold medals, but they made a dour, persevering side, based on a sound defence well marshalled by Jack McCarten, the best goalkeeper in the contest.

No outstanding alpine skier hogged the honours as Toni Sailer had done in 1956. Roger Staub won the giant slalom for Switzerland's first Alpine men's victory since 1948, Ernst Hinterseer took the slalom for Austria, and Jean Vuarnet of France came first in the downhill. Another Frenchman Guy Perillat was the most consistent performer, gaining a bronze in the downhill and finishing sixth in each of the other two events. The Austrians clearly slipped in the downhill. Sailer's heir-apparent, Karl Schranz, failed to fulfil expectations and was over-

One of Squaw Valley's assets as venue of the 1960 Winter Olympics was that almost all the events were within close walking distance. An added advantage was the California sun that shone throughout.

tomahawk, 22'. They say the tree is still there, but perhaps the etchings were obliterated by snow....

The cross-country skiing showed the two Olympic veterans Sixten Jernberg and Veikko Hakulinen to be still well up among the best. Sweden's Jernberg scored a gold and silver in the two shorter distances and came fifth in the marathon 50 km, won by the Finn Kalevi Hamalainen. Hakulinen gained the 50 km silver, got a bronze in the 15

km sprint, won by Norway's Haakon Brusveen, and was hero of Finland's remarkable victory in the relay. In a dramatic duel on the last 10 km leg, Hakulinen made up a 22 seconds leeway to pass Brusveen and win by just the length of a ski.

Although the men's cross-country events continued very much as the prerogative of Scandinavia, there was a major surprise when a German postman, Georg Thoma, emerged as winner of the Nordic combination, a stern test of all-round skill in cross-country and ski jumping. It was the first time a non-Scandinavian had won the event. And Germany was to defy the critics still more. Few expected Helmut Recknagel to win the spectacular 80 metres jumping, but he did it by a comfortable margin, impressing with his extra-rapid take-off and an outmoded orthodox arms-forward style. The sunshine on this calm day showed enormous shadows ahead of each silent jumper, further enhancing the theatrical effect that fascinated the awe-inspired crowds thronging the foot of the impressive jump hill.

The newly introduced biathlon, combining cross-country ski running and rifle marksmanship, was won by Klas Lestander, of Sweden, whose 20 shots without a miss made up for a lagging pace along the track.

Four Russians, headed by Marija Gusakova, filled the first four places in the women's 10 km race. Consequently the Soviet team's defeat by the Swedes in the relay was sensational, but this was mainly because a Russian racer fell and broke a ski during the first leg, so costing irretrievable time.

The gay informality of the closing ceremony reflected the true international friendship that the competitions and the off-stage Olympic village community had fostered. In contrast to the team-by-team parade on opening day, all the competitors at the end inter-mingled in such obvious harmony that one could not help but recall the famous words of Baron Pierre de Coubertin, pioneer of the modern Olympics: 'May the Olympic flame shed its light on all generations and prove a blessing to mankind on its journey ever upward to a nobler and braver world.'

Opposite, **Knut Johannesen led a spree of record-breaking in the 10,000 metres speed skating. He lowered the old mark by 46 seconds, and four others also bettered it. In second place was the Russian 5,000 metres gold medallist Viktor Kosichkin (1, on left). 2 Lidia Skoblikova became the first double gold medallist of the 1960 Games when she added the 3,000 metres title to the 1,500 metres, in which she set a new world record. 3 The Canadian pair Barbara Wagner and Robert Paul were convincing winners in the pairs figure skating. 4 Roger Staub's victory in the giant slalom came on the strangely named KT-22 mountain. 5 His fellow-Swiss Yvonne Ruegg won the women's equivalent.**

SQUAW VALLEY WINTER OLYMPIC GAMES, 1960
Gold Medallists

Nordic Skiing—Men			
15 kilometres	Haakon Brusveen	Norway	51 min 55.5 sec
30 kilometres	Sixten Jernberg	Sweden	1 hr 51 min 3.9 sec
50 kilometres	Kalevi Hamalainen	Finland	2 hr 59 min 6.3 sec
4 x 10 km relay		Finland	2 hr 18 min 45.6 sec
Combination	Georg Thoma	Germany	457.9 pts
80 metres jumping	Helmut Recknagel	Germany	227.2 pts
Biathlon	Klas Lestander	Sweden	1 hr 33 min 21.6 sec
Nordic Skiing—Women			
10 kilometres	Marija Gusakova	USSR	39 min 46.6 sec
3 x 5 km relay		Sweden	1 hr 4 min 21.4 sec
Alpine Skiing—Men			
Downhill	Jean Vuarnet	France	2 min 6.0 sec
Slalom	Ernst Hinterseer	Austria	2 min 8.9 sec
Giant Slalom	Roger Staub	Switzerland	1 min 48.3 sec
Alpine Skiing—Women			
Downhill	Heidi Biebl	Germany	1 min 37.6 sec
Slalom	Anne Heggtveit	Canada	1 min 49.6 sec
Giant Slalom	Yvonne Ruegg	Switzerland	1 min 39.9 sec
Figure Skating			
Men	David Jenkins	USA	1,440.2 pts
Women	Carol Heiss	USA	1,490.1 pts
Pairs	Robert Paul & Barbara Wagner	Canada	80.4 pts
Speed Skating—Men			
500 metres	Eugenii Grischin	USSR	40.2 sec
1,500 metres	Roald Aas / Eugenii Grischin	Norway / USSR	2 min 10.4 sec
5,000 metres	Viktor Kosichkin	USSR	7 min 51.3 sec
10,000 metres	Knut Johannesen	Norway	15 min 46.6 sec
Speed Skating—Women			
500 metres	Helga Haase	Germany	45.9 sec
1,000 metres	Klara Guseva	USSR	1 min 34.1 sec
1,500 metres	Lidia Skoblikova	USSR	2 min 25.2 sec
3,000 metres	Lidia Skoblikova	USSR	5 min 14.3 sec
Ice Hockey		USA	

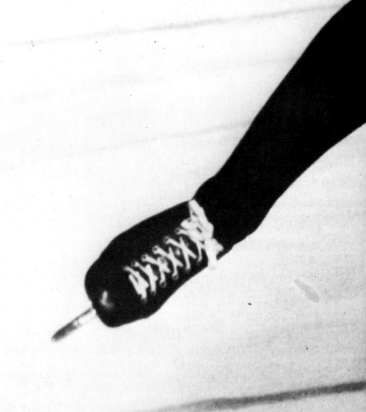

The anxiety of the long wait until the finish of the competition is etched on the face of Switzerland's teenage heroine, Marie-Therese Nadig, as she watches the opposition trying to beat her time in the giant slalom at Sapporo, where she won two gold medals.

Daily Telegraph Magazine

attended the Games, and they witnessed some thrilling events during the 12-day programme. The Russian speed skater Lidia Skoblikova won all four individual gold medals—the first woman to do so. In Alpine skiing, the French sisters Christine and Marielle Goitschel won a gold and a silver medal apiece. The biggest surprise came in the bobsleigh, when Tony Nash and Robin Dixon of Britain—a country with no courses for the sport —won Britain's first Olympic gold medal in the winter Games since 1952.

For the first time in the history of the winter Games, the opening ceremony was not held in an ice rink, but in the natural amphitheatre that formed the base of the scenic Bergisel ski jump, thus enabling more than 60,000 people to watch. There was a sad moment as the crowd stood silent in memory of Australian skier Ross Milne and Britain's tobogganist Kay Skrzypecki, who had both been killed in training before the Games.

The ceremony over, 1,186 competitors—the highest number ever at a Winter Olympics—from 36 countries set about winning the 34 gold medals at stake. The USSR, with 11 gold, 8 silver, and 6 bronze, claimed the lion's share, while the host nation, Austria, were the next best with 4 gold, 5 silver, and 3 bronze. The United States—the largest team present—did surprisingly badly, and Switzerland, a country whose name is synonymous with winter sports, did not obtain any awards at all.

The outstanding individual of the Games was Lidia Skoblikova, who was the 1960 champion over 1,500 and 3,000 metres. She won her four gold medals in four days and set three Olympic records—a feat that caused the 24-year-old blonde Soviet speedster to be acclaimed as the greatest woman ice racer ever seen. A surprising bronze medallist in the 3,000 metres speed skating was Pil Hwa Han of North Korea, who won her country's first ever medal in the Winter Olympics.

Two Olympic records were shattered in the men's speed skating. Richard McDermott, a Michigan barber, shaved a tenth of a second off the previous 500 metres record, finishing half-a-second ahead of three men who tied for the silver medal, including the former record-holder Eugeniv Grischin of the USSR. In the 5,000 metres the veteran Norwegian Knut Johannesen clipped 10.3 sec off the world mark.

With six out of nine judges giving her 5.9 marks out of a possible 6 for technical merit, the Dutch figure skater Sjoukje Dijkstra captured her country's first Olympic gold medal since 1948. It was the climax of a distinguished career for the 22-year-old Amsterdam girl, who turned pro-

1 Britain's Tony Nash and Robin Dixon propel their two-man bobsleigh down the Igls run to claim a surprise gold medal for their 'lowland' country—Britain's first Winter Games gold since 1952.
2 The flags of 36 competing nations dip at the colourful opening ceremony held in the natural amphitheatre which formed the base of the ski jump at Bergisel.

Innsbruck Winter Olympic Games
(1964)

The ancient Tyrolean city of Innsbruck experienced its mildest February for 58 years in 1964, just when snow was needed for the tenth winter Olympic Games. The Austrian organizers staged the Games with an efficiency belying their financial limitations, and with some astute re-timetabling and considerable help from the army they promoted a most successful Olympic celebration.

Nearly a million spectators

U.P.I.

fessional later in the year. Manfred Schnelldorfer took the men's title for the combined German team after seeing his French rival Alain Calmat fall twice. The classic skating of the veteran Russian pair, Oleg Protopopov and Ludmilla Belousova, won a tight struggle with the German world and European champions, Hans Bäumler and Marika Kilius. Protopopov's powerful lifts and his wife's control were decisive factors in the battle between the two best partnerships seen for years.

Five of the six Alpine skiing events were held at Axamer Lizum, about 10 miles south-west of Innsbruck, and the men's downhill on the Patscherkofel mountain near Igls. Austrian and French skiers won all six gold medals at stake, gaining three each.

The French sisters Marielle and Christine Goitschel scored a unique Olympic double: Christine beat her sister in the slalom by nearly a second over the two runs, and in the giant slalom it was Marielle's turn to win, with her sister sharing second place with the American Jean Saubert who had been third in the slalom. The Austrian women had a grand slam in the downhill event in which 20-year-old Christl Haas won the gold, Edith Zimmermann the silver, and Traudl Hecher the bronze.

In the three men's events, the German Ludwig Leitner, who was eighth in the giant slalom and fifth in the slalom and the downhill, was the best all-rounder. But in terms of medals the most successful skier was the Austrian Josef Stiegler, champion in the slalom and bronze medallist in the giant slalom. His team-mate Karl Schranz, who had surprisingly lapsed at the 1960 Games, recaptured some of his old form to take the giant slalom silver. But he had to concede first place by 0.38 seconds to François Bonlieu of France.

At Seefeld, a few miles up the Inn valley, the Nordic skiing fans were able to see the indefatigable Swedish veteran Sixten Jernberg win his third and fourth Olympic gold medals. The 50-km cross-country champion in 1956 and the 30-km champion in 1960, this grand old man of *langlauf* was greeted with sentimental cheers as he came home to win the 50-km, and as he won his fourth gold in the final Nordic skiing event, the 4 by 10 kilometres team event. The 35-year-old Swede thus brought his medal tally in three Olympic Games to four gold, three silver, and two bronze.

Had it not been for Jernberg's feat, the star of the Nordic events would have been Claudia Boyarskikh of the USSR who won golds in all three women's events. Yet another Russian success came in the men's biathlon, which had been introduced experimentally

for the 1960 Squaw Valley Games. Vladimir Melanin beat his compatriot Aleksandr Privalov by over three minutes in this skiing-shooting combination event.

The Commonwealth successes of Britain and Canada in the two bobsleigh events were something of a surprise, completely upsetting the form book, which favoured the Italians. The wins were, as the driver of the Canadian four-man bobsleigh, Vic Emery, was at pains to point out, 'a triumph for countries without a single course of their own'. Tony Nash and Robin Dixon, the British No. 1 two-man crew, had spent much time and money training together and really earned their gold medals. It was only Britain's third gold medal won at a Winter Olympic Games. They had perfected their run on the Igls course to the utmost degree, and won by just 12-hundredths of a second from the Italian No. 2 crew, Sergio Zardini and Romano Bonagura, with the Italian No. 2 bob piloted by the redoubtable Eugenio Monti in third place.

Germans took all of the men's single toboggan medals. The event, held at Igls, was won by 23-year-old Thomas Köhler, with Klaus Bonsack in second place. Köhler's aggregate time over the

four runs was less than 0.3 sec faster than Bonsack's. In the two-seater, the host nation, Austria, won both gold and silver medals, but the Germans were again victors in the women's single-seater, in which Ortrun Enderlein defeated the world champion Ilse Geisler.

The Innsbruck Games were the first at which luge tobogganing had been included, and for many onlookers it was a new experience to see the luge tobogganists adopt a sitting position, steering by skilfully transferring their weight and delicately controlling the sharp-edged runners, in contrast to the forward-prone position of the Cresta-style of the other tobogganists. Possibly because of the novelty of the event, some riders looked decidedly unsafe on their sleds, although the experienced German and Austrian experts seldom gave cause for anxiety.

The USSR, with seven wins and 14 points for seven games, appeared to win the ice hockey with plenty to spare from the Canadian team who won five of their seven games. In fact, the title was decided by Russia's final game, against Canada. Had Canada won, they would have finished equal on points with the USSR, and would have won the

gold medals because Olympic rules stated that, in the event of a tie between countries, the result of a match between the two would have decided the issue. As it happened, Russia beat Canada 3-2, and Canada were relegated to fourth position in the final table, Sweden taking the silvers and Czechoslovakia the bronzes. But there was no question that the best team—the only team to win all seven of its matches, and the team with the best goal average—won. The Russians were superbly fit—a factor that gave them superiority in the closing stages of their matches, were much better skaters than their opponents, while their forwards were adept at keeping possession of the puck until a clear scoring chance appeared.

A colourful finale to the Games was provided by the thrilling spectacle of 52 ski jumpers soaring silently over the Bergisel hill, the scene of the opening ceremony. After the Finn Veikko Kankkonen had beaten him and won the gold medal in the newly introduced 'little' 70-metre jump at Seefeld, the Norwegian Toralf Engan proved supreme in the traditional 90-metre event with Kankkonen second. In both ski-jumps Engan's team-mate Torgeir Brandtzaeg was third.

Associated Press

U.P.I.

INNSBRUCK WINTER OLYMPIC GAMES, 1964 Gold Medallists

Nordic Skiing—Men

15 kilometres	Eero Mantyranta	Finland	50 min 54.1 sec
30 kilometres	Eero Mantyranta	Finland	1 hr 30 min 50.7 sec
50 kilometres	Sixten Jernberg	Sweden	2 hr 43 min 52.6 sec
4 x 10 km relay		Sweden	2 hr 18 min 34.6 sec
Combination	Termod Knutsen	Norway	469.28 pts
70 metres jumping	Veikko Kankkonen	Finland	229.9 pts
90 metres jumping	Toralf Engan	Norway	230.7 pts
Biathlon	Vladimir Melanin	USSR	1 hr 20 min 26.8 sec

Nordic Skiing—Women

5 kilometres	Claudia Boyarskikh	USSR	17 min 50.5 sec
10 kilometres	Claudia Boyarskikh	USSR	40 min 24.3 sec
3 x 5 km relay		USSR	59 min 20.2 sec

Alpine Skiing—Men

Downhill	Egon Zimmermann	Austria	2 min 18.16 sec
Slalom	Josef Stiegler	Austria	2 min 11.13 sec
Giant Slalom	Francois Bonlieu	France	1 min 46.71 sec

Alpine Skiing—Women

Downhill	Christl Haas	Austria	1 min 55.39 sec
Slalom	Christine Goitschel	France	1 min 29.86 sec
Giant Slalom	Marielle Goitschel	France	1 min 52.24 sec

Figure Skating

Men	Manfred Schelldorfer	Germany	1,916.9 pts
Women	Sjoukje Dijkstra	Netherlands	2,018.5 pts
Pairs	Oleg Protopopov & Ludmilla Belousova	USSR	104.4 pts

Speed Skating—Men

500 metres	Richard McDermott	USA	40.1 sec
1,500 metres	Ants Antson	USSR	2 min 10.3 sec
5,000 metres	Knut Johannesen	Norway	7 min 38.4 sec
10,000 metres	Jonny Nilsson	Sweden	15 min 50.1 sec

Speed Skating—Women

500 metres	Lidia Skoblikova	USSR	45.0 sec
1,000 metres	Lidia Skoblikova	USSR	1 min 33.2 sec
1,500 metres	Lidia Skoblikova	USSR	2 min 22.6 sec
3,000 metres	Lidia Skoblikova	USSR	5 min 14.9 sec

Bobsleigh

2-man	Tony Nash & Robin Dixon	Great Britain	4 min 21.90 sec
4-man		Canada	4 min 14.46 sec

Luge Tobogganing—Men

Single	Thomas Köhler	Germany	3 min 26.77 sec
2-man	Josef Feistmantl & Manfred Stengl	Austria	1 min 41.62 sec

Luge Tobogganing—Women

Single	Ortrun Enderlein	Germany	3 min 24.67 sec
Ice Hockey		USSR	

1 Hardly any snow is visible as this ski jumper soars over Innsbruck. **2** Lidia Skoblikova won all four women's speed skating golds. **3** Marielle Goitschel matched her sister's tally of one gold and one silver in Alpine skiing. **4** Thomas Köhler won the first Olympic luge tobogganing gold medal. **5** Awnings prevented the remaining ice from melting on the bobsleigh course.

U.P.I.

Central Press

Grenoble Winter Olympic Games (1968)

Sixty-thousand people packed the ampitheatre that had been constructed especially for the opening ceremony of the Tenth Winter Olympic Games. After France's President de Gaulle had declared the Games open, the temporary construction was dismantled—a typical example of the efforts of the French to provide a spectacular presentation for the first Olympic competitions held in that country since 1924.

The traditional Olympic pageantry was brought up to date when showers of artificial roses—the rose being the symbol of Grenoble—were dropped from helicopters; the five Olympic rings were woven in smoke in the sky; and Olympic flags fluttered through the air hanging from parachutes. Stereophonic music accompanied the 1,560 competitors from 37 nations as they marched past. Alain Calmat, the former world figure skating champion, brought in the torch that had been carried from Olympia, and Leo Lacroix, the French Alpine skier, took the oath of amateurism. It was a memorable ceremony, the start of 13 days of intense competition that were marred only slightly by the unseasonably mild weather that necessitated some rearrangement of the timetables of the bobsleigh, luge, and Alpine skiing events.

The Grenoble Games were dominated by Jean-Claude Killy, a French hotelier whose consistency brought him all three gold medals in Alpine skiing. His victories were among the most controversial in the history of the Olympics, for he had been accused of professionalism; but the charges were of a type that could never be proved or disproved satisfactorily. Then, after the slalom, Karl Schranz, the evergreen Austrian whose skiing career had extended to its eleventh season, asked for an inquiry after being disqualified for allegedly missing a gate during a second descent which gave him a faster aggregate time than Killy. Doubts were raised and feelings ran high, but the jury stood by their decision and disqualified Schranz, leaving Killy the champion.

These were not the only skiing controversies. The sport's very future was threatened by the demands of the International Olympic Committee's president, Avery Brundage, that trade marks and names on skis should be removed. Brundage's unenforced demand escalated an already inflamed situation concerning problems of professional involvement that remained unresolved for years afterwards.

But none of this marred the real Killy glory. Poor visibility impaired the view of the challenging Chamrousse courses, but the runs were good, technically difficult, and a fair test for the world's best skiers. On the awesome-looking downhill course Killy exceeded 60 mph to win by 0.08 sec, and he won the slalom equally narrowly—by 0.09 sec. His giant slalom victory was the most clear-cut: Killy had more than 2 seconds in hand over the Swiss runner-up Willy Favre. But even with Killy's supremacy and the silver medal in the downhill of his compatriot Guy Perillat, France lacked some of the dominance that had been so obvious two years previously in the world championships at Portillo in Chile. Switzerland, led by Favre, Jean Daetwyler, and Duman Giovanoli, and the Austrians—notably Schranz and Heinrich Messner—were a constant danger.

Canada's Nancy Greene was the most successful woman Alpine racer despite a suspect ankle that had hindered her in previous events that season. The winner of the first World Alpine Ski Cup the previous year, she regained peak form to take the giant slalom gold and the slalom silver.

Ahead of Miss Greene in the slalom was Marielle Goitschel, perhaps the greatest woman skier of all time, who was in 1968 nearing the end of a great career. Reaching her best form of the Games in the slalom she started each run with amazing speed, and steered her way carefully to the finish. Her style—with its distinctive body-lean and perfect turning technique—allied to her superb anticipation and tall, powerful build brought her her third Olympic medal in two Games.

In contrast to Mlle Goitschel, her diminutive team-mate Annie Famose was second in the giant slalom and third in the slalom. Isabelle Mir, runner-up in the downhill, was yet another French medallist. But it was the Austrian girls who shone in the downhill, with Olga Pall taking the gold and the veteran Christl Haas third. Spear-heading a British revival was Gina Hathorn, who missed a bronze in the slalom by just three-hundredths of a second.

The outstanding woman of the Grenoble Games was the Swedish cross-country skier Toini Gustafsson. She left the opposition standing in the 5 km event, which she won with over 3 seconds in hand, and took the 10 km by over a minute. To her two gold medals she added a silver in the 3 by 5 km relay, anchoring the Swedish trio who were second to Norway.

The Scandinavians were unexpectedly outpaced in the men's 30 km by an Italian, Franco Nones, but the other cross-country races went to Norwegians. Ole Ellefsaeter was only 16.7 seconds ahead of Russia's Viatches Vedenin after a savage duel in the

1 A crowd of over 50,000 was at St Nizier to watch Vladimir Beloussov win the 90 metres ski-jumping from Czechoslovakia's Jiri Raska, who won the 70 metres event.
2 The medallists in the men's figure skating. Left to right, Tim Wood (silver), Emmerich Danzer (gold), and Patrick Pera (bronze). 3 The man who dominated the Grenoble Winter Olympics—Jean-Claude Killy. He won all three alpine skiing events, the downhill, slalom, and giant slalom, to emulate Toni Sailer's grand-slam in 1956. 4 Overcoming an ankle injury suffered during her preparations for the Games, Canada's Nancy Greene won the giant slalom by an amazing 2.5 seconds and was second in the slalom behind, 5 Marielle Goitschel, whose victory was the culmination of her fine career. In 1964, she had won the gold medal in the giant slalom. Third in the slalom and second in the giant slalom was another French skier Annie Famose. 6 Austria's Olga Pall won the women's downhill convincingly from Isabelle Mir of France and the Austrian Christl Haas, the defending Olympic champion.
7 An Austrian competitor in the 70 metres jumping, which was held at Autrans. Only the ice hockey and skating events were held in Grenoble itself.

50 km, and Harald Groenningen was less than 2 seconds faster than Finland's experienced Eero Maentyranta in the 15 km. The two Norwegians were joined by Odd Martinsen and Paal Tyldum in the winning 4 by 10 km relay team. The individual biathlon was also won by a Norwegian, Magnar Solberg, but his team were second to the Russians in the relay.

Franz Keller underlined a rising of West German strength in Nordic skiing when he won the 15 km and ski-jumping combination gold medal. Scandinavian pride was hurt further in the special jumps. On the 70 metres hill at Autrans, Jiri Raska leapt to a surprise victory for Czechoslovakia, followed by two Austrians, Reinhold Bachler and Balder Reiml. Björn Wirkola, the great Norwegian world champion of 1966, finished fourth.

A crowd of 58,000 people watched the spectacular climax of the ski-jumping from the 90 metres tower at St Nizier, where once more the Norwegians were put to shame. With the two best jumps of the contest, Russia's Vladimir Beloussov beat Jiri Raska, who proved his earlier win from the 70 metres tower was no flash in the pan. In fact, the successes in Nordic skiing were more widely

distributed than ever before, with Austria, Czechoslovakia, and Italy gaining their first Olympic medals in this branch of the sport.

The bobsleigh events were held at Alpe d'Huez, and provided a fitting climax to the long career of the Italian driver Eugenio Monti, the sport's outstanding exponent who had previously won no less than nine world titles but never an Olympic victory. This time, aged 40, he made no mistakes and in a memorable farewell performance clinched both two-man and four-man titles. The two-man was a real cliff-hanger: the West German boblet piloted by Horst Floth equalled Monti's aggregate time for the four runs and both he and Monti thought that two sets of gold medals would be awarded. But the regulations clearly stated that the fastest single run would decide such a tie, and although it was disappointing for Floth, popular sentiment rejoiced over Monti's triumphant finale. The weather interfered with the four-man bobsleigh. Although the floodlit course had three artificially frozen bends, the sun melted so much of the rest of the course that very early morning starts became inevitable, and the result was decided over two runs instead of the normal four.

The luge tobogganing at Villard-de-Lans was similarly inconvenienced. The woman's winner, Erica Lechner of Italy, prevented the Austrians and the two German teams from gaining a monopoly of the medals. That traditionally strong nation in this event, Poland, was completely overshadowed. Manfred Schmid of Austria narrowly pipped the East German Thomas Köhler to win the men's singles, but Köhler, partnered by Klaus Bonsack, reversed the order in the two-seaters. The clear, blue Olympic skies were momentarily clouded by the disqualification of the East German women's team by the Polish judge for heating the runners of their toboggan. The East Germans roundly condemned this 'capitalist, revanchist conspiracy', but to no avail.

The speed skating arena was enlivened to a cup-tie atmosphere by bands of Dutch and Norwegian supporters armed with rosettes, banners, motor horns, and bells. Predictions that the outdoor skating oval would not provide such a fast surface as similar rinks at higher altitudes were confounded as Anton Maier of Norway set a world record in the 5,000 metres and as no fewer than 52 improvements were made on the Olympic records. An important contribu-

tory factor to fast times may have been the ideally moist ice which had been chemically softened and demineralized to match ice formed naturally at mountain rinks. Maier, the 5,000 metres champion, was beaten by 1.2 seconds in the 10,000 metres by Sweden's Johnny Hoeglin. In the 1,500 metres Kees Verkerk defeated his fellow-Dutchman Ard Schenk, and Erhard Keller of West Germany took the 500 metres sprint.

The Netherlands' high reputation in women's ice racing was upheld by Johanna Schut and Carolina Geijssen, who won the 3,000 and 1,000 metres respectively. But their much-fancied compatriot Stien Kaiser managed only to win two bronze medals in the 1,500 and 3,000 metres after apparently reaching top form too early. Russian women speed skaters, previously renowned, had only one medallist: Ludmilla Titova won the 500 metres and was second in the 1,000 metres. An unprecedented event occurred in the 500 metres when the three United States competitors—Jenny Fish, Dianne Holum, and Mary Meyers—tied for second place and were all awarded silver medals.

The indoor Olympic Ice Stadium, a spacious and pillarless masterpiece of modern architec-

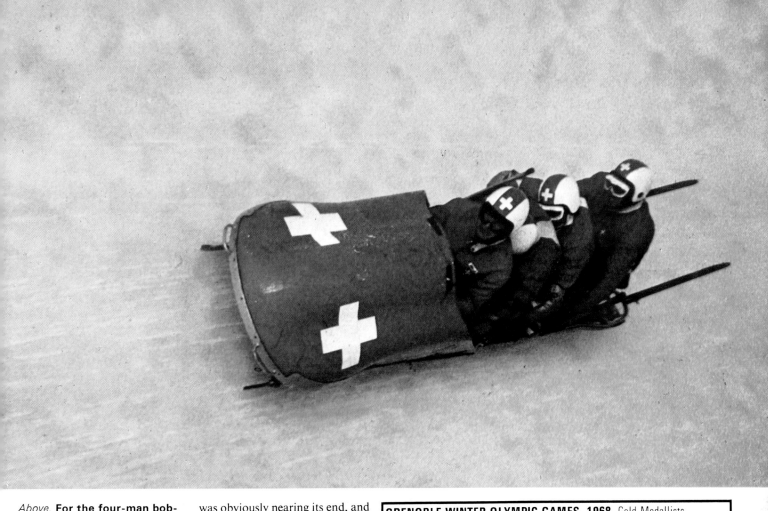

Above, **For the four-man bob-sleigh events, only two runs instead of the customary four decided the event as the sun melted so much of the course.** *Left,* **The ice hockey gold was won by the Russians (red).**

ture, was designed to seat 11,500 people, but this figure was exceeded at all three free skating events and for all the crucial ice hockey games.

A general trend of upsets of form extended to the men's figure skating when Emmerich Danzer, the world champion, dropped to fourth place, and his fellow-Austrian Wolfgang Schwarz, long accustomed to being Danzer's 'shadow', took the gold medal with a dominant display of free-skating highlighted by well-timed triple salchow, double axel, and double flip jumps.

A feature of the women's free-skating was the contrasting techniques of the classical, frail-looking winner, Peggy Fleming of the United States, and the robust runner-up, East German Gabriele Seyfert. The outcome was never in doubt because of Miss Fleming's substantial lead in the figures, but her slender frame belied a remarkable stamina which sustained a widely varied repertoire of gracefully fast spins, and smooth landings from her double jumps.

The retention of the pairs title by the Soviet husband and wife partnership Oleg Protopopov and Ludmilla Belousova was a commendable achievement in view of their ages: 35 and 32 respectively. Their long and successful career

was obviously nearing its end, and loud applause greeted their skilfully timed split lutz lift and characteristic one-handed death spiral.

The Russian stick-handlers began the eight-team ice hockey contest in unbeatable fashion, outclassing Finland 8-0 and East Germany 9-0. But they did not appear such clear favourites when they just beat Sweden 3-2. Then, in the outstanding match of the series, Czechoslovakia beat them 5-4 in a tense end-to-end affair which kept the excited spectators on the edges of their seats. Had the Czechs not drawn 2-2 with Sweden in the penultimate match of the tournament they would have been level with the Russians on points, in which case the result of the USSR-Czechoslovakia match would have decided the final order and not goal average. So the Russians did not win as easily as had been anticipated: they had 12 points from seven games, followed by Czechoslovakia with 11, and Canada with 10. Anatolii Firsov was the Soviet Union's star, being top scorer with 12 goals in the competition.

In common with the Innsbruck Games four years previously, the diverse nature of the terrain and the distances of up to 20 miles between venues caused considerable discomfort and frustration. But a most rewarding feature of the Games was that the Grenoble authorities had the foresight to build the Olympic facilities so they could be readily converted for the use of the people of the town after the Games had finished.

GRENOBLE WINTER OLYMPIC GAMES, 1968 Gold Medallists			
Nordic Skiing—Men			
15 kilometres	Harald Groenningen	Norway	47 min 54.2 sec
30 kilometres	Franco Nones	Italy	1 hr 35 min 39.2 sec
50 kilometres	Ole Ellefsaeter	Norway	2 hr 28 min 45.8 sec
4 x 10 km relay		Norway	2 hr 8 min 33.5 sec
Combination	Franz Keller	West Germany	449.04 pts
70 metres jumping	Jiri Raska	Czechoslovakia	216.5 pts
90 metres jumping	Vladimir Beloussov	USSR	231.3 pts
Biathlon	Magnar Solberg	Norway	1 hr 13 min 45.9 sec
Biathlon relay		USSR	2 hr 13 min 2.4 sec
Nordic Skiing—Women			
5 kilometres	Toini Gustafsson	Sweden	16 min 45.2 sec
10 kilometres	Toini Gustafsson	Sweden	36 min 46.5 sec
3 x 5 km relay		Norway	57 min 30.0 sec
Alpine Skiing—Men			
Downhill	Jean-Claude Killy	France	1 min 59.85 sec
Slalom	Jean-Claude Killy	France	1 min 39.73 sec
Giant slalom	Jean-Claude Killy	France	3 min 29.28 sec
Alpine Skiing—Women			
Downhill	Olga Pall	Austria	1 min 40.87 sec
Slalom	Marielle Goitschel	France	1 min 25.86 sec
Giant slalom	Nancy Greene	Canada	1 min 51.97 sec
Figure Skating			
Men	Wolfgang Schwarz	Austria	1,904.1 pts
Women	Peggy Fleming	USA	1,970.5 pts
Pairs	Oleg Protopopov &		
	Ludmila Belousova	USSR	315.2 pts.
Speed Skating—Men			
500 metres	Erhard Keller	West Germany	40.3 sec
1,500 metres	Kees Verkerk	Netherlands	2 min 3.4 sec
5,000 metres	Anton Maier	Norway	7 min 22.4 sec
10,000 metres	Johnny Hoeglin	Sweden	15 min 23.6 sec
Speed Skating—Women			
500 metres	Ludmila Titova	USSR	46.1 sec
1,000 metres	Carolina Geijssen	Netherlands	1 min 32.6 sec
1,500 metres	Kaija Mustonen	Finland	2 min 22.4 sec
3,000 metres	Johanna Schut	Netherlands	4 min 56.2 sec
Bobsleigh			
2-man	Eugenio Monti &		
	Luciano De Paolis	Italy	4 min 41.54 sec
4-man		Italy	2 min 17.39 sec
Luge Tobogganing—Men			
Single	Manfred Schmid	Austria	2 min 52.48 sec
2-man	Klaus Bonsack &		
	Thomas Kohler	East Germany	1 min 35.85 sec
Luge Tobogganing—Women			
Single	Erica Lechner	Italy	2 min 28.66 sec
Ice Hockey		USSR	

Sapporo Winter Olympic Games
(1972)

Grenoble in 1968 had seen the problems of professionalism and commercialism brought out into the open as the competitors gathered for the opening ceremony. Then the centre of the controversy was the flamboyant French skier Jean-Claude Killy, against whom charges could never be proved and who went on to a 'grand slam' of skiing gold medals.

Four years later, at Sapporo, status again set off controversy and for a time threatened the first Winter Olympics held in Asia. At the centre this time was the veteran Austrian, Karl Schranz, one-time heir apparent to the great Toni Sailer and usurped by Killy. Now he was to return home hailed as the hero—not because of any medal haul, but because he wore the mantle of the martyr.

In a week of bitterness, wrangling, probes into commercialism and professionalism, Schranz's suspension for allegedly profiting from advertising was the spark that set off the boycott threats, and endangered the Games that were costing the Japanese £17 million to stage. Perhaps it was just wild talk engendered by the high winds that blustered around Sapporo; perhaps it was because of the long distances travelled by competitors; perhaps it was courtesy to the host nation. Whatever the reason, there was no boycott and the controversy, seemingly customary as an *hors d'oeuvre* to modern major sports encounters, subsided to make way for the pageantry of the opening ceremony.

An entry of 1,128 competitors (911 men, 217 women), from 35 countries, had gathered by February 3 for the 11th Winter Olympics when Emperor Hirohito of Japan declared them open, and some 18,000 balloons took to the air, replacing the customary pigeons who, in turn, were mere substitutes for the doves of peace. A nice touch to the ceremony was the choice of the injured French skier, Ingrid Lafforgue,

1 Karl Schranz, the veteran Austrian star whose suspension just before the Olympics sparked the boycott threats at the Sapporo Games.
2 Britain's Galina Hathorn in the women's downhill, in which she finished 25th.
Opposite page: The Asians try their hand at Nordic skiing—the 15 km cross-country.

1 America's 16-year-old Anne Henning, the youngest gold medallist at Sapporo and the first competitor to set a Winter Olympic record twice in the same event—the women's 500m speed skating. 2 Marie-Therese Nadig—17-year-old schoolgirl double gold medallist, in the downhill and giant slalom. 3 Exhilaration and grace from the 70-metre tower.

to carry in the Olympic flag. Such moments of sympathy and the emotion of the ceremony itself helped to push less sporting matters into the background.

In the absence of a Killy, the star of the Sapporo Games emerged not in the alpine skiing but in the speed skating. Ard Schenk, a strongly built, blond Dutchman with a long, sweeping stride, took three of the four speed skating golds and in two events, 1,500 metres and 10,000 metres, set Olympic records to stamp his personality on both the Games and the sport. His compatriot Kees Verkerk, 1,500 metres gold medallist at Grenoble, was runner-up in the 10,000 metres; while Roar Gronvald with silvers in the 1,500 and 5,000, and Sten Stenson, with bronzes in the 5,000 and 10,000, kept Norway well to the fore.

There was another Olympic record in the 500 metres, to the reigning champion, Erhard Keller of West Germany, and all four women's speed skating events brought new records. Amazingly the sprint record went twice; to 16-year-old American Anne Henning, who was allowed a second attempt after being baulked in her first record-breaking run. The Russians Vera Krasnova and Ludmila Titova had to be content with the minor medals. Miss Henning added a bronze to her 500 metres gold in the 1,000 metres, which was won by Monika Pflug by just a hundredth of a second from Atje Keulen-Deelstra of the Netherlands. The latter showed her tremendous all-round ability with bronze medals in the 1,500 metres and the 3,000 metres, and was sixth in the sprint. Further proof of Dutch superiority came with the gold of Stien Baas-Kaiser in the 3,000 metres and her silver in the 1,500 metres behind America's Dianne Holum, who in turn followed Mrs Baas-Kaiser in the longer distance.

The alpine skiing, so often the centre-piece of the Winter Olympics, produced only one dual winner—and an amazing one at that. Marie-Therese Nadig, a 17-year-old Swiss schoolgirl, had not won a major race throughout the season, but she chose Sapporo to oust Austria's Anne-Marie Proell, the favourite, in both the downhill and the giant slalom. Heavy snow slowed the track in Miss Nadig's favour, but nonetheless hers was a most impressive performance. America's Susan Corrock took the bronze in the downhill and Austria's Wiltrud Drexel placed third in the giant slalom. The slalom went to

America—and Barbara Cochran —for their first alpine gold medal since 1952, and then only just: there was a mere two-hundredth of a second between the winner and France's Daniele Debernard. The French also took the bronze through Florence Steurer, which compensated in a small way for the disappointments of the season. In addition to Ingrid Lafforgue, the strong French team had lost Patrick Russel, Jacqueline Rouvier, and Francoise Macchi through injuries—Francoise Macchi's, coming during training at Sapporo, being the cruellest of all.

Nor was there any joy for the French in the men's alpine. There, the surprise was Francisco Fernandez-Ochoa, whose victory over Italy's Theoni brothers in the slalom—it was his first win in a major international—made him Spain's first Winter Olympic gold medallist. Gustavo Thoeni, the holder of the World Ski Cup, took the silver ahead of his brother Rolando, but showed true form in his second run in the giant slalom. For the first time, the Olympic event was decided on a two-runs aggregate, and after finishing third on his first run, Thoeni produced the fastest run next time round. With Norway's Erik Haaker,

fastest first time down, falling, it was left to the Swiss Edmund Bruggmann and Werner Mattle to take the minor medals. The Swiss finished 1-2 in the downhill with Bernhard Russi and Roland Colombin in that order, while Heini Messner, another of Austria's veterans, helped salvage some of his country's honour by finishing third despite a heavy attack of 'flu.

In the other ski sport, Nordic skiing, the inroads made into the Scandinavian dominance at Grenoble continued. This was not especially so across country, where the Norwegians and Swedes shared a virtual monopoly

with the Russians, but it was most definite in the jumping. A home hat-trick in the 70 metres jump was given an enthusiastic welcome as Yukio Kasaya, Akitsugo Konno, and Seiji Aochi took the medals in that order. The 1968 gold medallist, Jiri Raska of Czechoslovakia, could finish only fifth. But if home advantage could be given as a reason for the Japanese triumph, there could be no such excuse for the magnificent and brave jumping of Poland's Wojciech Fortuna from the 90-metre tower. His first leap of 367 feet left the others with too much to do, and Switzerland's Walter

Steiner outjumped Rainer Schmidt of East Germany for the silver medal.

There was gold, however, for the East Germans in the combined ski-jumping and 15 km cross-country. A Japanese, Hideki Nakano, led after the jumping section from Finland's Miettinen, but while the Finn sustained his challenge across country, the Japanese somewhat ironically came in last. East Germany's Ulrich Wehling came through to win the gold with Miettinen separating him from his compatriot Karl Luck in the medal order.

But for Sweden's Sven-Ake Lundback in the 15 kilometres, the men's cross-country would have been all Norway and Russia. Fedor Simaschov and Ivar Formo respectively gave Russia the silver and Norway the bronze behind Lundback, while in the 30 kilometres Vyacheslav Vedenine came through in a final powerful burst to relegate the Norwegians Paal Tyldum and Johs Harviken to minor placings. Surprisingly, considering Russia's 10-second success over Norway in a thrilling 4 x 10 kilometres relay, Vedenine's gold was only the second by a non-Scandinavian in the men's cross-country. Tyldum gained his revenge in the 50 kilometres, but Vedenine split Magne Myrmo and Reider Hjermstad to prevent Norway taking all three medals.

In the women's cross-country, the Russians, so supreme since Olympic ski-racing was introduced in 1952, dominated both events in the person of Galina Koulakova, 5 kilometres bronze medallist at Grenoble. In the 5 kilometres she led from the start, the other medals going to Finland's Marjatta Kajosmaa, 34-year-old mother of 11-year-old twins, and the Czech Helene Sikolova. Over the longer distance Miss Koulakova was followed home by fellow-countrywoman Alvetina Olynina, with Mrs Kajosmaa third. For Miss Koulakova there was a further taste for gold in the relay, the silver going to Finland and the bronze to Norway.

The biathlon gold medals went to the same recipients as in 1968: the individual to Magnar Solberg of Norway; the relay to Russia. Silver and bronze medallists, respectively, were Hansjoerg Knauthe of East Germany and Sweden's Lars Ardwidson in the individual; Finland and East Germany in the relay.

When the final tally of medals was reckoned, the 14 to East Germany was an appropriate reminder of its growing power in all international competition. However, of those 14, eight came in the luge tobogganing—a remarkable monopoly of three races. Wolfgang Scheidel attacked the 14-curve run from the first and held his position throughout, while Harald Ehrig and Wolfram Fielder shut out the opposition. Incredibly, the remaining member of the East German squad, Klaus Bonsack, took fourth place. The two-man luge ended in a dead-heat, and to some extent, therefore, the Italians Paul Hildgartner and Walter Plaikner broke the East Germany monopoly. They shared the same two-run aggregate as Horst Hornlein and Reinhard Bredow, while Bonsack and Fiedler followed their individual showings with the bronze. In the women's, the three East German entrants Anna Muller, Ute Ruhrold, and Margit Schumann finished in that order.

In the bobsleigh it was the other Germany who held the stage, taking gold and silver in the two-man and bronze in the four. Wolfgang Zimmerer steered both the gold and bronze medal winning sleds, while his opposite number in the leading Swiss sled, Jean Wicki, accomplished the same feat but in reverse order.

1 Home-crowd support for a Japanese entrant in the women's 10 km cross-country. Both the women's cross-country events were won by the Russian, Galina Koulacova, who won a third gold with the relay team. 2 Jean Wicki drives his four-man bob to victory and the security of the finishing line. 3 The two-man bob saw West Germany come out on top through Wolfgang Zimmerer and Peter Utzschneider.

Colorsport

Colorsport

The figure skating was memorable for the superb figures traced by Austria's Trixi Schuba. If she lacked the uninhibited freestyling of Canada's Karen Magnussen (silver) and America's Janet Lynn (bronze), the tall Austrian took full advantage of her superiority in the compulsory section. There was some controversial scoring, as there often is, but few knew how to react to the maximum six awarded to Janet Lynn for artistic impression after her fall.

There was a notable fall in the men's event, too. Ondrej Nepela, while attempting a triple toe loop jump, fell for the first time in four years, but this did not prevent the Czech, whose performance included an excellent triple salchow, from winning the gold medal. France's Patrick Pera failed to hold his position in the freestyle and had to be content with the bronze medal behind Sergei Tchetveroukhin of Russia.

The pairs, for so long the preserve of Oleg Protopopov and Ludmilla Belousova, saw two Russian pairs battle for their Olympic crown and ended with victory for Moscovites Alexei Ulanov and Irena Rodnina over the Leningrad pair, Andrei Suraikin and Ludmila Smirnova. East Germany's Uwe Kagelmann

and Manuela Gross added a bronze to their country's medal tally.

For the first time since the inaugural Winter Olympics, Canada did not compete in the ice hockey—the problem again being the question of status. As expected, the Russians won the gold medal, and only Sweden, with a 3-3 draw, stopped them winning every game. That draw, however, could have opened the way for the Czechs, had they not gone down 5-1 to the young United States team. Consequently the Czechs had to beat Russia in the final match, which they were unable to do. America's upsetting of the form book gave them the silver medal over the Czechs, as both finished the group with 6 points. In Group B, West Germany topped the table ahead of Norway and Japan.

Success in the ice hockey gave the Russians their eighth gold medal, and they ended the Games with 16 medals (five silver, three bronze), two ahead of East Germany (4-3-7). Once again, however, the dividing problems had remained unsolved, and the suspension of Schranz did little except rob the Games of a leading personality. With the threat of possible walk-outs and boycotts at forthcoming winter Olympics, plus the prohibitive cost of staging the events, it was not surprising that so few venues were coming forward to host the Games and it remained with the administrators to put the Olympic house in order long before the competitors arrived for the 1976 Winter Olympics at Innsbruck.

1 Italy (left), Switzerland and West Germany at the four-man bob medal ceremony.
2 Practising Soviet-American relations in the ice hockey.
3 Alexei Ulanov and Irena Rodnina. 4 Trixi Schuba.

SAPPORO WINTER OLYMPIC GAMES, 1972 Gold Medallists			
Nordic Skiing—Men			
15 kilometres	Sven Lundback	Sweden	45 min 28.24 sec
30 kilometres	Vyacheslav Vedenine	USSR	1 hr 36 min 31.15 sec
50 kilometres	Paal Tyldum	Norway	2 hr 43 min 14.75 sec
4 x 10 km relay		USSR	2 hr 04 min 47.94 sec
Combination	Ulrich Wehling	East Germany	413.34 pts
70 metres jumping	Yukio Kasaya	Japan	244.2 pts
90 metres jumping	Wojciech Fortuna	Poland	219.9 pts
Biathlon	Magnar Solberg	Norway	1 hr 15 min 55.50 sec
Biathlon relay		USSR	1 hr 51 min 44.92 sec
Nordic Skiing—Women			
5 kilometres	Galina Koulacova	USSR	17 min 00.50 sec
10 kilometres	Galina Koulacova	USSR	34 min 17.82 sec
3 x 5 km relay		USSR	48 min 46.15 sec
Alpine Skiing—Men			
Downhill	Bernhard Russi	Switzerland	1 min 51.43 sec
Slalom	Francisco Fernandez-Ochoa	Spain	1 min 49.27 sec
Giant slalom	Gustavo Thoeni	Italy	3 min 09.62 sec
Alpine Skiing—Women			
Downhill	Marie-Therese Nadig	Switzerland	1 min 36.68 sec
Slalom	Barbara Cochran	USA	1 min 31.24 sec
Giant slalom	Marie-Therese Nadig	Switzerland	1 min 29.90 sec
Figure Skating			
Men	Ondrej Nepela	Czechoslovakia	2,739.1 pts
Women	Trixi Schuba	Austria	2,751.5 pts
Pairs	Alexei Ulanov and Irena Rodnina	USSR	420.4 pts
Speed Skating—Men			
500 metres	Erhard Keller	West Germany	39.44 sec
1,500 metres	Ard Schenk	Netherlands	2 min 02.96 sec
5,000 metres	Ard Shenk	Netherlands	7 min 23.61 sec
10,000 metres	Ard Shenk	Netherlands	15 min 01.35 sec
Speed Skating—Women			
500 metres	Anne Henning	USA	43.33 sec
1,000 metres	Monika Pflug	West Germany	1 min 31.40 sec
1,500 metres	Dianne Holum	USA	2 min 20.85 sec
3,000 metres	Stien Baas-Kaiser	Netherlands	4 min 52.14 sec
Bobsleigh			
2-man	Wolfgang Zimmerer and Peter Utzschneider	West Germany	4 min 57.07 sec
4-man		Switzerland I	4 min 43.06 sec
Luge Tobogganing—Men			
Individual	Wolfgang Scheidel	East Germany	3 min 27.58 sec
2-man	Horst Hornlein and Reinhard Bredow	East Germany	1 min 28.35 sec
	Paul Hildgartner and Walter Plaikner	Italy	
Luge Tobogganing—Women			
Individual	Anna Muller	East Germany	2 min 59.18 sec
Ice Hockey		USSR	

Montreal (1976)

'We have every intention of presenting to the world in 1976 an Olympic Games worthy of man, with a proper balance between the spirit and the reality, rewarding to the present generation and beneficial to generations of the future.'

The words belong to Roger Rousseau, President and Commissioner General of the Organizing Committee of the Montreal Olympics, and the success of the XXIst Olympiad, indeed the very future of the institution, depends on that 'balance' being achieved. With the uneasy sound of politics reverberating around Mexico City and Munich, culminating in the horrible violence of guerrilla warfare, with amateurism becoming a term outdated in definition and concept, the scales have been heavily tilted to a harsh 'reality', away from the original 'spirit'.

That the challenge of redressing that balance belongs to Montreal has been in itself a source of controversy. The capital of Quebec appeared to be a makeweight in the bidding for the Games alongside the more obvious candidates, Moscow and Los Angeles. However, due almost entirely to the efforts of one man, Mayor Jean Drapeau, Montreal received the nomination, a decision that immediately met criticism from both inside and outside Canada.

The internal complaint concerned finance, but it was a charge that the ambitious M. Drapeau emphatically rejected: 'Some people feared that a high price in taxes would result. They were afraid that the games would cost so much in public monies. It was a natural enough reaction, we understood it, but it was of course wrong. We promised them that no public funds would be spent. We promised them that the Montreal Games would be wholly self-financed. We promised that the Games in Montreal would be on a smaller scale, an event with charm.'

Understandably, after Munich the major fear concerned, and will continue to concern until the end of the closing ceremony, security. Montreal has extreme housing problems and a high rate of unemployment, with an estimated 120,000 inhabitants below the poverty line. With a split population of two-thirds French speakers to one-third English, it

Models of Montreal, 1976.
Left: **The Olympic Village, which, instead of spreading outwards, was designed to soar skywards, providing a breathtaking view of Montreal.** *Following pages:* **The Olympic Stadium, a sporting complex in itself.**

Ed Lacey

Britain's performances in the 1974 European Championships may have given a somewhat false impression of Britain's athletics strength. However, there were performances which suggested that some of their leading athletes would be in the medal list. Among them were: 1 sprinter Andrea Lynch, 2 400m hurdler Alan Pascoe (331), and (3) the new 'golden girl', Donna Murray.

has a history of separatist rebellion which culminated in the murder of a Government minister and the kidnapping of a British diplomat. In 1972 outsiders infiltrated West Germany; in 1976 there is a potential threat from within as well.

Mayor Drapeau recognises the problem from first hand; 'I know a lot about terrorists from personal experience. A few years ago, the Quebec independence people blew up my house in the middle of the night. But I am not going to have Montreal Olympic complex turned into an armed camp.'

As soon as Montreal's status as Olympic hosts was confirmed though, security became a top priority. A group of senior police officers from the city were sent to Munich to study the work of Dr Manfred Schreiber, Munich's chief of police. One of Dr Schreiber's main recommendations was a lesson bitterly learned at the XXth Olympiad; the guerrillas who invaded the quarters of the Israeli team had arrived in Germany well before the Games. As a result Quebec and Ontario began rigorous surveillance of all persons arriving in the provinces, with a special watch kept on all immigrants.

M. Rousseau takes a realistic

view of the problem of preventing the squabbles of the world reaching the Olympic arena: 'What happened in Mexico and in Munich is something you've got to live with. This is the type of society in which we are living. But we must be prepared, and we have the professionals to cope with the situation. It is up to them.' What is not clear is how M. Drapeau's plan for security to blend into the surroundings will manifest itself. In mounting operations of such a massive nature, law enforcement agencies tend to prefer to show their strengths, and it is difficult to envisage the Montreal Games taking place without a police force being very much in evidence.

The International Olympic Congress, at their 1973 gathering in Varna, made a considerable attempt to cut back on the volume of competition in Montreal and thereby ease at least to some extent the numbers who have to be protected. Though all 21 sports of Munich will be represented in Canada, the IOC recommended cutbacks in ten of them, including athletics and swimming.

In athletics the walking events, in which Great Britain has always provided competitors capable of winning medals, are to be removed from the Olympic calendar. The 50 kilometres event is to be dropped, and though there will be a 20 kilometres walk in Montreal it is not to be retained for the 1980 Games. In the Olympic pool there will be no more men's and women's 200 metres individual medley events, and the men's 4 x 100 metres freestyle relay has been dropped too—a decision which makes Mark Spitz's achievement in Munich even more invincible, one of his

seven gold medals being won in that event. Also, in a positive move to curb the number of competitors at the Games, the men's swimming teams have been reduced from a maximum of 38 to 33 and the women's from 35 to 30.

Team numbers are to be reduced in other sports also. In fencing, for example, each country may bring only 18 entrants instead of the previous 20. Only 12 teams will contest the hockey finals instead of the 16 in 1972, though surprisingly the number of qualifying soccer teams has been upped from 12 to 16, but some of that increase will be absorbed in a reduction of the size of each squad. Now each nation must compete with only 17 players rather than the 19 of past years.

In shooting, the 300 metres event has been dropped, as has the tandem race in the cycling competition; in addition each country will be allowed only one entrant in the sprint instead of two. Both canoeing and gymnastics will be re-organised too. There will be a reduction in the slalom events, though there will be some new races to compensate, while the gymnastics competition is to be revamped to include fewer competitors fighting for fewer medals. The archery events are to be restricted from three entrants, per country per event, to two.

Although most of the proposed cut backs have met with strong protests from the international governing bodies of each sport that has suffered, keeping the final running order of the Olympic programme in some doubt, there is no denying the validity of the principle on which the IOC have acted. Such has been the four-

yearly increase in pressure on the glamorous balloon of the Olympics that further growth could expand it to beyond bursting point. Munich's cake of 9,000 competitors and officials surely turned the spectacle from a feast to sporting gluttony.

The recommendations made in Varna in October 1973 were geared to reduce the numbers by as many as 1,000, enough perhaps to justify Mayor Drapeau's boast that Montreal's Olympics will be on a smaller scale and that the organizers would, 'produce an Olympics to prove that small countries, even poor countries such as those in Africa, might someday play host to the Games'.

The foundation of Jean Drapeau's incredible optimism, which inspired his lone fight to bring the games to Montreal, is based on his belief that this slightly smaller extravaganza can be self-financing. Those who attack the Olympic institution in its present form claim it is wasteful expenditure in the cause of sport. The modern facilities of Mexico City provided an appallingly stark contrast to the poverty of the country. The Games brought prestige to Mexico, but many thought that government money could have been used for more directly humanitarian reasons—on improving the life of the population. Even in the more affluent surrounds of Munich, in the white elephant that was once the Olympic Village, the cost of purchasing accommodation has been quite prohibitive to the private individual, and makes the charge of wastefulness seem very real.

Montreal has one considerable advantage in staging the Olympics. The Organizing Committee insists that as much as 70 per cent

Ed Lacey

Ed Lacey

of the necessary buildings is already in existence; installations that were the core of the Expo exhibition in 1967. Although this does not include the lavish stadia that will be the focal point of the games, it certainly does embrace much of the roads and transportation that is essential in maintaining communications and access for both crowds and competitors.

However, most of Parc Maisonneuve, the central area for competition, is new. Set in a middle-class residential area on the east side of the city, it has been a site of round-the-clock building for the last four years, and the result is a complex of original concept and design, a creation which is at least three buildings in one. Visually most impressive is a skyscraper tower which the Canadians call 'the mast'. Over 500 ft high it contains sixteen stories, each of which provides training space for an individual sport; one floor for boxing, one for judo, one for wrestling etc. The architects claim there will be a total of 200,000 feet of floor space for preparation areas; and on the remaining stories there will be all manner of catering facilities, each enabling the visitor to eat or drink while marvelling at a breath-taking view.

At the bottom of this immense tower is the swimming centre in which again the need for preparation has not been neglected; alongside the 50 metre pool, in which the Olympic competition will take place, is another training pool of similar dimensions. The diving pool will be fully equipped for one, three, five, seven and a half and ten metre diving, and 9,000 spectators will be able to view the best swimmers and

divers in the world.

It is the stadium itself, though, adjoining the mast and the swimming centre, which is the most futuristic in design. Not only will the 70,000 spectators for the athletics finals all be completely under cover, but if the weather turns sour, the competitors too will be protected. Such is the design that the play area can be covered or uncovered within a quarter of an hour by the unrolling of a light membrane sheet, a perfect protection should the Games be threatened by summer squalls and showers—although the Organizing Committee have not made it quite clear who, or what circumstances, will dictate the use or absence of their umbrella. Against the demands of winter weather the roofing can be fixed on by a more permanent means, making the stadium a truly all-weather centre.

A series of politically motivated strikes disrupted the construction of the campus and social order in the city. Plumbers, pipe-fitters and electricians all downed tools and in May 1975 serious doubts arose about the ability of Montreal to stage the Olympics, but again Mayor Drapeau's optimistic philosophy rebuffed such suggestions by insisting that the main stadium had to be ready by January 1976, in order to sort out the inevitable teething troubles, particularly in the use of the roof.

Only the yachting, which will take place at Kingston on Lake Ontario, is far from the main competition area. Other principal sites will be the Montreal Forum, with a capacity of 18,000, which is to house basketball, gymnastics, boxing and volleyball, and Montreal University, where the hockey tournament will be based;

both are only a few kilometres from Parc Maisonneuve.

More central is the Olympic Village, situated within simple access of the main complex, and in itself another source of conflict between Mayor Drapeau and the citizens of Montreal. The land on which the Village now stands was the Montreal Municipal Golf Course, an area which formed part of the city's green belt. It was another argument which the strong-willed Mayor won, and now the Municipal Golf Course is sited elsewhere, while the Village hopefully will measure up to the boast that it will 'coddle the athletes. One must be certain that the atmosphere does not damage their spirits or their muscles.'

Spirits are unlikely to be damaged by the decision to erect no barriers between the men's and women's dormitories, another example of Montreal's thinking towards an open and friendly Games. The director of the Village has claimed that the athletes should be able 'to mingle, to be together, to love and to have fun. After all, this is the 1970s'.

Equally original is the scheme to store the world's press— perhaps as many as 4,000 journalists will cover the Olympics—on a fleet of luxury liners moored on the St Lawrence River adjacent to the Expo site. The idea has several advantages, especially in that no unnecessary permanent constructions need to be built to house reporters, while luxury cruisers are fitted generously with all the trappings and facilities of a first class hotel. The cost of hiring the vessels too will be considerably less than providing new installations. This is another arrow in Mayor Drapeau's quiver

to fire against those who still insist that it is economic madness for Montreal to stage the Olympic Games. The organizers also insist that a realistic estimate of total expenditure is 310 million dollars, excluding the necessary improvements to roadways and rail access to the Parc Maisonneuve. They are emphatic that this total can be covered without the burden being transferred to the taxpayers.

Of the projected income of $310 million, $250 million is hoped-for 'seniorage' from issuing commemorative coins. It is a system which brought considerable revenue to the Munich Games, and is based on producing coins of legal tender. The Royal Mint makes the coins at a cost which is less than face value, sometimes as little as 40 per cent depending on the current market price of the constituent metals, and the difference between the cost of production and that face value is normally profit for the Federal Treasury. However, the Canadian Government gave its assent to the profits on the special issues of Olympic coins going directly to the Organizing Committee. In all there will be 28 different coins issued in sets of four on seven separate occasions.

Although there was an overwhelming response to the first issue, which was sold out within a few days to buyers from all over the world, certain economic experts have cast doubts about the $250 million profit level being attained. Around $420 million worth of these coins must be sold to achieve such a level of revenue, and the population of Canada may not be sufficiently large to absorb a dominating proportion of them; the coins must sell heavily all over the globe, or at above market price to

151

collectors, to bring in the amount of money that the organizers are looking for. The general rise in world metal prices is another factor which might work against the scheme, with each increase chipping away at the amount of profit to be made on every coin.

A similar plan is to be operated on postage stamps, although this is expected to swell the funds by only $10 million. A much larger boost is expected to come from a sweepstake lottery which has already been very popular in Canada. Draws have been held every few months and the attraction of a top prize of $1 million has been magnetic; the first draw in April 1974 was sold out within a few days, 2,500,000 tickets being put on the market, from which the Organizing Committee creamed off a profit of $10 million. The original estimate was a total profit of $32 million from the lottery—in fact it may be substantially more. The scheme, however, has a dual benefit; five per cent of all gross receipts is ploughed back into domestic amateur sport in Canada so that the host country, winners of just two silvers and three bronze medals in 1972, have a more prosperous foundation on which to rear their competitors for battle on their doorstep.

With another $10 million forecast from ticket sales, the income position looks healthy enough on paper, but since a Treasury board predicted in 1973 that the loss on the Games would be over $200 million there has been continual scepticism. Much of the criticism has been amplified by the Committee's refusal to be specific in any way about their projected outlays. By far the largest lump in the original budget of their expenditure comes under the wide umbrella of 'construction'— an estimated cost of 250 million dollars. But as to actual details about stadium seating and floodlighting, the equipment for the swimming pool and the fitting for the training area, an overwhelming atmosphere of generality has prevailed.

The feeling of the sceptics has often been best summed up by John Robertson, a well-informed columnist of the *Montreal Star* who wrote in the American magazine, *Sports Illustrated*: 'Sometimes I think that the Games are being run by a ship of fools run by Captain Kangeroo and Walter Mitty; they won't tell anyone anything. Water is the price of fine wine but the Olympics cost nothing at all. These guys operate like the politicians of Paris; have some wine, have some conversation, things run by themselves, open another bottle of wine, everyone buy a brick— and there we've built a stadium. We don't know what the stadium may cost; we don't know what the Olympic Village is going to

cost. I don't know why there is such secrecy. If you talk about the real cost of the Olympics I'd say maybe a billion dollars if you counted the subway extensions. But who really knows? My guess is that no one really knows, no one at all. On the other hand I, like almost everyone else in Montreal, have an incredible sense of inevitability about all of it. Drapeau will bring it off somehow, and I doubt whether we will ever know what it's costing. And maybe we won't even care. That's the way it is with Drapeau's dream.'

However, it is a sense of inevitability not shared by the Canadian Federal Government. Very early in the history of Montreal's status as Olympic hosts they asked for assurances that they would be under no obligation to cover any debts from the Games—those assurances were received.

Although Mayor Drapeau and his team of organizers have a direct influence in the financial success or failure of Montreal, they will have less sway in the political arena into which the Olympics have now become drawn. The new President of the IOC, the Irish peer Lord Killanin, has admitted that 'the politicians have taken over', and that much of his first four years in office in succession to Avery Brundage has been spent amidst bickerings about political matters.

Perhaps the most telling remark of the entire 1972 Games came from the secretary general of the Organization for African Unity, who after winning the fight to expel Rhodesia from Munich said: 'Sport is not an end in itself'—seven words in total conflict with the original ideal behind the Olympics. There will be similar feelings in Montreal, and it is extremely unlikely that Rhodesia and South Africa will be represented.

There have been significant attempts to raise the bamboo curtain that was lowered between China and the IOC in 1958 when China left the movement, having withdrawn their contingent of athletes from the Melbourne Games two years earlier for political reasons. Since then the Chinese representation has come from Taiwan, which has competed under the titles of Formosa and Republic of China. Taiwan has never objected to China competing alongside it at the Games, but the Peking delegation has always insisted that Taiwan is part of China, and therefore that there should be no separation, just one team representing the flag of one nation.

The IOC, staunchly led by Mr Brundage, put their support behind Taiwan until a succession of events after the Munich

tournament reconstituted China's position. First the International Weightlifting Federation and then the International Fencing Federation accepted membership applications from China, whilst rejecting those from Taiwan. This gave China international recognition in six sports—ice hockey, skating, volleyball and rowing were the others—one more than the minimum required by the IOC for admission to the Olympic movement.

In September 1974 the Asian Games took place in Teheran with the blessing and patronage of the IOC, and again China competed to the exclusion of Taiwan. Since then China has made applications for international recognition in a range of Olympic sports. Although Lord Killanin, in Varna in 1973, had spoken out against Japan for adding their support to China, the political considerations were already beginning to outweigh any other factor. Sport once again was not being an end in itself.

Another crack in the Olympic ideal has concerned the question of amateur status, and the hypocrisy which allows 'soldiers' from Eastern Europe and 'college students' from the United States to compete with true amateurs who finance their own training themselves; and who lose money if they have to take time off from work to compete.

Here Lord Killanin has taken a more progressive viewpoint. His Executive Committee of the IOC proposed in 1974 that there should be radical changes to Rule 26 of the Olympic code— the rule which states that no athlete must spend more than 60 days each year training or competing when he is being subsidised financially. This law has never affected the full-time 'soldier' or 'student', who has all the facilities he needs all the year round. But it affects any national governing body who wishes to improve the prospects of its athletes by sending them, expenses paid, to a competition or a training area.

The IOC Executive proposed that athletes should be allowed to train and compete as often as they choose to do so in any year, and that they should be allowed to receive broken-time payments for any loss of income incurred while performing. The way was being paved towards the 'full-time' amateur. The suggestions provoked a favourable reaction from Great Britain's outstanding Olympic athlete, David Hemery: 'It is a marvellous suggestion and a very positive step in the right direction.'

It is, moreover, a step that could improve substantially Britain's chances of increasing their medal tally in future Olympic Games. In Montreal, however, the only

nation really likely to challenge the now predictable battle between Russia and the United States for medals is East Germany, whose athletes have achieved consistently high levels of performance in many Olympic sports in the four years since Munich. But the European Athletics Championships held in Rome in the late summer of 1974 did offer some hope of gold medals for Britain on the track at Parc Maisonneuve.

Within the space of a few hours on the final day of competition in Rome, Brendan Foster and Ian Thompson produced performances of the very highest calibre. Foster destroyed a field which included the double gold winner of Munich, Lasse Viren, to win the 5,000 metres in a devastating display of front running in which he led from gun to tape. Already the world-record holder for two miles, he was on a schedule for another world's best until the imposing heat edged him outside it.

Ian Thompson's victory was even more remarkable from an uncomplicated runner whose history is straight out of fairy-tale fiction. An average club athlete in middle-distance running he entered a marathon to help his club out, and became British champion. He also took the Commonwealth Games gold medal in New Zealand, and made it four wins in his only four attempts at the race when he became champion of Europe by more than a quarter of a mile in gruelling heat. Given normal luck both Foster and Thompson should be medal contestants in Montreal.

Whatever happens to individuals, however, the greatest test in 1976 is to be faced by the Olympic Games itself. From July 17 to August 1, the glare of the world's spotlights will be focused on the centre of French Canada. As well as the floating village of reporters, there will be, after considerable squabbling about the costs of the rights, world-wide television coverage, meaning that there will be an even greater audience than the estimated one billion who viewed the events in Germany. As such a spectacle it is extremely vulnerable.

But if the Olympic Games are to continue into the 1980s and beyond, it must be equal to any outside forces who may threaten to repeat the mayhem of that bloody event in the Village in Munich. More than that, the Olympic movement must conduct its own affairs with the dignity and grace of a true sporting occasion; it must be a vehicle for sportsmanship in a world where the word has become more associated with weakness than strength. That is the real challenge for Montreal.

59
Illustrated
NATIONAL PARKS

100TH ANNIVERSARY
of the National Park Service

Celebrating 100 Years of Wilderness and Wonder

WITH ORIGINAL POSTER ART BY ANDERSON DESIGN GROUP

SPECIAL THANKS TO:

David Anderson, Julian Baker, Kai Carpenter, Andy Gregg, Aaron Johnson, and Michael Korfhage: for collaborating as a team to create such a beautiful & comprehensive collection of National Park poster art.

Michael Korfhage: kudos for doing more posters than all of us put together!
Kai Carpenter: for producing 12 gorgeous oil paintings in record time.
Edward Patton: for your expert typography, design, photo searching and layout of the book interior.
Dawn Verner: for your many hours of research, photo searching and proofreading.
Jamie "Flip" Blaine: for editing Nathan's writing and adding creative direction to the narrative.
Dick Koonce: for your keen eye as a proofreader, and your encouragement as a friend.
Rick Smith, Former Superintendent & Ranger for 5 National Parks: for helping us connect with other retired park officials who provided a wealth of information and wonderful quotes.
Retired National Park Officials: for fact-checking, offering insight, perspective and years of service.

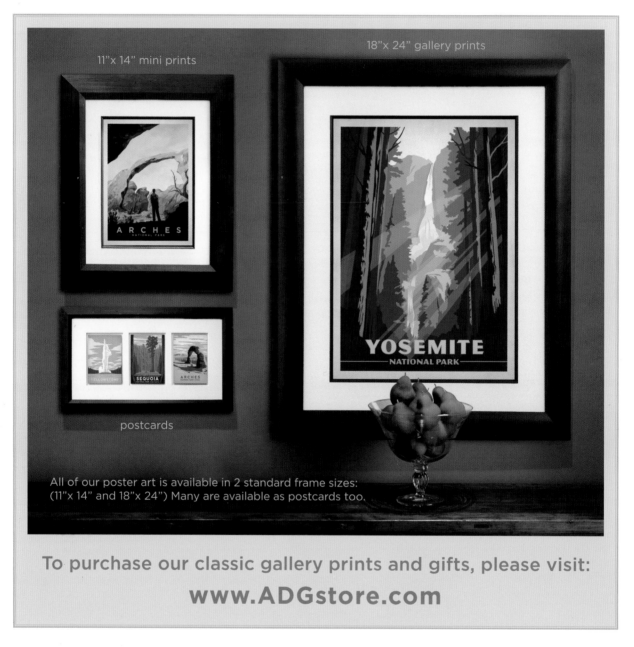

To purchase our classic gallery prints and gifts, please visit:

www.ADGstore.com

Cover, interior design, and all posters created by Anderson Design Group, Inc.
116 29th Avenue North, Nashville, Tennessee 37203 • Phone: 615-327-9894 • www.AndersonDesignGroup.com • www.ADGstore.com
All photos used by permission. Printed & bound in the U.S.A.

Published by Anderson Design Group, Inc..

Table of Contents

A Word from the Author...

I WAS 18. I had just finished high school, broken up with a girlfriend, and suddenly felt like the whole world was new and waiting for me to survey it. I loved to travel as a child, and I grew up with an insatiable wanderlust: to see what I hadn't yet seen, to go somewhere I'd never gone before. My dad and I shared this longing. To celebrate my graduation, he dropped everything from his busy graphic design schedule to take me on an adventure to Yellowstone National Park, a place we knew hardly anything about. But that made the trip all the more exciting. We were Lewis and Clark, journeymen into the Great Unknown. We packed our bags and headed West.

That trip would leave an indelible impression on me, revealing a type of freedom and wilderness unimaginable back east. We gawked as wild bison (real bison!) crossed the road, bringing Park traffic to a standstill. Boiling baths of pink, orange, blue, and green simmered beneath our glued-to-the-boardwalk feet as we crossed "Colter's Hell". We thrashed our rental car on a dirt road outside Jackson Hole, an enticing pot-holed trail that promised nothing more than an invitation to explore. I watched yellow wildflowers dance in the wind before a silent audience of Teton Mountains. I shivered in the moonlit fog as an elk silhouette knelt to graze. We lunched like Provencal Frenchmen on the banks of a stream. We camped beneath a sky of silken starlight. These moments of living poetry opened my eyes to a brand of wonder I'd only experienced second-hand in movies or books. This was real. Yellowstone was my gateway into the world of America's National Parks and I couldn't get enough.

But it wasn't just the novelty of the Park that stuck with me. It was enjoying this awe-inspiring land with someone I loved, someone I wanted to make memories with. The spirit of the National Parks is communal; yes there are moments of sheer bliss in solitude, but often the memories that stay with you are ones that are shared with others. Moments that bind you together, to be recalled later. People visit Parks together for these precious moments. That's the magic of the National Park experience: they were always meant to be shared. The Parks are our inheritance, diamonds

of nature woven into the tapestry of America. We are wrapped up in the folds of this cloth together, to enjoy the wonders we were born into.

As we celebrate the 100th anniversary of the National Park Service, it's important to remember that the Parks haven't always existed. And they are not permanent unless we keep them that way. We hope that as you leaf through these pages, you will be filled with a desire to go. Treat this book like an invitation in coffee table book format. You are invited to 59 of the world's greatest natural landscapes, all within the borders of the United States. They are wild yet fragile, wonderful places that needed protection from human nature before it was too late.

Each Park has a unique story, featuring characters that discovered transcendent beauty and then worked relentlessly to preserve it for future generations. The most glorious scenery in America was made accessible by a handful of people who valued service over possession. They envisioned a future for a special plot of American soil and sought to make that vision a reality. We are the beneficiaries of their dreams.

The National Parks are your inheritance, treasures that are yours by birthright. If you are an American citizen, the Grand Canyon is yours. The Yosemite Valley is yours. The world's longest cave system is yours to explore. The world's tallest trees are yours to gaze up into. Acadia, Crater Lake, Glacier, Arches, Hawai'i Volcanoes, the Smokies: all yours. As you look at the posters we've created for each of these places, as you read the stories for each one, we hope you will be inspired to go and witness what makes our country so unique. Our art pays tribute to this great gift. Celebrate this great land with us and protect these jewels of creation for our children and our children's children. You will not be disappointed.

This book is dedicated to my fiancée Kamalani, who let me borrow her card table as a writing desk and her Weimaraner as a muse. Your love and encouragement kept me going when writing this book felt like scaling Mount Denali (I look forward to actually doing that with you someday). Thank you for lifting me up on the hardest days. You are my greatest adventure, and I can't wait to explore the world with you.

A special thanks to author and fellow Parks enthusiast Michael Joseph Oswald, whose work *Your Guide to the National Parks* was a primary resource for this book. Your attention to detail, investigative spirit, and first-hand experience were invaluable tools in my attempt to describe the riches of our National Park heritage.

—Nathan Anderson, *Writer*

A Word from the Artist...

DRIVING AN RV was just one of the fun/scary/crazy experiences that helped to shape this book. Only a few months before I put my life on hold to finish this project, my amazing wife Patty and I took turns driving a borrowed RV (affectionately dubbed Large Marge) from Nashville to the Grand Canyon, Zion, Bryce, Petrified Forest and back. I relished days of conversation with my wife of 29 years, who is also my best friend and the mother of our kids. I dedicate this book to her (Patty—not Large Marge). While our four kids relaxed in the 90s-era upholstered living room on wheels, Patty and I watched the scenery change through the windshield. The green rolling hills of Tennessee gave way to the open plains of Arkansas and Oklahoma, which gradually morphed into the painted deserts of New Mexico, Arizona and Utah. At each stop, my family explored canyons, rafted down rivers, and stood in awe of jaw-dropping sunsets and panoramic vistas. We laughed and hiked and ate and posed for family photos. We took full advantage of wonderful National Park visitor centers, scenic roads and trails, exhibits and coin-operated campground showers (with 7-minute limits). Thanks to dedicated people we have never met, we enjoyed unspoiled, expertly-managed parks full of natural wonders, protected and preserved as our national heritage. We shared a universal human and Divine experience walking in reverent silence along the rim of the Grand Canyon with people from all over the globe. It was the greatest family adventure we've ever had.

I was a king for those 2 weeks, enjoying the things I love most in life—the great outdoors, my country, and my family. It also was a much-needed break from the long hours I'd been spending in the studio creating poster art and running my design firm. After working for more than 5 years

to create a complete series of National Park poster art, this was the perfect way to celebrate the final stretch of a long process.

Several months before our trip, I read that the National Park Service would be celebrating its 100th anniversary in 2016. So my oldest son Nathan, an avid hiker, history buff, and a very talented writer agreed to help me produce an NPS Centennial coffee table book that would feature all 59 of my National Park posters, plus his own compilation of insights, facts, travel tips, and historical information.

During and after our RV trip, Nathan worked tirelessly researching information, checking facts, and writing a rich narrative about each of the 59 parks. He tackled the task of summarizing the 100 year history of the National Park Service, making it accessible and interesting. As a father-son duo, we visited parks, pored over dozens of books, travel guides, maps and websites. We watched the National Park documentary by Ken Burns which we found to be one of the finest compilations of history, narrative and imagery ever assembled on the subject.

Finally, I engaged my design firm's all-star team: Edward Patton, Dawn Verner and Aaron Johnson to help me lay out the book. The result is a celebration of our national heritage expressed in poster art, photography and the written word. It is a love letter to America by a group of creative people, outdoor enthusiasts, and history lovers. It is a call to our fellow citizens to venture out and experience the wilderness and wonder that has been set aside for us to enjoy. America's natural sanctuaries have been made accessible to everyone thanks to the sacrifice, foresight, and dedication of park rangers, politicians, philanthropists, naturalists, and ordinary people. Our National Parks exist today thanks to public servants who have worked tirelessly to protect and preserve some of the most beautiful outdoor spaces on our planet. Happy 100th Anniversary, National Park Service! Think of this book as a 160-page birthday card!

—Joel Anderson, *Graphic Artist and founder of Anderson Design Group, Inc.*

The Anderson family (left to right) Joel, Nathan, David, Patty, Benji, Mimi

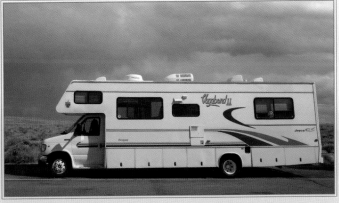

"Large Marge," the Mother Ship for our 2015 National Park adventure

OUR POSTERS LOOK OLD,

as if they were produced generations ago and then recently discovered in an estate sale. Folks often confuse our art with vintage posters that are in the public domain. That's because we have spent years studying the rendering techniques, typography, color palettes, and style of art done in the 1920s, '30s and '40s. We create original poster art, but we strive to make our designs look like they were done by artists from another era.

During my first year as an illustration major in art school, I fell in love with the iconic imagery created during the Golden Age of Poster Art—a glorious era of commercial art from the late-1800s to the mid-1900s. I was especially captivated by the romance and adventure of travel poster art. Back before the age of photography or computers, designers and illustrators used their masterful hand-rendering and hand-lettering skills to catch the attention of the viewer, to draw them into a scene, and inspire them to take a trip to some exotic destination. The colors, fonts, rendering styles and general aesthetic were beautiful even though in their day, these posters were nothing more than everyday advertisements created to be pasted up on a wall out in a public space. (In those days, architecture, packaging, even street lamps were ornate, intricate, and crafted with artistic attention to the smallest detail).

Today, in an era of computerized art, photography and cost-conscious efficiency, our culture craves simplicity and vintage craftsmanship. We desire authenticity, excellence, and anything hand-crafted. So it's no surprise that we now decorate with yesterday's ordinary advertising art and accept it as historic and beautiful, a legitimate, nostalgic and emotionally engaging art form.

One of my favorite series of prints from the Golden Age of Poster Art was created in a response to a crisis. During the Great Depression, the Works

Progress Administration sought to help unemployed artists by commissioning posters that were intended to inspire Americans to visit National Parks. I still remember the very first time I saw a WPA National Parks print. I was with my son Nathan in the Visitor Center at

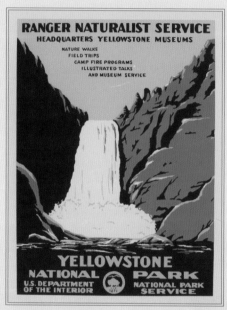

Above: The first WPA print I ever bought. Below: The first National Park print my team produced.

Yellowstone National Park, and my eye was drawn to a simple yet iconic poster that was screen printed in a limited color palette. The clean composition drew my eye to Yellowstone Falls and summed up the experience my son and I had enjoyed earlier that week. I had taken

lots of photos, but this poster did what no camera could—it eliminated all the unnecessary details and it focused my attention on the canyon, the majestic waterfall and the open sky above, adding a typographical appeal to see the sights and experience the wonder of Yellowstone. I immediately bought that poster, and I took it home as a treasured souvenir of the amazing week I spent with my son.

Visiting National Parks with my family inspired me to collect more WPA poster art that would capture the awe and wonder of America's most beautiful places. I began to notice the powerful compositions, selective focus on iconic imagery and the integration of hand-lettering. These classic posters promoted the parks, romanticized nature, and inspired Americans to travel and explore our great country. But as I soon discovered, only a few of these National Parks prints were ever created, and many of the ones that were produced had been lost or damaged over the decades. For the surviving WPA National Park posters we enjoy today, we owe a debt of thanks to seasonal park ranger Doug Leen, who in 1973 found a WPA Grand Teton poster in a pile of trash being hauled out during NPS renovations. He began scouring the country for other surviving prints and negatives. As it turns out, only 14 parks had ever commissioned a WPA poster, and of those 14 parks, only 11 poster designs have survived. After years of searching, Doug and his team carefully restored and reproduced the designs they had salvaged, saving a treasure trove of delicate and deteriorating art from extinction, and making fresh reproductions available to the public once more. I will always be grateful to Ranger Doug for having the foresight to hunt down the WPA park posters and for making the designs available to a new generation.

Once I realized that no one had ever

Shown above are a few of the surviving WPA National Parks prints. These images were provided by the Llibrary of Congress.

created a complete collection of National Parks posters, I had an idea. Why not create a whole new generation of original poster art inspired by those classic WPA prints? Why not produce an original illustrated poster design for each of the 59 parks? As an artist, an outdoor enthusiast, and a proud American, I couldn't think of a more inspiring or exciting way to merge my passion and talents.

I decided to pick up where the WPA artists left off by creating a few prints of my own favorite parks. I shared the list with my illustration team, who at the time included staff artist Andy Gregg, intern Julian Baker, and free-lance artist Michael Korfhage. Over a five-year period, I assigned specific park posters to each of my artists, providing them with direction, reference and inspiration. In the last few months before assembling this book, Michael Korfhage created 20 of the designs at a pace that resembled the buzzing productivity of the old WPA poster art studios. Kai Carpenter produced 12 oil paintings in a classic, romantic travel style. My son David Anderson was working as an intern at

my studio while he was in art school, so he worked on a few of the prints along with staff illustrator Aaron Johnson. We surpassed my original goal of 59 posters and produced a series of National Parks prints that now includes over 70 designs!

All along the way, we kept the designs iconic, simple, and beautiful. Our goal was to produce art that would catch your eye from a distance, and then speak to your soul upon closer inspection. We wanted to inspire everyone to fall in love with adventure, to protect and preserve nature, and to celebrate the rich heritage that is ours as citizens of this grand and beautiful country.

After working on this series with the aid of modern technology, I am amazed at the beautiful prints the WPA artists cranked out in an era before photography was widely used in advertising art. They did their jobs creating temporary art that was produced to be pasted onto a wall or taped up in school classrooms. By necessity, their art had to be bold, iconic, emotive, and easily read in a split second. It had to be created in a very limited color palette. Ironically, the WPA

artists were just glad to have work to do during the Great Depression. They never dreamed that their work would be collected and prized by future generations like ours.

We use the computer as a finishing tool, but I still insist that my artists draw and sketch to create art that is as authentic and iconic as the classic 20th Century works that inspire us. There is no quick or simple way to do this kind of art. Just like in the old days, each of our posters starts with a clever idea, and takes 30 to 60 hours to render. Years ago, poster art was disposable, (that is why the few surviving vintage posters are so rare and valuable today). And that is why we are creating a new generation of poster art which hopefully will not suffer the same fate of being pasted up on a wall, only to fade in the sun, peel in the wind, and disintegrate in the rain!

As you'll see in this book, everything we do is a labor of love, rooted in our appreciation of classic American advertising art. I hope you enjoy the art as much as we enjoyed creating it!

JOEL ANDERSON *was born in Denver, Colorado in 1965. His family moved every few years to places such as Dallas, Curacao, El Salvador, New York, and South Carolina. Joel studied at Ringling School of Art & Design in Sarasota, Florida where he concentrated on Illustration and Design. After graduating with honors in 1986, Joel moved to Nashville and worked for 7 years at Carden & Cherry advertising agency. While there, Joel won several ADDYS and an Emmy Award for his work on a Saturday morning TV show; independently, he exhibited & sold his paintings in local galleries. Joel co-founded Anderson Thomas Design in 1993 with David Thomas. The firm worked on numerous award-winning projects for clients like Universal Studios, DreamWorks, Hasbro, and Harper Collins. After David retired in 2007, Joel retooled the company as Anderson Design Group and narrowed the focus to illustrative design, publishing and poster art. Joel has published over 600 posters and 12 books.*

Our National Park Service: Celebrating 100 Years

IT ALL BEGAN with a strange, bubbling region in the remote territory of northern Wyoming. Established in 1872, Yellowstone National Park was America's first National Park, featuring a vast and mysterious frontier laced with geysers, hot springs, waterfalls, and lonely stretches of wilderness. It was also an area that could be easily exploited: hunters would massacre Yellowstone's bison population while crafty businessmen would purchase scenic plots of land and charge tourists a hefty toll to see the Park's wonders. This National Park would exist to protect Yellowstone's wilderness from and for mankind. The historic Senate bill read: "Be it enacted … that the tract of land … lying near the headwaters of the Yellowstone river … is hereby reserved and withdrawn from settlement, occupancy, or sale under the laws of the United States, and dedicated and set apart as a public park or pleasuring ground for the benefit and enjoyment of the people."

Though Yellowstone was created 44 years before the National Park System was born, this initial Park set the precedent for the 58 that followed. It was the conception of the American Park idea, answering the questions: what is the function of a National Park? What is its purpose? Why do we intentionally set aside vast areas of our own land that could otherwise be used for commercial or agricultural development? Yellowstone

was the seed planted into the American consciousness, pointing out not only our fleeting existence but the fragility of nature. Yellowstone caused us to look at ourselves and think ahead. What will be left of this country for our children? For our grandchildren? The first Park made us consider the natural wonders we possessed, and asked us how we, as a nation, would care for these gifts. The ancient canyons, geysers, waterfalls, and mudpots pointed out our youth in the shadow of the Earth's age. We did not create the land, but we became

> **"It is not what we have that will make us a great nation; it is the way in which we use it."**
> *-- Theodore Roosevelt*

stewards of it.

The origins of the National Park System would be incomplete without mentioning a humble Scottish sheepherder named John Muir. A self-taught naturalist, fearless mountain climber, poet, prophet, and champion for exploited wilderness, John Muir's life and work borders on an American legend. He was a simple man who surrendered his life to Nature, to experience the living world like very few "Westernized" people ever would. He climbed Douglas fir trees, slept on Alaskan glaciers, sledded down an avalanche, and scaled slippery waterfalls out of an unquenchable curiosity with the natural world. Yosemite Valley was Muir's backyard, classroom, and playground in the later years of the 1800s. It was here that John Muir studied the plants and animals of the Sierra Nevada Mountains with a religious fervor. He taught Yosemite's visitors to appreciate what was free for all mankind to enjoy. He wrote essays and letters, celebrating the vibrant life that poured down from the peaks and pleaded for their protection. He was a defender of the defenseless, a voice crying out in the wilderness.

Muir studied America from the woods, where he gained a unique perspective on American greed. Enterprising lumber companies decimated irreplaceable tree groves in California and Washington State. Hunters and sports-

---

A 100-Year Timeline of the National Park Service: 1916-2016*

Fifty-nine current parks have been formed since our nation began preserving land for the enjoyment of future generations. Nine of them were set aside before the National Park Service was created in 1916 to manage the parks. Over the years, Presidents protected tracts of land by designating them as national monuments. Often in the face of opposition by corporations and private citizens, Congress acted to establish these protected areas as National Parks, creating a legacy of wilderness and wonder for all of us to cherish.

1875

1872
Yellowstone

1890 Sequoia
1890 Yosemite

* It was surprisingly difficult to determine the actual order of when each of the 59 parks were established. Since all of our sources varied, this timeline portrays the most recent establishment dates of each current National Park (as opposed to authorization dates). Parks that have been dissolved and reestablished are dated accordingly.

men killed thousands upon thousands of bison on the Great Plains. Gray wolves and grizzly bears were shot to near extinction. Ancient pre-American artifacts were robbed from ancestral Indian homes as souvenirs. Miners lusted for gold and blasted into mountains (no matter how scenic) in search of precious minerals. Muir observed a young country that, though exploding with industry and achievement, was gouging itself with unbridled commercialism. We were quickly becoming victims of our own success, and Muir watched as we consumed our timeless and fragile wilderness spaces in the name of progress. The eccentric mountain man of Yosemite sounded the alarm, and his psalms of natural splendor resonated in the hearts of countless Americans. Because of early advocates such as John Muir, the National Park idea caught momentum in our nation's capitol. We needed a system to save us from desecrating ourselves irreparably.

The bones of the National Park Service began to assemble with the passing of the Antiquities Act in 1906. This ruling gave the President of the United States the ability to designate land as national monuments. Theodore Roosevelt would sign this Antiquities Act into law, and he carried out his new capacity with relish. Many of our National Parks today originated as national monuments, including the Grand Canyon, Zion, Acadia, and Carlsbad Caverns. Roosevelt's passion for conservation set the tone for future Americans as the National Parks idea came into fruition. By the end of his presidency, Theodore Roosevelt had created 5 National Parks, 18 national monuments, and placed over 280,000 square miles of U.S. land under federal preservation. The Antiquities Act now allowed the federal government to begin collecting and protecting places of national and natural significance for the country's enjoyment.

What's the difference between a national monument and a National Park? A national monument usually contains one primary resource of cultural, scientific, or historic interest worth preserving. This could be a recreational area, a wilderness or forested area (such as Muir Woods or Glen Canyon), a military site (such as Pearl Harbor), pre-American ruins (at Chaco Canyon),

or a patriotic site (Mount Rushmore or the Statue of Liberty). A National Park is composed of several resources and scenery (wildlife, forests, canyons, geysers, waterfalls) that are all federally protected from any private commercial use. National monuments could be created

without Congressional approval, so many early champions of the National Park idea went straight to the President with their requests to protect America's uniquely beautiful landscapes.

A magnetic, wildly successful businessman named Stephen Mather would become the first director of the National Park Service. With his enthusiastic knack for promotion and love for American Parks, Mather would convince the

1900 1903 Wind Cave 1915 Rocky Mtn. 1916 Lassen Volcanic 1919 Acadia 1919 Grand Canyon 1919 Zion 1925 1929 Grand Teton 1934 Great Smoky Mtns.

1899 Mt. Rainier 1902 Crater Lake 1906 Mesa Verde 1910 Glacier 1916 National Park Service is established 1917 Denali 1921 Hot Springs 1928 Bryce Canyon 1930 Carlsbad Caverns 1935 Shenandoah

9

country of the need for one department to oversee the country's greatest natural treasures. Accompanied by his young assistant Horace Albright, Mather convinced senators, congressmen, railway barons, and average American families to first familiarize themselves, then cherish the National Parks. Touring across the country, Mather and Albright brought the Parks into the public limelight, promoting tourism and encouraging more convenient lodging and travel options for Park guests. Their tireless efforts gave Americans a sense of ownership and responsibility for these

beautiful places. And, on August 25, 1916, President Woodrow Wilson would sign the Organic Act, bringing the National Park Service into existence. Its fundamental purpose would be to "conserve the scenery and the natural and historic objects and the wild life" of the Parks, and "provide for the enjoyment of the same in such manner … as will leave them unimpaired for the enjoyment of future generations." The National Park System was born, and Stephen Mather would lead the way into a new age of natural preservation, building the first Park system of its kind on the planet.

With this new conservation administration in place, the National Parks Service now had the written power to protect America's precious landscapes from commercial abuse. Enforcing this authority, however, would prove to be an enormously difficult task. As World War I raged on, calls to support the troops with federally-protected lumber, minerals, and livestock grew louder and louder. Private logging companies eyed the national forests of the Great Smoky Mountains and Mount Rainier. Ranchers pushed to raise sheep and cattle on the lush fields of Yosemite. But Mather and Albright withstood the attacks, and the National Park Service continued to add more Parks to the fold from all over the country, wilderness wonders from Utah,

Alaska, Maine, Colorado, North Carolina, and Tennessee. Roadways and railways were developed to bring more and more visitors into the Parks. When Stephen Mather passed away in 1930, an

> "We have fallen heirs to the most glorious heritage a people ever received, and each one must do his part if we wish to show that the nation is worthy of its good fortune."
> -Theodore Roosevelt

experienced Horace Albright championed Mather's legacy to preserve and promote America's National Park System in the midst of a financial crisis.

As America plunged into the Great Depression of the 1930s, President Franklin Delano Roosevelt did his part to keep the Park system alive too. He reorganized federal protection of national monuments, forests, war memorials, and preservations by placing them under National Park jurisdiction. This expansion of power added incalculable significance to the National Park Service. They were

A 100-Year Timeline of the National Park Service (1916-2016)

1938 Olympic	1941 Mammoth Cave	1944 Big Bend	1950	1960 Haleakalā	1962 Petrified Forest	1968 North Cascades / 1968 Redwood	1971 Arches / 1971 Capitol Reef	1975	1978 Badlands / 1978 Theodore Roosevelt
	1940 Kings Canyon / 1940 Isle Royale	1947 Everglades		1956 Virgin Islands	1961 Hawai'i Volcanoes	1964 Canyonlands	1972 Guadalupe Mtn.	1975 Voyageurs	

now sole stewards of America's historical and natural treasures. A new Wildlife division was added too, with a greater emphasis on protecting the Park's animal populations, spearheaded by young zoologist George Melendez Wright. When 1 out of every 4 American workers lost their jobs during the Depression, Roosevelt's New Deal programs put more than 3 million people back to work. Groups such as the Civilian Conservation Corps improved roads and campsites, built trails and visitor centers, and planted trees throughout the Park system.

Progress slowed as the nation entered World War II and many young men were sent overseas, but the Parks continued to be a place of solace as the war raged on until 1945. With a renewed sense of pa-

triotism and relief, Americans flooded back into the National Parks after the war. By 1955, annual visitor attendance topped 62 million. In response to this massive influx of tourism, National Parks Director Conrad Wirth proposed a 10-year, $787 million plan to dramatically develop the Parks' infrastructure and keep the Parks from being "loved to death." This proposal was named Mission 66, and would be completed by the Park System's 50th birthday in 1966.

The grooming and growing of Mission 66 paid off, and the Parks continued to add valuable landmarks and wilderness

regions to its ever-widening fold. Secretary of the Interior Stewart Udall lead the charge, urgently persuading Congress to create Parks such as North Cascades, Redwood, Canyonlands, and Guadalupe Mountains. He would also help establish protected waterways, seashores, and trailways such as the Appalachian Trail and the Pacific Crest Trail. Udall embodied the National Park's motto of preservation for future generations, stating: "Each generation has its own rendezvous with the land, for despite our fee titles and claims of ownership, we are all brief tenants on this planet. By choice, or by default, we will carve out a land legacy for our heirs." Udall's efforts would take the National

Park Service to new heights; over 165 million people would visit the 38 National Parks and 200 historic sites and monuments by 1972. In 1980, President Jimmy Carter would invoke the Antiquities Act in Alaska, controversially setting aside 47 million acres of pristine Alaskan wilderness. Seven enormous National Parks would be carved out of America's Last Frontier.

Since then, Congress has established 11 more National Parks, bringing the Park Service's total to 59 as of 2015. Each place is a unique depiction of American freedom: a refuge for wildlife, geological phenomena, and vast woodlands. They are also our playgrounds, where people of all backgrounds, races, and creeds can enjoy communion with nature. The tension between tourism and preservation continues to affect how the Parks are managed. As our world changes, these areas of timeless beauty must be maintained to protect that healthy balance. The National Park Service has fought to keep the "legacy of the land" for future generations, and as Americans we should embrace our Park heritage. Go and enjoy these 59 wonders of nature. They were set aside just for you.

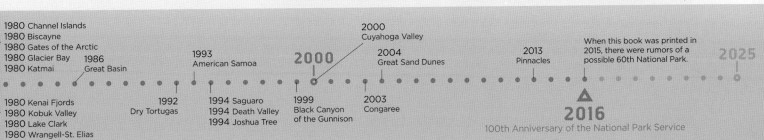

Olympic **21**
32 North Cascades
4 Mount Rainier
8 Glacier

WA

MT

ND

39 Theodore Roosevelt

OR

5 Crater Lake

ID

1 Yellowstone

SD

33 Redwood

17 Grand Teton

WY

Wind Cave **6** **38** Badlands

10 Lassen Volcanic

NE

Great Basin **49**

UT

Rocky **9** Mountain

Yosemite **3**

Bryce Canyon
Capitol Reef
Arches **34**

CO

Pinnacles **59**

CA

NV

16
35
31

Black Canyon **55** of The Gunnison

KS

Kings Canyon **22**

Canyonlands

14 Zion

2 Sequoia

7 Mesa Verde **58** Great Sand Dunes

Death Valley **53**

13 Grand Canyon

Channel Islands **40**

Joshua Tree **54**

Petrified Forest **30**

OK

AZ

NM

52
Saguaro

Carlsbad Caverns **18**

36
Guadalupe Mountains

TX

25 Big Bend

Alaska

Kobuk Valley **46** **42** Gates of the Artic

AK

11 Denali

Lake Clark
Wrangell-St. Elias
47 **45** **48**

Katmai **44**
Kenai Fjords
43
Glacier Bay

Hawaii

28 Haleakalā

HI

29
Hawai'i Volcanoes

Find Your Favorite Parks!

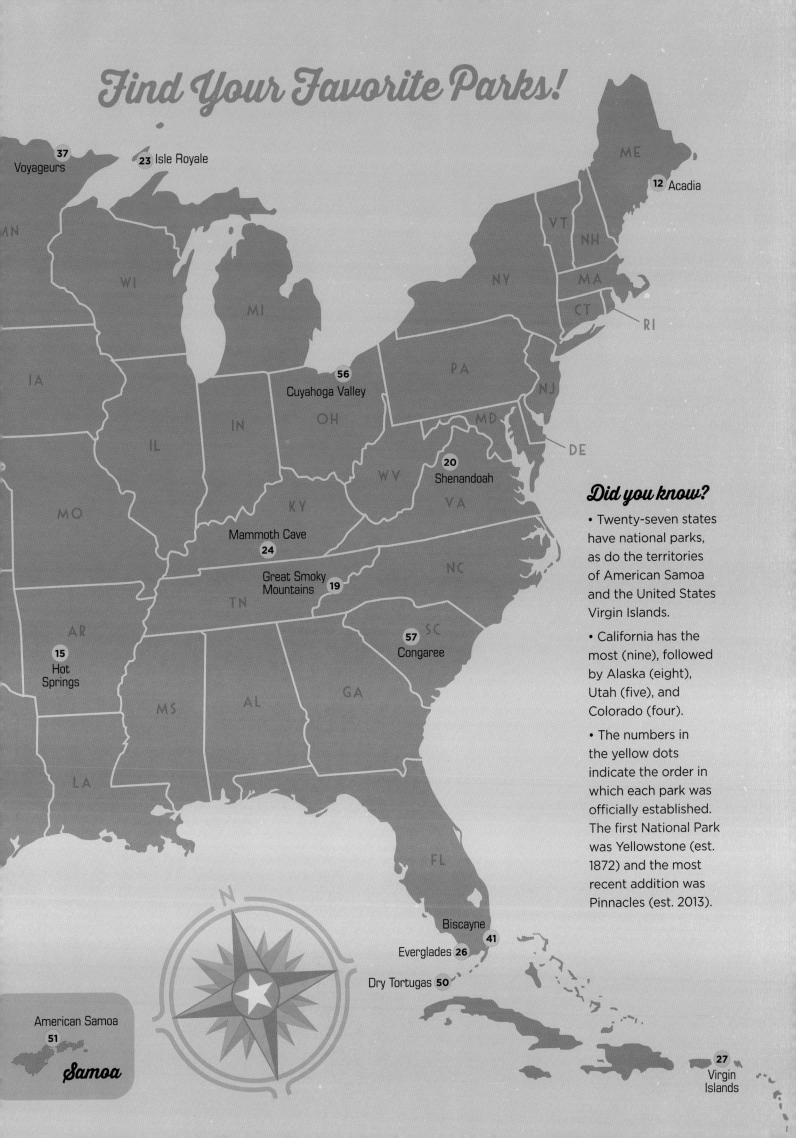

37 Voyageurs

23 Isle Royale

12 Acadia

56 Cuyahoga Valley

20 Shenandoah

24 Mammoth Cave

19 Great Smoky Mountains

15 Hot Springs

57 Congaree

41 Biscayne

26 Everglades

50 Dry Tortugas

51 American Samoa

Samoa

27 Virgin Islands

Did you know?

• Twenty-seven states have national parks, as do the territories of American Samoa and the United States Virgin Islands.

• California has the most (nine), followed by Alaska (eight), Utah (five), and Colorado (four).

• The numbers in the yellow dots indicate the order in which each park was officially established. The first National Park was Yellowstone (est. 1872) and the most recent addition was Pinnacles (est. 2013).

YELLOWSTONE
— NATIONAL PARK —

YELLOWSTONE

MASSIVE. Strange. Iconic. These are just a few of the many superlatives belonging to America's first national park. With over 2.2 million acres of real estate, Yellowstone is enormous. It is a Park bubbling (figuratively & literally) with life. Due to it's convenient location above an active supervolcano, the Yellowstone Caldera, the Park possesses over 10,000 geothermal features within its boundaries. Perhaps most famous of these are the geysers, with household names like **Old Faithful**. The Park also contains a vast array of otherworldly wonders: technicolor hotpots of emerald green and Tahoe blue, pasty gray cauldrons of boiling mud, bleached-white terraces of sulphuric springs, and a canyon made of golden rock.

John Colter, an explorer formerly associated with Lewis and Clark, came across the Yellowstone region in the first decade of the 1800s while trapping for the Missouri Fur Trading Company. Colter's tales of the steaming pools, evil smelling bowls of boiling mud, and gush-

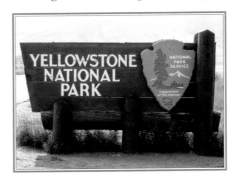

ing fountains were laughed off by many. Yet the myth of "Colter's Hell" spread, drawing Ferdinand Hayden, head of the Geological and Geographical Survey of the Territories, and his ambitious team

of scientists into the region in 1871.

Fully prepared for what he might find, Hayden made sure to bring along landscape painter Thomas Moran and photographer William Henry Jackson to document the team's discoveries. Through the eyes and hands of these artists, the world saw Yellowstone. Moran painted dreamscapes of color: water, rock, and light dancing together. Jackson's dramatic black and white photographs of bursting geyser fountains and hot springs revealed an untamable wilderness. Through the diligent practice of art and science, Hayden's team brought national attention to the region.

Hayden convinced Congress that the elevated, volcanic land would never be good for mining or agriculture. A pub-

Est. 1872

1ST National Park

WYOMING *Equality State*

BEST TIME OF YEAR: March to May or September to November – mild weather & fewer crowds.

DID YOU KNOW? Human history of the Yellowstone region goes back more than 11,000 years.

Look for **BISON**

<YELLOWSTONE 18" X 24" Limited Edition Print created in 2010 by Julian Baker & Joel Anderson

lic park, one protected from exploiters and profiteers, would be more suitable. Without government protection, however, Yellowstone would become a commercialized tourist attraction and its strange grandeur would be diminished. Congress was convinced and President Ulysses S. Grant would sign the first National Park into existence on March 1, 1872.

Exploring Yellowstone is a meditation on the odd, a journey that requires time but produces a type of awe that few other places on Earth can. In the early years, the Park was protected by the U.S. military, who built roads while staving off lawless poachers and prospectors. These access roads were eventually united into the single

Grand Loop Road, a 142-mile figure eight that connects guests to all of Yellowstone's most popular regions. From this sweeping roadway, visitors experience the natural panorama of Yellowstone. Steamy geyser basins such as **West Thumb**, **Midway**, and **Norris** line the south and middle regions, displaying a wide variety of color, form, and volatility. Boardwalks lead to the world-famous Old Faithful geyser on the **Upper Geyser Basin**. The **Grand Canyon of the Yellowstone** is another wonder, a heart-stopping display of power as the Yellowstone River dashes into the golden-walled gorge below. The eerie **Mammoth Hot Springs** lie on the north end of the park.

While geothermal abnormalities

abound in this unconventional ecosystem, plants and animals of all shapes and sizes do too. Outside of Alaska, Yellowstone has the densest concentration of non-human mammals in the United States. Over 67 different species of mammals populate the park, ranging from bison and grizzly bears to gray wolves, big horn sheep, moose, elk, lynx, and wolverines. The hot springs act as a beachside resort for the tiny thermophile ("heat-loving") organisms and lichens that flourish in and alongside the boiling-hot basins. The Park has also become a safe place to bring back the dead: the gray wolf, nearly eliminated from the lower 48 states, was reintroduced to Yellowstone National Park in 1995.

"I always think of Yellowstone as North America's Serengeti. No other place in the lower 48 has such an amazing variety of wildlife. The geysers, hotsprings and mudpots are the bonus visitors get when traveling through this amazing place. It truly deserves the distinction of being the world's first national park."
— Rick Smith, Retired Seasonal Ranger in Yellowstone from 1959-1969
(total years of NPS service: 31)

YELLOWSTONE FALLS 18" X 24" Limited Edition Print based on an oil painting by Kai Carpenter created in 2015 >

YELLOWSTONE
— NATIONAL PARK —

SEQUOIA

NATIONAL PARK

General Sherman THE WORLD'S BIGGEST TREE

SEQUOIA

Congress set aside Sequoia as a National Park in 1890, and Fry would go on to become one of Sequoia's most enthusiastic Park Rangers.

The old forest beckons: over 15,800 sequoia trees still loom in Sequoia and the neighboring Kings Canyon National Park. These Parks are home to the world's two largest trees. **General Sherman**, the emperor of the evergreens, can be approached in Sequoia National Park. **General Grant**, the second largest, reigns in the southwest corner of Kings Canyon. Along with its mighty forests, the High Sierra also features a wide array of lakes, caves, vistas, and meadows. Take in the mountain views from **Moro Rock** or rest your legs after a steep hike to the pristine **Eagle Lake**. Climbing Sequoia's lofty Mount Whitney is on many avid hikers' bucket lists. Wherever you choose to explore, Sequoia is a quiet reminder of our smallness and youth in the presence of Earth's elderly giants.

THE SOLEMN forest of Sequoia National Park rests on the western slope of the Sierra Nevada Mountains in California. As the second oldest National Park in the system, Sequoia set a precedent for America's "best idea," the preservation and enjoyment of our natural wonders. Roads are few here. This is a backpacker's paradise, an area of ancient beauty where some of the world's grandest trees live and grow. It is also home to the tallest mountain in the lower 48 states, **Mount Whitney**. The giant in American conservation, John Muir, once wandered these woods. Much of his zealous early writing was charged from the abuse he saw amongst these trees.

In 1876, Muir described the Sequoia tree groves as "God's First Temple." This wooded cathedral was Muir's refuge from the rapidly developing world of California. And, like a prophet disgusted with man's treatment of the holy temple, so Muir reacted to the careless and greedy actions of encroaching enterprisers. Sheepherders were burning down swaths of forest to create pasture, while loggers, understandably impressed by the immense size of the trees, took to chopping them down by the square mile. Two thousand year old trees were ripped from the ground to build rocking chairs and room for more sheep to graze. Muir would not let this temple be desecrated by ignorance. Logger-turned-conservationist Walter Fry would aide in Muir's dream, using his first-hand experience with the fragile trees to advocate their need for protection.

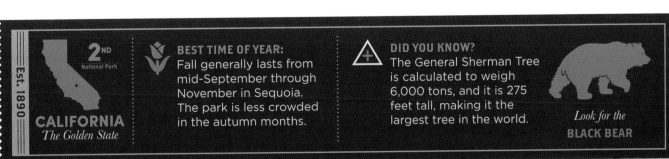

Est. 1890
CALIFORNIA
The Golden State

2ND
National Park

BEST TIME OF YEAR:
Fall generally lasts from mid-September through November in Sequoia. The park is less crowded in the autumn months.

DID YOU KNOW?
The General Sherman Tree is calculated to weigh 6,000 tons, and it is 275 feet tall, making it the largest tree in the world.

Look for the
BLACK BEAR

<SEQUOIA 18" X 24" Limited Edition Print created in 2012 by Julian Baker & Joel Anderson

National Parks Timeline ·
1900   1950   2000
1890

19

YOSEMITE
NATIONAL PARK

YOSEMITE

SO MUCH of John Muir's work was inspired by the mystic grandeur of Yosemite National Park. His psalms of creation welled up from the base of **Yosemite Falls** and echoed off the granite face of **El Capitan**. He attempted to describe the indescribable. Muir's passion for places like Yosemite left an indelible mark upon America, teaching us how to hold onto a beautiful space: not too tight and not too loose, to savor and to share. We are left with his legacy in writing and in the preservation of 1,190 square miles of picturesque Sierra high country. One of the country's oldest National Parks, Yosemite is now

a place of solace and inspiration for families and adventurers from all across the world. The National Park System's healthy tension between preservation and tourism began here. This tension is still felt today as the mile-wide, 7-mile long **Yosemite Valley** welcomes millions of visitors each year who begin their wilderness adventure from the valley floor.

Yosemite is a shapely diamond in the Sierra's mountain crown, and was first the sacred home to the Ahwahneechee Indians. A battalion of soldiers, seeking the Indians, stumbled across the untarnished majesty of Yosemite Valley

in the 1850s. Whispers of such beauty would draw men with varying ideas on how to use it. Former gold miner James Mason Hutchings saw that there was money to be made, and began heading up tours and nature trips into the valley in 1855. He soon built a ramshackle hotel to house his guests. Galen Clark was also enamored by Yosemite's glory, but instead sought to protect it from commercial abuse. His letters to Congress were eventually backed by California Senator John Conness, and President Lincoln would place Yosemite Valley and **Mariposa Grove** under state control in 1864.

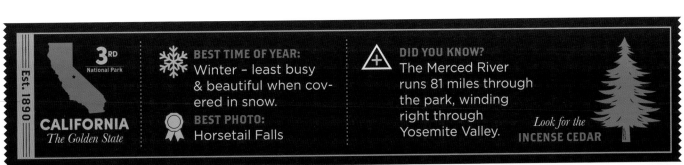

Est. 1890

CALIFORNIA
The Golden State

3RD National Park

BEST TIME OF YEAR:
Winter – least busy & beautiful when covered in snow.

BEST PHOTO:
Horsetail Falls

DID YOU KNOW?
The Merced River runs 81 miles through the park, winding right through Yosemite Valley.

Look for the
INCENSE CEDAR

<YOSEMITE 18" X 24" Limited Edition Print created in 2010 by Andy Gregg & Joel Anderson

Clark became the park's first caretaker while Hutching's squatting tourist business became illegal. Hutchings kept at it, however, and eventually hired a wandering shepherd named John Muir to run his sawmill. Muir found a home among the tall trees of Yosemite, building a cabin at the foot of Yosemite Falls. He too was fascinated by Yosemite's wonders, and would accompany Hutchings' few customers on hikes when not tramping through the wilderness alone. Soon Muir was an attraction himself, and park visitors followed Muir around to try and see the Sierras through his eyes.

Tourism grew by leaps and bounds as the years went on, and the ever-changing state government began to neglect the protection of Yosemite. Land was leased to farmers, loggers, and ranchers. Tourists built enormous bonfires and spilled them down the cliff face at **Glacier Point** to create "fire falls." Muir was outraged. He realized that the only way to save

Yosemite was through Washington: "Through all the wonderful, eventful centuries since Christ's time -- and long before that -- God has cared for these trees, saved them from drought, disease, avalanches, and a thousand straining, leveling tempests and floods; but He can-

---

"I have here seen the power and glory of a Supreme Being; the majesty of His handy-work is in that 'Testimony of the Rocks.'"
-Dr. Lafayette Bunnell, Yosemite: 1851

---

not save them from fools -- only Uncle Sam can do that." Muir got his wish in 1890 when Congress designated Yosemite as a National Park.

Muir would rejoice knowing the vast

backcountry of Yosemite still remains unspoiled today. Visitors can experience many of the same views and vistas that Muir once described with such reverence. Popular hiking routes spring from the busy Yosemite Valley, such as **Mist Trail** which leads visitors up to classic viewpoints at **Vernal** and **Nevada Falls** and eventually to the very peak of spectacular **Half Dome**. **Tunnel View** is a must-see for photographers. There are many ways to dive in and escape the huge summer crowds. Drive into the heart of the Sierras via **Tioga Road** to access the exquisite lakes and alpine meadows of the high country. From **Hetch Hetchy Backpackers Camp**, see the notorious dam that filled the one valley Muir loved most but could not save. And don't forget to visit the sleeping giants at Mariposa Grove, where the mighty sequoia continue to grow thanks to the efforts of John Muir, Galen Clark, and the National Park Service.

"I never tired of going to work and looking up at the walls of Yosemite Valley. Depending on the season or the time of day, no two views were the same. How fortunate we are as Americans that those who came before us had the wisdom and foresight to preserve and protect this wonderful place. We would be poorer as a nation had they not done so." — Rick Smith, Retired Park Ranger at Yosemite from 1971-1976 (total years of NPS service: 31)

YOSEMITE VALLEY 18" X 24" Limited Edition Print based on an oil painting by Kai Carpenter created in 2015 >

YOSEMITE
NATIONAL PARK

MOUNT RAINIER

NATIONAL PARK *Washington*

MOUNT RAINIER

Volcano and glacier, fire and ice: **Mount Rainier** is a poetic duality. The almighty colossus of the Cascade Range, Mount Rainier stands nearly three miles tall. Before the American expansion westward, Rainier was a sacred place to nearly a dozen Indian tribes who called the mountain Tahoma - "the great mountain where the waters begin." The snowy crown of the Great Mountain glowers over Washington's verdant valleys and lower mountain heads. Rivers of ice course down the steep slopes. The Park hosts 25 major glaciers, an icy cover-up for the layers of magma and ash that once poured out of the Rainier volcano, just 50 miles southeast of Seattle. The occasional earthquake reminds visitors that the primeval Rainier is still potent. Its last eruption was only 120 years ago after all. Despite the mountain's angry past, the mood most visitors encounter at Mount Rainier National Park is one of

> "Climb the mountains and get their good tidings. Nature's peace will flow into you as sunshine flows into trees. The winds will blow their own freshness into you, and the storms their energy, while cares will drop off like autumn leaves."
> *-John Muir*

ebullient bliss. Cheerful woodlands and meadows wreathed in foliage cause many to consider this region of the Cascades "the American Alps."

The Park contains a glorious blend of alpine lakes, evergreen forest, brilliant wildflowers, and heavy snowfall. Walk through this extensive montane dreamscape on a week-long backpacking trip along **Wonderland Trail.** This 93-mile trail circles the entirety of Mount Rainier and provides quiet communion with wilderness at the foot of such overwhelming grandeur. Park rangers built and completed this beloved pathway in 1915, utilizing it as an efficient (and scenic) route to traverse the thick Rainier backcountry and protect the land from poachers and vandals. Rangers built patrol cabins along the way, some of which are still used today. In 2015, Mount Rainier National Park celebrated the 100th anniversary of Wonderland Trail. It is a

Est. 1899

4TH National Park

WASHINGTON
The Evergreen State

BEST VIEW:
Ride the Mt. Rainier Gondola at Crystal Mountain – 2,500 vertical feet to the summit.

DID YOU KNOW?
Bear, elk, goats, and cougars elude the average visitor, but squirrels, marmots and birds are easier to spot.

Look for ELK

<MOUNT RAINIER 18" X 24" Limited Edition Print created in 2013 by Michael Korfhage & Joel Anderson

prized possession of the National Park System that has taught self-reliance and a deeper appreciation for nature for over a hundred years.

In the late 1800s, Mount Rainier's thick forest groves were caught in the center of a conservation war. Under the Forest Reserve Act, Presidents could set woodlands aside for national protection without hindrance from Congress. Rainier's forests came under U.S. protection in 1893. The question was: how should "protection" be defined? Chief forester Gifford Pinchot believed in the "conservation by use" philosophy, that through responsible cutting American forests could be preserved. Pinchot proposed to implement this theory on the lush forests of Rainier. The ever-present John Muir stood in his way. Muir refused to see this rejuvenating land used for anything other than enjoyment and quickly called for the establishment of a National

Park. Support came from a variety of parties with a variety of motives. The National Geographic Society wanted to study Rainier's volcanoes and glaciers. The Northern Pacific Railroad Company saw a National Park as an opportunity for more tourism and train ticket sales. Despite the Park's private bolsters, the federal government was hesitant to give

its blessing and overrule Pinchot. Congress had to be assured Rainier would never be suitable for farming or mining and that they wouldn't have to spend another dime to manage it. The bill finally passed in 1899 and Rainier became the Pacific Northwest's first National Park.

The Park itself circles the base of the mountain, providing magnificent views of the mountain centerpiece from many different angles. Plunge into the rainforests and hike along smooth-stone glacial streams at **Carbon River.** Walk beneath thousand year old trees at the **Grove of the Patriarchs** or enjoy a picnic beside the subalpine lakes in the **Sunrise region.** Abundant bouquets of wildflowers are enjoyed throughout the summer in the busy **Paradise area.** And for those that are willing, Mount Rainier invites you to climb straight up its 14,410 foot slope and look down upon this Alpine Elysium.

"Few national parks in the contiguous United States provide the diversity of resources that Mount Rainier offers. From walks through old growth 'rain forests' along crystal clear streams to high alpine glacier climbing — and everything in between. This park has it all for visitors." — Bill Wade, Retired Park Ranger at Mount Rainier from 1967-1970 (total years of NPS service: 30)

RAINIER: MOMENT IN THE MEADOW 18" X 24" Limited Edition Print based on an oil painting by Kai Carpenter created in 2015 >

MOUNT RAINIER
— NATIONAL PARK —

CRATER LAKE
National Park OREGON

America's Deepest Lake

CRATER LAKE

A POOL of blue perfection glitters before you at Crater Lake National Park. As with many of the National Parks, the now tranquil Crater Lake had a violent geological past. A stormy volcano named Mount Mazama erupted here about 7,700 years ago. The eruption was so devastating, the volcano imploded and left a five-mile wide, 1,943-foot deep crater (or caldera). The walls of the caldera were sealed watertight by Mazama's lava and left to cool high up in the Cascade Mountains. With the Park's average annual snowfall of 44 feet per year, it wasn't long before the spacious caldera was filled with the purest, cleanest mountain water. Now it is the deepest lake in the United States and enjoyed by about half a million people each year.

William Gladstone Steel was an early champion of preserving the lake. As a Kansas teenager in 1870, Steel read about Oregon's "sunken lake" from a newspaper he had wrapped his lunch in. The description captured his imagination and he vowed to visit someday. Fifteen years later, Steel got his chance. He was astounded: "Imagine a vast mountain six by seven miles through, at an elevation of eight thousand feet, with the top removed and the inside hollowed out, then filled with the clearest water in the world, to within two thousand feet to the top ... and you have a perfect representation of Crater Lake." Steel kept this "hollowed out mountain" in the forefront of his mind for the next seventeen years as he lobbied, campaigned, and promoted

Crater Lake as America's next National Park. In 1902, Crater Lake became a Park and Steel's newspaper dream had been saved for the pure enjoyment of future generations.

As expected, the lake is the centerpiece of this sublime Park. Trails wind up into the surrounding mountains, offering hikers rousing views into the crystalline waters below. Hike up **Mount Scott** to the highest point in the Park and take in the unblemished landscape of Crater Lake. Down by the shore, ferries carry the curious to **Wizard Island**. The **Rim Drive** is an incredible 33-mile round trip speckled with scenic overlooks and picnic areas around the lake. The road is open only in the summer and early fall before snow envelops the area once more.

Est. 1902

5TH
National Park

OREGON
The Beaver State

👍 **WINTER ACTIVITIES:**
In the winter, ranger-led snowshoe hikes are offered on weekends, usually beginning in late November and running through late April.

⚠ **DID YOU KNOW?**
Its depth of 1,943 feet (592 meters) makes it the deepest lake in the United States, and the ninth deepest lake worldwide.

Look for
PRONGHORN ANTELOPE

<CRATER LAKE 18" X 24" Limited Edition Print created in 2015 by David Anderson & Joel Anderson

WIND CAVE

NATIONAL PARK

EXPLORE ALL OVER AND UNDER **SOUTH DAKOTA**

WIND CAVE

ACCORDING to Lakota Sioux legend, the world's first bison stepped out the mouth of Wind Cave. Wind Cave National Park is still home to many of America's bison today, though you probably won't find any milling about underground. While the Park is named after its whistling subterranean chasm, the gorgeous Black Hills of South Dakota should not be missed. Though (or because) the Park is small, the concentration of wildlife is great. In fact, Wind Cave is one of the most photo-friendly places in the Park System. Bison, prairie dogs, elk, falcons, and the black-footed ferret all dwell on the plains and in the ponderosa pines of the Black Hills. And of course, there's the cave itself.

Thanks to its quirky ability to knock off hats, Wind Cave was rediscovered by a pair of brothers in 1881. The "cave wind" is created by uneven air pressure; when the cave's air becomes more pressurized than the atmosphere outside, great bursts

of wind will rush out the cave's only entrance. News of this cave spread and the South Dakota Mining Company laid claim to the area a few years later, hiring J.D. McDonald to live above ground and mine for gold below. No gold was found but the resourceful McDonald and his 16-year-old son Alvin began offering cave tours. Alvin kept finding new passageways and his dad saw that there was money to be made in tourism.

In 1891, the McDonalds partnered with a local businessman named John Stabler to start a cave improvement company, building staircases and walkable trails along the known passageways. They also built a hotel and facilitated a stagecoach taxi service that carried guests to and from the cave mouth. Tragedy and discord soon broke the partnership, however. Alvin McDonald died of typhoid at the age of 20, and Stabler began to make claims of the land previously leased to

the McDonalds. Stabler tried to drive J.D. out of the partnership altogether, and the feud caused such a ruckus that the U.S. Department of the Interior got involved. The government found that neither party had legitimate claims to the cave, and instead had the land established as a National Park in 1903.

Much like Mammoth Cave in the Southeast, Wind Cave is a relatively dry cave with few stalagmite or stalactite formations. The tunnels do contain a wide variety of strange minerals, including the rare boxwood, which looks like a freakish wasp's nest of calcite. You can go back in time and explore the cave by **candlelight tour**: Park Rangers lead a small group of visitors along the old trails of Alvin McDonald with only a candle bucket to guide you. If you'd prefer the sunlight, above-ground trails at **Boland Ridge** and **Lookout Point** will give you excellent views of the gentle Black Hills.

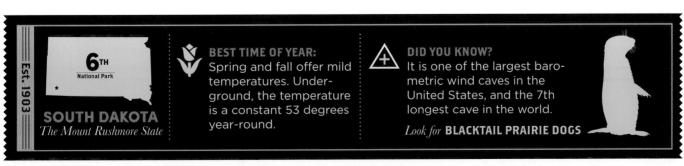

Est. 1903

6TH National Park

★

SOUTH DAKOTA
The Mount Rushmore State

BEST TIME OF YEAR:
Spring and fall offer mild temperatures. Underground, the temperature is a constant 53 degrees year-round.

DID YOU KNOW?
It is one of the largest barometric wind caves in the United States, and the 7th longest cave in the world.

Look for **BLACKTAIL PRAIRIE DOGS**

<WIND CAVE 18" X 24" Limited Edition Print created in 2015 by Michael Korfhage & Joel Anderson

SEE THE ANCIENT CLIFF PALACE

MESA VERDE
NATIONAL PARK · COLORADO

MESA VERDE

UNDER the infinite skies of southwestern Colorado, a Pueblo city called Mesa Verde ("Green Table") has slept in the canyon walls for almost a thousand years. The ghostly remains of this Puebloan metropolis help us understand where these ancient Indians worked, what they ate, how they worshipped, and where they slept. It also highlights the ingenuity of their 12th century architects, who designed homes of all shapes and sizes into the soft rock. As such, this Park was the first one established to protect a manmade prehistoric site. The priceless artifacts found at Mesa Verde National Park challenged us to value pre-American antiquity and to protect it from plundering.

Quaker cowboys were the first to excavate the Puebloan cliff dwellings. The Wetherhills, five brothers from Kansas, were a curious group of young men who stumbled across Mesa Verde while tending their cattle in 1889. It didn't take long for them to realize the rich significance of the place and their obligation to protect it. Al Wetherhill wrote: "To know you are the first to set foot in homes that had been deserted for centuries is a strange feeling. It is as though unseen eyes watched, wondering what aliens were invading their sanctuaries and why."

As novice archaeologists, Al and his brothers did their best to dust off ancient pottery and utensils, carefully labeling the artifacts and noting where they had found them. Their digs soon became a full-time job, lead by their ambitious eldest brother Richard. Unfortunately, word spread of their findings and their precious site became host to vandals and treasure hunters. The brothers reached out for help from the Smithsonian and the U.S. government to no avail. Meanwhile, an enthusiastic Swedish scientist named Gustaf Nordenskiöld taught the brothers how to properly dig and preserve the Pueblo artifacts (and took some back home with him in the process). Activist groups arose, lead by the Colorado Cliff Dwelling Association, to highlight the prehistoric city's need for protection. And in 1906, President Theodore Roosevelt would sign the bill, preserving Mesa Verde for future generations as a National Park.

Ranger-led tours of the Pueblo homes are offered throughout the summer. The regal **Cliff Palace** contains 150 individual rooms. This structure alone hosted about 100 people, and many of their living spaces and ceremonial rooms (called "kivas") are still intact today. There are 5,000 known archaeological sites in the park, and 600 of them are cliff dwellings. Tours into the **Balcony House** and **Long House** are also excellent ways of getting a feel for how the Ancestral Pueblo people lived out their daily lives.

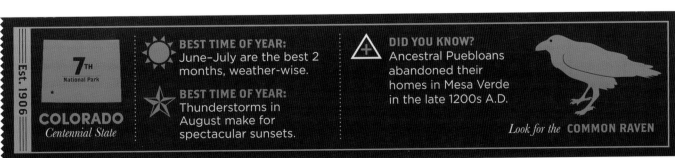

Est. 1906

7TH National Park

COLORADO *Centennial State*

BEST TIME OF YEAR: June–July are the best 2 months, weather-wise.

BEST TIME OF YEAR: Thunderstorms in August make for spectacular sunsets.

DID YOU KNOW? Ancestral Puebloans abandoned their homes in Mesa Verde in the late 1200s A.D.

Look for the **COMMON RAVEN**

<MESA VERDE 18" X 24" Limited Edition Print created in 2014 by Michael Korfhage & Joel Anderson

GLACIER

NATIONAL PARK

MONTANA

GLACIER

NOTHING compares with the icy peaks of Glacier National Park. You feel so tiny, an insignificant speck with a backpack before such giants. The mountain air is bracing and a sense of awe-struck wonder overwhelms you as you ride along the **Going-to-the-Sun Road**. This 50-mile engineering marvel carries drivers and red vintage tour buses deep into the Park, curling around stark vistas and tunneling into the very mountains themselves. Every bend in the road reveals something new, one wondrous detour after the next. Glacial lakes mirror jagged mountain teeth, grizzly bears and mountain goats wander the hillsides foraging for their next meal, and frantic waterfalls race hundreds of feet to the valley below. The beauty is celestial. Park advocate George Bird Grinnell put it best when he called

Glacier the "Crown of the Continent".

Glacier is enormous, occupying over 1,000,000 acres of northern Montana. It is adjacent to Alberta's Waterton National Park across the Canadian border. In 1932, the two Parks partnered together to become the world's first International Peace Park. The Parks are administered separately but share in the study and management of the area's unique wildlife population. Hikers can now traverse national lines on the **International Peace Park Hike**, lead by Rangers from both countries. Don't forget your passport!

Way before the land was set aside as a National Park, Blackfeet Indians lived here, at the foot of a lone peak they called Chief Mountain. This land was a sacred place for the Blackfeet; they would hunt for bison in the nearby valleys and climb the mountains to pray. It was a quiet and

solitary region for hundreds of years until an 1890s mining boom brought greedy prospectors into the area, seeking wealth from the Northern Rocky Mountains. The Blackfeet could do little to slow the invasive gold rush and were soon forced to sell 800,000 acres of their land for federal protection. George Bird Grinnell was Glacier's most passionate conservationist and a friend to the Blackfeet. Grinnell had climbed and named many of the area's glacier-formed mountains and creeks. He called for fair treatment of the Blackfeet Indians while also promoting the area as an ideal place to form a National Park. His fervor won out, and Grinnell's campaigns convinced Congress to add Glacier as a National Park in 1910.

With the area now under Washington's jurisdiction, the next question was how to draw people out to this

Photo by Joel Anderson

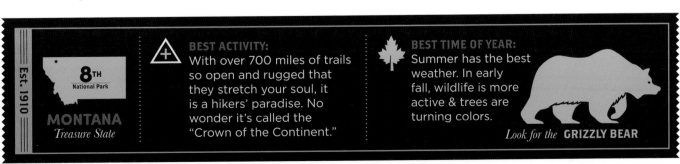

<GLACIER 18" X 24" Limited Edition Print created in 2012 by Michael Korfhage & Joel Anderson

National Parks Timeline ·
1900
1950
2000
▲
1910

35

remote Montana wilderness. Many of the wealthier American families around this time were taking summer trips to Europe. The Great Northern Railway, among other American railroad companies, saw the creation of National Parks as an excellent way to keep vacationing Americans in the States and on their luxurious railcars. They promoted the Park to Easterners with dramatic artwork of Glacier's vistas, and hired Blackfeet Indians to perform ritual dances and songs in theater halls all across the eastern U.S. The railway's motto was "See America First." The national promotion was a major success, and train-riding tourists arrived in droves.

The Park System's first director Stephen Mather recognized the value of American

tourism, not only from the obvious financial and patriotic standpoints, but also as someone trying to save the land. Busy parks meant more government funding,

which would help to keep private mining and logging companies away from the unmarred, now public wilderness.

Glacier National Park is a hiking epicenter, with over 700 miles of trails and hundreds of campsites scattered about the vast backcountry. **Logan Pass** and **Many Glacier** are both excellent locations to start a backpacking adventure in the central area of the Park. Twenty-five active glaciers still carve out the mountain passes of these highlands. Peering into **Hidden Lake** is worth the hike (the summer crowds thin out the higher you climb). And for an end of the day respite, the lovely **Lake McDonald** and **St. Mary Lake** lie alongside each Park entrance. These are great spots for relaxing after a long drive through Glacier.

"Glacier National Park is a hikers' paradise and as a young ranger I learned the trails and the strengths of the mountains and valleys of the east side of the Park. All my stress and the problems of the sub-district in the summers would fade away and the quiet peace of the Park would revive me every time I hit the trails. Once you have experienced the beauty and majesty of this place you will return again and again to recharge yourself and re-create the feelings you experienced."
— Bill Pierce, Former Ranger at Glacier from 1972-1975
    (total years of NPS service: 38)

∧ **GLACIER NATIONAL PARK: GOING TO THE SUN ROAD** 18" X 24" Limited Edition Print created in 2013 by Joel Anderson
GLACIER: A VIEW TO REMEMBER 18" X 24" Limited Edition Print based on an oil painting by Kai Carpenter, created in 2015 >

GLACIER
NATIONAL PARK

ROCKY
MOUNTAIN
NATIONAL PARK

ROCKY MOUNTAIN

ALPINE bliss awaits you at Rocky Mountain National Park. This incredible mountain chain in Colorado epitomizes the West: lofty snowcapped peaks, crystal lakes, fields of elk and moose, rugged trails inviting high adventure. The Rocky Mountain's clean air and fresh wilderness have been cherished by Americans for centuries. The Park is only a two-hour drive from Denver, making it a favorite of local weekenders all year round. And, as to be expected in Colorado, there are a wide variety of activities in this relatively small Park: rock climbing, horseback riding, backpacking, fishing, camping, cross-country skiing, and of course hiking. So many ways to experience a Rocky Mountain High!

The National Park System exists because of a handful of tireless Americans who put their passion for nature ahead of personal gain or glory. The common, everyday people that saved the Parks for millions of others are often themselves left forgotten or unheralded. Enter Enos Mills. Enos was a clean-cut outdoorsman and nature writer who, as a sickly boy, had been transplanted to the Rockies in the late 1800s. As he grew up, he gained his strength from the pure mountain air at **Longs Peak**, the tallest of more than sixty 12,000+ foot peaks in the area. An avid spokesman and believer in nature's healing power, he opened an inn and lead his guests on strenuous hikes to the heights of his beloved mountain range. The scourge of reckless logging as well as a chance encounter with John Muir motivated Enos to soon seek out public protection for his adopted home. He began a crusade to save the Rockies, pointing to the now-elderly Muir as his inspiration. When Muir died in 1914, his passion for conservation was remem-bered well; with the death of the "Father of the National Parks", Congress hastened to pass a bill establishing Rocky Mountain National Park, in memory of Muir.

Though the Park's size is one-eighth of Yellowstone, it receives just as many visitors each year. Utilizing a shuttle bus or early morning parking spot will get you away from the crowds and up into the tundra. Lakes are a major highlight of the Rockies, many of which reflect the dramatic mountain skylines. Strolls around **Bear Lake** up to **Dream Lake** are lovely, especially in the early fall. **Nymph** and **Emerald Lake** can also be accessed from the Bear Lake trailhead and make for a great family hike. Reaching **Chasm Lake** is more challenging but well worth the view. Don't forget to drive the spectacular **Trail Ridge Road** if you visit in the summer!

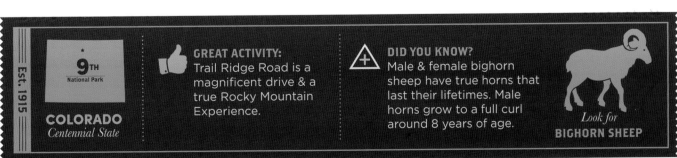

Est. 1915

9TH
National Park

COLORADO
Centennial State

GREAT ACTIVITY:
Trail Ridge Road is a magnificent drive & a true Rocky Mountain Experience.

DID YOU KNOW?
Male & female bighorn sheep have true horns that last their lifetimes. Male horns grow to a full curl around 8 years of age.

Look for
BIGHORN SHEEP

<ROCKY MOUNTAIN 18" X 24" Limited Edition Print created in 2013 by Michael Korfhage & Joel Anderson

LASSEN VOLCANIC
NATIONAL PARK

CALIFORNIA

LASSEN VOLCANIC

A VOLCANO quietly seethes at the dragon tail end of the Cascade mountain range in California. Birds sing while black bears roll in the grass beneath breezy conifers surrounding the gray pyramid peak. The alpine tranquility and lack of tourist crowds make this small Park a serene getaway. All seems calm now, but the silent mountain has a violent history. In 1915, Lassen exploded, firing off a series of eruptions that devastated the surrounding area. An awe-struck photographer named B.F. Loomis caught the explosion on film and documented the dangerous scene:

"The eruption came on gradually at first, getting larger and larger until finally it broke out in a high roar like thunder. The smoke cloud was hurled with tremendous velocity many miles high, and the rocks thrown from the crater were seen to fly way below the timberline before they were followed by a comet-like tail of smoke which enabled us to tell definitely the path of their flight."

This volcanic outburst cloaked the forest in ash. Fortunately, no one in Loomis's party was seriously hurt. Their survival story paired with Loomis's photographs did grab national attention though. While Lassen's Peak ominously rumbled for 5 more years, Congress converted the then-national monument into a full-fledged National Park in 1916. Though Lassen Volcanic was now a Park, the government did not see fit to fund it. One senator explained, "it should not cost anything to run a volcano."

The Park is lightly populated throughout the year with snows closing off many of the main trails in the wintertime. Similar to Yellowstone, Lassen Volcanic contains several strange geothermic features, bubbling up through the Park's thin crust. Follow the boardwalk through **Bumpass Hell** to see roiling mudpots and smelly hot springs, and the ghastly shore of **Cold Boiling Lake**. Take in the Park's dramatic vistas from the **Juniper Lake** region or lace up your hiking boots to climb the dormant **Lassen Peak** itself.

Est. 1916

10TH
National Park

CALIFORNIA
The Golden State

BEST TIME OF YEAR:
Snow lingers into May and starts again as early as October. Wildflower season peaks in early summer.

DID YOU KNOW?
Lassen Peak and Mount St. Helens were the only two volcanoes in the continental United States to erupt during the 20th century.

Look for the RED FOX

<LASSEN VOLCANIC 18" X 24" Limited Edition Print created in 2015 by Michael Korfhage & Joel Anderson

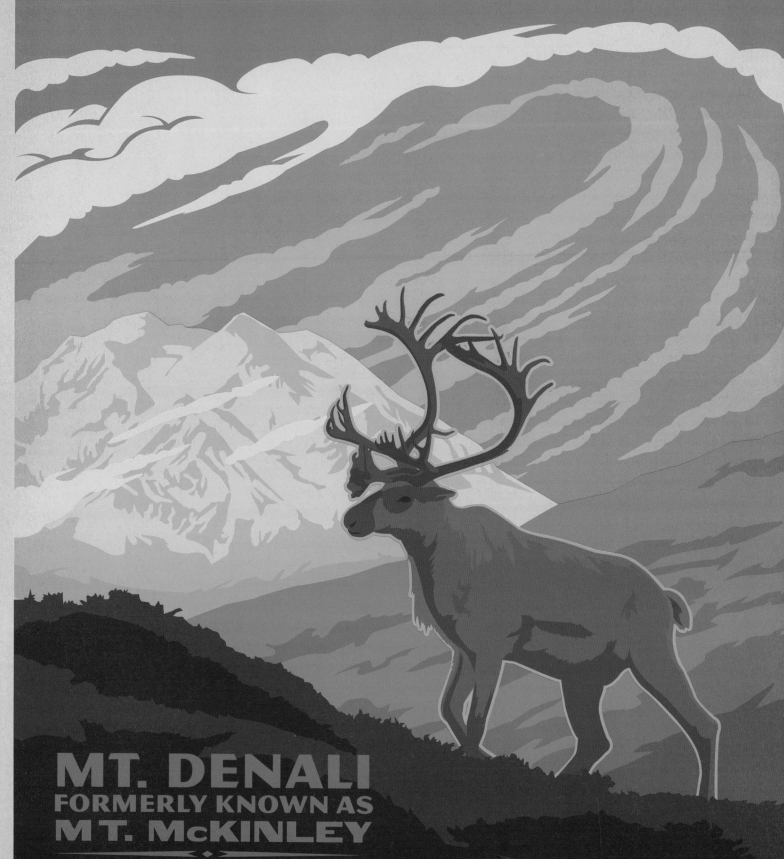

Denali NATIONAL PARK

MT. DENALI
FORMERLY KNOWN AS
MT. McKINLEY
THE TALLEST POINT
IN NORTH AMERICA

DENALI

SIX MILLION acres of sweeping Alaskan wilderness fill the borders of Denali National Park. The Park feels almost as wide as it does tall: Denali's central feature is the mighty **Mount Denali**, North America's tallest mountain. Reaching at well over 20,000 feet, Mount Denali is a colossus that beckons only the bravest to scale its icy slopes. Stories have been told, photographs faked, and flags planted by intrepid climbers atop "The High One," formerly known as Mount McKinley. Early mountaineers, along with an influential bohemian naturalist named Charles Sheldon, put this Alaskan wilderness on the map as America's Last Frontier. A 92-mile **Park Road** now winds through the foothills of Mount Denali, allowing guests to see the wild Dall goats Sheldon studied with such devotion as they clambered over the foot of the great mountain.

Denali, like Alaska, is a land of extremes, a brand of wildness that far exceeds man's ability to control it. A grizzly bear carries food back to her den at **Sable Pass**, while hungry wolves stalk a large herd of caribou on the **Plains of Murie.** Wildflowers carpet the valley, dancing golden beneath a cloud-cloaked Mount Denali. It was here,

in a cabin beside the **Toklat River,** that Charles Sheldon lived and observed the unadulterated wilderness around him for an entire year. Much of Alaska was still unknown territory to most Americans in 1915, but Sheldon knew this land was sacred, a place that represented the idea of freedom like nowhere else. Sheldon and his mountaineer guide Harry Karstens spent a long, sunless winter discussing the possibility of a Park here, of an organized American effort to guard Alaska's enormous wildlife population from prospectors and over-eager sportsmen. While the tundra was vast, more and more people were beginning to flock to Denali. A railroad from Anchorage to nearby Fairbanks was almost complete, and miners were already tramping into the area. Sheldon knew Congress would need to act fast, so he moved to Washington full-time to campaign for his beloved mountain and the wildlife that surrounded it. In 1917, Mount McKinley National Park was established. The Park would be expanded and renamed Denali in 1980.

Harry Karstens knew the power of Mount Denali first-hand. Karstens, along with two others, climbed the mountain's

South Peak in 1913, the first group to reach the ceiling of the continent. Karsten's ascent is imitated today, as climbers from all over the world still attempt to reach the lofty summit. Park visitors can also savor Denali's grandeur from a campsite at **Wonder Lake** or soar above the glacial mountains on an unforgettable **flightseeing tour.** Whether from the sky above or the valley below, Denali National Park is a rare glimpse of untamed America.

11TH
National Park

Est. 1917

ALASKA
The Last Frontier

BEST TIME OF YEAR:
The most popular time to visit is the summer, when the weather is warm, the wildlife is most active, and the flowers are in bloom.

DID YOU KNOW?
There are approximately 400 different types of flowering plants in Denali National Park.

Look for the **GRIZZLY BEAR**

<DENALI 18" X 24" Limited Edition Print created in 2010 by Andy Gregg & Joel Anderson

Visit Beautiful

ACADIA

NATIONAL PARK · MAINE

BASS HEAD HARBOR LIGHTHOUSE

ACADIA

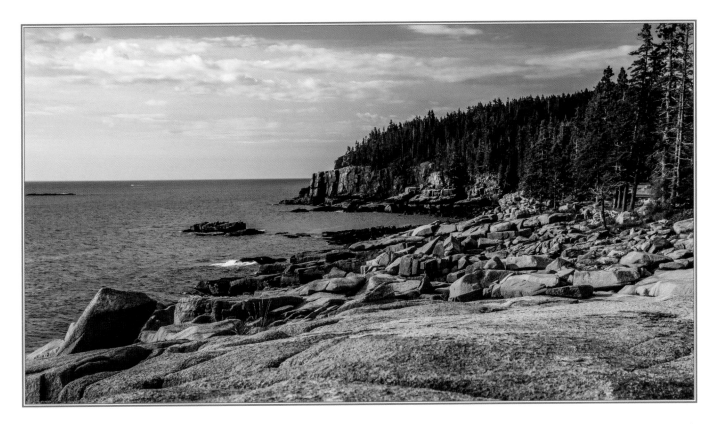

WITH ITS GRANITE clifftops and thick pine trees jutting right up to the craggy coastline, Acadia is a New England paradise. What once was a rich man's summer playground has become a quiet public refuge from the busy and crowded city life of the Northeast. A glacier-formed archipelago, Acadia National Park (located on Mount Desert Island) features one of the largest mountains on the East Coast and America's only known fjord in the Atlantic Ocean. Acadia is not just a place of natural phenomena, however. It is also a living story of an American ideal: selflessness for the benefit of future generations. What was long a fertile hunting and gathering place of the native Abenaki ("People of the Dawn"), Mount Desert Island was spotted and claimed by French sea captain Samuel de Champlain in 1604. Champlain, seeing the bald tops of the granite cliffs, chris-

> ## "The sea, once it casts its spell, holds one in its net of wonder forever"
> *-Jacques Yves Cousteau*

tened the place "l'Isle des Mont Déserts" or "the island of the bare mountains." The name stuck throughout the years, though Mount Desert Island (MDI) was nothing more than a remote hiking and fishing destination until painters Thomas Cole and Frederic Church began capturing Acadia's wild beauty in the mid-19th century. Their powerful images of the Atlantic coastland enticed many of New England's upper-class families, seeking a secluded vacation spot not too far from home. Many of these wealthy elite purchased large tracts of land to build their mansions (or "cottages" as they called them). And yet from these American aristocrats would arise the willingness to sacrifice their slices of paradise so that millions of future Americans could enjoy them. John D. Rockefeller Jr., son of the billionaire oil baron, spent his summers playing in the lush forests and

Est. 1919

12TH National Park

MAINE
Pine Tree State

BEST TIME OF YEAR:
Visitors & locals rave about May–the cooler weather for hiking, fantastic trout fishing & bird watching. 42–65°

DID YOU KNOW?
You can explore 45 miles of scenic carriage roads built in the '20s & '30s by bike –the finest examples of broken-stone roads designed for horse-drawn vehicles.

Look for
HARBOR SEALS

<ACADIA 18" X 24" Limited Edition Print created in 2013 by Michael Korfhage & Joel Anderson

National Parks Timeline ·   1900   1950   2000

1919

45

sea-soaked puddles of Mount Desert Island. As an adult, he recognized the need to protect Acadia's pristine wilderness. He spent over $3.5 million to expand the Park, donating some 11,000 acres while also building 57 miles of broken-stone carriage roads for public use. These roads give hikers, bikers, and horseback riders a uniquely Acadian experience without the interruption of motorized vehicles (still banned from the carriage roads to this day).

Another pivotal character to the creation of Acadia National Park was founding father George Dorr. Dorr grew up in a family of wealthy "cottagers" who spent their summers on MDI. As he grew older, Dorr realized that his beloved Acadia, currently divided up into the hands of private owners like himself, would be safer from exploitation if given over to the fledgling National Park Service. With the idea

of preserving this natural wonder for future generations, Dorr convinced scores of his wealthy neighbors to donate their vacation home property to create this patchwork Park. In 1919, Acadia National Park was officially recognized and George Dorr would spend

the next 25 years as the Park's Superintendent, earning a monthly wage of $1. During this time, Dorr blazed many of the hiking trails still enjoyed today. The tallest mountain in the Park was

named after Dorr, to honor his tireless efforts to conserve Maine's rugged and majestic coastline. When George Dorr passed away in 1944, his ashes were scattered from a seaplane over MDI, the island he had given his life to protect and preserve. Park visitors now have a divine New England shoreline to savor thanks to men like Rockefeller and Dorr.

Early birds should grab a blanket with some coffee and hike (or drive) up **Cadillac Mountain** to see the sun rise over the Atlantic. Take in the dramatic coastal vista from **Schoodic Point** via **Schoodic Head Trail**. Wander with your thoughts down the tranquil **carriage roads**. Face your fears and witness Maine's rugged coastline from an incomparable angle atop **Champlain Mountain** via **Precipice Trail**. Don't forget to check out the 19th century lighthouse (and the view that inspired our Acadia poster) from **Bass Harbor Head**.

"Acadia National Park is truly a national treasure steeped in beauty for all seasons. Fall colors grace the mountain landscape, winter snows cap Cadillac Mountain, tireless waves crash the craggy shoreline, and a maze of carriage paths and trails provide ample opportunities to experience this natural wonder. All this coupled with a touch of "down east hospitality" on Mt. Desert Island provide both a natural and cultural experience beyond compare."
— Roger Rudolph, Former Park Ranger at Acadia from 1979-1981
    (total years of NPS service: 34)

ACADIA: OTTER CLIFFS 18" X 24" Limited Edition Print based on an oil painting by Kai Carpenter created in 2015 >

ACADIA
NATIONAL PARK

GRAND CANYON

NATIONAL PARK

GRAND CANYON

over a mile deep. It is pure: visibility on a clear day averages between 90 and 110 miles. It is old: rock dating back to almost 2 billion years lies on the canyon floor.

Spread over 1,218,375 acres of protected land, the Grand Canyon is unspeakably glorious, transcending any human attempt to imagine or explain it. The canyon impresses without even having to try. Playful light and shadow splash their hues upon a mass canvas of stone. Like the sunsets, each view of the Grand Canyon is unique depending on the weather and time of day. Though there are a large variety of ways to encounter it, almost any angle will give you the same experience: a reverent sense of

STANDING ON THE EDGE

of the Grand Canyon, a zealous President Theodore Roosevelt beseeched Americans to recognize what a wonder we possessed within our borders. "In the Grand Canyon, Arizona has a natural wonder which is in kind absolutely unparalleled throughout the rest of the world. I want to ask you to keep this great wonder of nature as it now is. I hope you will not have a building of any kind, not a summer cottage, a hotel or anything else, to mar the wonderful grandeur, the sublimity, the great loneliness and beauty of the canyon. Leave it as it is. You cannot improve on it. The ages have been at work on it, and man can only mar it."

The beauty of the National Park System is that the Parks were specifically created as a "democratic inheritance" for all

Americans to enjoy. If you are an American, the Parks are yours. They belong to you. They belong to your children and your children's children. They are not meant for just a wealthy few, but for all to enjoy. You go to the Parks to see outside of yourself, to suddenly become small in the midst of such majesty. In no place does this sensation feel more apparent than at Grand Canyon National Park. Songs have been written, photographs taken, and conversations stalled in the attempt to describe it. The Grand Canyon is just as fitting for poetry as science. It is vast: 277 river miles long, up to 18 miles wide, and

smallness. And while it can never be fully understood, the Grand Canyon beckons to be explored. All you need to do is go. The **South Rim** is a popular destination for 90% of the Park's 5 million annual visitors. Though crowded in the summer, especially around **Bright Angel Lodge,**

<GRAND CANYON 18" X 24" Limited Edition Print created in 2010 by Andy Gregg & Joel Anderson

with a little hiking you can escape the crowds for a quiet overlook along the **Rim Trail.** Trails into the Canyon such as **Bright Angel** and **South Kaibab** are accessible from the South Rim as well. Reaching the **North Rim** requires a 220-mile journey by car, but visitors savor the North Rim's less congested, alpine-forested area. The North Rim is 1,000 feet higher than the South and provides the highest vista in the park from **Point Imperial** (8,803 feet above sea level).

Rafting on the **Colorado River** through the Grand Canyon, as described by Eric Henze in his book *RVing With Monsters,* is "truly a defining moment in anyone's life. It is an experience that moves beyond words, resets your definitions of awe and wonder, brings a restful peace to the soul and at times puts you in moments of unholy terror that -- on getting to the other side of -- help remind you just how awesome it is to be alive." Though it will require a reservation up to a year in advance (and nerves of steel), rafting the Colorado is yet another unforgettable way to experience one of America's greatest treasures.

"The Canyon is more than a National Park or a global icon. It is more than what can be revealed through a photograph or the turn of words. For some, it is just a deep hole in the landscape. For others, it is a spiritual connection with creation. For me, it is all of that and more. I was born in a small two room clinic on the South Rim because my father was just starting his career with the National Park Service and my mother, with clear intention, chose that place to have her first born. When I returned to Grand Canyon as Superintendent, my connection was very special because of this. It was a place of beginnings; a place that transcended origins and endings. I knew of the importance to care for it, to protect it and to preserve it, which is what my job required. But, I also knew it was my birthplace and represented the start of a three generation family history protecting national parks which made my job even more important to me. Both of my parents now lie in the Pioneers Cemetery on the South Rim having returned to the Canyon for their final journey. And, the power of the Canyon continues, always greater than the visitors who experience it and the people who have lived with it and cared for it over the years."

— Robert Arnberger, Superintendent of Grand Canyon 1994-2000 (total years of NPS service: 34)

GRAND CANYON VISTA 18" X 24" Limited Edition Print based on an oil painting by Kai Carpenter created in 2015 >

GRAND CANYON
— NATIONAL PARK —

SEE KOLOB ARCH AT

ZION
NATIONAL PARK

ZION

ease of access into the region. Though the Great Depression staggered the U.S. in 1929, it would soon create an incredible opportunity for unemployed Americans to cultivate Zion's matchless splendor. Teams of Civilian Conservation Corps

> "Wherever we go in the mountains, or indeed in any of God's wild fields, we find more than we seek."
> *-John Muir*

tunneled through solid rock to carve out roadways that confound imagination. The CCC built new campgrounds, managed flood control of the Virgin River, and even blazed one of the most hair-raising hiking trails in the National Park

CENTURIES before Mormon settlers discovered this lush oasis in southeastern Utah, Zion National Park was known to the natives as "Mukuntuweap" or "straight-up land." Unlike the Grand Canyon where visitors usually view the spectacular rock formations from above, the Navajo sandstone giants of Zion are mainly experienced from the "ground-up." These cliffs, sculpted by incessant wind and rain, surround your peripheral as the effervescent **Virgin River** flows between canyon walls and across the valley floor. You cannot help but feel a little unworthy in this sacred tabernacle of natural beauty. The mountains themselves seem to have been dramatically summoned from the dry landscape, called to protect an American slice of Eden.

Up until the 20th century, Zion was too remote a destination for tourism. Only through sheer determination did Native Americans and Mormons traverse and settle scant portions of this rugged landscape. With only old wagon trails for roads this natural sanctuary remained an enigma. In 1904, a traveling painter named Frederick S. Dellenbaugh permanently changed that. His dreamscape portrayals of cream and red-colored canyons caught the country's attention at the St. Louis World Fair. In only a few years time, President Taft would declare the region a national monument. President Wilson and the U.S. Congress would add more land and declare the protected area a National Park in 1919. With the same awe-filled determination of Zion's former residents, Zion National Park's new stewards paved roads and brought

Photo by Joel Anderson

Est. 1919

14TH
National Park

★

UTAH
The Beehive State

🌷 **BEST TIME OF YEAR:**
Late spring or early fall is the best time to explore Zion.

⚠ **DID YOU KNOW?**
The Virgin River carries millions of tons of sediment to the Colorado River each year.

Look for
ROCK SQUIRRELS

<ZION 18" X 24" Limited Edition Print created in 2013 by Michael Korfhage & Joel Anderson

National Parks Timeline · 53 →

1900   1950   2000

△
1919

Photos by Joel Anderson

System. Thanks to the tireless efforts of CCC work crews, roads such as **Zion Canyon Scenic Drive** and **Zion-Mount Carmel Highway** now bring delight and wonder to millions of visitors each year.

Exploring the southern area of Zion is simple thanks to the Park's convenient shuttle bus system that carries guests from the visitor center to various trailheads along Zion Canyon Scenic Drive. You can imagine the painter Dellenbaugh setting up his easel across many of the roadway's fantastic vistas. The busy shuttles drive through this single asphalt artery into the heart of Zion National Park. A network of hiking trails stem from this road and lead guests through a living liturgy of wilderness psalms. The Virgin River whispers joyfully beneath the Park's storybook peaks and even invites you to enter the river on trails

---

> **"Everybody needs beauty as well as bread, places to play in and pray in, where Nature may heal and cheer and give strength to body and soul alike."**
> *-John Muir*

---

such as **the Narrows**. With walking stick in hand, you can splash through the shallow river and enjoy the stunning smooth-rock bluffs that bless each and every turn. A divine section of the Virgin River murmurs beneath the mountains at **Big Bend**. Here the riverbanks are strewn with colored stones and visitors feel hemmed-in by the gigantic rock castles of **Heaps Canyon**. Look up and witness the spine-tingling climb to **Angel's Landing** from below. This trail was crafted by the CCC and includes switchbacks, thousand-foot drop offs, and a single chain handrail to lead you to the very roof of Zion National Park. Backpackers are rewarded with the astonishing glory of **Kolob Arch** in Zion's vast backcountry. Enter in and witness the splendor of this consecrated canvas on the Colorado Plateau.

"The scenic grandeur of Zion National Park has long brought a feeling of wonder and awe to those fortunate enough to have experienced it. The towering sandstone walls formed by the Virgin River were viewed as somewhat formidable by the early Southern Paiutes who named it Mukuntuweap or straight canyon. Issac Behunin, an early Mormon settler thought of the canyon as Little Zion, a place of reverence and peace. That name stuck and the park now carries the name of Zion. Today's visitors can experience those same feelings as the park preserves a sanctuary for them and for future generations, providing a place of life and hope."
— Donald A. Falvey, Former Superintendent of Zion from 1991-2000
   (total years of NPS service: 28)

ZION: VIEW FROM THE TOP 18" X 24" Limited Edition Print based on an oil painting by Kai Carpenter created in 2015 >

ZION
NATIONAL PARK

SEE BEAUTIFUL
HOT SPRINGS
National Park ★ Arkansas

HOT SPRINGS

A STEAMY reservoir of mineral water boils beneath the porous hills of central Arkansas. For centuries this basin has accumulated rainwater, slowly creating a deep underground well where water is boiled pure and spouted back out via geothermal energy. Forty-seven hot springs now flow out of Hot Springs Mountain, and humans have found ways to promote this "fountain of youth" for centuries. A National Park-protected resort city has sprung up around the mountain, and health and beauty-conscious individuals have flocked here ever since.

Both the Spanish and the French ventured into this region way before Arkansas became a state. Native Americans introduced the explorers to this "Valley of the Vapors," which America acquired through the Louisiana Purchase in 1803. President Thomas Jefferson sent scientists to explore this fabled hot springs region soon after. The men found the springs, and the dream of a hot springs health spa began. People started moving in to build log bathhouses,

claiming the healing powers of the boiling streams for themselves. This led the Arkansas Territory to ask President Andrew Jackson to set aside the Hot Springs region as a national reservation in 1832.

The mineral waters now belonged to the U.S. government, but that did not stop ambitious entrepreneurs from building hotels and bathhouses to tap into this moneymaking stream. By the late 1800s, Hot Springs was a bustling resort town containing opulent Victorian bathhouses, an elegant park for strolling, and underground pipes to keep the hot water flowing. The town's heyday ran well into the 1940s when as many as 24 bathhouses were open for business, giving more than a million baths in a single year! Celebrities, famous and infamous, poured into town to soak and sweat in the mineral baths all along Bathhouse Row. Al Capone was one notable repeat visitor. Director of the National Park Service Stephen Mather was also a regular

at the bathhouses and commissioned the construction of a free bathhouse for all of the town's guests. He also persuaded Congress to redesignate the town as a National Park in order to continually protect Hot Springs Mountain's precious resource.

With the advancement of medicine, the hot springs of Arkansas are no longer worshipped as miraculous, but they are certainly still enjoyed by those seeking relaxation. Walk the **Grand Promenade** up to one of the most sumptuous former bathhouses, **The Fordyce,** which now serves as a museum and the Park Visitor center. Guests needing a break from the baths may climb the mountain reservoir itself on a trail up **Hot Springs Mountain** where a tower offers panoramic views of the Ouachita Mountain range. Tranquility is the norm in the nation's smallest National Park. Whether you prefer a stroll through the woods or a soak in the tub (or both), you will find a relaxing escape at Hot Springs National Park.

Est. 1921

15TH
National Park

★

ARKANSAS
The Natural State

BEST TIME OF YEAR:
Year-round. And if it's cold outside, you can stay warm enjoying the 4,000-year-old thermal waters!

DID YOU KNOW?
It was a hangout for mobsters Al Capone, Frank Costello, Bugs Moran & Lucky Luciano.

Look for
SPOTTED SALAMANDER

<HOT SPRINGS 18" X 24" Limited Edition Print created in 2013 by Michael Korfhage & Joel Anderson

National Parks Timeline

1900

1950

2000

△
1921

57 →

BRYCE CANYON
NATIONAL PARK • UTAH

BRYCE CANYON

STEPPING out of a dry pinewood forest, you find yourself on a gusty alien planet. A congregation of castles bake red in the sun, their pointed turret heads all turned in your direction. You feel like an intruder, but you cannot help wandering further into their presence. A single, slippery pathway switchbacks down into the limestone unknown like a winding desert snake. Dust cakes your shoes as you try not to make too much noise, slipping and sliding down the crushed pottery-like road. You are being watched. You glance up at the spindly spire faces that adorn the castle escarpments. Their ruddy rock eyes stare blankly back at you. Cold. Mute. Like the frost that so faith-

fully eats away the residents' rock bodies beneath an endless ceiling of starlight each night. The solemn wind courses through their conical colonies. You step out of their shadow and into their world.

Bryce Canyon National Park is home to the hoodoo tribes. Piled like drips of wet beach sand, these towering stone fingers silently invite you to explore their fairyland, crafted by the impartial hands of water, wind, and time. The hoodoos speak wordlessly to one another, standing just wide enough apart for you to climb between their knobbed knees. Wander along the serpentine **Navajo Trail** for an intimate glimpse of this multi-lithic wonderworld. Each twist and turn in **Queen's**

Garden brings hikers into the presence of another gangling giant, painted rusty in the sun. Secret passageways burrow into the castle walls. Curious travelers, young and old, quickly find themselves tempted by these textured towers and run up to nestle in a soft stone embrace.

A farmer named Ebenezer Bryce first wandered into this soundless city in 1875. Pursuing wayward livestock through the area, he exclaimed that this was "one hell of a place to lose a cow." The Mormon Church had sent Bryce into this remote region of southwestern Utah and he took it upon himself to live peacefully amongst the silent natives. He built a cabin for his family just below the

Est. 1928

16TH
National Park
★

UTAH
The Beehive State

🌷 **BEST TIME OF YEAR:**
Late spring through early fall is ideal for hiking and seeing the wildflowers.

✚ **DID YOU KNOW?**
The famous hoodoo rock formations at Bryce Canyon are caused by constantly freezing and melting water.

Look for **PRONGHORN ANTELOPE**

<BRYCE CANYON 18" X 24" Limited Edition Print created in 2013 by Michael Korfhage & Joel Anderson

massive hoodoo amphitheater, a timeless gathering place for thousands of red and cream turrets. The farmer and his family would wake in view of this stoic congregation of stonework each day. Life among the rocks was hard and winters were harder for the Bryce family, but they persisted to till the soil and graze their livestock on the scrubby dirt mounds. Locals began calling the area "Bryce's Canyon." The Bryce family eventually moved on to a more forgiving landscape, and the secret gatherings of the area's inhabitants carried on undisturbed.

Decades later, murmurs of the mythic Bryce Canyon reached the ears of Stephen Mather and the National Park Service. Alongside his colleague and friend Horace Albright, Mather entered the vast stronghold of the hoodoo nation in 1918. They sat upon the sloping hillside at

Inspiration Point and pondered for hours the strangeness of this eccentric community. The spires themselves greeted the two men without a word, eying their vista with soulless apathy. "Marvelous; exquisite; nothing like it anywhere," Mather laughed with glee. The two friends agreed this unearthly landscape was worth savoring and made a point to share it with the outside world. In 1928, Congress established Bryce Canyon National Park, a protected playground for Americans of all ages. Work crews built roadways and blazed trails into the minaret metropolis during the Great Depression, and today the limestone kingdom of the hoodoos hosts millions of dumbfounded visitors each year.

"It was wonderful to work at Bryce Canyon, where my father started his NPS career and my parents 1934 honeymoon cabin is still used as employee housing. Even now when asked to describe Bryce Canyon and its unique hoodoos, I share the feelings of a 1920's visitor to Zion, Grand Canyon and Bryce Canyon National Parks. He wrote of his feelings of majesty and wonder looking upward in Zion and feeling that he was looking down into the red infernos of hell as he stood on the Grand's rim. He acknowledged however that the enchanting and delicate beauty of Bryce Canyon could not be described. Like him, I note: there are not words, you must go and see for yourself."
— Fred J. Fagergren, Superintendent of Bryce from 1991 – 2002 (total years of NPS service: 34)

BRYCE CANYON: HOODOO HEAVEN 18" X 24" Limited Edition Print based on an oil painting by Kai Carpenter created in 2015 >

BRYCE CANYON
— NATIONAL PARK —

GRAND TETON

NATIONAL PARK • WYOMING

GRAND TETON

JUST south of Yellowstone National Park, a lofty mountain range rises from the flat Wyoming plains. No foothills impede the view; the lonely granite-gray peaks of the Tetons dominate the skyline, mirrored by glacial lakes at their exposed base. Many rugged outdoor adventures have begun with these snow-capped peaks looming in the distance. An invigorating desire for discovery permeates the young and old, all those who are willing to climb up one of the Park's spectacular vistas or wash themselves with glorious scenery from the **Snake River**. Grand Teton National Park is a place both unique from and intertwined with its older sister Yellowstone. Large elk herds winter beneath the shadows of the Tetons, while a wide variety of waterfowl swim and nest in the glittery waters of **Jackson Lake**. A Park that was originally formed from struggle and well-intended deception is now one of the finest natural wonderlands in the West.

French fur trappers first christened the "Grand Tetons" in the 17th century, and spent much time in the area exploring and hunting for the area's prolific beavers. Winters were harsh but a few hardy frontier families and trappers, such as David Jackson, persisted to live in the valley beneath the mountains. The town became known as Jackson Hole.

An enthusiastic Yellowstone superintendent named Horace Albright united with billionaire John D. Rockefeller, Jr.

to set aside the Tetons as a National Park in the mid-1920s. Rockefeller's sincere devotion to the Park idea lead him to quietly purchase large parcels of private Jackson Hole land around the mountains. Disguised as a Utah land company, the scheme worked at first. But when locals discovered Rockefeller's deceit, they refused to give him another inch, outraged by his sly attempt to 'steal' their land for Washington's use. Though the Teton Mountains themselves would be designated a Park in 1929, Congress would not accept Rockefeller's land donation and the valley's resplendent meadows and wetlands would remain in limbo until 1943. That year, despite Wyoming's furious refusal to comply, President Roosevelt invoked the Antiquities Act, officially grafting Jackson Hole's pristine valley into Grand Teton National Park. Rockefeller's land would

be added to the Park in 1950. Anti-park sentiment was strong throughout the state for a few more years but would eventually fade as tourism increased. Now the majestic Tetons are enjoyed by 3 million people each year and the mountains take center stage at this much-loved National Park.

The Teton experience is just as incredible now as it was back in the fur-trapping days. Take in the unforgettable mountain views from **Inspiration Point** and peer into the enchanting **Jenny Lake,** where lazy ferries carry visitors across the lake's picturesque shoreline. For a more daring exploit, hike up one of the many Teton peaks. A gorgeous view from trails such as **Amphitheater Lake** and **Signal Mountain** is well worth your effort, and a float down the Snake River at sunset is a perfect way to end your day in the wild Wyoming countryside.

Est. 1929

★ **17**TH
National Park

WYOMING
Equality State

🌷 **BEST TIME OF YEAR:**
Early fall - the weather is comfortable, crowds are small, and elk are abundant. The males bugle to attract females.

⊕ **DID YOU KNOW?**
Be careful driving in the park. Moose, elk, bison, and mule deer often use roads as corridors, too!

Look for **BEAVERS NEAR LAKES & RIVERS**

<GRAND TETON 18" X 24" Limited Edition Print created in 2010 by Andy Gregg & Joel Anderson

National Parks Timeline · · · · · · · · · · · · · · · · · · 1900 · · · · · · · · · · · · · · · · · 1950 · · · · · · · · · · · · · · · · · 2000 · · · · · · · · · · ⟩→ **63** →

▲
1929

WALK THE HALL OF GIANTS AT

CARLSBAD CAVERNS
National Park

CARLSBAD CAVERNS

A SHRIEKING swarm of bats rushes out into the New Mexican twilight. Beneath the Chihuahuan Desert is a vast series of chambers, summer home to over 400,000 Mexican free-tailed bats as well as some of the most ethereal stone architecture you will ever encounter. Dripping from the limestone ceiling are ghoulish cave wraiths: sharp stalactite and stalagmite fingers reach out to touch one another, while swirling helictites and gypsum chandeliers look like they could reach down and wrap their wraith-white arms around you. Carlsbad Caverns Na-

tional Parks hosts a hive of cave systems beneath the Guadalupe Mountains. Sulfuric acid and mineral-bearing rainwater honeycombed these tunnels into the Earth, and the startling cave formations give testament to this wondrous work of persistence. The overarching theme of this Park was stated succinctly when the Department of the Interior sent photographer Robert Holley to investigate. Holley was brought to his knees by the "deep conflicting emotions of fear and awe" that emanated from the caves like summer bat clouds pouring out into the desert night.

Bats lured the first-known explorers into Carlsbad. Intrigued by their nightly feeding frenzies, a young Jim White climbed down into their subterranean home in the late 1890s. He took a liking to their dank and strange living quarters, delving deeper into Carlsbad's depths by candlelight. He familiarized himself with the bats' home, dubbing the eerie landmarks and chambers. He began to seek out customers for spelunking trips, with little success. Of the few brave souls that showed interest in Jim's caving adventure, one would be invaluable to the Park's future. Photographer Ray V. Davis would enter Carlsbad Caverns in 1915 and capture the ghastly underworld on film. The New York Times published his photographs in 1923, producing a surge in tourism to see this supernatural landscape. President Calvin Coolidge set the cave aside as a national monument in 1928, and Con-

gress would declare Carlsbad Caverns a National Park two years later.

Carlsbad Caverns may still host an enormous bat population, but that shouldn't keep you away from exploring their illustrious abode. The bats leave guests alone, sleeping during the day and feasting on tasty mosquitos and other flying pests by night. Self-guided and ranger-led trails are both available

> ## "The Grand Canyon with a roof on it."
> *-Will Rogers*

at Carlsbad. Peer into the **Bat Cave** and sneak past **Witch's Finger** on the **Natural Entrance Tour.** See the dramatic stone candelabras and limestone draperies of **Queen's Chamber** on the **King's Palace Tour.** Enter a world untouched by the sun in the mystic tunnels of Carlsbad Caverns National Park.

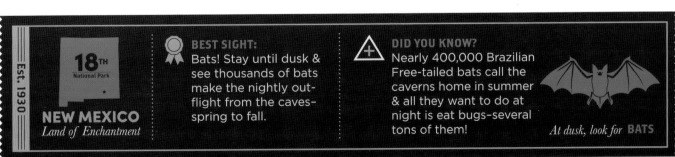

Est. 1930

18TH
National Park

NEW MEXICO
Land of Enchantment

BEST SIGHT:
Bats! Stay until dusk & see thousands of bats make the nightly outflight from the caves-spring to fall.

DID YOU KNOW?
Nearly 400,000 Brazilian Free-tailed bats call the caverns home in summer & all they want to do at night is eat bugs-several tons of them!

At dusk, look for **BATS**

<**CARLSBAD CAVERNS** 18" X 24" Limited Edition Print created in 2013 by Michael Korfhage & Joel Anderson

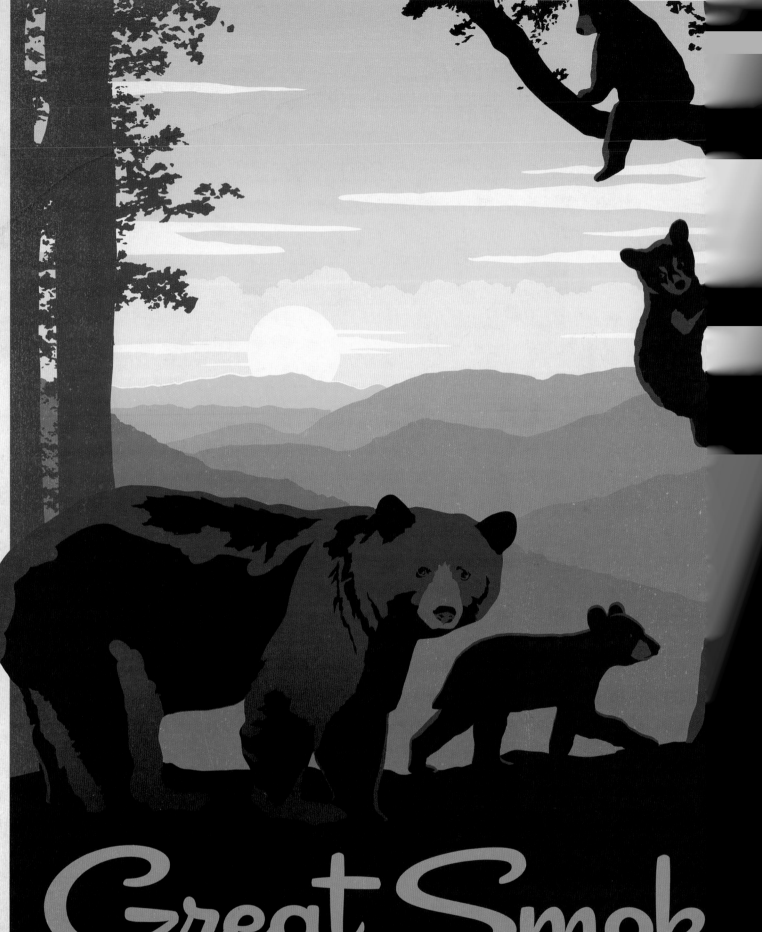

Great Smok
MOUNTAINS

AMERICA'S MOST VISITED **NATIONAL PA**

GREAT SMOKY MOUNTAINS

THE DUSKY blue hills of the Smokies roll off into the distance from the view atop **Clingman's Dome** at Great Smoky Mountain National Park. This scene is a glimpse into the old Appalachian country, a moment that could have been made a thousand years ago when the woods were young. Hemlock, oak, red spruce, fraser fir, and tulip poplar still populate the old forests today, housing one of the most diverse populations of plants, animals, and insects of any temperate climate in the U.S. The Park ranges in elevation some 6,000 feet and spreads across 800 square miles of Tennessee and North Carolina backcountry. The glory of the Appalachian Mountains is encompassed here: in a single hike

from bottom to top, you'll experience a range of ecosystems equivalent to hiking from Georgia to Maine. The trees make the Smokies, but they were not always treated with such reverence; the brink of deforestation awoke local Americans to reroute the seemingly inevitable. Now the Smokies are at the center of the National Park experience in the East. A third of the entire U.S. population lives within a day's drive of the Park. Add to that the Park's well-maintained road system connecting travelers to two mid-major southern cities and it's no wonder why over ten million people visit the Smokies each year.

What is now a prime tourist destination was once a hideaway for social outcasts and the estranged: isolated farming fam-

ilies, moonshiners, former Confederate soldiers, convicts, and Cherokee Indians that refused to march the Trail of Tears. It was in this Appalachian melting pot that Horace Kephart found refuge in 1904. Once a brilliant Ivy League scholar and entrepreneur, Kephart was now a broken man. Having lost his family, his business, and nearly his mind, he fled to the Smokies for renewal. In the mountains, he found solitude, rest, and time to write. His books about camping and life in Appalachia were a national success, providing Kephart a platform for advocating the protection of his adopted home. Meanwhile, large Eastern logging companies ate up the Smoky Mountains with locust-like ferocity. Stripping a patch

19TH
National Park

Est. 1934

TENNESSEE
The Volunteer State

BEST VIEWS:
The spectacular colors of autumn light up the Smokies for 7 weeks or more—from the highest elevations to the foothills.

DID YOU KNOW?
Fall colors are so amazing in the Smokies because of the diversity of trees—over 100 species of native trees.

Look for **WHITE-TAILED DEER**

<GREAT SMOKY MOUNTAINS 18" X 24" Limited Edition Print created in 2013 by Michael Korfhage & Joel Anderson

of old forest clean, they'd move on to the next area, hiring local townspeople at each stop. Kephart and his new friend, a Japanese immigrant turned Asheville photographer named George Masa, set out to survey the mountains and advocate their salvation. Masa's stunning photography alongside Kephart's essays moved millions, and the state governments of Tennessee and North Carolina soon joined their rally cry for a park. President Calvin Coolidge would designate the Smokies as a Park in 1926, with the sole condition that no government funding be necessary to create or maintain it. Large tracts of private land still needed to be purchased to keep the Park from dying at birth. Local communities, rich and poor, all joined together to raise the $10 million necessary to keep the dream alive. John D. Rockefeller Jr., son of the wealthiest man in America and a devoted lover of the Parks, would also contribute,

donating $5 million to the cause. Then, in the year of the stock market crash of 1929, President Franklin D. Roosevelt completed the task, purchasing the last $1.5 million worth of private land in order to firmly establish a national park in the Great Smoky Mountains. This would be the first time in history that the U.S. government would purchase private land for a National Park. The efforts of the great and the small, public and private, capitals and churches, made the Smokies what they are today. It seems only fitting that these old woodlands in the Appala-

chian hills are now so deeply cherished by tens of millions of American people.

Nature abounds in the Great Smoky Mountains. Over 1,500 species of wildflowers carpet the Park, and the vantage points from which to see them are almost as numerous. Hike along **Cades Cove Nature Trail** for chance encounters with the areas teeming wildlife. The Smokies are an opulent home for black bears, white tailed deer, wild turkey, squirrels, fox, salamanders, and (in the summer) fireflies. Waterfalls sing praises throughout the Park, especially at **Ramsay Cascades** and **Rainbow Falls.** Experience elevated elation from a hike up **Chimney Tops** or take in the timeless vista that so inspired Horace Kephart and George Masa from Clingman's Dome. Thanks to early advocates like Kephart and Masa, the Smokies remain a people's park: an accessible yet unspoiled sanctuary for American wilderness.

"The Smokies are a wilderness crown found between Tennessee and North Carolina. You really feel the majesty of the mountains and forests as you explore the top of the Appalachian range. You also sense the history of the area as you discover the valleys where people lived for ages. Cataloochee was one of those valleys where I always experienced a journey back through time when families lived in the valley for many generations with very little contact with the rest of the world."
— Bill Pierce, Former Ranger at Great Smoky Mtns from 1977 — 1981
   (total years of NPS service: 38)

GREAT SMOKY MOMENT 18" X 24" Limited Edition Print based on an oil painting by Kai Carpenter created in 2015 >

GREAT SMOKY MOUNTAINS
— NATIONAL PARK —

SHENANDOAH
—NATIONAL PARK—

STONY MAN CLIFF

SHENANDOAH

FAWNS grazing in the quiet hollows of Virginia's Shenandoah recall a simpler time, when communion with nature was a daily occurrence in our young country. This Park, tucked away in the tumbling Blue Ridge Mountains, is only 75 miles from Washington D.C. It has served as an old world refuge from the flummoxed eastern life for over a century. The main artery of the Park is **Skyline Drive**, a 105-mile ribbon of road that laces through a narrow sheet of protected forest, mountain, and meadow in the Blue Ridge highlands. Atop these mountain peaks are crowns of lichen-clad boulders, providing climbers a breathless view of the Virginian valleys below. Four seasons circulate the Park's scenery each year, drawing over a million annual visitors to watch the endless transformation. A sea of burning orange, yellow, and red foliage ignites the forest each fall, and delicate new life flowers from the snowmelt in spring. Time has the ability to move and stand still simultaneously here. Change and changeless, these are the unique traits of Shenandoah.

The Park itself has a rich American history, and it played an important role in one of our poorest decades. The region was at one time a patchwork of private land, over a thousand independent tracts owned by farmers, loggers, posh resort proprietors, even the President of the United States. With such close proximity to the capital, Shenandoah hosted a wide variety of political galas, weekend getaways, and private conferences for Washington's elite. However, when the stock market crashed in 1929 and the nation hurtled into the Great Depression, the Park also became a haven of renewal. President Hoover, along with hundreds of the area's residents, handed over their homes and their land to the state of Virginia. The state then placed Shenandoah National Park under federal protection in 1935. During the bleak 1930s, President Franklin D. Roosevelt commissioned ten CCC camps to facilitate and enhance the Park for all people to enjoy. They went to work blazing trails, building visitor centers and facilities, and fashioning walls and guardrails along Skyline Drive. FDR envisioned this Park as a place of "recreation and re-creation". Shenandoah rose from the ashes of the depression and became a natural refuge for so many weary Americans.

Although Shenandoah's most prominent feature is Skyline Drive, it is by no means the only highlight. The main road connects visitors to several of the Park trailheads, from which 200,000 acres of pristine woodlands and meadows can be accessed and explored. Opportunities to camp, hike, bird-watch, and ride horseback abound here, and the 511 miles of trails vary from a family-friendly nature walk at **Fox Hollow** to the heart-pounding ascent of craggy **Old Rag.** Visit the abandoned homesteads of Shenandoah's former residents on **Limberlost Trail.** You can dine like an aristocrat on a chic-rustic retreat to **Skyland Resort** or sleep like a black bear under the oak and hickory trees along the **Appalachian Trail** (which runs straight through Shenandoah). Whether high above the misty hills or deep within the valley, the sights and sounds of Shenandoah National Park will instill in you a sense of gratitude and love for this beautiful country.

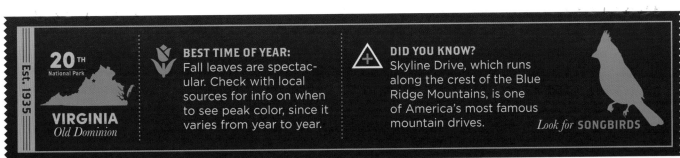

20TH National Park

Est. 1935

VIRGINIA *Old Dominion*

BEST TIME OF YEAR: Fall leaves are spectacular. Check with local sources for info on when to see peak color, since it varies from year to year.

DID YOU KNOW? Skyline Drive, which runs along the crest of the Blue Ridge Mountains, is one of America's most famous mountain drives.

Look for **SONGBIRDS**

<SHENANDOAH 18" X 24" Limited Edition Print created in 2013 by Michael Korfhage & Joel Anderson

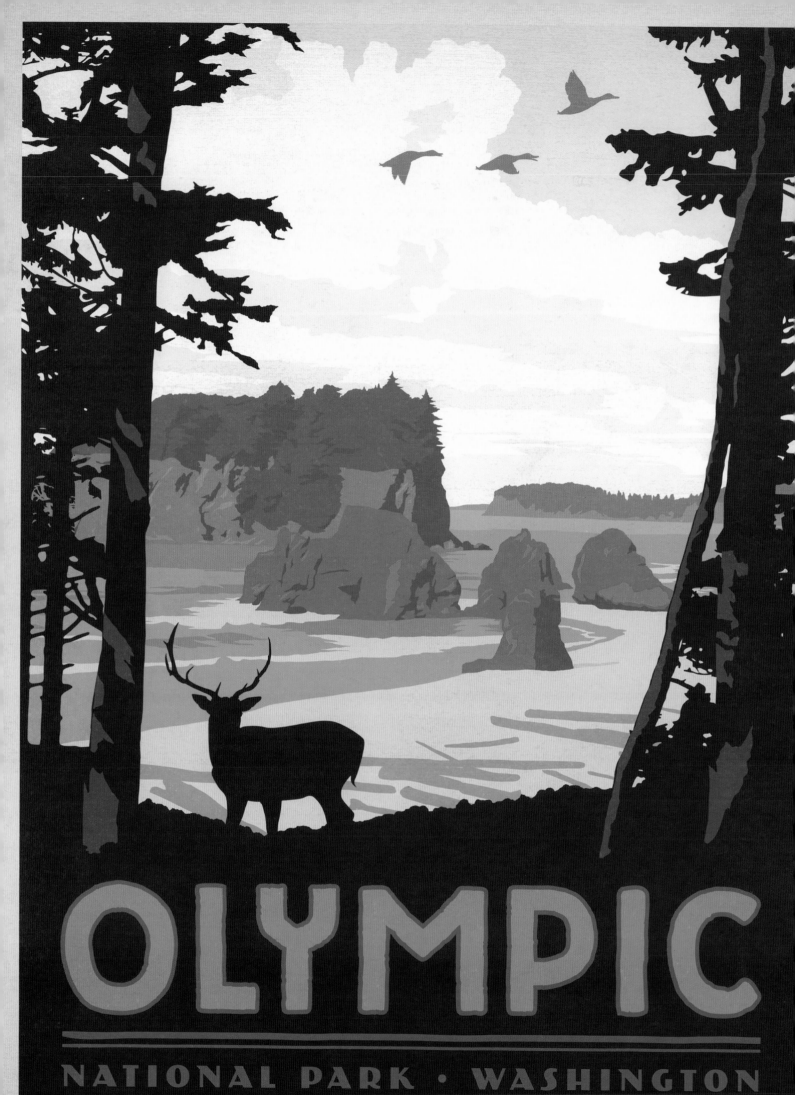

OLYMPIC

NATIONAL PARK · WASHINGTON

OLYMPIC

A **TEMPERATE** rainforest practically spills into the Pacific Ocean from the northern peninsula of Washington state. Blankets of moss drape the old forests, sumptuously clothed before the regal Mount Olympus. Drinking around 200 inches of precipitation each year, the trees at Olympic National Park are dripping with life. Thirteen rivers ring around the mountain, bubbling beneath untouched groves of western hemlock, red cedar, and giant sitka spruce. These woodlands house a large community of wildlife: black bears and Roosevelt elk, mountain goats and marmots, beavers and salamanders, osprey and bald eagles. Olympic also boasts 73 miles of pebbled Pacific coastline, dotted with intertidal ecosystems. Purple crab and sprawling starfish lounge in the shallows. Further out, gray whales breach in the springtime. This is a Park where ocean meets forest, and the whole Earth seems to rejoice at this union.

Olympic National Park swells with opportunities to explore, and people have gravitated towards the pristine mountains and beaches for millennia. Native Americans have occupied the Olympic peninsula for over 12,000 years. Five distinct tribes still dwell alongside the Park's rugged coast. Western explorers floated by these shores for centuries, slowing their ships to marvel at the mesmerizing peak of Mount Olympus. A lieutenant named Joseph P. O'Neil sought a closer encounter with Olympus, and led an expedition into Olympic's rainforests from the town of Port Angeles in 1885. His month-long, 17-mile journey brought him to **Hurricane Ridge**, an overlook that is now arguably the most scenic vista in the Park. Today, Park visitors may reach this gusty ridgeline by car, and the view continues to refresh and reward those who venture up.

Highway 101 now circles the Park, providing outlets to the Park's various regions around Mount Olympus. Olympic National Park is divided into two distinct regions: a coastline and a mountainous mainland. From the mainland, guests may hike up the foothills of Olympus, staring up into its snow-capped peaks from trails such as **Hurricane Hill**. Wander through the lush **Hall of Mosses** at **Hoh Rain Forest** to learn about this region's distinct (and rainy) ecology. Backpack beneath enormous cedar and spruce trees in the southwestern **Quinault region**, or soak it up in the natural hot springs of **Sol Duc**. Out on the Pacific coast, another 'forest' awaits. Bleached driftwood splays out along the shore at **Rialto Beach** like old whale-bones. Strange fins of stone congregate in Rialto's shallows while beachcombers meander through the **Hole in the Wall**, a natural tunnel carved into the shore's sloping hillside. From the beach shallows up to the top of Mount Olympus, this Park is an immersive introduction to the Pacific Northwest. Dive in and soak up this lush wonderland of water, tree, and stone.

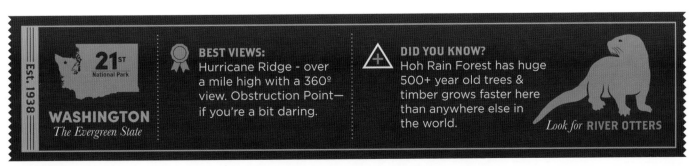

Est. 1938

21ST National Park

WASHINGTON
The Evergreen State

BEST VIEWS:
Hurricane Ridge - over a mile high with a 360° view. Obstruction Point— if you're a bit daring.

DID YOU KNOW?
Hoh Rain Forest has huge 500+ year old trees & timber grows faster here than anywhere else in the world.

Look for RIVER OTTERS

<OLYMPIC 18" X 24" Limited Edition Print created in 2013 by Michael Korfhage & Joel Anderson

ZUMWALT VALLEY

KINGS CANYON
NATIONAL PARK

KINGS CANYON

THE VENERABLE redwood trees of Kings Canyon populate the thick forests just north of Sequoia National Park. A diminutive scrap of this region was initially set aside as General Grant National Park in 1890. This small thumb of a Park included the **General Grant sequoia**, the second largest tree in the world, and the illustrious grove of trees harboring this giant. Kings Canyon National Park would spring from this patch of revered woodlands and grow into a distinguished destination for a Californian backcountry adventure.

The vision for an "extended" Sequoia began as early as the 1880s, but would not come into fruition until 1940. On a jaunt through the Sierras, Secretary of the Interior Harold Ickes was shaken by the timelessness of Kings Canyon. The elderly trees, laughing rivers, yawning caves, and solemn canyons inspired him beyond words. This unadulterated freshness felt different than other Parks. By this time, roadways laced several of America's National Parks. Everyday families could drive up and through these natural wonders within a few hours. Ickes desired to establish a Park that would be left undeveloped, impenetrable to the meandering automobile. He wanted a place that would require its guests to get out of their cars and onto the trails: a landscape of stillness, of nature's song uninhibited by the noise of mankind. Ickes saw this exquisite possibility up here in the Sierra Nevada, and endorsed Kings Canyon as a National Park, to be left as it was found. Only a single road was built to bring visitors into the woods. The rest would need to be explored on foot.

The undeveloped nature of Kings Canyon remains to this day. Sequoia trees still grow wild on the slopes of the Sierras. **Grants Grove** stands taller than ever, quietly stretching heavenward in the southwest corner of the Park. **The Pacific Crest Trail** runs straight through the canyon, guiding backpackers along weatherworn mountain passes and glacial streams. Lakes dot the Park like alpine puddles after a winter's thaw. Leave your car at Road's End and begin a refreshing journey into the High Sierra along **Rae Lakes Loop**, where concealed natural beauty waits to be uncovered. Kings Canyon seems to exist outside of time, as it was intended. Enter in and get lost for a while.

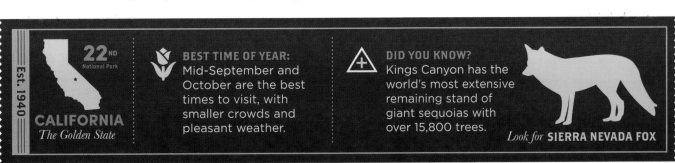

Est. 1940

22ND National Park

CALIFORNIA
The Golden State

BEST TIME OF YEAR: Mid-September and October are the best times to visit, with smaller crowds and pleasant weather.

DID YOU KNOW? Kings Canyon has the world's most extensive remaining stand of giant sequoias with over 15,800 trees.

Look for **SIERRA NEVADA FOX**

<**KINGS CANYON** 18" X 24" Limited Edition Print created in 2015 by Michael Korfhage & Joel Anderson

ISLE ROYALE

NATIONAL PARK • MICHIGAN

ISLE ROYALE

ABOARD a ferry ship, you find yourself on a vast inland sea blanketed in thick fog. You cannot see more than a dozen feet ahead in any direction. The chill of mist and the unknown tingles your spine as the seconds, minutes, hours pass ... and then, there in the ghost cloud, a lighthouse looms. The yellow-white light is faint but familiar, guiding the ferry on a hidden pathway towards harbor. More than 25 ships lost sight of the light, running aground or sinking in the treacherous Northern waters of Lake Superior. As the lighthouse takes form, you are aware of a lushly wooded shoreline. All is still. You have entered Isle Royale National Park.

Isle Royale is the most remote National Park in the lower 48 states, floating just below the Canadian border in the northwest corner of Lake Superior. The island is a 45-mile long, 9-mile wide stronghold of wildlands, a remote hermitage for moose, gray wolf, red fox, and loon. The lake's notoriously rough waters secure the island's seclusion from the casual passerby, but hardy backpackers and kayakers now have access to this guarded gem by way of ferry or seaplane. While the average visit to most National Parks is 4 hours, guests visiting Isle Royale commit to the long haul. An average visit to Isle Royale lasts 3.5 days, including the 4 to 6-hour ferry ride to and from Michigan's mainland. No automobiles ever reach the island; to visit Isle Royale is to give yourself over to the northern wilderness, where hikers share the trails with the island's untamed residents.

The primal nature of the isle has remained constant thanks to Detroit reporter Albert Stoll, who, in the 1920s, campaigned for the island's admission as a National Park. Lusty mining and lumber companies eyed the island as a prime source for copper and hardwood. For over a decade, Stoll fought off their pandering attempts from his post at Detroit News, writing fiery articles that campaigned for Isle Royale's federal recognition. Finally, as Americans crawled out of a financial crisis in 1940, President Franklin D. Roosevelt used money generated by the New Deal to purchase the island, sustaining the mysterious archipelago for the next generation of explorers.

A trek to Isle Royale requires preparation, flexibility, and commitment. The Park is not easy to access or leave. Ferries from Minnesota and Michigan tow Park guests over the precarious Lake Superior, with trips usually lasting around 2-6 hours one-way. On the island, hiking is your only means of transportation. Trails such as **Greenstone Ridge, Stoll Memorial,** and **Rock Harbor** wind through the conifer forests and along Isle Royale's scenic ridgelines. Over 36 campgrounds dot the backcountry, providing multiple opportunities to take in the Park's unmarred solitude overnight. Kayaking is also very popular along the shoreline. Explore tiny islets off the main coast at **Five Finger Bay** or a north shore estuary at **McCargoe Cove.** For those with warm blood and a taste for nautical history, dive into the depths of frigid Lake Superior on a SCUBA tour into a watery shipwreck graveyard. The lonesome wilderness of Isle Royale awaits.

Est. 1940

23RD
National Park

MICHIGAN
The Great Lakes State

WILDERNESS HIKE:
Greenstone Ridge Trail is a 4-day, 3-night 40-mile hike that traces the spine of this wild and remote Lake Superior island.

DID YOU KNOW?
The waters surrounding the island contain 10 major shipwrecks and several lesser ones.

Look for the elusive GRAY WOLF

<ISLE ROYALE 18" X 24" Limited Edition Print created in 2015 by Michael Korfhage & Joel Anderson

National Parks Timeline · ▶ 77 →

1900   1950   2000
▲
1940

WORLD'S LONGEST CAVE SYSTEM

MAMMOTH CAVE

NATIONAL PARK • *Kentucky*

MAMMOTH CAVE

DRIVING up I-65, you would never know the longest cave system on Earth lies just below the rolling Kentucky hills. Mammoth Cave is gargantuan. Carved into porous limestone, the cave is over 400 miles long. And scientists believe there's still plenty more to discover. Despite its immensity, Mammoth Cave somehow maintains a humble disposition, instilling in its spelunking guests a simple giddiness for exploration. It is not garish (no "mood" lighting or music). The lighting installed along the underground trails reveal only what it is: a wondrous labyrinth of stone. It is also a place that epitomizes the American struggle for freedom.

Mammoth Cave played a pivotal role in protecting America's existence in the War of 1812. Mammoth contained large deposits of saltpeter, which could be mined out and easily converted into gunpowder. In fact, Park Rangers will tell you that a majority of the American ammunition used in the war came straight from this cave. Sadly, the miners of Mammoth Cave's minerals were slaves, people who would be unaffected by an American victory over England. Slaves worked in the damp darkness of the cave 10 to 12 hours a day, mining for a precious resource that would keep them in their squalor. All Americans today owe our enslaved forefathers a great debt, for through them the wonders of Mammoth Cave would be opened and our nation's freedom to enjoy it protected.

You cannot visit Mammoth Cave without hearing the name Stephen Bishop. Stephen was a Kentucky slave in the 1830s and one of the cave's first and greatest tour guides. He was bright, witty, and brave; working with a Louisville cartographer, he mapped out roughly 10 miles of the cave he had explored from memory. Park visitors can still purchase a copy of his extraordinary "memory map" in Mammoth's Visitor Center. When the nephew of the cave's wealthy owner foolishly left Stephen's tour group looking for a lost hat, Stephen went back for him. The young man was lost in the dark for 38 miserable hours before Stephen found him. With his trademark enthusiasm, Stephen named many of Mammoth's key landmarks and passages. You can still see his signature written in ash on walls throughout the underground Park.

Mammoth is not your typical cave. You won't find many stalagmites dripping from the ceiling or glittery quartz in the walls. The beauty lies in its simplicity. It is a tunnel of stone: vast, cool, and deep. Inviting wisps of mist rise from the cave's mouth throughout the hot Southern summer. About 15 miles of the cave is open to the public. Park Rangers, brimming with anecdotes and geology lessons, lead tour groups along the trails. Tours include a family-friendly saunter to **Frozen Niagara** and the fascinating **Historic Tour**. Mammoth Cave even has something for guests with an adrenaline itch: the pitch-black, belly-crawling, why-did-I-sign-up-for-this **Wild Cave Adventure.**

Est. 1941

24TH
National Park

KENTUCKY
The Bluegrass State

BEST TIME OF YEAR:
The cave is a constant 60 degrees all year, so come when it's too hot or too cold to enjoy the outdoors!

DID YOU KNOW?
Most of the shrimp and fish that live in caves do not have eyes, since they spend their entire lives in darkness.

Look for **EYELESS CAVE FISH**

<MAMMOTH CAVE 18" X 24" Limited Edition Print created in 2015 by Michael Korfhage & Joel Anderson

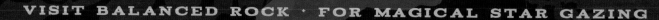

BIG ● BEND

NATIONAL PARK ★ TEXAS

VISIT BALANCED ROCK · FOR MAGICAL STAR GAZING

BIG BEND

DEEP in the sunbaked desert of southwestern Texas lies a limestone canyon carved out by the **Rio Grande**. The river serves as the boundary between the United States and Mexico, and the isolated wilderness surrounding its banks reinforces the idea of a no-man's land. Big Bend, named after the horseshoe curve of the river around the Park, is lightly visited throughout the year because of its remote location. But this is no mere desert: Big Bend National Park is home to over 5,000 species of plants, trees, and animals, including some 450 types of migratory birds. The highlands of the **Chisos Mountains** combined with the floodplains of the Rio Grande make for a diverse and highly enjoyable landscape when visiting in the cooler seasons of fall or spring. Climb up into these secluded Texas canyonlands to see how life blossoms in the desert.

For centuries, Big Bend's territory belonged to the Native Americans as an oasis in the Chihuahuan Desert. The Indians survived by farming and hunting the river valley's abundant wildlife. As the years went by, the Rio Grande would eventually soak the shoes of many different types of people, wading across with various ambitions. The conquest-driven Spanish crossed the river from Mexico in the late 16th century, searching for gold and new lands. Comanche Indians later blazed a trail through the Park at **Persimmon Gap** and across the river, traversing back and forth while raiding Mexican villages. Mexican and American settlers established homesteads and ranched on both sides of the Rio Grande. Dangerous outlaws, bandits, and Mexican revolutionaries fled through Big Bend's canyons to avoid arrest. The region was a place of epiphany for rancher Everett Ewing

Townsend in the early 1900s. The Texas mountains roused Townsend to political action, and he would spend the next two decades lobbying for a Park at Big Bend. Roosevelt's New Deal sent a CCC team to the Rio Grande in the 1930s. The workers faced a daunting task, to bring infrastructure and access to a desolate area with no electricity and blazing summer heat. Despite the challenge, the men got it done and Townsend's dream was realized in 1944.

Thanks to Townsend and the CCC, much of Big Bend's arid beauty is now accessible by hiking and roadways. Detour for the magnificent vistas of **Santa Elena Canyon** and **Mule Ears** along **Ross Maxwell Scenic Drive.** Lace up your hiking boots and climb the Chisos Mountains via **Lost Mine Trail.** Find the famous "balancing rocks" in the **Grapevine Hills' backcountry.** There's no better way to finish off your long day of desert hiking than a soak at the **Hot Springs natural spa** beneath an infinite tapestry of Texas starlight.

25TH National Park

TEXAS
The Lone Star State

Est. 1944

BEST TIME OF YEAR: Winter - dry & mild, daytime 65°+

BEST HIKE: Lost Mine Trail

DID YOU KNOW? The park has more types of birds, bats & cacti than any other in the U.S. It's also one of the most remote parks in the lower states.

Look for the **MOUNTAIN LION**

<**BIG BEND** 18" X 24" Limited Edition Print created in 2014 by Michael Korfhage & Joel Anderson

National Parks Timeline · **81**

1900   1950   2000

△
1944

Everglades
NATIONAL PARK

FLORIDA

EVERGLADES

A TRANSITIONAL landscape blurring the lines between water and earth, the Everglade wetlands soak up over 1.5 million acres of southwestern Florida. Park visitors can experience one of the most unique ecosystems in the country from a canoe, gliding along the shallow waters of the **Wilderness Waterway** where alligators and manatees, ibises and egrets, cypresses and mangroves all thrive in the balmy coastal marsh. Over 350 species of birds live within the watery confines of the Park, making for a grand bird-watching getaway. Despite developers' never-ending attempts to stem its slow tide, the mighty Everglades persistently roll on towards the sea. Life, though threatened, continues to flourish in the swamplands.

The Everglades' past is a troubling one. In the early 1900s, innumerous Floridian birds were killed and plucked to decorate women's hats. Local politicians and big businessmen also saw the region as a site to be drained and developed. Dikes, dams, and levees were built outside the confines of the Park, diverting essential freshwater flow from Lake Okeechobee and the Kissimmee River. Everglades National Park, differing from its western counterparts, is an area set aside primarily for the protection of a threatened ecosystem rather than breathtaking scenery. In a part of the country that's so thickly populated and developed, the Everglades continue to hang on for survival. Sadly, more than 50% of the original Everglades region has already been destroyed and reclaimed for human use. The Park today protects a portion of what remains. Time will only tell how much longer these teeming Florida wetlands will exist.

The Everglades have lived in a state of contention for almost a century. Due to their lack of stunning vistas and obvious natural beauty, the region is often written off by many as a mosquito-ridden wasteland. But a few believed this was a place worth saving. A journalist named Marjory Stoneman Douglas along with a visionary conservationist named Ernest F. Coe would stand toe-to-toe with South Florida's land-hungry investors and commercial developers in defense of the swamp.

A former land developer himself, Coe was drawn to the Everglades and soon treasured the slow-moving rivers of life that flowed into the Gulf. He was shocked that people were so quick to destroy such a unique ecosystem, where rare wildlife, orchids, and tropical trees depended on the shallow flooding. He called for the creation of a National Park that included not only the Everglades, but the Big Cypress Forest to the north and Key Largo to the southeast as well. The

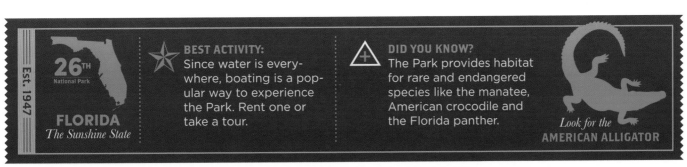

Est. 1947

26TH
National Park

FLORIDA
The Sunshine State

BEST ACTIVITY:
Since water is everywhere, boating is a popular way to experience the Park. Rent one or take a tour.

DID YOU KNOW?
The Park provides habitat for rare and endangered species like the manatee, American crocodile and the Florida panther.

Look for the
AMERICAN ALLIGATOR

<EVERGLADES 18" X 24" Limited Edition Print created in 2010 by Andy Gregg & Joel Anderson

feisty Marjory Stoneman Douglas, journalist for the Miami Herald, supported his vision. Douglas spent five whole years studying the Everglades before publishing her perspective in 1947. Her poetic commentary, matched with her witty barbs against good old boy politics, gave a major boost to society's outlook on the wetlands. She wrote:

"There are no other Everglades in the world.... Nothing anywhere else is like them; their vast glittering openness, wider than the enormous visible round of the horizon, the ... sweetness of their massive winds, under the dazzling blue heights of space.... The miracle of the light pours over the green and brown expanse of sawgrass and water, shining and slow-moving below, the grass and the water that is the meaning and central face of the Everglades of Florida. It is a river of grass."

In December, Coe and Douglas's struggle for the Everglades finally paid off. Florida legislature raised the $2 million necessary to purchase the remaining private swampland, and Congress desig-

nated the Everglades as a National Park.

Though this Park is more accessible by canoe than foot, Park Services have built a few excellent trailways from which to experience the incredible Everglade ecosystem without getting wet. An easy, highly rewarding nature walk along **Anhinga Trail** provides up-close opportunities to (safely) meet an alligator, while birds of many shapes and sizes can be watched at **Eco Pond.** Take the 15-mile **Tram Road** to a 45-foot tall observation tower that overlooks the glistening wetlands. You'll also be standing at the highest point in the Park, as the Everglades' elevation never exceeds more than 8 feet above sea level. Be sure to plan your visit for the wintertime as heavy rain, hurricanes, and swarms of mosquitoes make a summer trip to the Everglades much less enjoyable. The Park is a reminder to us of nature's fragility, that water is life. May it continue to flow through the complex and now preserved biosphere of the Everglades.

"The Everglades is all about water. It is difficult to truly understand the fragile nature of the park without being on the water or in the water. My favorite memories were canoeing or slogging through the sloughs, and looking for rookeries in Florida Bay—only the sounds of birds broke the silence."
— Maureen Finnerty, Former Superintendent of Everglades from 2000–2004 (total years of NPS service: 32)

SILENT EVERGALDES 18" X 24" Limited Edition Print based on an oil painting by Kai Carpenter created in 2015 >

EVERGLADES

NATIONAL PARK

VIRGIN ISLANDS
NATIONAL PARK

VIRGIN ISLANDS

A JEWEL NECKLACE of emerald isles graces the neck of the Caribbean. Each gem is a living paradise, a divine getaway for thousands of visitors each year. Sugar white beaches, thick leafy jungles, and a lustrous coral reef teeming with colorful fish crown the tropical dreamscape known as the Virgin Islands. Within this lovely archipelago is St. John's Island, home to Virgin Islands National Park. Though seemingly flawless today, the sugar mill ruins on St. John's Island give testament to a darker time, when these islands were populated with slaves rather than sun-starved tourists. The Park protects these monuments of the past, reminding us of an ugly era in human history. And yet, just as jungle reclaims the abandoned sugar fields, new life replaces the old. Virgin Islands National Park seems to redeem this once-exploited land and promote hope in all who wash up on its ivory shores.

On a voyage to the West Indies, Christopher Columbus first christened the numerous and undefiled Virgin Islands in 1493. Opportunistic Europeans set sail for this mythical island chain soon after.

Danish sugar planters laid claim to St. John's and soon turned the island into a sugar and rum-producing powerhouse. More than 80 plantations smothered the island, choking out native plants and animals to cultivate the sugar stalks. African slaves tended these fields for 150 years. Relics of these plantations, factories, and mills are scattered throughout the Park, serving as reminders of the Danish sugar empire and the plight of the Africans forced to run it. The sugar boom ended in the mid-1800s with tired island soil and the emancipation of the slaves. At the height of World War I, the United States purchased St. John's and 50 other Virgin Islands to protect the mainland from German naval attacks. The war ended and vacationers soon discovered the tropical appeal of these isles. Developers began building posh resorts as more and more tourists flocked to the sunny Caribbean. Once

again, the island's forests were threatened by commercialization. In the 1950s, billionaire conservationist Laurance Rockefeller purchased 5,000 acres, or half of St. John's Island, and donated it to the U.S. government as a National Park.

Today, Virgin Islands National Park is a nature haven for a large variety of birds, sea turtles, dolphins, forests of seagrass, palm, and the coral reef's bustling fish communities. Safe from exploitation, the land and sea now flourish with life. Investigate the vivacious coral reefs firsthand by snorkel or SCUBA in **Waterlemon Cay**. Experience the rich history of St. John's along the **Reef Bay Trail**, and finish off with a refreshing dip in the cove. Pop a tent on the shores of **Cinnamon Bay** for one of the most idyllic campgrounds in the United States. Reconnect yourself to nature and spend a day in the sand at Virgin Islands National Park.

Est. 1956

27TH National Park

VIRGIN ISLANDS
United in Pride & Hope

BEST TIME OF YEAR:
Anytime of the year is great for visiting this tropical paradise.

DID YOU KNOW?
Most of St. John's original vegetation was clear-cut in the colonial period for sugar-cane production. Fortunately, it has all grown back!

Look for the
BOTTLENOSE DOLPHIN

<VIRGIN ISLANDS 18" X 24" Limited Edition Print created in 2013 by Michael Korfhage & Joel Anderson

WITNESS SUNRISE AT HALEAKALĀ CRATER

HALEAKALĀ
NATIONAL PARK ◪ HAWAI'I

HALEAKALĀ

YOU STAND in the silent twilight atop a dormant volcano. Sleep stings your eyes as you squint into the expanse. A cloud quilt lies rumpled over the yawning valley below. You shiver in the wind, glancing at the bleary-eyed tourists around you, all awaiting the arrival of the morning star. And slowly the silken cloud sea begins to glow orange and yellow. Jagged cliff silhouettes darken as the sky ignites, and the Pacific sparkles in the new light. Morning has dawned. Welcome to Haleakala, the House of the Sun.

Hawaiian legend has it that the demi-god Maui once heard his mother sigh and say that the island days were too short, that the sun did not stay up long enough for her laundry to dry. Clever Maui happened to know that the sun lived atop Mount Haleakala, and he climbed up to the mountain's summit. Using his sister's hair, he made a lasso and yanked down the sun. He would

only let go if the sun agreed to cross the sky more slowly. The sun pled for mercy and agreed that he would make the days longer in the summertime. Satisfied, Maui released the star and descended the mountain. Sun has generously splashed his rays on the islands ever since. Playful silversword plants laugh in the breeze, blooming beneath clear mountain summit skies. Down the mountainside, in verdant Kipahulu Valley, waterfalls shimmer and tumble into the coves.

Haleakala National Park is divided into two wholly distinct areas, the exalted moon-desert summit and the lush beach jungles of **Kipahulu**. No road connects the two regions, so it's best to take a few days to fully enjoy this diverse display of Hawaiian wilderness. The summit is actually two volcanic valleys that melded after erosion ate away the mountain's peak. This supervalley formed a "crater" basin, 2,720 feet deep. Ambitious

hikers may now descend into this steep depression via **Halemau'u** and **Sliding Sand Trails.** Most Park guests are content to simply watch the sunrise from the crater rim at **Pu'u'ula'ula Summit**.

If you're not into high-altitude volcanic wastelands, you're in luck. Haleakala features an incredible ocean-side Eden at Kipahulu. While you cannot actually swim in the ocean here, water-lovers can splash in the sumptuous pools of **'Ohe'o Gulch.** Many of these jungle baths are formed by Kipahulu's magnificent waterfalls, of which the greatest is 400-foot **Waimoku Falls**. Access the misty wonder of Waimoku from the luscious **Pipiwai Trail,** considered one of the best hikes in Hawai'i. Walk through thick bamboo forests and breathe in the island air. Volcanoes and waterfalls await you on this jewel of Maui. Escape the mundane and savor the sunshine at Haleakala National Park.

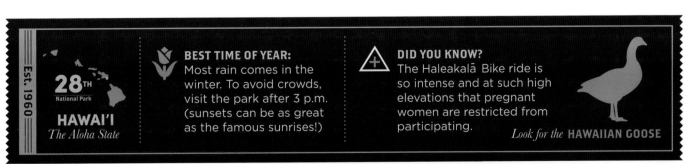

Est. 1960

28TH
National Park

HAWAI'I
The Aloha State

🌷 **BEST TIME OF YEAR:**
Most rain comes in the winter. To avoid crowds, visit the park after 3 p.m. (sunsets can be as great as the famous sunrises!)

⚠ **DID YOU KNOW?**
The Haleakalā Bike ride is so intense and at such high elevations that pregnant women are restricted from participating.

Look for the **HAWAIIAN GOOSE**

<HALEAKALĀ 18" X 24" Limited Edition Print created in 2015 by Michael Korfhage & Joel Anderson

National Parks Timeline · · · · · · · · · · · · · · · · · · 1900 · · · · · · · · · · · · · · 1950 · · · · · · · · · · · · · 2000 · · · · · · · · **89**

1960

HAWAI'I
VOLCANOES
NATIONAL PARK

HAWAI'I VOLCANOES

LAVA and ocean intertwine at Hawai'i Volcanoes National Park. Huddled on the southeastern corner of the Big Island, this Park is governed by the volatile cycle of destruction and renewal. The Big Island itself is a product of this volcanic process, and the Earth's red-hot magma that formed the islands continues to create new land in the South Pacific. Hawai'i Volcanoes is a place as steeped in history as volcanic debris: Polynesian and Tahitian immigrants have occupied the islands for over 1,500 years. Petroglyphs etched in lava by ancient Hawaiians and fossilized footprints of native soldiers killed by a volcanic eruption shroud the Park in mystery. A more recent historical figure would bring national (and tourist) attention to the South Pacific. Mark Twain's clever and lurid accounts of the island helped spark an interest in preserving Hawai'i's mountains of fire.

Two mountain behemoths dominate the Park. **Mauna Loa** lies on the northern end, a sheer monster of volcanic rock. The base of the mountain sits at the bottom of the Pacific Ocean and rises some 30,000 feet from the ocean floor (13,679 feet above sea level). When measuring Mauna Loa's sheer girth, it is one of the largest mountains on the planet. Hawaiians of old paid reverence to their volcano goddess Pele at **Kilauea**, the second and most active of the Park's

two volcanoes. Kilauea erupted as recent as 1983, and has stayed in a grumbling, cantankerous state ever since. Always up for a new adventure, Mark Twain once stayed at the Volcano House Hotel on Kilauea's summit. At night he would watch as lava lit up the night sky:

"I turned my eyes upon the volcano again.... For a mile and a half in front of us and half a mile on either side, the floor of the abyss was magnificently illuminated ... like the campfires of a great army far away.... It looked like a colossal railroad map of the State of Massachusetts done in chain lightning on a midnight sky. Imagine it -- imagine a coal-black sky shivered into a tangled network of angry fire!"

Hawai'i Volcanoes National Park has several trails from which to explore the island's multidimensional landscape. Rainforest, desert, lava fields, arid mountaintops, and volcanic beaches can all be experienced here. And since the Park rests on an active volcano, it is constantly changing. Witness the smoldering activity of Kilauea from the **Kilauea Iki Trail.** Pay close attention to trail and road closures as lava flow and noxious gases can make parts of the Park inaccessible. If open, drive the scenic **Crater Rim Drive** for a chance encounter with spouting liquid magma in **Halema'uma'u Crater.** Follow in the footsteps of Twain and the ancient Hawaiians as you gape at the power of this land on fire.

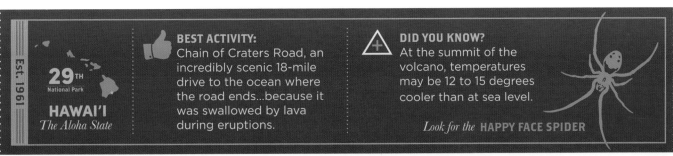

Est. 1961

29TH
National Park

HAWAI'I
The Aloha State

BEST ACTIVITY:
Chain of Craters Road, an incredibly scenic 18-mile drive to the ocean where the road ends...because it was swallowed by lava during eruptions.

DID YOU KNOW?
At the summit of the volcano, temperatures may be 12 to 15 degrees cooler than at sea level.

Look for the **HAPPY FACE SPIDER**

<HAWAI'I VOLCANOES 18" X 24" Limited Edition Print created in 2013 by Michael Korfhage & Joel Anderson

PETRIFIED FOREST
NATIONAL PARK

PETRIFIED FOREST

THE ANCIENT and sleepy wonders of Petrified Forest National Park rest only a few miles off I-40 and Route 66 in northeastern Arizona. Though now a silent fossilized wasteland, scientists believe that this area was once a lush subtropical jungle. Fossils of some of the world's earliest dinosaurs have been found here, while the wood-turned-stone trees the Park is famous for still lie scattered about (rather than a 'standing' forest, as might be expected). For those who enjoy anthropology, the remains of an ancestral Pueblo Indian neighborhood lie on the north end of the Park. Though much remains unknown, stories told by these ancient people are etched into nearby rock walls. This Park is a detour into days of old. Driving through the sluggish Route 66 towns remind you that this was once a place of vitality. Now, as with the trees themselves, a heavy sense of nostalgia sprawls across the hills of **the Painted Desert**, inviting you to reflect on ages long gone.

Americans have John Muir and Pres-

ident Theodore Roosevelt to thank for preserving the remarkable antiquities of the Petrified Forest. If it wasn't for the efforts of these two men, the remaining 250 million year old trees would have been picked apart bit by bit until none remained. Opportunists found all sorts of ways to turn the crystallized wood into a souvenir: from paperweights and bookends to stools, lamps, even table-tops. Gem collectors would blast logs of the petrified wood in search of precious crystals. John Muir noticed this while exploring the area in 1906. With his trademark ability to frustrate businessmen, Muir began a new crusade to save the fossilized forest. Thanks to a close friendship with President (and fellow nature enthusiast) Theodore Roosevelt, Petrified Forest was declared a national monument in 1906 and later

became a National Park in 1962.

One 28-mile main road takes you from the north entrance to the south with a visitor center on each end. The petrified wood, **Crystal Forest**, and **Agate Bridge**

can be found in the southern section of the park while the Painted Desert, **Blue Mesa, Pueblo villages**, and **petroglyphs** are located in the north. The crystal sarcophagi of primeval trees await your inspection throughout Petrified Forest National Park. Take the time to wander through their final resting places, and watch as their colors awaken in the rain.

Photo by Joel Anderson

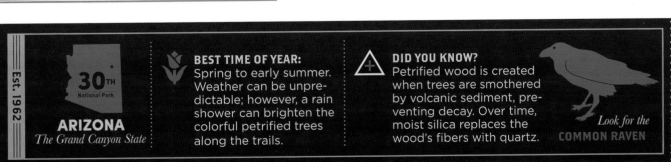

Est. 1962

30TH
National Park

ARIZONA
The Grand Canyon State

BEST TIME OF YEAR:
Spring to early summer. Weather can be unpredictable; however, a rain shower can brighten the colorful petrified trees along the trails.

DID YOU KNOW?
Petrified wood is created when trees are smothered by volcanic sediment, preventing decay. Over time, moist silica replaces the wood's fibers with quartz.

Look for the
COMMON RAVEN

<PETRIFIED FOREST 18" X 24" Limited Edition Print created in 2015 by Michael Korfhage & Joel Anderson

VISIT ANGEL ARCH

CANYONLANDS
NATIONAL PARK

CANYONLANDS

DESERT and water intertwine to create art upon the southeastern Utah canvas of Canyonlands National Park. Two roaring rivers have slowly devoured the landscape for millennia, carving and carrying away ancient sediment from the many-layered canyon walls. The **Colorado** and **Green Rivers** collide in the center of this Park, dividing the region into three separate areas: **Island in the Sky, Needles,** and the **Maze District**. The Park's variety of pinnacles, mesas, arches, and alien-like fins and spires is immense and often overlooked; though Canyonlands is Utah's largest National Park, it is also the least visited.

Canyonlands is a prime example of rocky Utahn backcountry. Life is sparse, difficult, persistent. Junipers grip the earth with their gnarled roots, squeezing out an existence on a few drops of water. Lizards bake in the sun as the shadows of massive buttes stretch out across the sandstone valley. It is rich in its barrenness. Prehistoric natives left a masterpiece of petroglyph artwork upon the walls at **Horseshoe Canyon**. This region has been explored by miners, missionaries, cowboys, Indians, geologists: people all searching for life among the rocks.

Weapons were sought out here too. During the Cold War, government-hired prospectors scoured Canyonlands for uranium. Miles and miles of roadways were built for discovering and transporting the ore. Little uranium was found, however, and the initial ravaging for ammo in fact brought about the Park's permanent protection. Bates Wilson, the then-superin-

tendent of Arches National Monument, advocated for preservation of Canyonlands and lead backcountry jeep tours to prove his point. A vacationing Secretary of the Interior Stewart Udall took one of these tours and brought tales of Utah's beauty back to Washington. President Lyndon B. Johnson would sign Canyonlands officially into the National Park fold in 1964.

Though isolated, Canyonlands National Park offers a long menu in high adventure. The collision of the Colorado and Green Rivers provides an exhilarating white-water rush down the rapids at **Cataract Canyon**. Hiking and four-wheeling are both excellent ways to explore Island in the Sky's elevated terrain. An easy hike will bring you to the dramatic **Mesa Arch** right off the main road. A journey into Needles provides a more intimate encounter with the quirky stonescape of the canyon. Here the mythic **Druid Arch** and **Angel Arch** can be accessed.

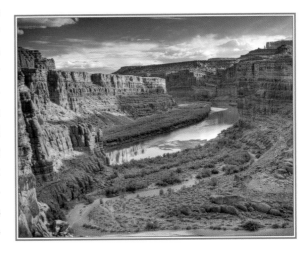

Est. 1964

31ST National Park

UTAH
The Beehive State

★ **BEST ACTIVITY:**
If you have only one day, do not miss the Island in the Sky.

⚠ **DID YOU KNOW?**
Some of the rock art in Horseshoe Canyon was painted over 3,000 years ago.

Look for the
MOUNTAIN LION

<CANYONLANDS 18" X 24" Limited Edition Print created in 2014 by Michael Korfhage & Joel Anderson

National Parks Timeline · · · · · · · · · · · · · · · 1900 · · · · · · · · · · · · · · · 1950 · · · · · · · · · · · · · · · 2000 · · · ➤➤ 95 →

△
1964

NORTH CASCADES

NATIONAL PARK

AMERICA'S ALPS · WASHINGTON

NORTH CASCADES

PEER UP INTO the snowy chiseled peaks of the American Alps. Breathe in the pure air, seasoned with hints of cedar and snowmelt. You feel like you are the last human on Earth here. The solemn peaks surround you, hemming you in with their glacial glory. Over 300 glaciers still work their craft in this Park today, patiently shaping and molding the Cascade Range in the Pacific Northwest. These mountains received their name from the innumerable waterfalls that rush down their rocky slopes, feeding the Park's cerulean lakes. North Cascades National Park is a glacial wonder, a continuous work of wilderness art. It is a paradise locked away from civilization by its own design: the Cascades are notoriously difficult to access here, making this region one of the least visited Parks in the lower 48 states. Still, the invitation to explore is especially tantalizing in a place like this. With over 400 miles of wooded and riv-

er-laced trails, the opportunities abound to unlock the treasures of the Cascades.

Today, a single highway spans North Cascades National Park. Travelers are regaled with angular, seemingly inaccessible mountain beauty as they drive through **Rainy** and **Washington Pass** in the Park's northern region. Even the hardiest fur trappers grew pale at the feet of these harrowing Cascade giants in the early years. "A more difficult route to travel never fell a man's lot," growled trapper Alexander Ross in 1814. With mountain names such as Mount Despair, Damnation Peak, and Mount Terror, the area's daunting reputation precedes itself.

Nonetheless, the Cascades' fearless inhabitants went to work, uniting old miner roads and exploration routes to form the stunning **North Cascades Highway,** completed in 1972. This road pierces the Cascade Range by way of the **Skagit River,** which feeds into the Park's

cherished lake system. Canoes, kayaks, and ferries carry passengers across the chilly waters of **Lake Diablo** and **Lake Ross** (both belonging to the North Cascades' Ross Lake Recreational Area). The gravelly **Cascade River Road** brings you into the Park's rugged southern region, where day hikers find a rejuvenating thrill in the climb to **Cascade Pass.**

Keep a sharp eye out for the North Cascades' lighthearted mascot, the mountain goat. These furry rock climbers thrive on the ridgelines. Salmon leap up the Skagit River to their spawning beds each fall. This annual spectacle draws a gawking host of tourists and bald eagles, eager to catch (and eat) a piece of the action. Though only a few hours from Seattle, this magnificent region remains a well-kept secret within the Park system, where undefiled wilderness awaits you. Climb up and enter the solitude of North Cascades National Park.

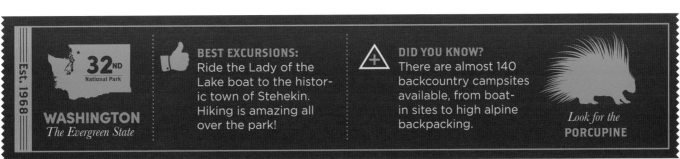

Est. 1968

32ND National Park

WASHINGTON
The Evergreen State

👍 **BEST EXCURSIONS:**
Ride the Lady of the Lake boat to the historic town of Stehekin. Hiking is amazing all over the park!

⚠ **DID YOU KNOW?**
There are almost 140 backcountry campsites available, from boat-in sites to high alpine backpacking.

Look for the
PORCUPINE

<NORTH CASCADES 18" X 24" Limited Edition Print created in 2013 by David Anderson & Joel Anderson

REDWOOD
NATIONAL PARK

REDWOOD

DENSE MORNING FOG rolls slowly over a lush grove of coastal redwoods. The sun filters through the tree mist, shedding a smattering of sunlight across the forest floor. Roosevelt Elk call out to one another in the meadow as sleepy sea lions slip out from their coves in search of breakfast. Gloomy and alive, Redwood National Park encompasses 133,000 acres of Pacific coastland. Old

> **"The redwoods, once seen, leave a mark or create a vision that stays with you always."**
> *-John Steinbeck*

growth forest once dominated this landscape. As late as 1850, over 2 million acres of thick redwood coated Northern California. Today, the Park protects what remains of these resplendent woodlands. Some of the world's tallest and oldest trees grow in this forest. Despite their shallow root systems, the redwoods can grow taller than the Statue of Liberty (many already have) and live for more than two millennia. The tallest tree in Redwood is **Hyperion**, towering 379 feet high as a spectacular example of undisturbed growth. The Park's proximity to the Pacific Ocean keeps the region cool and foggy, a near perfect environment for the long life of a thirsty giant. While this Park now contains a landscape of prehistoric serenity, it was once in danger of being logged completely bare. Conservationist groups would struggle for decades to salvage what was left of these mossy behemoths.

Native American tribes thrived within the redwood forests for over 3,000 years. Using the wood from fallen trees, the natives built entire villages and fleets of canoes. They lived off the land, picking berries, hunting elk, and fishing for salmon off the shores of the Pacific. Evidence of their complex and harmonious societies can still be found along the coast. When gold became king in the 1850s, settlers and prospectors swarmed into Northern California, wiping out many of the Native American villages and pushing the people onto reservations. Some natives resisted, hiding in the redwood groves. Their ancestors continue to live within the Park to this day.

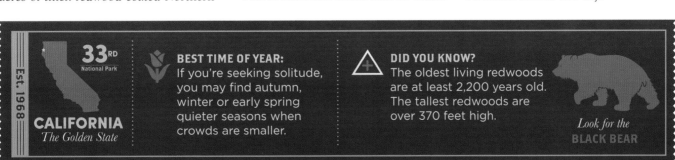

Est. 1968

33RD
National Park

CALIFORNIA
The Golden State

BEST TIME OF YEAR:
If you're seeking solitude, you may find autumn, winter or early spring quieter seasons when crowds are smaller.

DID YOU KNOW?
The oldest living redwoods are at least 2,200 years old. The tallest redwoods are over 370 feet high.

Look for the
BLACK BEAR

<REDWOOD 18" X 24" Limited Edition Print created in 2013 by Michael Korfhage & Joel Anderson

National Parks Timeline · · · · · · · · · · · · · · · · · 1900 · · · · · · · · · · · · · · · · 1950 · · · · · · · · · · · · · · · · 2000 · · · →99→

1968

As unlucky gold miners lifted their eyes from their pans to the surrounding forests, a new lucrative scheme entered their heads. A logging mania overtook the region as wide swaths of old forest were decimated and sold up and down the booming West Coast. The incessant buzzing of the sawmills grabbed the attention of early 20th century conservationists. Alarmed at the rate of the forest's destruction, a group of naturalists formed the Save-the-Redwoods League. They rallied support from all over the country, and the state of California soon responded with the establishment of three state-protected parks. The loggers kept chewing up trees until 1968 when President Lyndon B. Johnson commissioned Redwood National Park, finally silencing the saws once and for all.

The woods would need years to recover. Thankfully, a massive redwood replanting and cultivation project began in 1978 and continues today. Redwood National Park is now enjoyed by nearly half a million people each year. Many come just to see the tree kings that reign in this part of the country. Grab a permit and walk beneath the outstretched arms of these titans on the **Tall Trees Trail**. Enjoy a leisurely loop through the forest on the **Lady Bird Grove Trail** or spend an afternoon by the sea at **Crescent Beach**. In time, these wild forests will take back the barren patches and cloak the hills once more in fresh redwood glory.

"Every time I walked through a grove of redwoods I sensed the hushed majesty of these giant trees. I always felt as if I had entered a cathedral where all my senses were alive with the feeling of a timeless forest of the tallest trees in the world. I could sense the centuries these trees had stood and drew on this timelessness to strengthen my resolve to protect them."
— Bill Pierce, Former Superintendent of Redwood National Park from 2003-2006 (Total years of NPS service: 38)

REDWOOD: AMONG THE GIANTS 18" X 24" Limited Edition Print based on an oil painting by Kai Carpenter created in 2015 >

REDWOOD

NATIONAL PARK

ARCHES
NATIONAL PARK • UTAH

ARCHES

LOCATED IN THE HIGH desert country of the Colorado Plateau, Arches National Park is like wandering into a natural stone arch convention. Spires, balancing rocks, stone fins, and the namesake arches all abound here, congregating together underneath a sweeping Utah sky. No other place in the world offers such a high concentration of stone arch work: more than 2,000 of these natural formations populate the park. This region is home to a variety of celebrity arches, such as **Landscape Arch** (longest arch in North America, second longest in the world) and the rockstar of all natural arches, the **Delicate Arch** (as seen on many a Utahn license plate as well as our poster art). Thanks to diligent park planning, many of these stone celebrities can be admired up-close. One main Park road delves deep into the heart of the region, introducing guests to new curved skylines at every turn. Whether you are an avid hiker or prefer seeing the sights by car, the main characters of this panoramic Park beckon to be explored.

Famed nature writer Edward Abbey was a Park Ranger at Arches in the 1950s. His lucid and lonesome accounts of wilderness life helped spark a movement towards greater environmental awareness, to protect vulnerable places like Arches from pollution and irresponsible use of natural resources.

He understood humanity's desperate need for nature. From the silence of the Utah desert, Abbey penned *Desert Solitaire*, and with Muir-like cognizance he wrote: "Wilderness is not a luxury but a necessity of the human spirit, and as vital to our lives as water and good bread. A civilization which destroys what little remains of the wild, the spare, the original, is cutting itself off from its origins and betraying the principle of civilization itself."

Abbey recognized that few places on Earth contain more originality than Arches. And sadly, time is limited. As the years roll on, the creative force of the arches will also destroy them: erosion will one day bring its fragile

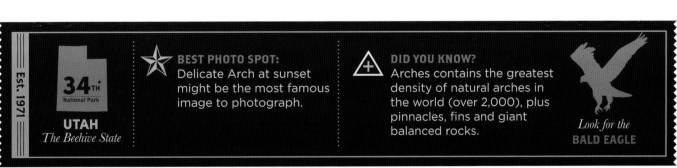

Est. 1971

34TH
National Park

UTAH
The Beehive State

★ **BEST PHOTO SPOT:**
Delicate Arch at sunset might be the most famous image to photograph.

⊞ **DID YOU KNOW?**
Arches contains the greatest density of natural arches in the world (over 2,000), plus pinnacles, fins and giant balanced rocks.

Look for the
BALD EAGLE

<ARCHES 18" X 24" Limited Edition Print created in 2010 by Julian Baker & Joel Anderson

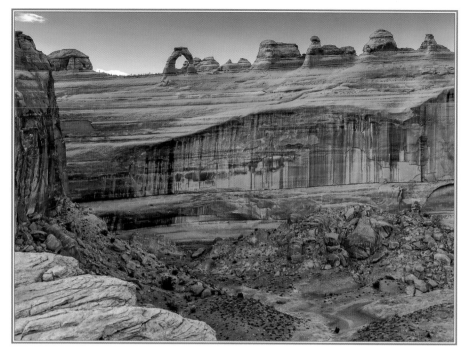

handiwork crumbling back to earth. No one knows for sure how much longer we will have these incredible feats of nature, so Park Rangers are especially adamant on visitor responsibility.

Carefully-laid trails lead to many of the popular formations throughout the Park, several of which are only a short hike from the main road. The payback for exploring Arches is great: one hike usually packs in several photogenic spots. Trails such as **Park Avenue** and **Devils Garden** are loaded with can't-miss moments. The illustrious (and especially fragile) Landscape Arch is accessible from the Devils Garden Trailhead. This Golden Gate of stone bridges is the longest arch in North America at 306 feet from base to base. The **Windows Section** features an easy climb to the awe-inspiring **Double Arch,** a natural phenomena where visitors may scramble up under its sinuous arms and experience the arches from directly beneath.

Perhaps the most iconic image in all of Utah is the Delicate Arch. A three-mile, strenuous hike will bring you to the foot of this sandstone beauty. Especially gorgeous at sundown, this arch lives up to the hype. Bring plenty of water and pa-

> "The farther one gets into the wilderness, the greater is the attraction of its lonely freedom."
> *-Theodore Roosevelt*

tience: the trail to Delicate Arch is one of the Park's most popular. Make time for some memorable meandering through the stone maze at **Fiery Furnace**. This beloved section of Arches is a ranger-led adventure and will put your all-terrain skills to the test.

"The location of the greatest concentration of stone arches and the largest free standing arch in the world is a wonderland of mystical rock formations that should be viewed not only in daylight but by moonlight."
— Walt Dabney, Former General Superintendent of Arches from 1991-1999 (total years of NPS service: 30)

ARCHES: LANDSCAPE ARCH 18" X 24" Limited Edition Print based on an oil painting by Kai Carpenter created in 2015 >

ARCHES
— NATIONAL PARK —

CAPITOL REEF

National Park

SOUTH CENTRAL UTAH ✦ **RED ROCK COUNTRY**

CAPITOL REEF

A PANOPLY of crafted stone beauty awaits you at Capitol Reef National Park. Best to leave your snorkel at home for this Park; Utah's Capitol Reef is actually named after a unique geological phenomenon called **the Waterpocket Fold**. This dramatic, 100-mile tilted rock spine snakes across the length of the Park from north to south. Geologists call this structure a monocline, a "wrinkle" in the Earth's crust pocketed with water-catching basins. Shifting tectonic plates, water, and time would create the rolling "waves" of the reef, as well as a vast portfolio of sculpted domes, cliffs, canyons, arches, and monoliths. Though no doubt an impressive collection, this lengthy museum of eroded art gave early Mormon pioneers and railway planners a colossal headache, preventing passage much like an ocean reef would to a ship. Though this area would always remain remote, appreciation would someday replace agitation, and life would be cultivated beneath the winding shadows of Capitol Reef.

The **Fremont River** flows across the north end of the reef, slipping a lush lifeline into this thirsty wilderness. For centuries, the small river valley would serve as a desert oasis, a safe haven for Native Americans and weary explorers, seeking a route across the Utah desert. By the 1800s, Mormons had settled in the valley, building villages, fertilizing the fields, and planting an orchard of fruit trees along the river banks. One enthusiastic Mormon Bishop named Ephraim Pectol convinced his brother-in-law that their slice of arid paradise would make a prime tourist destination. In 1921, they began promoting the region as Wayne Wonderland, named after their nearby home in Wayne County. Pectol was elected to the state legislature a few years later and immediately reached out to President Franklin D. Roosevelt about commissioning Wayne Wonderland National Monument. Though stipulating a name-change, Roosevelt agreed and set aside 37,711 acres of Utah canyonlands for the creation of Capitol Reef National Monument. Under the (unpaid) care of first custodian Charles Kelley the park would grow and withstand a ravishing for uranium during the Cold War. A Park-friendly government program called Mission 66 brought substantial development and paved roadways to this remote area, dramatically increasing tourism. In 1971, Congress passed a bill to protect the entirety of the Waterpocket Fold along with the surrounding territory. President Nixon signed it and Capitol Reef National Park was born on December 18, 1971.

Over 3,000 fruit trees still fill the fragrant orchard campground of **Fruita**, and Park guests may pick a snack there before heading into the canyons. Trails lace the northern regions of the Waterpocket Fold, allowing hikers to witness a wide variety of the Reef's gloriously eroded stonework. Take in panoramic views of the wavy gorge from **Goosenecks** and **Sunset Point**. Grab a few apricots before setting out on a 3.5-mile hike to hidden **Cohab Canyon**. Follow the scenic trail to a lofty natural archway at **Hickman Bridge** and continue on up the **Rim Overlook Trail**. Traverse this vast landscape of sloping stone. It is now a protected wonderland set aside just for you.

Est. 1971

35TH
National Park
★

UTAH
The Beehive State

BEST TIME OF YEAR:
From spring to fall, the park offers several ranger programs at no charge.

DID YOU KNOW?
The cliffs, canyons, domes and bridges in the Waterpocket Fold are part of a wrinkle on the Earth which extends almost 100 miles.

Look for the
COYOTE

<CAPITOL REEF 18" X 24" Limited Edition Print created in 2015 by Joel Anderson

GUADALUPE PEAK • THE HIGHEST NATURAL POINT IN TEXAS

GUADALUPE MOUNTAINS

★ NATIONAL PARK ★

GUADALUPE MOUNTAINS

OCEAN AND DESERT. Reefs and peaks. Sponges and pine. Guadalupe Mountains National Park, at one time or another, contained all of these. This is a relatively obscure Park with a rich geological and cultural history. The waterless landscape in west Texas was once a shallow sea, home to a 400-mile long horseshoe reef that is now a fossilized mountain range. Today, the two highest points in Texas jut out of this Park's ancient coral shoal. At 8,749 feet, **Guadalupe Peak** is the tallest mountain in Texas and its neighbor, **El Capitán**, looms 8,064 feet high and can be seen from up to 50 miles away.

Life still abounds in these mountains, a desert oasis above the harsh Chihuahuan wastelands. Where primordial fish, coral polyps, algae, and sponges once thrived is today a haven for elk, black bears, roadrun-

ners, and, of course, backpackers. Those who make the trek out to these oft-overlooked Texas highlands will discover a landscape brimming with adventure.

The Guadalupe Mountains have never been a hospitable landscape for human life, but stone age artifacts have been found in the area dating some 12,000 years. Petroglyphs and pottery are all that remain of these ancient nomads. In more modern times, Apache Indians used to hide out in the mountain caves and hunt for game when not raiding nearby homesteads. They would live in isolation from white men until the mid-1800s when Texan prospectors sought out a pathway through the mountains.

American dreams of transcontinental railways and a cross-country mail road were brought into western Texas, and the era of the Apache Indians soon came to a close. U.S. militiamen were sent in to drive out the natives and clear a safe passage for the mail coaches. In the midst of this bloody war, two brothers built a house at **Frijole Ranch** in 1876. This building would serve as the area's main community center and post office for the next 70 years until it was purchased by successful banker-turned-rancher J.C. Hunter. Along with petroleum geologist Wallace Pratt, Hunter purchased thousands of acres around the Guadalupe Mountains. Hunter and his son raised goats in the Park's mountain highlands, while Pratt built family summer homes within the stunning **McKittrick Can-**

yon. These men recognized the unique beauty of their backyards and, in time, donated their land to the National Park Service to create Guadalupe Mountains National Park, which opened in 1972.

Thanks to the generous donations of the Hunters and the Pratts, the Guadalupe Mountains are now accessible for all to enjoy. Witness bright fall foliage in the Texas highlands on the **McKittrick Canyon Trail** in late October. This trail is considered one of the best hikes in the Lone Star State no matter what month it is. Get personal with the state's highest point on a pebbled pathway up to Guadalupe Peak or backpack into a secluded conifer forest for a night under the stars at **Pine Top.** Streams of life still flow through the Guadalupe Mountains. Venture up and wash yourself in the hidden wonders that await you.

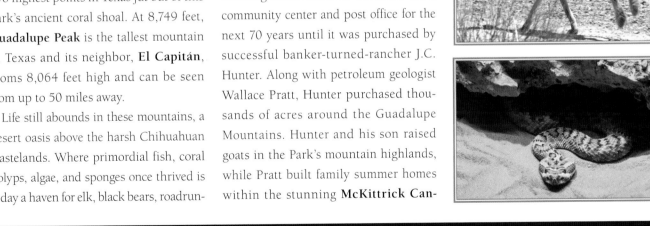

<**GUADALUPE MOUNTAINS** 18" X 24" Limited Edition Print created in 2013 by Michael Korfhage & Joel Anderson

National Parks Timeline · · · · · · · · · · · · · · · · · · 1900 · · · · · · · · 1950 · · · · · · · · 2000 · · · **109**

1972

VOYAGEURS

NATIONAL PARK

ELLSWORTH ROCK GARDENS

MINNESOTA

VOYAGEURS

A SPIRIT of adventure pulses through the web of waterways at Voyageurs National Park. This was once an 18th century fur trappers' paradise, and the French Canadian "voyageurs" were masters of these channels. They romped across the region's 30 lakes singing merry songs and smoking pipes, camped out beneath the stars of the North Country, and hunted for beaver pelts, whose pelts were then at the pinnacle of European fashion. Only the hardiest of men could sail with the voyageurs, as the trappers often paddled up to 16 hours a day and endured the brutal Minnesota cold each winter. But these explorers were responsible for charting much of the continent's northwestern territory, and their zealous energy pervades the Land of 10,000 Lakes to this day.

Modern day paddlers still find never-ending adventure among the 900+ islands of this National Park in northern Minnesota. Though remote, Voyageurs was once in danger of losing its natural features to land development. Loggers ravaged the region's timber and miners blasted for gold. Dams were built, suffocating the lake country in the noose

> **"Nature is always lovely . . . All scars she heals, whether in rocks or water or sky or hearts."**
> *-John Muir*

of progress. In the 1930s, a local conservationist named Ernest Oberholtzer stepped in to save what was left of these pristine lakelands. As a founder and councilman of the nationally-recognized Wilderness Society, Oberholtzer's cries for preservation soon reached federal ears. Park recognition would take

decades, but in 1975, Congress created Voyageurs National Park to permanently protect this Minnesota treasure.

With less than 10 total miles of roadway, this Park is meant to be explored by boat. Beavers, bald eagles, gray wolves, loons, and moose can all be encountered through kayaking the inlets or hiking along the island trails. Don't forget your fishing pole; this Park has some of the best fishing in the Midwest. Explore the Park's 4 major lakes (**Kabetogama, Namakan, Rainy,** and **Sand Point**) and end your day unwinding in one of the 200 shoreline campsites. Reenact the voyageur life in a 26-foot canoe and learn about these hardy French Canadian sailors on a free ranger-led **North Canoe Voyage**. Test your boating skills, enjoy the summer sunshine, and experience the ultimate lake country at Voyageurs National Park.

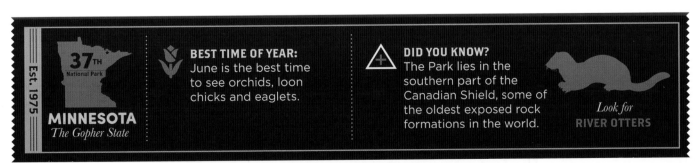

37TH National Park

Est. 1975

MINNESOTA
The Gopher State

BEST TIME OF YEAR:
June is the best time to see orchids, loon chicks and eaglets.

DID YOU KNOW?
The Park lies in the southern part of the Canadian Shield, some of the oldest exposed rock formations in the world.

Look for
RIVER OTTERS

<**VOYAGEURS** 18" X 24" Limited Edition Print created in 2015 by Michael Korfhage & Joel Anderson

National Parks Timeline · ≫ **111** →

1900   1950   2000

△
1975

ENJOY THE GOOD LIFE

Visit

BADLANDS

NATIONAL PARK ◆ SOUTH DAKOTA

BADLANDS

LIFE, death, and the solemn beauty of decay are themes represented on the rugged plains of Badlands National Park. Just off I-90 in southwestern South Dakota, Badlands entertains over one million guests a year with stories of its tumultuous geologic past. The largest protected prairie in the National Park System is found here, as is one of the richest fossil beds of mammals on the planet. The treasures of the past are buried beneath a landscape so harsh and stubborn that Spanish explorers, French fur trappers, and Lakota Sioux Indians all called it the same name: "the bad lands". Though you won't find a farmer trying to plow the soil around here, Badlands National Park nevertheless protects and provides for over 250 species of wildlife. And thanks to the ancient forces of deposition and erosion, the Badlands continues to surprise and delight paleontologists, naturalists, and tourists with its natural treasures each day.

The air and earth at Badlands is thick with the past. What is now canyon and spires of limestone and soft mudstone was once covered by a shallow sea. The water teemed with fish, turtle, and squid. As geological forces changed the landscape of the American Great Plains, the water drained out of the area, leaving a lush subtropical environment. Fossils of sabertooth tigers, giant lizards, mammoths, camels, and hornless rhinos reveal a once exuberant locale. While scientists are still discovering the bones of extinct animals underground, endangered species still breathe and roam free throughout the Park. Hard-to-find bison, swift fox, and black-footed ferret all call the Badlands their home.

Built in the 1930s, **Badlands Loop Road** is a 42-mile lifeline for the Park's visitors. From this road much of the awe-inspiring **Badlands Wall** can be accessed and enjoyed. Hiking trails such as **Door**, **Notch**, and **Saddle Pass** draw adventurers into the Wall itself, and the commanding views of the prairie are a fresh reminder of life past and present in the Badlands. Overlooks at **Yellow Mounds** and **Pinnacles** are must-stops for nature-lovers; watching bighorn sheep climb the eerie yellow hills will leave you entranced. With so much to see from one main access road, exploring the inhospitable Badlands is now more enjoyable than ever before.

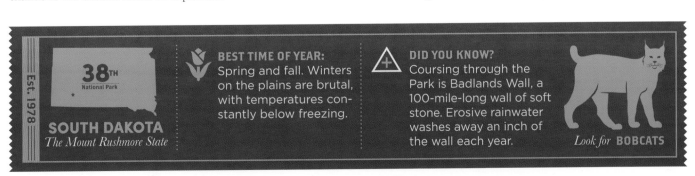

Est. 1978

38TH
National Park

SOUTH DAKOTA
The Mount Rushmore State

BEST TIME OF YEAR:
Spring and fall. Winters on the plains are brutal, with temperatures constantly below freezing.

DID YOU KNOW?
Coursing through the Park is Badlands Wall, a 100-mile-long wall of soft stone. Erosive rainwater washes away an inch of the wall each year.

Look for BOBCATS

<BADLANDS 18" X 24" Limited Edition Print created in 2013 by Michael Korfhage & Joel Anderson

National Parks Timeline · ≫ 113 →

1900   1950   2000

△
1978

THEODORE ROOSEVELT
NATIONAL PARK

MEDORA NORTH DAKOTA

THEODORE ROOSEVELT

ONE OF THE STRONGEST personalities in American history found his calling here in the Badlands of North Dakota. The landscape is pure Western prairie wilderness, home to wild horses, prairie dogs, buffalo, and pronghorn. The broken hills and weathered rock formations give testament to the region's incessant wind erosion, creating a strange and timeless aura to the Park. It is a near perfect place to feel connected and refined by unpolished nature. The **Little Missouri River** churns through colorful canyons and buttes across the

> ## "I never would have been President if it had not been for my experiences in North Dakota."
> *-Theodore Roosevelt*

valley floor, leaving a lush cottonwood and juniper-dotted riverbed in its wake. It was here, near the banks of the Little Missouri, that a young and sickly boy named Theodore Roosevelt became a man, finding a hidden toughness and respect for the wild. Roosevelt sought healing on the plains of North Dakota, and the vitality this region brought him changed the course of National Park history forever.

Theodore Roosevelt first arrived in Medora, North Dakota in 1883. He was a skinny, bespectacled 25 year old rich kid from New York City with one thought

on his mind: to bag a bison. The American buffalo population was already dwindling, but TR was enamored with the cowboy lifestyle of the West from the start. Though the local ranchers made fun of his city slicker background, Roosevelt's limitless energy soon impressed his peers and he bought into the rigorous life of a cattle rancher. His homestead at **Maltese Cross Ranch** is preserved to this day as a time capsule to Roosevelt's developing time in the Badlands. The

following year, back in New York City, TR lost both his wife and his mother on the same day. Overwhelmed with grief, Roosevelt returned to the northern plains where he built **Elkhorn Ranch** and faced a brutal North Dakotan winter that wiped out more than half of his cattle. Though suffering great loss on all accounts, Roosevelt discovered an inner strength and a deep passion for America's wilderness that would alter the course of his life. The lessons he learned in North Dakota, and the ability to connect with the common man, eventually transformed the young Roosevelt into the President of the United States and a founding father of the National Park System. In his memory, this Park was established in 1978, preserving forever the rugged landscape that shaped an incredible life.

Opportunities for solitude abound at Theodore Roosevelt National Park. Explore the grassy hills and curved canyons on horseback, just like TR did 100 years ago. This Park is one of the few parks in the country that is almost completely accessible for horses, and a great place to saddle up is at **Peaceful Valley Ranch.** If you'd prefer an air-conditioned perspective, take the **Scenic Loop Drive** that winds through some of the most breathtaking regions of the North and South units of the Park, including the much-loved **Prairie Dog Towns.** Be sure to stop and stretch your legs at the **Caprock Coulee Pullout** for a glimpse of some eerie mushroom-shaped hoodoos along the trail. Let the wild winds of the northern plains reinvigorate you, just as they did for our resilient 26th President, Theodore Roosevelt.

Est. 1978

39TH
National Park

NORTH DAKOTA
Rough Rider State

BEST TIME OF YEAR:
Summer is the most popular time to visit the park, since the days are very long.

DID YOU KNOW?
The park is home to animals such as bison, prairie dogs, wild horses, mule deer, elk, pronghorn and numerous bird species.

Look for **FERAL HORSES**

<THEODORE ROOSEVELT 18" X 24" Limited Edition Print created in 2014 by Michael Korfhage & Joel Anderson

PICTURESQUE VIEWS AT ANACAPA ISLAND

CHANNEL ISLANDS

NATIONAL PARK

CHANNEL ISLANDS

THE PACIFIC OCEAN dashes against a chain of rocky isles off the coast of Southern California. It's hard to believe there's still undeveloped land so close to one of our nation's largest cities. Flocks of brown pelicans, seagull, and puffin glide on the salty gales to their cliff-side nests. Pods of dolphin chase after anchovies as blue whales trundle through underwater forests of sea kelp. Boisterous colonies of sea lion bicker and bark on the pebbled beaches. Bright yellow kayaks dot the glittery coasts, wandering in and out of the islands' many sea caves. This is Channel Islands National Park, an island refuge sanctified from the smog of Los Angeles. Often referred to as the "Galapagos of the North," this wilderness archipelago presents a living picture of life in Southern California before Americans moved in.

The Chumash Indians lived on the Channel Islands for thousands of years, sailing back and forth from present-day L.A. in redwood canoes while hunting for seals. Their quiet way of life was forever altered when Spanish explorers discovered their island villages in the mid-16th century. Though friendly trade partners at first, the Europeans soon over-hunted and exploited the islands' natural resources, and their foreign diseases decimated the Chumash. Mexico later claimed the islands as a prison and sheep ranch before the U.S. military took possession in the early 1900s. Today, Channel Islands National Park and Marine Sanctuary still protect the original wildlife of these coastal islets and the wonders that live below the surface of the azure Pacific.

Your island adventure begins on the mainland at **Ventura Harbor's visitor center**. Here, Park Rangers have developed a unique interactive program to teach visitors about the Channel Islands' exquisite sealife. Donning microphone-equipped SCUBA gear and handheld cameras, rangers dive into the Park's thick kelp forests off the coast of nearby **Anacapa Island**. Standing dry in the visitor center, Park guests have the opportunity to see what the divers see and ask questions about the aquatic ecosystems on-screen. Waiting in the harbor are a fleet of ferry boats, ready to carry passengers across the rough coastal channel to the Park's five islands: Anacapa, **Santa Cruz, Santa Rosa, San Miguel**, and **Santa Barbara**. Visitors must bring in their own water and food for the trek out to this windswept archipelago. The remoteness of these islands generates its own special appeal; out here you feel thousands of miles away from any trace of urban sprawl. Watch the rowdy mob of sea lions congregate at **Point Bennett** on San Miguel. Climb up to a dramatic 150-foot cliff above the roaring Pacific at **Inspiration Point** on Anacapa or paddle into a chilly sea cave at **Scorpion Beach** on Santa Cruz Island. Take a trek out to these rustic Californian islands and discover a world where the ocean still reigns supreme.

Est. 1980

40TH
National Park

CALIFORNIA
The Golden State

BEST TIME OF YEAR:
Summer is the best time for diving, snorkeling, swimming, kayaking, and sailing.

DID YOU KNOW?
Channel Islands National Park consists of 249,354 acres, half of which are under the ocean.

Look for the
ISLAND FOX

<CHANNEL ISLANDS 18" X 24" Limited Edition Print created in 2015 by Michael Korfhage & Joel Anderson

National Parks Timeline · · · · · · · · · · · · · · · ·   1900   · · · · · · · · · · · · · · · · ·   1950   · · · · · · · · · · · · · · ·   2000   · · · · ·   117

1980

BISCAYNE

A TEEMING South Florida metropolis lies just off the coast of Miami. Coral reefs replace skyscrapers and swarms of colorful fish replace the bustling city traffic. Only 30 miles away from Florida's largest city is one of the world's largest coral reef systems, home to a multitude of aquatic life. Forty shimmering islets bask in the Florida sunlight at Biscayne National Park. These tiny islands represent only 5% of the Park's protected area; if you want to truly experience Biscayne, you'll need to grab a paddle and a snorkel.

The islands of Biscayne, with their strategic location off the southeast corner of Florida, hosted pirates and mutineers for over three centuries. Early Spanish galleys, stuffed with gold from the New World, were prime targets for the Caribbean's fierce privateers. Memories of the area's violent past remain intact at **Caesar Creek**, named after the legendary African pirate Black Caesar who supposedly buried 26 bars of solid gold on one of Biscayne's islands (yet to be found).

The Park was also home to a little-known African-American entrepreneur named Israel Jones. Jones moved to South Florida in 1892, taking a variety of odd jobs as a handyman and lime farmer. Jones learned quickly and was shrewd with his savings. In 1898, Jones purchased **Old Rhodes Key**, where he immediately went to work clearing the thick gumbo limbo trees and thorny under-

brush, uncovering a rich soil base perfect for growing key limes. The family lime business boomed and Jones soon purchased neighboring **Totten Key** to grow pineapples with his two sons, Lancelot and Arthur. As Jones grew older, his sons acquired the fruit business. Lancelot was also an expert fisherman, and his services were sought after by patrons such as President Herbert Hoover and Richard Nixon. Lancelot was keenly aware of the unique natural splendor of his island home. As developers threatened to build roadways across the Keys, Jones eventually decided to sell his land to the National Park Service, who in turn allowed him to continue living in Biscayne and teach visitors about the ocean's wonders for the rest of his life.

A dark green sea turtle waddles down from the shoreline before gliding into the reef. Aquatic wildlife is on full display here at Biscayne: over 500 species of fish, crab, clam, and lobster, not to mention dolphin and manatee, reside in this lively seascape. Enjoy the wild coral beauty on a **ranger-guided snorkeling trip** or spend a lazy day paddling in Lancelot's backyard at **Jones Lagoon**. Watch South Florida's top windsurfers work their craft on the waves at **Convoy Point**. Learn about the reef's infamous shipwreck history on the underwater **Maritime Heritage Trail** where divers can explore the wreckage of six unlucky vessels from as early as 1878. Soak in the rich history and luxuriant beauty of Biscayne National Park.

Est. 1980

41ST National Park

FLORIDA *The Sunshine State*

BEST TIME OF YEAR: Summer. Waters are clearer, making for fantastic viewing in a glass bottom boat tour or snorkeling.

DID YOU KNOW? As the largest marine park in the NP system, Biscayne NP is more than 95% covered by water.

Look for the **BROWN PELICAN**

<BISCAYNE 18" X 24" Limited Edition Print created in 2013 by Michael Korfhage & Joel Anderson

GATES
of the
ARCTIC
NATIONAL PARK

SEE BEAUTIFUL ALASKA

GATES OF THE ARCTIC

IN THE FAR REACHES of America's Last Frontier is a National Park the size of Switzerland. Northern Alaska is the purest form of desolation. Formidable mountain crags cast their shadows over the dark rivers, ribboning across the treeless tundra. A lonesome caribou herd calls out into the gloom. Aurora glow sweeps across the night sky. The Rocky Mountain range ends here, at the northernmost National Park in the United States. Gates of the Arctic National Park lies completely above the Earth's Arctic Circle, where the sun never seems to set throughout the short summer and refuses to rise on a long and brutal winter. Much like the landscape, the weather is tempestuous and fickle. A snowstorm can occur any time of the year. Only the stoutest adventurers would even consider visiting a place

like this. There are no trails or campgrounds. There are no roads in or out of the Park. Access into the Gates is possible only by air taxi or on foot. But the harsh Alaskan landscape is nonetheless incomparable for its unspoiled backcountry and poetic simplicity.

In the 1930s, writer and forest conservationist Bob Marshall journeyed up Alaska's **Koyukuk River** to the North Fork. There he encountered two lofty sentinels, **Frigid Crags** and **Boreal Mountain.** Following the river between these two behemoths, Marshall quietly acknowledged that he had entered the Gates of the Arctic. Marshall studied this vast glacial wilderness, utterly void of human development. His work would eventually inspire Congress to set aside this region as a National Park in 1980. Grizzly bear, wolf, caribou, and fox continue to scratch out a meager living on the boggy taiga. Six rivers flow through the Park, providing a wild rafting adventure for those daring enough to enter the frigid rapids. The **Kobuk** and Koyukuk rivers are two of the more popular routes to float through the boundless Alaskan backcountry. The Gates welcome the bold. Enter and be amazed.

> *In the early morning when the first faint light*
> *Cuts the murky blackness of the cool calm night,*
> *While the gloomy forest, dismal, dark, and wild,*
> *Seems to slowly soften and become more mild,*
>
> *When the mists hang heavy, where the streams flow by*
> *And reflects the rose-tints in the eastern sky,*
> *When the brook trout leaps and the deer drinks slow,*
> *While the distant mountains blend in one soft glow,*
>
> *'Tis the precious moment, given once a day,*
> *When the present fades to the far-away,*
> *When the busy this-time for a moment's gone,*
> *And the Earth turns backward into Nature's dawn."*
> *-- Bob Marshall*

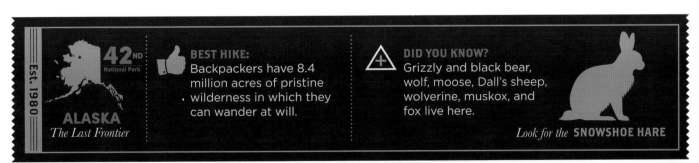

Est. 1980

42ND National Park

ALASKA
The Last Frontier

BEST HIKE:
Backpackers have 8.4 million acres of pristine wilderness in which they can wander at will.

DID YOU KNOW?
Grizzly and black bear, wolf, moose, Dall's sheep, wolverine, muskox, and fox live here.

Look for the **SNOWSHOE HARE**

<GATES OF THE ARCTIC 18" X 24" Limited Edition Print created in 2015 by David Anderson & Aaron Johnson

GLACIER BAY
NATIONAL PARK

ALASKA

GLACIER BAY

A GREAT THUNDERING crystal world of ice envelops the southeastern Alaska coastlands. Dark peaks poke up through their shawls of snow. The 3 million-plus acres of Glacier Bay National Park may be a bundled world of frost, but nature has recently provided a pathway for humans to enter this icy chamber. Less than 300 years ago, Glacier Bay did not exist. What is now a cruise ship-welcoming inlet was once a glacier-choked frozen mass. Since 1794, the region's glaciers have shrunk back more than 60 miles, unveiling ever-transforming terrain that invites you to peek beneath the icy armor of Alaska and find a vibrant body of new life.

Accompanied by a group of Tlingit Indian warriors, John Muir once canoed the 800 miles from Fort Wrangell to Glacier Bay in 1879. Glaciers had fascinated Muir for years, inspiring him to write dozens of essays on their extensive sculpting of his beloved Sierra Nevada Mountains in California. In Alaska, Muir felt he had returned to the Earth's Ice Age. He gasped in awe as icebergs cracked off the fro-

into another." Muir's arduous initiation to the Alaskan wilderness stoked in him a deep-seated passion for Glacier Bay.

Eleven years later, at the age of 52, Muir returned for a 9 day solo excursion despite a chronic cough. Ever the optimist in nature's healing powers, a drenched and sunblind John Muir decided to camp out atop a tidewater glacier. He awoke to find his cough gone and his health restored. "No lowland microbe can survive on a glacier," he said. Baffled by this eccentric adventurer, the local Tlingits began calling him "Great Ice Chief." The Ice Chief would later have an imposing glacier named after him. Since then, Muir's glacier has melted back into the valley where it resides to this day. **Muir Inlet** invites kayaks and canoes to explore the freshly melted waterway left in the glacier's wake.

Adventure awaits on land as well. Delve into a newly established forest on the **Bartlett River Trail**, where a wide variety of wildlife play and eat on the banks of the estuary. Be sure

"Glacier Bay is a time machine. To travel its waters from Icy Strait to Marjorie Glacier is to leap—in just a few hours—from a mature rain forest to the Little Ice Age. It is a dynamic, ice-carved world where rising land seems to expand in relief, eased of its glacial burdens. It is the homeland of the Tlingit peoples. And as a national park, it belongs to all Americans, its citizen-owners, in perpetuity." — Cherry Payne, Retired Park Superintendent at Glacier Bay from 2007-2010 (total years of NPS service: 34)

a pristine fjord flanked with rainforest and lichen-coated hillsides. Otters feast on fresh crab legs while a riot of sea lions bask out on the sunlit shores. Humpback and killer whales breach further out in the thawing estuaries. Glacier fragments break off and crash into the sea (called "calving"). Glacier Bay National Park is an zen slopes and exploded into the water. He pondered the paradox of creation by destruction: "... Nature is ever at work building and pulling down, creating and destroying, keeping everything whirling and flowing, allowing no rest but in rhythmical motion, chasing everything in endless song out of one beautiful form to bring a rain jacket and wear layers. Even in the summer the climate is cool and wet. Take a boat tour of the bay's interior fjords, where dramatic glacial splash-shows rock the walls of **Tarr** and **Johns Hopkins Inlets.** An unforgettable adventure awaits you in this Alaskan cocoon of water and ice.

Est. 1980

43RD
National Park

ALASKA
The Last Frontier

★ **BEST ACTIVITY:**
Sea kayaking is the easiest way to explore. Visiting the bay on a cruise ship is also an amazing experience!

DID YOU KNOW?
An iceberg's color can reveal its makeup; dense bergs are blue, and white ones are filled with trapped air bubbles.

Look for
HUMPBACK WHALES

<GLACIER BAY 18" X 24" Limited Edition Print created in 2012 by Michael Korfhage & Joel Anderson

KATMAI

THE RIVERS RUSH WHITE down the great Alaskan mountain ranges. Shimmering upstream, sockeye salmon wriggle their way towards their nesting grounds. They leap out of the strong currents, progressing up the stair-step waterfalls that impede their way home. The salmon are tired and desperate. Huddled around the slippery river staircase is the salmon's second obstacle: a barricade of hungry brown bears, fur matted and streaming with beads of frigid mountain water. They stand in the gushing current and wait. A mother glances towards shore to eye her two cubs wrestling in the shallows. She turns back to the foamy falls as a silver flicker darts past. Another flops her nose. She bares her yellow fangs and licks her lips. A third bounces from the water and she snatches it by the tail. It writhes and squirms. The mother cranes her neck and flicks the fish to its broad side, securing it in her mouth. Cameras click and tourists ahh. The mother clears

her nostrils and lumbers back to her cubs. Just another summer day at **Brooks Falls** in Katmai National Park.

Away from the fishing frenzy, a quiet stone valley slopes gently up to the base of Katmai's volcano range. The stillness is a cover-up for a once terrifying display of violence. In 1912, the peninsula of Katmai shuddered in torment as the rocky cap burst off the top of **Novarupta Volcano.** Ash and flaming rock spewed out and smothered the valley in 700 feet of debris. Small seaplanes now hum through an atmosphere once choked in ash. Seattle residents, 1500 miles to the south, washed their sidewalks of Novarupta's ashy eruption. The National Geographic Society sent a team of scientists into the volcano range to examine the devastation four years later. What they found was astonishing and deadly. Poisonous gases curled up from the rubble blanket through fumarole vents. Gas mask-donning scientists crept into the cooling basin. The gaseous wraiths

made quite an impression on botanist Robert Griggs, who named the desolate landscape the **Valley of Ten Thousand Smokes**. Griggs brought his findings back to Washington, where Congress created Katmai National Monument in 1918. In 1980, Katmai would be included in the Alaska National Interest Lands Conservation Act and become a National Park. Today, hikers may safely explore the volcanic ravine's 40-square miles, where ebullient rivers have since carved pathways into this valley of destruction.

Air taxis carry thousands of people into Katmai each year. This region is home to some of the best animal watching in the National Park System. Strategically-placed porches and secure campgrounds are available for guests to feel safe while they observe the Park's 2,000 brown bears. Whether you hike, fish in the crystal streams, or simply sit and watch the furry locals fish, you'll never forget a day spent here on the Alaskan coast.

44TH National Park

Est. 1980

ALASKA *The Last Frontier*

BEST TIME OF YEAR: July is the best time to watch bears fishing at Brooks Falls.

DID YOU KNOW? In Katmai, bear cubs will generally stay with their mothers for 2.5 years.

Look for the **SOCKEYE SALMON**

<KATMAI 18" X 24" Limited Edition Print created in 2015 by Aaron Johnson & Joel Anderson

KENAI FJORDS

National Park

EXPLORE THE ALASKAN WILDERNESS

KENAI FJORDS

RIVERS OF BLUE ICE flow through Kenai Fjord's granite mountains and crumble into the sea. Glaciers, leaving cavernous fjords in their wake, hew Alaska's southern coast. Dramatic, slate-colored cliffs swarming with seabirds wall the fjord inlets. The most notable residents are the clown-faced puffins, air-to-water acrobats that collect fish with their brightly colored beaks. The fjords are also home to thousands of seals and sea lions. You can find whole communities splayed out together on the sloping shorelines. Mountain goats, in their creamy white coats, scamper along the dark ridges. Waterfall rivulets dance down the mountain faces. These streams flow from the slowly receding ice of the highland glacier fields. The ice king of Kenai Fjord is the indomitable

Harding Icefield, the largest glacier field in the country. The icefield's vast frozen ocean stands more than a mile high and covers more than 300 square miles with blue-white waves. Thirty-eight glaciers stream down from this single artic reservoir. Each glacier has quietly sculpted Kenai's terrain over time. As the glaciers melt away, their work is revealed in smooth cliffs and new meadows. Hosts of tour boats enter the Park via **Resurrection Bay** from the nearby town of Seward just to gaze at the living artwork of Kenai Fjords. The rich aquatic life and stunning fjord vistas make this National Park a boater's delight.

Visitors who wish to see Kenai Fjords on foot may drive up from Seward and park their cars beside Harding's little toe, **Exit Glacier**, in the northeast corner

of the Park. Stretch your legs on a paved trail up to the overlook of this small but impressive icefield extremity. Willing hikers may climb further up into conifer forests and frozen wastelands on the arduous yet rewarding **Harding Icefield Trail**. The Park also features a myriad of inlets and islands to explore by kayak. A 9-hour ferry ride will bring you to the pristine **Northwestern Lagoon**, a frosty coastal paradise for the adroit kayaker. Rustic campsites dot the shore where weary paddlers spend their evenings beneath crisp Alaskan starlight. Slightly closer to civilization is **Aialik Bay,** an accessible inlet riddled with forested coves, perfect for a day of adventure. The frozen earth is alive at Kenai Fjords National Park. Grab a paddle and enjoy this watery world of Alaskan splendor.

Est. 1980

45TH
National Park

ALASKA
The Last Frontier

BEST VIEW:
The Harding Icefield is the Park's dominant feature and one of the major reasons for the creation of the Park.

BEST ACTIVITY:
Kayaking is a great way to see the wonders of Kenai Fjords.

Look for ORCAS

<KENAI FJORDS 18" X 24" Limited Edition Print created in 2015 by Aaron Johnson & Joel Anderson

KOBUK VALLEY
NATIONAL PARK · ALASKA

KOBUK VALLEY

ABSOLUTE, DESOLATE wilderness awaits the brave at Kobuk Valley National Park. This is a backpackers' toughest challenge, to explore the merciless and unpredictable landscape of northwestern Alaska. There are no roads here. There are no visitor centers here. You may enter the Park only by plane or boat. You must carry in everything you need to survive on the endless tundra. It is the least visited National Park in America, averaging just about 3,000 visitors per year. And with good reason. Neighboring Gates of the Arctic National Park, Kobuk Valley lies completely above the Arctic Circle. It is a land of extremes: winter temperatures steadily stay below freezing and the chilling arctic winds make it feel even colder. Summer is the best time to visit but be prepared for the nefarious swarms of mosquitoes.

You may be wondering, *Why on earth did we turn this place into a National Park?* Though barren and isolated, this region is an ancestral home to one of Alaska's most majestic creatures, the caribou, and the native people that have lived off these herds for nearly 10,000 years. And for travelers seeking an escape from developed America, this is about as far away as you can get.

Kobuk Valley lies between two mountain ranges: the **Baird Mountains** to the north, and the **Waring Mountains** to the south. The wide, placid **Kobuk River** flows gently across the valley floor. This is the region's lifeline, the heart of the region's wildlife activity. The most prolific residents of Kobuk Valley are the wooly caribou. Numbering more than half a million, the vast herds of caribou cross the Kobuk River twice each year, migrating to and from their breeding grounds. Within the Park's 2 million acres reside about a dozen small Eskimo communities. With time-honored tradition and respect, the natives still hunt the caribou during the caribou's migration period. The Eskimos rely on the meat to feed their families and the skins to keep warm throughout the harsh winters. Park guests may witness the mass exodus of the caribou at a river bend called **Onion Portage,** a ford where the herds have crossed for millennia.

To the south of the Kobuk River, at the foot of the Waring Mountains, is **Great Kobuk Sand Dunes.** Sometimes referred to as "the Sahara of the Arctic", this rippling desert stretches out for over 25 square miles. The dunes are a mountainous collection of ancient dust, by-product of glacial grinding from the last Ice Age. The caribou herds must cross this gusty desert twice each year. Incessant wind, like an Alaskan Etch-a-Sketch, quickly erases all evidence of the caribou's mass-migration. Park visitors can experience the lonely solitude of the dunes on a round-trip 4-hour hike as part of their weeklong rafting trek across the Park. The 80 miles of river will carry you from the eastern town of Ambler to Kiana in the west, with plenty of hiking opportunities along the way. A trip like this will require extensive planning, but few wilderness encounters can match the solitary communion with nature found at Kobuk Valley National Park.

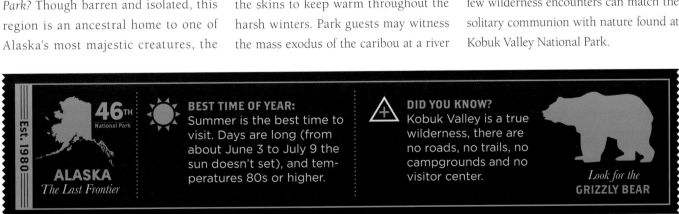

Est. 1980

46TH National Park

ALASKA *The Last Frontier*

BEST TIME OF YEAR: Summer is the best time to visit. Days are long (from about June 3 to July 9 the sun doesn't set), and temperatures 80s or higher.

DID YOU KNOW? Kobuk Valley is a true wilderness, there are no roads, no trails, no campgrounds and no visitor center.

Look for the **GRIZZLY BEAR**

<KOBUK VALLEY 18" X 24" Limited Edition Print created in 2015 by Joel Anderson

National Parks Timeline · · · · · · · · · · · · 1900 · · · · · · · · · · · · 1950 · · · · · · · · · · · · 2000 · · · · · · · **129**

1980

LAKE CLARK
NATIONAL PARK

SEE ALASKAN WILDLIFE AT CHINITNA BAY

LAKE CLARK

FOUR MILLION ACRES of the best Alaskan countryside await you at Lake Clark National Park. Bush pilots from Anchorage fly visitors into the Park via seaplanes. These small aircraft provide their passengers with an awe-inspiring aerial view of Lake Clark's natural glory. Cerulean lakes, glacier-flooded mountain passes, thick coastal rainforest, fish-rich rivers, and wind-swept tundra all play their part in the natural symphony that is Lake Clark. Three distinct mountain chains, peppered with secluded lakes and streams, unite within Park boundaries. Two active volcanoes, **Iliamna** and **Redoubt**, regularly vent reminders of their presence. Fishermen from all over the world cast their lines into Lake Clark's streams each summer. This Park is an anglers' paradise; rainbow trout, arctic grayling, northern pike, and five unique types of salmon can all be caught within Lake Clark. The native Dena'ina Athabascan people have worked, played, lived, and died here for thousands of years. Their name for this region is Qizhjeh Vena, "a place where people gathered." Protected by the National Park Service, the Athabascan way of life continues to this day. Park visitors too can now gather together to enjoy this serene slice of Alaskan coastland.

A log cabin on the shore of **Twin Lakes** stands as a testament to Alaska's hardy, self-reliant residents. Richard L. Proenneke, a nature writer and master craftsman, built his lakeside cottage

by hand in the 1960s. For the next 3 decades he lived alone in this cabin, exploring, filming, and writing about Lake Clark's unrefined grandeur. He was a man who did everything by hand, living solely off the land and streams with simple tools. In his journals, collected in Sam Keith's book *One Man's Wilderness: An Alaskan Odyssey*, Proenneke wrote: "I enjoy working for my heat. I don't just press a button or twist a thermostat dial. I use the big crosscut saw and the axe, and while I'm getting my heat supply I'm working up an appetite that makes simple food just as appealing as anything a French chef could create." This wry, do-it-yourself attitude, paired with a deep admiration for nature's power,

allowed Proenneke to preach the message of wilderness conservation to millions of readers. He is remembered to this day by the National Park Service as a champion steward of Alaska's natural resources. Park visitors today can visit his log cabin and read his joyful, down-to-earth recollections of daily life in remote Alaskan backcountry.

In a Park so rich in outdoor activities, opportunities abound for an intimate connection with Lake Clark's wilderness. Try your hand at salmon fishing on the **Tlikakila River,** or take a wild whitewater-rafting trip down the **Chilikadrotna.** A more peaceful boating tour sails on the turquoise waters of **Lake Clark** itself, where steep mountain slopes hem you in from both shores. Hire a guide and trek into the hilly Alaskan outback via **Telaquana Trail,** a path used by the Athabascan people for centuries. The grand wilderness of southwestern Alaska lies wide open before you at Lake Clark National Park. Enter in and enjoy the many charms of this arctic utopia.

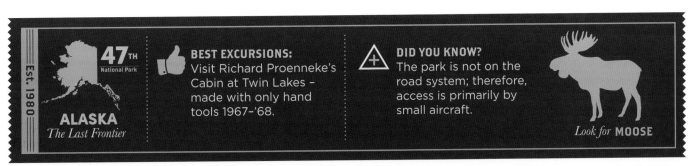

Est. 1980

47TH National Park

ALASKA *The Last Frontier*

BEST EXCURSIONS: Visit Richard Proenneke's Cabin at Twin Lakes – made with only hand tools 1967–'68.

DID YOU KNOW? The park is not on the road system; therefore, access is primarily by small aircraft.

Look for **MOOSE**

<LAKE CLARK 18" X 24" Limited Edition Print created in 2015 by Michael Korfhage & Joel Anderson

WRANGELL-ST. ELIAS
NATIONAL PARK & PRESERVE

LARGEST NATIONAL PARK IN THE UNITED STATES

WRANGELL-ST. ELIAS

THE ALASKAN COLOSSUS

of Wrangell-St. Elias National Park is as big as it gets. Looming over the Canadian Yukon border in southeastern Alaska, the sweeping 13 million acres of Wrangell-St. Elias has it all. Sawtooth peaks claw at the infinite sky. Deep chasms puncture fields of blue ice. Gluttonous glaciers swallow up entire mountain ranges in frozen excess. Foaming streams and alpine lakes sparkle in the summer sun. Boreal forests of spruce, aspen, and poplar furnish the leafy foothills. Bison, moose, grizzlies, Dall sheep, gray wolves, bald eagles, and caribou all thrive in this virgin wilderness, broadly untouched and unexplored by mankind. It is America's largest National Park, six times the size of Yellowstone. And, unlike many of its Alaskan counterparts, Wrangell-St. Elias is accessible by car. Two gravel roads bring Park visitors into the midst of incomprehensible majesty. They also quietly remind guests of the region's rich history in copper and gold mining. Today, the **Nabesna** and **McCarthy Roads** run past the remains of desolate mining villages and into a vast undisturbed kingdom of water, tree, and stone.

Three monstrous mountain ranges form the backbone of this National Park. The glacier-gutted **Wrangell Mountains** lie to the north, the **Chugach range** to the south, and the **St. Elias range** to the east. Nine of the 16 tallest peaks in America stand in these three lustrous mountain ranges. North America's second largest is the Park's southeastern peak Mount St. Elias. Russian explorers were some of the first non-natives to enter Wrangell-St. Elias, arriving in the early 1700s. Hired by the Russian Czar, Danish adventurer Vitus Bering led a fleet of Russian ships across the channel from Siberia to Alaska (the route is now known as the Bering Strait). On the feast day of St. Elias, Bering and his men laid their eyes on a magnificent snow-capped pinnacle tumbling down into **Icy Bay.** Overwhelmed by the peak's sheer magnitude, Bering named the mountain "St. Elias" in honor of the day it was discovered.

A century later, Russian governor and naval officer Baron Ferdinand Petrovich von Wrangel governed the Russian colonies in Alaska. Life was never easy for Wrangel as he battled three native tribes to maintain control of the **Copper River region**, an area rich in fish, furs, and minerals. The tenacious Baron Wrangel kept the colonies intact until 1867, when Russia sold their Alaskan territory to America once and for all. Wrangel's legacy of courage would be forever remembered by his American successors. The Park's primary mountain range, along with several landmarks along the coast, are named after the fearless Russian governor.

There is no better way to experience the sweeping icy expanse of Wrangell-St. Elias than on a **flightseeing tour.** Small bush planes carry passengers over some of the most exquisite landscape on Earth, sights Vitus Bering or Baron Wrangel could only dream of. Like other Alaskan Parks, WSE also hosts some of the finest fishing spots on the continent. Copper River is a premier destination for anglers looking to land the big one. Boundless natural beauty occupies the nation's largest National Park. Come and explore this indescribable treasure, now part of our American heritage forever.

Est. 1980

48TH National Park

ALASKA
The Last Frontier

BEST TIME OF YEAR:
May is prime time for mountaineering excursions.

DID YOU KNOW?
Parts of the Park are so remote and unexplored that mountains, glaciers, and passes remain unnamed.

Look for **MOUNTAIN GOATS**

<WRANGELL-ST. ELIAS 18" X 24" Limited Edition Print created in 2015 by Michael Korfhage & Joel Anderson

LEXINGTON ARCH

GREAT BASIN
NATIONAL PARK

GREAT BASIN

WAVES OF PARCHED sagebrush sigh in the high desert wind of central Nevada. Painted in the driest of watercolors, this landscape persists to exist in arid beauty. A lonely summit, worn ragged by the elements, looms over the tumbling basin valley. **Mount Wheeler** is a 13,000-foot sentinel for this barren wilderness, centerpiece to Great Basin National Park. The Park represents a much larger Great Basin region of the American West, a vast system of "bowls" scooped into the states of Nevada, Utah, Idaho, Oregon, and California. These valleys are inland water traps, collecting scant rainfall and mountain streams in mudflats and salted lakes while providing no outlet to the ocean. The result is a bone dry, gusty environment where only the toughest, most adjusted wildlife survives. Gnarled, weathered roots of the world's oldest trees anchor themselves against the ruthless gales. Great Basin's bristlecone pines are

natural phenomena, a small grove of pine-trees older than King David that cling to the rugged highlands of Mount Wheeler. Shaped and polished by the wind, these pines symbolize Great Basin's wondrously rugged character where life continues to defy its harsh environment.

Great Basin National Park was once home to an industrious gold-miner-turned-rancher named Absalom Lehman. A mining failure in California but a smashing success in Australia, Lehman knew from firsthand experience how to thrive in difficult circumstances. After his wife and daughter passed away in Australia in the 1880s, Lehman moved to Nevada where he lived his first summer "under a pine tree with Indians for neighbors." He quickly adjusted to his new surroundings, remarried, and established a ranch in the Park's northeastern corner. Friends, relatives, and newcomers all flocked to Lehman's ranch and the

homestead became a bustling village and orchard. While out on a jaunt one day, Lehman stumbled upon a small series of caves beneath the foothills of Mount Wheeler. He soon began guiding lantern tours into **Lehman Caves**. Park visitors can still enter this limestone sanctuary beneath the desert today.

Encounter the stark determination that defines this National Park atop Mount Wheeler. Ascend the exposed summit via **Wheeler Peak Trail**, where winded climbers are rewarded with an incredible panoramic view of the Basin. **The Bristlecone Forest Loop** lies just below the summit and invites guests to ponder their own finite existence in the midst of such ancient life. Plunge into the subterranean world of Lehman Caves on the **Grand Palace Tour**, where dangling chandeliers of stone await you. Through struggle rises brilliance on the wastelands of Great Basin National Park.

49TH National Park

Est. 1986

NEVADA
The Silver State

BEST DRIVE:
The 12-mile Wheeler Peak Scenic Drive for unparalleled views of the mountains and surrounding valleys.

DID YOU KNOW?
The park is home to Lexington Arch, one of the largest limestone arches in the western United States.

Look for the **RED-TAILED HAWK**

<GREAT BASIN 18" X 24" Limited Edition Print created in 2015 by Michael Korfhage & Joel Anderson

DRY TORTUGAS

WHITE SEAPLANES bob gently on the shores of a 19th century fortress. Seventy miles southwest of Key West, a ruddy stronghold lined with arches and cannon punctuates the Gulf's crystal teal waters. Though the U.S. Navy no longer utilizes the fortress at Dry Tortugas National Park, the historical significance of **Fort Jefferson** makes this tropical site indispensable. Less than 500 feet away from this citadel of warfare is a natural bird sanctuary. **Bush Key** swarms with black-capped sooty terns and other sea-birds, finding respite and a meal on the shores of this desert island. Park visitors may bird-watch from the fort's ramparts, or take a stroll along the **seawall** and moat where stingray, starfish, and gray snapper loiter in the still waters. Once an ammunition-heavy stronghold, the island fortress and archipelago at Dry Tortugas National Park now exist as an aquatic playground.

Spanish explorer Juan Ponce de León supposedly moored on these islands in the early 1500s. He and his men feasted on the region's prolific turtle population, inspiring a full-bellied León to name the keys "Las Tortugas." Spanish ships made these islands a regular stop on their route to the Americas, producing a spike in piracy and shipwrecks along the isles' hidden reefs. Divers today can explore the 260-foot remains of a Norwegian sailboat called *Avanti* or "The Windjammer" just south of **Loggerhead Key.** As the turtle population waned and the United States rose to power, Las Tortugas

became more than just an idyllic spot for turtle soup. American military strategists chose the island's **Garden Key** as a premier location for a coastal fortress.

Dry Tortugas National Park now protects the stout brick hexagon of Fort Jefferson. Standing at 45 feet tall with a circumference of nearly half a mile, this imposing bulwark guarded America's trade ships from pirates in the Gulf of Mexico through the latter half of the 1800s. During the Civil War, Union forces also used the isolated location of this Florida Key as a prison for deserters. One famous inmate was Dr. Samuel Mudd, who had bandaged and splinted the leg of John Wilkes Booth immediately after Booth had assassinated President Lincoln at Ford's Theater. As a prison, Fort Jefferson was difficult to maintain as no fresh

water was available on the island and tropical storms wreaked havoc on the fort's exterior. The archipelago's utter lack of freshwater earned it the unfavorable description "dry". President Franklin D. Roosevelt designated Dry Tortugas as a National Monument to protect the birds and sealife in 1935. The islands would become a National Park in 1992.

Strap on some flippers and snorkel in the shallows around Garden Key, where coral reef and forests of sea grass await your inspection. Venture further out on a SCUBA tour into **Sherwood Forest,** a lively community of coral, crustaceans, turtles, and fish of many hues. Kayaking opportunities also abound in the glittery waters of the Gulf. Experience the history and natural splendor of this National Park in the sunny Florida Keys.

50TH National Park

Est. 1992

FLORIDA
The Sunshine State

BEST TIME OF YEAR:
Year-round. Temps range from the mid-80s to the low 50s– in April and May, visitation is at its peak.

DID YOU KNOW?
Access is by boat or seaplane. Boat passage from Key West takes about three hours; 45 minutes by air.

Look for **SEA TURTLES**

<DRY TORTUGAS 18" X 24" Limited Edition Print created in 2015 by Michael Korfhage & Joel Anderson

SEE POLA ISLAND

✳ NATIONAL PARK OF ❯
AMERICAN SAMOA

AMERICAN SAMOA

AN ISOLATED diamond in the South Pacific, American Samoa is one of the most picturesque and hardest to reach Parks in the system. The five volcanic islands are nothing more than tiny dots on a map, some 2,600 miles southwest of Hawai'i. Its remote location and tradition-focused inhabitants preserve the island's tropical and laid-back culture. Though convenience isn't a theme here, unadulterated natural beauty certainly is. These islands are the only U.S. Park (or property of any kind) below the equator, and they host five distinct rainforest ecosystems: lowland, montane, coast, ridge, and cloud. The Samoan fruit bat and a variety of tropical birds flit through the trees. Out in the water, coral reefs line the coast, concentrated especially around the **island of Ofu.** These reefs are home to over 950 species of fish.

As distinct as the islands themselves, the bilingual Samoan people are both proud and conscientious of their land. They have partnered up with the National Park Service to protect many of Samoa's rainforests, coral reefs, and beaches. Laws were passed to prevent non-Samoan investors from exploiting the land to build resorts and timeshares. Though there are a few hotels on the main island of **Tutuila,** the National Park of American Samoa provides travelers with a unique lodging experience that cannot be found anywhere else: the **Homestay Program.** For a modest fee, guests can live, eat, and play alongside a Samoan family while learning about the rich cultural history of the native people. Sort of like a bed-and-breakfast, island family style. The host families set the cost of accommodations and activities, regulated by the National

Park. This is a highly recommended experience for curious travelers comfortable with stepping out of their comfort zones.

Though much of the protected region is still inaccessible, there are a few trails from which to explore American Samoa's volcanic coastline. North of the primary city of Pago Pago is the trailhead to scenic **Mount 'Alava.** Resting in nearby Vai'ava Strait, the beloved **Pola Island** receives lots of photographic attention from hikers. Snorkeling is another way to experience the island's abundance. Though unpopulated and difficult to reach, the island of Ofu has some of the most beautiful (and secluded) reefs and beaches in the Park. **Si'u Point from Ta'u Island** dazzles visitors with emerald sea cliffs towering over the brilliant blue South Pacific.

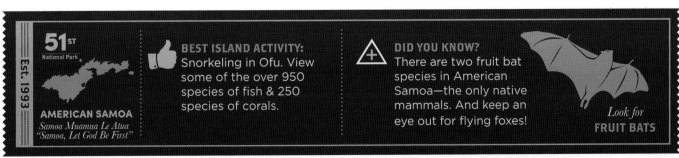

51ST National Park

Est. 1993

AMERICAN SAMOA
Samoa Muamua Le Atua
"Samoa, Let God Be First"

👍 **BEST ISLAND ACTIVITY:** Snorkeling in Ofu. View some of the over 950 species of fish & 250 species of corals.

⚠ **DID YOU KNOW?** There are two fruit bat species in American Samoa—the only native mammals. And keep an eye out for flying foxes!

Look for **FRUIT BATS**

<AMERICAN SAMOA 18" X 24" Limited Edition Print created in 2015 by Michael Korfhage & Joel Anderson

WALK AMONG THE GIANTS

ARIZONA

SAGUARO
NATIONAL PARK
▲▼▲▼▲▼ ARIZONA ▼▲▼▲▼▲

SAGUARO

THE ROYAL KINGS of all cacti, the saguaro reign over the Sonoran Desert in southern Arizona. This cactus species is synonymous with the American Southwest and a seemingly ever-present prop in Western films. Flanking the eastern and western sprawl of Tucson's suburbs, Saguaro National Park protects over 1.5 million of these spiked monarchs. They are benevolent as they are regal: the sweeping arms of the saguaro cactus protect many of the region's vulnerable wildlife from the harsh desert climate. Woodpeckers, elf owls, warblers, and Harris hawks all build their nests on or inside the hollow cacti.

Students and faculty at the University of Arizona first showed interest in protecting their needled neighbors back in 1920. Tucson was then a quiet frontier town, and ranchers allowed their cattle to rummage through the fragile cacti forests just 15 miles away. Tourists removed young saguaro plants as souvenirs, while locals uprooted the saguaros for their own home landscaping purposes. Teenagers carved their names into the waxy trunks. Grazing cows stamped the soil solid, preventing the diminutive saguaro seeds from germinating. Something needed to be

to take shape. CCC teams built scenic roads in the 1930s. President Kennedy added 25 more square miles of dense saguaro forest from the Tucson Mountains in 1961. Finally, in 1994, Congress declared Saguaro a National Park.

"The tall Saguaro cactus may be one of the most iconic symbols of the West. Yet, it has limited range and is only found in key ecosystem niches in Arizona and northern Mexico. It is really the symbol of the Sonoran Desert, the majority of which lies in Mexico. In places in this park are found the best and largest specimens living within an area that ranges from lush desert to high islands in the sky peaks. The park bookends the East and West sections of the Tucson metropolitan area offering not only a place to hike and escape to but a reminder of a rich desert heritage that needs constant protection."
— Robert Arnberger, Superintendent of Saguaro from 1983-1987 (total years of NPS service: 34)

The saguaro's ruby-red fruit feed nocturnal foragers such as the pig-like javelina, fox, and desert tortoise. Each spring, the saguaro plants are adorned with brightly colored blossoms that bloom in the setting sun, to the delight of timely Park visitors. These cacti are desert Goliaths, growing up to 50 feet tall and weighing up to 16,000 pounds. Their waxy skin and spongy flesh take advantage of the rare Arizona rainstorms, absorbing and storing 200 gallons of water inside their rigid frames. When the saguaro flourish, the wilderness rejoices. The only threat to this cacti kingdom is humanity.

done before this desert forest was irreparably damaged. University of Arizona's president Homer L. Shantz, a botanist, championed the cause, envisioning an outdoor laboratory for students in the university's own backyard. With the help of Tucson newspaperman Frank Hitchcock, Shantz drew national recognition to the plight of the cacti. Hitchcock's political connections in Washington paid dividends in 1933 when Herbert Hoover invoked the Antiquities Act to set aside Saguaro as a National Monument. In the care of the U.S. Forest Service, the framework for a National Park continued

Enter the realm of desert splendor on the **Cactus Forest Drive** in the eastern **Rincon Mountain district**. You can cool off from the desert heat on a hike up into the Rincon Mountain range via **Tanque Verde Trail**, where groves of ponderosa pine and Douglas fir shelter black bear and white-tailed deer. Take a family stroll along the **Desert Discovery Trail** in the Park's western **Tucson Mountain district**. Here you can learn all about the unique survival skills of the plant and wildlife in this arid corner of the country. The outstretched arms of the Saguaro welcome you in at Saguaro National Park.

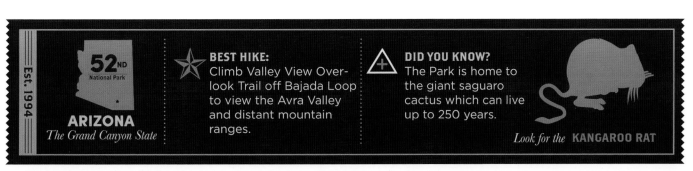

Est. 1994

52ND National Park

ARIZONA
The Grand Canyon State

BEST HIKE:
Climb Valley View Overlook Trail off Bajada Loop to view the Avra Valley and distant mountain ranges.

DID YOU KNOW?
The Park is home to the giant saguaro cactus which can live up to 250 years.

Look for the **KANGAROO RAT**

<SAGUARO 18" X 24" Limited Edition Print created in 2014 by Michael Korfhage & Joel Anderson

National Parks Timeline · 1900 · · · · · · · · · · · · · · · 1950 · · · · · · · · · · · · · · · 2000 · · · · · · · »141→

1994

MYSTERIOUS SAILING STONES

DEATH VALLEY

NATIONAL PARK ⊟ CALIFORNIA

DEATH VALLEY

BLEACHED BOULDERS lie still on the flatlands, baking beneath a torrid sun. The land is barren. The empty lake basin looks like a monotone mosaic, countless dirt patches held together by a raw web of cracks. Across this vast mesa race the immobile rocks, their pathways marked by the dusty trails they've left in their wake. They are the **Sailing Stones** of Death Valley National Park. Though no one knows for sure, scientists believe these stones travel by atypical rainstorms or by strong winter winds slowly pushing the stones across the frozen flats. But rain seems nonexistent here. Averaging right around 2 inches of rainfall per year, Death Valley is without a doubt one of the driest regions in America. Any moisture is a gift for this parched landscape and the sun seems to blaze hotter here than anywhere else. Average highs in August are 115 degrees Fahrenheit. You can descend into the lowest point on the continent at **Badwater Basin**, 282 feet below sea level. Death Valley is dry, deep, and vast: it is

the largest National Park south of Alaska, 3.4 million acres of chapped mudflats and desolate mountain ranges. And yet, this forsaken wilderness has learned to blossom with very little. The valley needs only a few raindrops in the cooler winter months to clothe the naked earth in spring wildflowers, some of the most spectacular you will see anywhere. The night skies glisten all the brighter when you're standing on the valley floor cloaked in soft white starlight. Despite the harsh environment, Death Valley National Park welcomes over a million guests each year who discover enchantment in the heat.

Imagine getting lost in a place like this. A team of Midwestern '49ers, drawn to California by rumors of gold, hitched together 100 wagons and wandered into this remote region on their way to the coast. Two months later, they were still in Death Valley, unable to find a way out. The Panamint and Amargosa mountain ranges had the travelers completely hemmed in. The men were haunted by

"hunger and thirst and an awful silence." Having to abandon their wagons and eat their own oxen, the parched pilgrims finally escaped the basin on foot via **Emigrant Pass,** wishing good-bye and good riddance to this "Death Valley". Other visitors to the valley left far more fortunate. Before signing on as the National Park Service's first director, Stephen Mather made millions of dollars raking up borax from the valley floor. Mather named his company 20 Mule Team Borax after the long mule trains that tramped across Death Valley, hauling out 10 tons of borax each time.

Visit Furnace Creek to learn about the Park's rich mineral history and ascend one of the valley's most scenic vistas at sun-drenched **Zabriskie Point.** Enter the off-road void at the **Racetrack,** where a four-wheeler or high clearance vehicle grants you access into a waterless sea skimmed by Sailing Stones. Arid mystery and promising potential simmer down here in the desert valley.

53RD National Park
Est. 1994
CALIFORNIA *The Golden State*

BEST TIME OF YEAR: Fall through early spring while temps are moderate.

DID YOU KNOW? The salt pan on the floor of Death Valley covers more than 200 sq. miles. It is 40 miles long and more than 5 miles wide.

Look for the **DESERT IGUANA**

<DEATH VALLEY 18" X 24" Limited Edition Print created in 2013 by Michael Korfhage & Joel Anderson

JOSHUA TREE

NATIONAL PARK ◆ CALIFORNIA

JOSHUA TREE

IN SOUTHERN California, two deserts converge to form a strange and wonderful landscape. The "high" Mojave Desert tumbles down into the "low" Colorado, blending each ecosystem's plants and wildlife. The result is a lustrous desert ecosystem rich with smooth rocks, cacti and yucca plants, and an endlessly adaptable population of birds, reptiles, and mammals. Joshua Tree National Park is named after it's most iconic resident, the Joshua Tree. This yucca plant, with its quirky limbs, looks like a Dr. Seuss illustration come to life. The Joshua Trees thrive in the Mojave region of the Park where they reminded early Mormon settlers of the Biblical hero Joshua as he lead the Israelites into the Promised Land with outstretched arms. Joshua Tree now welcomes over a million visitors each year: rock climbers, painters, hikers, and stargazers all find a unique blend of solace and adventure here in the arid wilderness.

Originally home to violent cattle rustlers, ranchers, and gold miners, Joshua Tree captured the imagination of a well-to-do Southern woman from Mississippi named Minerva Hoyt. Growing up in high society, Hoyt married a doctor and moved to Pasadena in the early 1900s. There she involved herself in a number of civic clubs and nature groups, among them a society to protect the austere beauty of California's deserts. As a gardener in Southern California, Hoyt showed particular interest in Joshua Tree's 800 species of plants and flowers that thrived in the arid basins. She respected their ability to flourish when the odds were permanently against them. This lesson took on new meaning when she lost both her husband and her infant son. Thousands of miles from her Southern roots, she turned to the desert for solace. Joshua Tree too was in anguish as hundreds of motorists cruised through the valley, uprooting cacti for their homes

and burning the "grotesque" Joshua Trees for sport. Minerva Hoyt cried out for the suffering forests. She awoke to what would be her life-long calling, and with indomitable resolve organized world-wide botanical events. She introduced Southern California's distinct plant life to nature-lovers in New York, Boston, and London. Friends began calling her "the apostle of the cacti." Her impassioned articles and reports soon reached Washington, where Hoyt had the opportunity to speak directly with Franklin D. Roosevelt. Hoyt's zeal won him over, and Roosevelt commissioned Joshua Tree National Monument in 1936. President Bill Clinton added 200,000 protected acres and elevated the monument to a full-fledged National Park in 1994.

The San Andreas Fault, along with hundreds of other fault lines, stripe Joshua Tree National Park. Visitors can climb atop piles of raw boulders tumbled together by earthquakes and erosion at **Jumbo Rocks,** where the unforgettable **Skull Rock** and **Giant Marbles** bask out in the sunshine. Many of the pocketed monoliths so beloved by the Park's rock climbers are products of seismic agitation as well. Grab a slab on one of the Park's 400 formations and test your skills in this premier climbing destination. Go greet a friendly congregation of Joshua Trees in **Hidden Valley,** where a narrow trail leads you into a quarry of spartan desert splendor.

Est. 1994

54TH
National Park

CALIFORNIA
The Golden State

BEST VIEW:
Stargazing: city dwellers are astounded when they get their first glimpse of the night sky in its natural state.

DID YOU KNOW?
The famous San Andreas Fault bounds the south side of the Park and can be observed from Keys View.

Look for **JACK RABBITS**

<**JOSHUA TREE** 18" X 24" Limited Edition Print created in 2012 by Michael Korfhage & Joel Anderson

National Parks Timeline ·

1900   1950   2000

145

1994

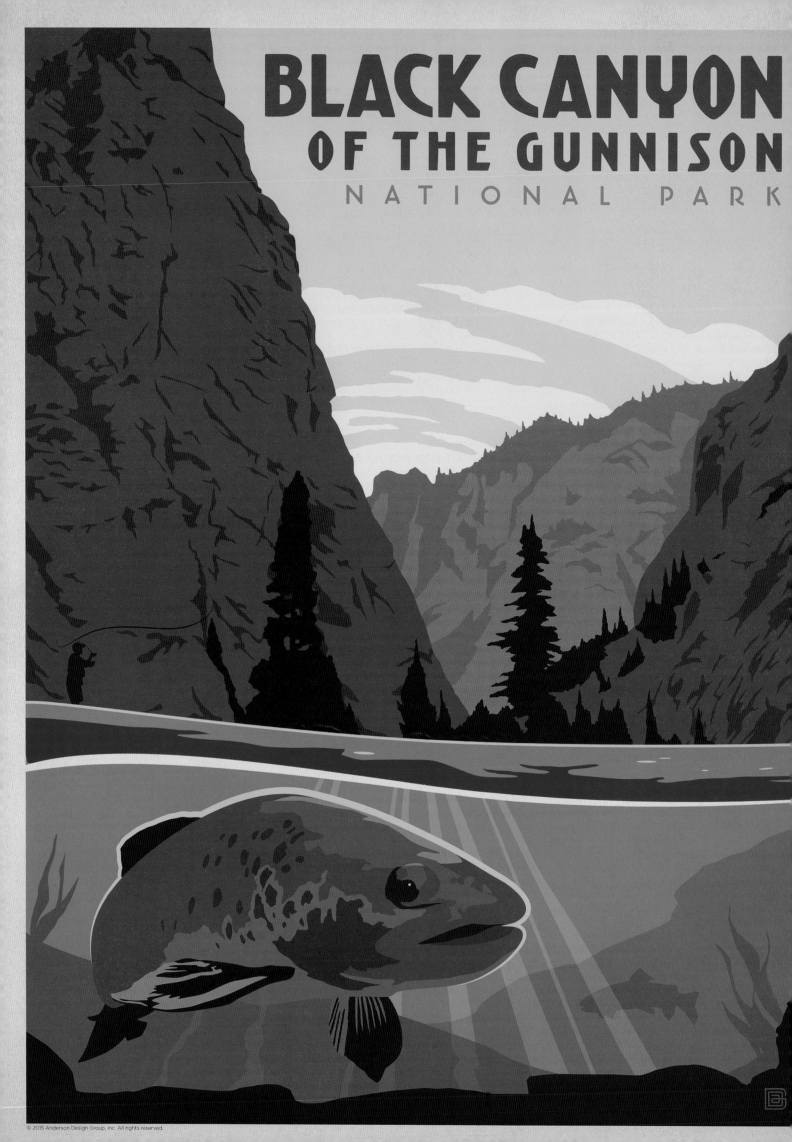

BLACK CANYON OF THE GUNNISON

YOU STEP INTO THE darkest of canyons, the sun blacked out by the narrow granite cliffs. The charcoal stone looks even darker in the cold shadows. The rapids' deafening sound pounds into your skull and echoes off the walls. Your descent was treacherous to say the least; pebbles and scree had you sliding down the steep, 2,000-foot slope to the riverbank. You and one other person, an electrician and photographer named William F. Torrence, are convinced that an irrigation tunnel can be drilled into this gloomy canyon, providing desperately needed water to the nearby Uncompahgre Valley. Hundreds of people are pinning their hopes of survival in the valley on your success. As a seasoned irrigation engineer and adventurer, you are willing to risk life and limb to divert water out of this hellish ravine. Having studied the Gunnison River for months, you've noted the rapids' steady descent of 95

feet per mile. The water seethes in confined fury. You've learned from the fatal journeys of previous Gunnison River runners that this is no simple task. You've packed lightly. Instead of a boat, you and Torrence climb aboard an air mattress. Your supplies, notebooks, and Torrence's camera equipment are stowed in rubber

---

> **"Eventually, all things merge into one, and a river runs through it."**
> *-Norman Maclean*

---

bags. With a hefty kick, you push off the bank and enter the wildest ride of your life on the bone-chilling rapids through the Black Canyon of the Gunnison....

Abraham Lincoln Fellows and William F. Torrence were the first people in history to run the entirety of the Black Canyon, traveling a sopping 33 miles

in 9 days. The men hiked, bouldered, swam, and rafted down the river on an air mattress. Though an equally miserable and hair-raising experience, their journey proved that an irrigation tunnel could be built. A 6 mile, 11 by 12-foot diversion tunnel was completed in 1909 thanks to the fearless efforts of these two men. The Gunnison River is now tamer than ever due to 3 dams built upstream from the National Park. And yet the rapids are still formidable, challenging only the most experienced rafters and kayakers to navigate their frothy fury.

For those who prefer to stay dry, Black Canyon of the Gunnison National Park offers plenty of opportunities to hike or drive along the canyon's north and south rims. The southern rim is more popular (and accessible) for tourists, and you will find plenty of pull-offs along the **South Rim Road** to stretch your legs and stare down into the chasm, 2,250 feet deep. **Painted Wall View** is one favorite stop as the dark granite wall face here is streaked with wispy strips of pink and white crystal. An 80-mile drive will bring you to the far less visited northern rim. Explore the cliff forests along **North Vista Trail** for a concealed communion with Colorado wilderness. There are even a few trails into the canyon itself, though they are incredibly strenuous. Apply for a permit to experience the heart-pounding descent like Fellows and Torrence from the **Red Rock Canyon Route** into the depths of the Black Canyon.

Est. 1999

55TH National Park

COLORADO *Centennial State*

BEST TIME OF YEAR: Winter is great for backcountry camping, cross-country skiing, and snowshoeing. Summer is best for hiking.

DID YOU KNOW? The Painted Wall is the highest cliff in Colorado. At 2,250 feet tall, it is 1,000 feet taller than the Empire State Building!

Look for ELK

<BLACK CANYON OF THE GUNNISON 18" X 24" Limited Edition Print created in 2015 by Michael Korfhage & Joel Anderson

SEE BRANDYWINE FALLS

Cuyahoga Valley

NATIONAL PARK ★ OHIO

CUYAHOGA VALLEY

A SHIMMERING RIVER weaves through the Cuyahoga Valley in northeastern Ohio. Verdant forest, bubbling waterfalls, mossy boulders, and a wide array of wildlife furnish the valley in splendor. Most Americans probably don't realize there's a National Park just outside Cleveland, but locals flock to this hidden gem of natural beauty. Gently winding out of Lake Erie, the Cuyahoga (Iroquois for "crooked") River was once a primary trade route for ships heading towards the Gulf Coast via the Ohio & Erie Canal. Engineers constructed a 101-mile long **Towpath Trail** for donkeys and horses to tow ships through the canal's various locks. The north to south riverside pathway is now a go-to attraction for Park visitors seeking a quiet stroll or bike ride.

Though serene today, Cuyahoga Valley National Park is a living reminder that unbridled production has consequences. Throughout the latter half of the 1800s, Cleveland's shipping industry boomed, choking the river with boat traffic and sewage. Wildlife soon fled from the toxic waters oozing with chemicals and waste. Several times the Cuyahoga even caught fire, earning it the ominous nickname "the river that burned." In 1969, after a scathing article by Time Magazine about Cuyahoga's pollution, local residents and environmentalists responded in what would be one of the most dramatic environmental turnarounds in American history.

Washington passed clean water laws, and Congress set Cuyahoga Valley aside as a National Recreation Area in 1974. Mass cleanup projects began all across the valley, and Ohioans worked tirelessly to bring the land back to life. Their rehabilitation efforts paid off: Cuyahoga Valley became a National Park in 2000 and a wide variety of plants and animals now occupy the landscape once more. River otters, tundra swans, turtles, white-tailed deer, blue herons, even bald eagles all dwell along the crooked river. As a Park, Cuyahoga Valley represents Americans at our worst and our best, failure and redemption. It is a landscape rescued from America, for America.

Not only is Cuyahoga Valley National Park veined by roadway and river but by rail as well. Park visitors can gaze out over Ohio's rolling hills and floodplain on board the **Cuyahoga Valley Scenic Railroad.** This charmingly vintage railway courses through the entire Park, picking up and dropping off guests at various stations along the way. Hiking is also a beloved pastime here in a Park with over 70 waterfalls. **Brandywine Falls** tops them all, a 60-foot display of foaming waterworks that draws a large crowd each year. The **Ledges Trail** is another prime hiking destination. It's hard to imagine you're still in suburban Ohio as you wander past mossy sandstone through a deciduous forest chiming with songbirds. Find refreshment and renewal in Cuyahoga Valley, where a river of life flows once more.

Est. 2000

56TH
National Park

OHIO
The Buckeye State

BEST VIEW:
Brandywine Falls attracts the most tourists – the less crowded Blue Hen Falls is also beautiful and secluded deep in the forest.

DID YOU KNOW?
This park is in northeastern Ohio, between the sprawling cities of Cleveland and Akron.

Look for the
GREAT BLUE HERON

<CUYAHOGA VALLEY 18" X 24" Limited Edition Print created in 2013 by Michael Korfhage & Joel Anderson

CONGAREE
NATIONAL PARK

S. CAROLINA

CONGAREE

OLD GROWTH forest thrives on the banks of the Congaree River. Over 75 species of trees vie for the sun's rays in the lofty canopy. Loblolly pines, some as tall as skyscrapers, mingle with the oak, bald cypress, water tupelo, and holly populations. Ferns and fungi coat the lush forest floor where the bizarre "knees" of cypress roots pop out of the ground. Gauzy veils of Spanish moss and sweltering humidity remind you you're in the American South. Congaree is a land outside of time, where birds, fish, insects, and reptiles revel on the floodplain. Humans are invited to observe this teeming ecosystem from the **Boardwalk Trail,** a 2-mile elevated pathway coursing into the watery woodlands of Congaree National Park.

The Congaree region was named after the Congaree Indians native to South Carolina some 500 years ago. Hunting and fishing along the lowlands, the Congaree people may well be the last successful human residents to have ever lived here. Most European settlers were repelled by the mosquito-thick floodplain but their brief visits still left a mark on the natives: smallpox wiped out the tribe in the late 1600s. After the Indians passed away, settlers had great difficulties planting and grazing their cattle along the river. With massive flooding up to 10 times each year, the soil was always soggy and often rinsed away. Loggers thought they might fare better and entered the dense woodlands

with axes and saws. They too would be disappointed as access roads were next to impossible to build and heavy logging equipment sank into the mire. Further frustration arose when loggers tried to float the few cut trees downriver. Too green to float, the leveled giants sank straight to the bottom. The woodpeckers laughed in their canopies.

It wouldn't be until the 1970s when the Congaree trees were threatened again. This time, loggers armed with lighter equipment took down the elderly trees with a vengeance. The Sierra Club soon learned of this scourge on the East Coast. Their pleas for one of America's last and largest remaining bottomland hardwood forests resulted in the establishment of a National Monument in 1976. Though Hurricane Hugo would ravage Con-

garee in 1989, the trees continue to command this South Carolina jungle. Congress designated the Congaree floodplain as a National Park in 2003.

Congaree is small, about 24,000 acres in size with only 20 miles of trailways. However, Rangers offer guests a unique opportunity to explore the Park on a **free canoe trek** down the Congaree River each weekend. Paddling and bird watching are the primary activities here. Over 170 species of bird flutter through the gloomy treetops. The ranger-led **"Owl Prowl"** is a popular nocturnal activity where guests are invited to seek out the forest's array of hooting inhabitants. Though miniscule, Congaree is an animal kingdom that has always protected its own. Wander into this floodplain forest of the Old South and see for yourself.

Est. 2003

57TH
National Park

SOUTH CAROLINA
The Palmetto State

BEST ACTIVITY:
At night in the fall and spring, Rangers lead visitors on an "owl prowl," to hear the calls of barred owls and see the glowing fungi that grow on cypress trees.

DID YOU KNOW?
It is not a swamp, but a floodplain that floods about 10 times a year. Wild boar live in the park, as do feral pigs which are invasive pests.

Look for the
WILD BOAR

<CONGAREE 18" X 24" Limited Edition Print created in 2015 by Aaron Johnson & David Anderson

SAN LUIS VALLEY·COLORADO

GREAT SAND DUNES
NATIONAL PARK

GREAT SAND DUNES

GUSTY FINGERS comb the tresses of a vast golden dune. All is in motion. All is still. A dance sways ever on in the wild silence between sand and wind at Great Sand Dunes National Park and Preserve. These playful dunes imitate their stoic thirteen thousand-foot parents, the **Sangre de Cristos Mountains**, hovering in the background. Incessant gales blow down from the mountains to craft and shape this sandscape. What now appears to be a desert scene straight out of North Africa was once a sediment-rich lake. The **San Luis Valley** is all that remains of Lake Alamosa, which glistened between the Sangre de Cristos Mountains to the east and **San Juan Mountains** to the west. The Park's concealed alpine lakes attest to an ancient time when water was abundant in southern Colorado. The Park today seems perfectly content to exist as a para-dox, a sweeping scene of both constancy and change. Though the sandy patterns toss and turn like waves on a tumultuous sea, the vast dunes themselves seem to loom immobile. A hiker's footprints along the ridgeline are soon wiped clean by the shifting breezes. Surface temperatures on the dunes can range from a scorching 150 degrees in the summer to 20 below on the coldest winter nights. The highest of the dunes is **Star Dune**, a 750-foot tall giant that peers out over the entire dunefield, home to the largest dunes in North America. Atop these golden peaks you can experience the riveting silence that explorer Zebulon Pike once felt as he peered over this billowing sea of sand and pondered a way across. Most people today are more bent on enjoying the sand: hiking, sledding, sandboarding, or sprinting down these rippled hills are all favorite pastimes among Park visitors.

Though sand is the primary attraction (and there's plenty to be had), Great Sand Dunes National Park and Preserve also features a complex ecosystem of wetlands, grassy plains, mountain forests, and tundra. Camouflaging amphibians, circus beetles, and kangaroo rats make their homes in the mountains of dust. Bison, face-painted badgers, and pronghorns roam the grasslands. Pika, mountain lions, snowshoe hare, and bighorn sheep scrape out a living beneath the pines and firs of the Cristos highlands. You can explore all of these environments with the help of a sturdy pair of hiking boots and an all-terrain vehicle for traversing **Medano Pass Primitive Road.** For a more low-key escapade, build a sand castle and take a refreshing dip in **Medano Creek.** This lively waterway courses straight into the dunefield to rejuvenate both man and animal in the high desert. Make the journey to this isolated National Park and find new life atop these shimmering piles of sand in southern Colorado.

58TH
National Park

★

COLORADO
Centennial State

Est. 2004

👍 **BEST ACTIVITY:** Sandboarding!

⚠ **DID YOU KNOW?** The sand can heat up to 150º

⚠ **DID YOU KNOW?** Located in the high mountain desert of the San Luis Valley, it's North America's biggest dune field.

Look for **MOUNTAIN LIONS**

<GREAT SAND DUNES 18" X 24" Limited Edition Print created in 2014 by David Anderson & Joel Anderson

National Parks Timeline ·
1900
1950
2000
2004
153

BEAR GULCH RESERVOIR

PINNACLES
NATIONAL PARK

PINNACLES

A REFUGE of magnificent beauty is carved into the hills of Coastal California. Copper spires and castles of volcanic rock crown the tumbling bluffs in glory. Only an hour outside Monterey, Pinnacles National Park looks and feels like Middle Earth, a land fit for an epic tale of adventure. Condors, like kings of old, spread their massive wings and levitate over their dominion: prehistoric remains of a volcano fractured by the San Andreas Fault. The windy gusts these condors glide on have fashioned the stone palisades and fortresses for thousands of years. Merry streams trickle down from the highlands and churn into basins and narrow canyons. Earthquakes transformed some of these canyons into talus caves, deep gorges roofed by toppled boulders that wedged into the fractures. Fourteen species of bats inhabit these caves. The soft darkness of **Bear Gulch Cave** and **the Balconies** is especially vibrant with these furry colonies. Out in the sunshine, bees and butterflies busy themselves in the swaths of spring wildflowers that pop up out of the scrubby chaparral. Pinnacles National Park is a realm of joyful and unblemished solitude.

Native Chalon and Mutsun Indians have delighted in the valleys and colonnades of Pinnacles for centuries. The Natives lived off the landscape's abundant provision; acorns, wildflower seeds, rabbit, deer, and elk kept the natives clothed and well-fed, while the region's unique plant and tree species provided a variety of medicines and materials.

Through small fires and strategic harvesting, these early Californians cultivated the lavish landscape. In time, Spanish monks and homesteaders settled the surrounding countryside, forever altering the Indians way of life. The native population dwindled as European diseases ravaged the coast.

A century later, a young Michigan transplant named Schuyler Hain moved into Pinnacles with his family. Fascinated by the dream-like stonework, Hain began leading tours into **Bear Valley** and the nearby caves. He wrote articles and letters, exclaiming the wonders of this stone garden. "Here the cliffs of many-colored rock rise hundreds of feet in sharply defined terraces, or great domes or pinnacles. Beyond, and scattered over an area of some six square miles is a mass of conglomerate rocks wonderful in extent and in fantastic variety of form and coloring." Hain's letters attracted the attention of Stanford University, whose president helped him connect with National Forester Gifford Pinchot. Through Pinchot's recommendation, President Theodore Roosevelt established Pinnacles National Monument in 1908. CCC groups developed Hain's dream in the 1930s, building trails into the stone walls and paving roadways. One hundred and five years after Roosevelt's initial protection, President Barak Obama designated Pinnacles as America's 59th National Park. Today, a breathtaking ascent to **High Peaks** will introduce you to this serrated land of mythical grandeur, crafted by nature for the permanent enjoyment of all mankind.

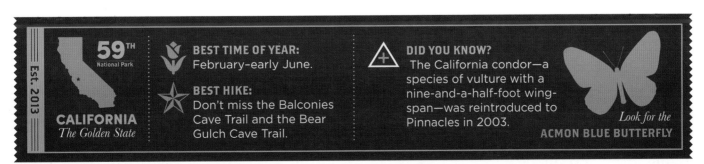

<PINNACLES 18" X 24" Limited Edition Print created in 2015 by Michael Korfhage & Joel Anderson

How the Art is Made...

WE WORK AS A TEAM of artists. As founder of Anderson Design Group, I've had the great pleasure of collaborating with creative friends to accomplish artistic feats that none of us could do alone. I was trained as an illustrator, so when possible, I enjoy rendering a poster from start to finish. But for this project, I realized the best way to produce 70+ National Park posters along with a book within 5 years was to act like the conductor of a chamber orchestra and write parts for each of my virtuoso players to perform. I started by creating a master list of poster themes. Then I assigned illustrations to different artists who I had trained as interns or who could draw, paint, and design in a classic style. During this process, several artists were always working on different posters at the same time. I would look at progress sketches and renderings, offer input and guidance, and then try to stay out of the way as much as possible to let everyone do what they were born to do. As soon as one of the illustrations was turned in, I would spend several hours on it adding finishing touches, creating continuity for the entire series of posters. Andy Gregg and Julian Baker created the first few poster designs for this collection back in 2010. Since then, Michael Korfhage, Kai Carpenter, Aaron Johnson and David Anderson have done the rest. Here is a behind-the-scenes look at how three of the artists created their art...

1. After I told Kai what I wanted, he created some rough sketches of different scenarios.
2. Once we settled on a composition, he drew a tighter sketch showing specific details.
3. He then began painting with oils on a canvas. See the progression of his work above.
4. Once the painting was dry enough to be handled, Kai took it to a photographer to have a digital photo made.
5. I added some subtle changes in Photoshop to create an area for the typography which I overlaid to finish the poster.

KAI CARPENTER grew up in the Pacific Northwest, and works from his Seattle studio. I still recall the first time I saw his work—I felt like I was looking at magazine cover art from the 1930s or '40s. His style and sense of lighting gave his art a look from a bygone era. I knew his paintings would be a great fit for the vintage-style poster series I was creating. A graduate of the Rhode Island School of Design, Kai has illustrated for a wide variety of clients including Wizards of the Coast and Harper Collins. Kai draws his inspiration from artists of the late 1800s to the 1940s, particularly the Golden Age illustrators.

1. I created a rough sketch to show Aaron my vision for the poster composition.
2. Aaron took my concept, did some research and expanded the idea in his own sketch.
3. Once we were happy with the composition, Aaron began rendering the illustration.
4. After experimenting with a few different sky colors, Aaron settled on a palette that bathed the scene in evening light.

AARON JOHNSON graduated from Watkins School of Art, Design & Film in Nashville, TN. He worked as an intern before joining ADG as a staff artist. Aaron prefers to draw and paint on a tablet which is hooked up to an iMac computer. He looks at the screen while he moves a stylus across the surface of the tablet on his desk. Using the same techniques and motions he would normally use with pencils and brushes, his digital workspace allows for unlimited editing with no pencils to sharpen, no paint to spill, and no brushes to clean!

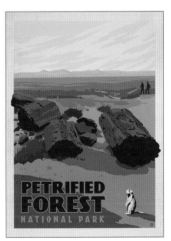

Michael's process and techniques are very similar to Aaron's. He starts with a pencil sketch and then moves to the computer to render his art digitally. Like the rest of us, he is also a fan of old-school poster and advertising art from the early to mid-20th Century.

MICHAEL KORFHAGE works in Nashville as a free-lance illustrator and commercial artist. After graduating from Watkins College of Art, Design & Film, he started collaborating with me as an independent contractor helping me produce poster art. I love working with him because, after working together on more than 100 posters, he knows exactly what I am looking for. Michael also works for magazines, ad agencies, and small businesses. His work is inspired by folk art, mid-century design, and storytelling.

About Anderson Design Group...

ANDERSON DESIGN GROUP has been around since 1993. My design firm originally excelled in CD and toy packaging, book covers, and logos. In 2003, I began creating poster art and training my interns and staff artists to emulate classic poster art styles from the 1920s, '30s and '40s. Our first poster series was the award-winning *Spirit of Nashville* collection—a series of prints that celebrated the history and charm of our hometown. Over time, Anderson Design Group morphed into an illustration and design studio with a poster shop on the ground floor. In 2010, after producing over 150 different Nashville designs, I began work on a new series of posters called *The Art & Soul of America*. This was to be a travel poster collection full of my favorite American cities, parks and historical sites. It started out as a small collection of illustrated prints depicting cities like Seattle, New Orleans, New York and Chicago. The prints were an instant success, and I began receiving requests from all over the USA for new art depicting other places that were special to people—places where history or memories were made, and souls were stirred.

After creating almost 200 different prints of U.S. cities and National Parks, I began experimenting with more diverse poster themes like World Travel prints, a coastal collection, posters about coffee, beer and wine, Mid-Century Modern designs, poster art for children, Southern expressions, vintage Americana advertising art, and even a Man Cave collection. By late 2015, the talented artists of Anderson Design Group had helped me produce over 600 different poster designs. Our art has been exhibited on every continent on the globe (except for Antarctica). Our prints have been purchased for display all over Europe, Australia, South Africa, Canada, and South America. They have been featured on movie and network TV sets, given as gifts to diplomats, hung in embassies and consulates, published in design journals, and displayed in homes and offices by poster art lovers everywhere.

What started in Nashville as a way to celebrate Music City and promote our little Nashville-based design firm has grown to become one of the largest bodies of decorative poster art ever assembled by one team of artists. It is still growing, and it's all available in the Anderson Design Group Studio Store located at 116 29th Ave. North, Nashville, TN 37203, or online at **www.ADGstore.com.**

Interior of the Anderson Design Group Studio Store in Nashville, TN

Joel Anderson sketching in his Nashville studio

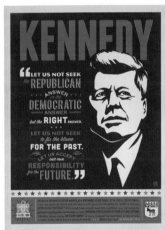

Shown above are prints from our various series—each one explores specific themes such as: Art & Soul of America, Man Cave, Coastal Living, Mid-Century Modern, the Spirit of Nashville, Political, World Travel, Lake & Lodge, Southern Sayings and Coffee.

INFORMATION SOURCES

All facts, figures, and quotes are derived from the sources below and the National Park Service website (www.nps.gov).

- Abbey, Edward. *Desert Solitaire: A Season in the Wilderness.* New York: Touchstone, 1990. Print. (Page 103)

- Biggers, Ashley M. "What's the Difference between National Parks and National Monuments?" *Outside Online.* Outside Magazine, 22 Apr. 2014. Web. 22 Sept. 2015. <http://www.outsideonline.com/1785161/what%E2%80%99s-difference-between-national-parks-and-national-monuments>. (Page 9)

- Brown, Phil, ed. *Bob Marshall in the Adirondacks: Writings of a Pioneering Peak-Bagger, Pond-Hopper and Wilderness Preservationist.* Saranac Lake: Lost Pond, 2006. Print. (Page 131)

- Duncan, Dayton, and Ken Burns. *The National Parks: America's Best Idea.* New York: Knopf, 2009. Print. (Pages 8-11, 15, 22, 29, 33, 41, 49, 60, 65, 67-68, 83-84, 91, 123)

- *Guide to National Parks of the United States.* 7th ed. Washington: National Geographic Society, 2012. Print. (Pages 14-153)

- Henze, Eric. *RVing with Monsters: The Complete Guide to the Grand Circle National Parks.* N.p.: Gone Beyond Guides, 2014. Print. (Page 51, 95, 107)

- "History." Ranger Doug: Ranger of the Lost Art. Ed. Ranger Doug's Enterprises. N.p., n.d. Web. 29 Sept. 2015. <http://www.rangerdoug.com/history>. (Page 6)

- Oswald, Michael Joseph. *Your Guide to the National Parks.* Whitelaw: Stone Road Press, 2012. Print. (Pages 14-153)

- Proenneke, Richard, and Sam Keith. One Man's Wilderness: An Alaskan Odyssey. Anchorage: Alaska Northwest, 1999. Print. (Page 131)

- Park Ranger quotes were provided by the following former NPS employees (in order of appearance) Rick Smith, Bill Wade, Bill Pierce, Roger Rudolph, Robert Arnberger, Donald Falvey, Fred J. Fagergren, Maureen Finnerty, Walt Dabney, and Cherry Payne.

- Park Ranger photos were supplied by retired rangers and have been used with their permission. (Pages 16, 22, 26, 36, 46, 50, 54, 60, 68, 84, 100, 104, 123, 141)

- All stock photography was purchased from Deposit Photos and Shutterstock.

- Historic images are courtesy of the National Park Service and the Library of Congress.

- Photos of Joel Anderson are by Alyssa Adams (Pages 7, 158)

- Where indicated, original photos of Yellowstone, Glacier, Zion, Bryce and Petrified Forest are by Joel Anderson (Pages 4, 5, 16, 35, 53, 54, 59, 60, 93, 157, 158)

- Original oil paintings are by Kai Carpenter

- Original posters are by Anderson Design Group: Joel Anderson, David Anderson, Julian Baker, Andy Gregg, Aaron Johnson and Michael Korfhage.